MANAGING INTERNATIONAL CONFLICT

FROM THEORY TO POLICY
A TEACHING TOOL USING CASCON

Lincoln P. Bloomfield
Allen Moulton

Both of the Massachusetts Institute of Technology

St. Martin's Press
New York

Sponsoring editor: Beth Gillett
Managing editor: Patricia Mansfield Phelan
Production supervisor: Scott Lavelle
Art director: Lucy Krikorian
Text design: Evelyn Horovicz
Cover design: Evelyn Horovicz
Cover art: John Labbe/The Image Bank

Library of Congress Catalog Card Number: 95-73316

Manufactured in the United States of America.

1 0 9 8 7
f e d c b a

For information, write:
St. Martin's Press, Inc.
175 Fifth Avenue
New York, NY 10010

ISBN: 0-312-13675-7

Acknowledgments

Some material in this book is adapted with substantial changes from writings by Lincoln P. Bloomfield which originally appeared in the following publications: *Controlling Small Wars* with Amelia C. Leiss (New York: Alfred A. Knopf, 1969); "Computerizing Conflicts," *Foreign Service Journal,* June 1988; "Twilight of Autarchy," *Harvard Magazine,* November/December 1988; *Rethinking International Cooperation* with Harlan Cleveland (Minneapolis, MN: Humphrey Institute of Public Affairs, University of Minnesota, 1988); "Coping with Conflict in the Late Twentieth Century," *International Journal* (Canada), Autumn, 1989; "Collective Security and U.S. Interests," in *Collective Security in a Changing World,* ed. Thomas G. Weiss (Boulder, CO: Lynn Riemer, 1993); "Policing World Disorder," *World Monitor,* February 1993; "Enforcing Rules in the International Community: Governing the Ungovernable?" in *Issues in Global Governance,* papers written for the Commission on Global Governance (London: Kluwer Law International, 1995); and "Debunking the New World Disorder," *The Washington Quarterly,* Summer, 1994.

Preface

Managing International Conflict is, we believe, a unique package that combines theory and policy with a proven analytic methodology and practical computer software. In a world where conflict between nations and within borders remains widespread, conflict management is essential to governments, international and nongovernmental organizations, and commercial enterprise. The combined text and software of *Managing International Conflict,* constituting an integrated whole, can be of proven help to students and scholars studying international relations and history, as well as to practitioners and analysts concerned with early warning and conflict prevention, and citizens interested in understanding the dynamics of conflict.

Part I provides an understanding of the nature and process of conflict based on theory and history. Part II explores the future global conflict agenda and policy options for managing their consequences. Chapters 1 through 8 by Lincoln P. Bloomfield draw on his extensive research and teaching at the Massachusetts Institute of Technology plus hands-on conflict management experience in the State Department and National Security Council. Part III develops a theory of conflict prevention and explains the CASCON method of computer-assisted conflict analysis designed and executed by Allen Moulton, visiting research scholar at MIT's Center for International Studies.

The CASCON computer software provides student, researcher, and policy professional with a computer tool for applying the methods explained in Chapters 9 and 10 to the analysis of ongoing and historical conflict situations. CASCON is designed as an aid to the memory and to the imagination. It is policy-oriented but does not attempt to replace human decision making. It is not a simulation or a game, nor does it attempt to predict future events. As a model, a method, and a rich repository of knowledge and judgments by diplomatic and scholarly experts, its purpose is to reinforce human reasoning about conflict. In 1988, an earlier version of CASCON received the Distinguished Software Award in Political Science from EDUCOM and NCRIPTAL (the National Center for Research to Improve Post-Secondary Teaching and Learning). With the publication of *Managing International Conflict,* CASCON is now made generally available for the first time.

For the student of international relations, foreign policy, or history, *Managing International Conflict,* together with the CASCON software and database included, provides a unique opportunity for understanding conflict from a policy point of view. As a course project, CASCON can provide the kind of hands-on experience that comes from the laboratory exercise in science and engineering education. A student interested in a professional career involving foreign policy can also gain insight into the kind of reasoning used by policy professionals. In a world of localized power relationships and conflict alongside globalized economic and commercial integration, students interested in an international business career may also find that studying international relations with a policy orientation will be invaluable.

The original case studies were prepared under the direction of Amelia C. Leiss; additional case studies were prepared by Brown and Shaw Research Corp. under John C. Hoagland, Jr.; and the precis were written by Iri Bloomfield. The earliest attempt at computerizing our historical-analytical dynamic conflict model was done by Cambridge Computer Associates. All subsequent versions of CASCON including the present one were created and developed by Allen Moulton in collaboration with Lincoln Bloomfield. Much of our basic research on local conflicts, as well as the systematizing of conflict data, was undertaken with the sponsorship of the U.S. Arms Control and Disarmament Agency. Support for research and additional case studies was provided over the years by a variety of sources including the University of Michigan, MIT's Project Athena, and the U.S. Institute of Peace.

The CASCON database captures knowledge and judgments of experts and officials, scores of whom have been involved in the coding of CASCON's database of 85 post–World War II conflict cases. During three decades of our research on conflict at the MIT Center for International Studies, many students, researchers, and professionals have experimented with the methodology and computer technology of CASCON. Faculty colleagues Hayward R. Alker, Jr., and Nazli Choucri were always generous in their advice and help. Active contributors to CASCON's development included Robert Beattie, Richard Barringer, Robert Ramers, Geoffrey Kemp, Priscilla Clapp, Lawrence Legere, Cornelius Gearin, James Foster, R. Lucas Fischer, Paul Giers, Dale Murphy, Pierre Chao, Eric Liebeler, James Panagos, and Brian Burgoon, and many other MIT graduate students assisted with the case studies.

The book also benefited from the comments of Ali Abootalebi, Union College; Daniel Austin, Edinboro University; Marc A. Levy, Princeton University; Witold J. Lukaszewski, Sam Houston University; Kenneth J. Mijeski, East Tennessee State University; Thomas J. Price, University of Texas at El Paso; and Henry A. Shockley, Boston University. More than any other collaborator, Amelia C. Leiss deserves credit for much of the basic research on which this book is based, including the fundamental concepts and models of conflict. Without Amy Leiss's efforts, both intellectual and managerial, the project and all its varied products would simply not have been possible.

Lincoln P. Bloomfield and Allen Moulton

Publisher's Note

Managing International Conflict: From Theory to Policy is a dynamic, interactive package designed to help students and others to explore conflicts between and within nations, and to better understand why they occur and what can be done to control them.

Managing International Conflict is ideal for courses in International Relations, National Security, Foreign Policy, and Peace Studies. As an innovative text/software package it has four features that make it a bold, new kind of supplement.

▶ *The CASCON program.* This award-winning computer program grew out of a need to computerize a historical-analytical conflict model and to provide students with first-hand practice in managing conflict. Over the years it has been redesigned for classroom use and has been exhaustively tested by the U.S. government, the United Nations, and many instructors. It is now completely updated as well as user-friendly.

▶ *A one-of-a-kind book on conflict.* The main text by Lincoln P. Bloomfield draws on many years of research and experience with conflict. It provides introductory chapters on violence and human nature, contemporary "small wars," an analysis of prospects and tools for coping with world disorder, and a unique annotated bibliography on conflict. Instructors and students alike will appreciate this brief, understandable text designed to give them the background knowledge and framework they need to analyze international conflict.

▶ *85 cases for analysis.* The computer program includes 85 cases in the CASCON database and 571 different factors that influence conflict. Students, concerned citizens, and instructors can get active experience in analyzing and dealing with conflict. These cases are suitable for ongoing projects, post tests, and lab assignments.

▶ *Expert author team.* Lincoln P. Bloomfield is author or co-author of nine books on international relations and foreign policy and has lectured in 35 countries. He has also served as a State Department official and as director of global issues in the National Security Council, and has years of classroom experience. Allen Moulton is on the research staff of the MIT Center for International Studies and a partner in CASCON's evolution and distinguished history for over 25 years. As a team, Bloomfield and Moulton have blended theory and practice into an innovative, useful project.

Contents

CHAPTER 9

CONFLICT ANALYSIS WITH CASCON   127

CHAPTER 10

THE CASCON USER'S GUIDE   149

LACK OF MEMORY IS AN INTOLERABLE DEFECT IN ANYONE WHO TAKES ON THE BURDEN OF THE WORLD'S AFFAIRS.

MONTAIGNE, ESSAYS (1580)

One ~

WHY CONFLICT?[1]

T wo contradictory images strike the eye at the close of the twentieth century. One image is that of the best educated, most technologically advanced generation in human history. Its members for the most part coexist with one another peacefully. They trade and communicate across the globe, and on every continent they tend civilization's panoramic and often breathtaking heritage of arts and culture. The competing image depicts groups—tribes, sects, states—nursing grievances, fostering prejudices, transmitting hatred to succeeding generations, and sometimes battling one another to the death across national boundaries or within their own society's shared space.

Many people thought that when the half-century of Cold War ended, the world would at last be freed of the tensions and bloodshed unleashed by the ideologues of fascism and communism. We are mercifully unburdened of the contingent threat of nuclear annihilation, but not of conflict. Witness, for only one sad example, the strife in the Balkans in the 1990s among the same unreconciled tribes that battled under the Austro-Hungarian and Ottoman empires, and whose unresolved differences go back even earlier to schismatic Christendom and the rise of Islam.

Whatever our moral preferences, it is empirically true that warfare is part of the human scene—and so is peace. Why should this be so? And where can we turn to understand why some—but not all—human groups struggle with other groups? Is it because they are groups? Is it the inherent nature of the political state that breeds conflict? Is it the uneven distribution of economic goods? Is there something innately conflict-prone about the international system? Or does a more convincing answer lie in the genetic material that codes our chromosomes and comprises what we call human nature?

EXPLANATIONS FROM INTERNATIONAL RELATIONS THEORY

A brief review of theories of international relations gives us at least partial explanations of the phenomenon of conflict.

According to "realist" theory, the behavior of organized political groupings is driven by a quest to attain or retain power. Since the seventeenth century, that power has been sought and fought over by states. Despite all the modern trends toward "globalization," realism still regards the state as the central actor in a fundamentally anarchic international system. On the moral plane, states are still driven by self-interest rather than by the norms of international organizations such as the United Nations. A closely related theme is that the special moral calculus appropriate for the state's decision making is distinct from the ethical norms of the moral individual. Indeed, according to the seventeenth-century English political philosopher Thomas Hobbes, individuals in a "state of nature" are not very moral either; in fact, they conduct a permanent war among themselves until they are restrained by creation of a state.[2] Thus realism implies pessimism about both human nature and the possibility of unbroken peace.

Political philosophy is studded with the icons of realist theory, starting with the Greek military historian Thucydides who described the Peloponnesian Wars as an interplay of impersonal forces and great leaders.[3] In the sixteenth century Niccolo Machiavelli wrote the original playbook for twentieth-century spin doctors, explaining *inter alia* that anything goes when the Florentine prince's aim is to get and keep power.[4] If Machiavelli was prescribing rules for success, modern realists claim to be simply describing the reality of "value-free" politics. In our times the moody and brilliant American diplomatist George Kennan made explicit realism's moral position. States must act in their interests, he stated, and cannot indulge in the kind of self-denying behavior (such as pacifism) that can be the individual's highest form of moral expression.[5] (Some theorists accepted the concept of interests but redefined it to embrace cooperative action.[6])

Hans Morgenthau cogently analyzed international politics as a struggle for power in an anarchic environment,[7] as did the insightful neo-Calvinist theologian Reinhold Niebuhr.[8] It is worth remembering that both Morgenthau and Niebuhr wrote during a pessimistic time when fascism and militarism were propelling the world toward a new Armageddon. Like Kennan, they saw peace as a function of balanced forces rather than of abstract ideals or hollow legalisms. The French writer Raymond Aron suggested that the choice between peace and war depended on resources[9]—a theme advanced by the geopolitics school (Sir Halford Mackinder, the Sprouts, Nicholas Spykman, et al.). Morton Kaplan made the peace–war equation downright Newtonian with his metaphor of states bouncing geometrically against one another like billiard balls.[10]

The school of political realism was not unconcerned with curbing the natural warlike inclination of states in an anarchic world system. However, unlike the internationalists and multilateralists, their prescription was not international rule-making of the sort embodied in the League of Nations Covenant and the United Nations Charter. What was the point of trying to curb international anarchy with peaceful norms to which the major states would not subscribe? Conflicts would be reduced, they argued, to the extent that a balance of power existed among the parts of the system that would ensure equilibrium. As Henry A. Kissinger wrote, the balance of power system was not meant to avoid crises or even wars, but "to limit both the ability of states to dominate others and the scope of conflict."[11] The motto was not reform but stability. Balance keeps the peace; imbalance is a prescription for conflict.

Since conflict is inherent in the system itself, the only "realistic" way to curb threats to stability and equilibrium is for responsible states to apply countervailing power when challenged. Among contemporary realists Kissinger had the unique opportunity to play the role not only of Machiavelli but also that of his princely client. Kissinger first articulated his concept of system stability in his study of the Congress of Vienna and the ensuing 70 years of relative peace in nineteenth-century Europe.[12] Then as national security adviser and secretary of state he helped implement a new geometric design—the U.S.–Soviet–China triangle—aimed at restoring the superpower balance. If a classic scenario of conflict is a situation in which the defenders of the status quo avoid anarchy by blocking those seeking change, the realist strategy is by definition profoundly conservative.

"Neo-realism" added greater sophistication to realism's state-centered analysis in an era that was more self-conscious about economic and resource factors as well as systems concepts. Kenneth Waltz, Hedley Bull, Steven Krasner, and Robert Gilpin (to name four major contributors) also started from the reality of international anarchy in which status quo and change are in tension. Waltz's "structural realism" employed the state's internal structure to analyze equilibrium based on distribution of capabilities in the system.[13] Gilpin described the cost-benefit calculation states make in deciding whether to challenge the status quo.[14] Neo-realists usually argue that systemic stability requires that a "hegemonic" role be played by a leading power committed to preserving the status quo.

The school of thought sometimes labeled "idealist" boasts considerably less scholarly doctrine than do the realists, doubtless because it has had a good deal less success in empirically validating its approach in a conflict-ridden world. But that depends on whether one sees the global glass as half-empty or half-full. Certainly the United Nations has had a major hand in reducing and containing conflict since 1945, and in Chapters 4 through 6 we will consider the potential and limits of international organizations in coping with future war and peace issues. But some other idealist approaches raise more questions than they answer.

We need not linger on the conflict-prevention utility of utopians who prescribe a perfect society as the solution to human conflict. Yes, democracies have learned habits of tolerance and compromise, and in that sense there may be a grain of historical nourishment in the optimism of the late eighteenth century's Count de Condorcet (infinite perfectibility of mankind) or the nineteenth century's Herbert Spencer (inevitable progress). But generalized prescriptions of nonviolence seem irrelevant in the face of armed aggression: even an unarmed

Costa Rica may be regarded as protected by U.S. power. On the international stage the pacifist persuasion has proved not only ineffective but also dangerously misleading in the face of determined aggressors from Hitler, Mussolini, and Tojo to Saddam Hussein.

Yet realism's scornful dismissal of idealism as sentimental nonsense also distorts the truth. Immanuel Kant's prescription of "perpetual peace,"[15] akin to the views of the French philosopher Baron de Montesquieu who so influenced the American Constitution,[16] featured republican forms of government. Today, as we will see in Chapter 3, many would agree that democratic governance is indeed a barrier to wars between states. The so-called functionalists, led by David Mitrany,[17] never could demonstrate that international cooperation on common problems of health, radio frequency allocation, airport rules, and the like would overcome basic political differences. But as with Sherlock Holmes's dog that did not bark in the night, such regimes doubtless account for the absence of some conflicts that might have ensued without such functional regimes.

A more explicit doctrine of conflict reduction came from the free-trade advocates of nineteenth-century Britain. Utilitarian economists from Adam Smith and John Stuart Mill to Alfred Cobden and Jeremy Bentham believed in free trade as a guarantor of peace. The axiom, "when goods cross borders, armed forces do not," was echoed by U.S. Secretary of State Cordell Hull in the 1930s. But as a working formula it had already turned sour when some of the world's prime trading nations tore one another apart in World War I.

It is within the boundaries of a state that conflict can sometimes be contained with methods that do not work in the interstate arena. Within the British-ruled India of Mahatma Gandhi or the American South of Martin Luther King, Jr., nonviolence proved to be a potent and eventually successful strategy of peaceful change. (Note that in both cases the status quo power was a democracy, however imperfect.) Similarly, the American philosopher William James's moral equivalent of war strategy[18] could help reduce conflict on the violent streets of American cities.

If the conservative school of realism has influenced much of modern international relations conflict theory, the radical school of economic determinism and dependency has attracted many intellectuals and early Third World leaders. Karl Marx formulated his theory of class struggle in the British Museum's reading room at the heart of Charles Dickens's London.[19] The social evils of early industrialization, of dog-eat-dog capitalism, and of poet William Blake's "dark Satanic mills" formed the backdrop for what was to become a widely influential concept of conflict based on the iron laws of Dialectical Materialism. History, it argued, is a story of economic warfare between haves and have-nots as the masses are exploited by the ruling class, first under feudalism, then under "monopoly capitalism" and imperialism, but eventually triumphing under socialism, at which point the dialectical process terminates.

Under this doctrine, war is a function of capitalist imperialism, and conflict is thus inevitable. When communist theory became the state philosophy of

Bolshevism in Russia, the concept of inevitable conflict became a self-fulfilling prophecy, both causing and explaining the hostility of the outside world. The notion of clashes between the imperialist states, expounded by Lenin in 1916, was increasingly difficult to demonstrate as the democracies cooperated while the Soviet Union itself became an imperialist state ruling restless "colonies" to its west and confronting another hostile communist giant—China—to its east. The doctrine of inevitability of war was discarded.

Like realist theories, radical theories contained more than a germ of truth. Western Europe's overseas colonies were originally a source of cheap raw materials for its industrial and commercial growth. Colonial liberation sometimes involved bloody conflict, as in Algeria, Indonesia, Cyprus, the Congo, and Kenya. But many more colonies were freed without violence, doubtless because most had long ceased to be an engine of profit for the metropolitan power.

The proponents of dependency theory located the source of conflict in the uneven economic development of former colonies compared with the evolution of the developed industrial countries. Norwegian Johan Galtung's conceptual map showed a wealthy and powerful status quo at the center, girdled by an exploited majority of societies lying in the "periphery."[20] Immanuel Wallerstein spelled out this evolving international division of labor that featured "unequal exchange."[21] (We will see echoes of this concept when we map concrete conflict situations in Chapters 2 and 3.)

Yet another general explanation of conflict has come from those who focus on the environment and natural resources. In early nineteenth-century England, the Reverend Thomas R. Malthus—the "Gloomy Dean"—challenged the optimism of de Condorcet with a pessimistic equation in which geometric population growth outran arithmetically increased food supply.[22] This laid down an early marker for latter-day scholars of the population–resources–conflict equation such as Nazli Choucri.[23] As we will also see in Chapter 3, future sources of conflict may arise from population pressures in combination not so much with a shortage of raw materials or even food, as with degradation of an over-abused physical environment.

These theories of conflict explain much. But clearly no universal law of political behavior yet exists, and the competing constructs remain useful but incomplete paradigms. In the real world, states mature and in the process revise their self-defined national interests. Traditional enemies, conquerors, and empire builders such as France, Great Britain, Germany, Italy, Belgium, Portugal, Austria, Spain, the Netherlands, and Sweden retain their identities—but war between them has become unthinkable. Yet, in the same world, disputes[24] persist between other historically quarrelsome pairs of states such as China–Vietnam, India–Pakistan, Israel–Syria, Peru–Ecuador, and Armenia–Azerbaijan.

Some ethnically distinct groupings within states have learned to coexist peacefully, if not always happily; witness Belgium, Romania, Malaysia, South Africa, the United States, even Canada, and perhaps someday Northern Ireland.

But in the late twentieth century, Orthodox Serbs, Catholic Croats, and Muslim Bosnians could still be incited from peaceful coexistence to mutual slaughter, as could East African Hutus and Tutsis, and Sri Lankan Sinhalese and Tamils. Oversize tyrannies such as the now-sleeping former Soviet Union and the now-awakening China can represent built-in potential for conflict. Gross economic inequality persists between center and periphery, and unfairness could be a watchword for new struggles. But parts of the periphery are outstripping some developed states, while negotiated trade rules together with common sense may keep other giants from driving the real global proletariat to rebellion.

International relations theory sometimes appears to belabor the obvious. It reflects the effort of scholars to think systematically about a vastly complex system composed of political units, economic and scientific forces, divergent histories, and human beings equipped with idiosyncratic patterns of behavior and morality. Extracting from that kaleidoscopic reality the factors that breed conflict, as well as those that minimize it, requires attention to virtually all the elements of political life cited in this chapter. (The Computer-Aided System for Analyzing Conflicts—CASCON—presented in Part IV of this book, which enables the reader to interact dynamically with multiple elements of conflict, rests on an appropriately broad range of explanatory "factors.")

In the end it is the unique quality of the human species that defines its social, economic, and political systems, and that supplies the most persuasive explanation of its often perverse political behavior. Other species on the planet also organize into groups, packs, tribes, even (for ants and bees) "factories." Normally, however, they respect one another's territory except when driven by hunger. In combat, they usually follow protocols of behavior that leave a victor satisfied with symbolic surrender of a "belly-up" adversary—leaving *Homo sapiens* the only species that gratuitously kills. The primary road to understanding the deepest sources of conflict is doubtless human nature itself.

VIOLENCE AND HUMAN NATURE

Is It in the Genes?

The human species has always displayed two faces, one pacific, the other bellicose. Diagnoses of our schizoid nature are plentiful.[25]

The one-time premier authority on human nature, Sigmund Freud, spoke for the pessimists when he asserted that "there is no likelihood of our being able to suppress humanity's aggressive tendencies."[26] Was Dr. Freud just thinking about his patients? No, according to biologist Edward O. Wilson: man's fate as war maker was sealed when the Darwinian dice were first rolled. His destructive hereditary traits were fixed in place when "a carnivorous primate . . . tribal and aggressively territorial," rather than some more benign form of animal, took over the earth.[27] It's a short step from that to the conclusion that conflict is simply built into the human DNA. This of course lets animals off the hook. But a school of ethologists led by Konrad Lorenz studied aggressive animal behavior and extrapolated it to the human species, noting the aggressive turf-defending instinct that his colleague Robert Ardrey called the "territorial imperactive."[28]

Biology also offers a nongenetic explanation. Aggressive human behavior was initially adaptive and functional—"something people are designed to do," according to a pair of experts on human violence.[29] In this argument, violence is not dysfunctional at all, but rather the condition for success in a Darwinian world, especially for men. More controversially, some evolutionary psychologists identify what they call biological markers of violent disposition measurable by one's level of the neurotransmitter serotonin (low is bad and tends toward impulsive violence).

The biological argument about man's innate nature is recapitulated in debates about man as a political animal. After all, political philosophy at root is shaped by the way a philosopher assesses human nature. To Thomas Hobbes, writing in 1651, it's a jungle out there. Humankind is driven by "a perpetuall and restlesse desire of Power after power, that ceaseth onely in Death." Without the presence of intimidating authority, it's a "warre . . . of every man against every man . . . and the life of man, solitary, poore, nasty, brutish, and short."[30]

Hobbes's dim view of the "state of nature" might be dismissed as coming from a mathematician trying his hand at political theory, and being shocked at the conceptual disorder he encountered. But Hobbes's pessimistic followers, ranging from Alexander Hamilton to twentieth-century neo-Calvinists, pretty much share the view that only a disciplined sociopolitical order can civilize the darker face of human nature, and that peace is maintained by organizing society so as to keep the inherently brutal individual under firm control.

The "peaceful individual" side of the historic argument has equally respectable philosophical roots. The *locus classicus* is French philosopher Jean-Jacques Rousseau's optimistic eighteenth-century concept of human nature if only coercive authority will let it alone. "Men . . . living in their primitive independence . . . cannot be natural enemies." War "can exist neither in the state of nature . . . nor in a [lawful] state."[31] Grounded on similar philosophical premises, liberal idealists from Thomas Jefferson to modern Wilsonians take as a given the innate civility and cooperative nature of humankind left to itself.

The flip side of that position is that humans organized into groups are more likely to behave in a destructive fashion. In our era, the most common current explanation for all the conflict is popular emotion based on ethnicity. As Friedrich Nietzsche once put it (with typical hyperbole), madness is the exception in individuals but the rule in groups. In the words of the Spanish diplomat Salvador de Madariaga, "Let us not forget that if individual human beings shudder at the idea of cannibalism, those collective human beings we call nations have practiced it in the past and would, alas, practice it again tomorrow."[32]

In the fifth century B.C., Aristophanes wrote *Lysistrata,* in which wives with-held their sexual favors until their war-prone husbands stopped fighting. Since then, others have argued that the benign aspect of human nature lies in its feminine side, in contrast to testosterone-driven, power-hungry males (with some obvious exceptions such as Britain's Margaret Thatcher's war on Argentina in 1982 and India's Indira Gandhi's on Pakistan in 1971). But historian Barbara Tuchman preferred the explanation of inadvertence. Dismissing complex deterministic theories of power, she saw conflict as "sometimes a matter of ordinary men wading into water over their heads, acting unwisely or foolishly or perversely as people in ordinary circumstances frequently do."[33] (She also once said of Americans: "Warlike, no; violent, yes.") The explanation of World War I as essentially inadvertent tied in persuasively with contemporary concern about the possibility of inadvertent nuclear war issuing from mutual misperceptions.

War

A leading student of warfare, Martin Van Creveld, believes that war is simply programmed into human nature. "[T]he real reason why we have wars is that men like fighting, and women like those men who are prepared to fight on their behalf . . . the only way to bring about perpetual peace would be to somehow eradicate man's willingness, even eagerness, to take risks of every kind up to and including death."[34] In the same vein, a British historian finds that in some societies war is not only an expression of culture, but also "the culture itself." "Warfare is almost as old as man himself, and reaches into the most secret places of the human heart, places where self dissolves rational purpose, where pride reigns, where emotion is paramount, where instinct is king."[35] It was in this spirit 2400 years ago that Thucydides reported the Athenians telling the Melians, "The strong do what they can and the weak suffer what they must." His contemporary, Heraclitus, agreed: "War is the father of all things."

The debates and theorizing about human nature and violence will continue. But theory and philosophy aside, the reality of war is undeniable, in the literal sense of the purposeful organization of technologically assisted killing power by political groupings that traditionally act as states and sometimes by groupings within states. It is *organized* warfare that sets the human species uniquely apart from the rest of the natural world (and shouldn't the self-glorifying name of our species—*Homo sapiens*—be revised to take account of our occasionally monumental *un*wisdom?)

The dominant culture has approached the matter of war in widely varying ways. Western analyses in the late nineteenth and early twentieth centuries regarded war as a rational instrument of influence-seeking or power-maintenance. The strategic change brought about since 1945 by nuclear weaponry has revolutionized the strategist's cost-benefit equations by setting nuclear warfare beyond any rational (not to say moral) framework. But the theorists of war who flourished a century or more ago saw warfare as value-neutral, and the issues they raised were not those of morality but rather of cost-effectiveness. The classic eighteenth-century text, *On War,* by Carl von Clausewitz, taught succeeding generations of students of power and *realpolitik* that war is the continuation of policy by other means.[36] For the German strategic thinkers of the day, Bismarck's achievement of German unification at the expected cost of wars against Denmark, Austria, and France was eminently cost-effective.

Some went considerably further and positively glorified war, moving the topic from analysis into the realm of the irrational, the emotional, and even the spiritual. The heavy breathers of German Romanticism seemed to believe that war is positively good for you. One writer claimed that "war is a biological necessity of the first importance."[37] Field Marshal Helmuth von Moltke announced that "war is an integral part of God's ordering of the universe. Freedom means that the manly instincts which delight in war and victory dominate over other instincts, for example, over those of 'pleasure.' "[38] Not to be outdone, Nietzsche blustered that "the human being who has become free spits on the contemplative type of well-being dreamed of by democrats. The free man is a warrior."[39]

Lest all this preoccupation with war be thought a German idiosyncrasy, imperial Britain long boasted of winning its wars on the playing fields of Eton (by teaching discipline and courage, taking cold showers, etc.). On the eve of Hiroshima a future British prime minister, Harold Macmillan, himself disabled in World War I, was heard to say, "I enjoy wars."[40] As Kissinger summed it up, early twentieth-century wars could be started "with a touch of frivolity" in the general belief that "periodic bloodletting was cathartic."[41]

Americans, whose ideology required that national interest be matched with a moral purpose, always had a harder time justifying the use of force. The pioneer naval strategic analyst Captain (subsequently Admiral) Alfred Thayer Mahan squared that vexing circle by writing that "the purpose of military power is to provide time for moral ideas to take root" since "war now not only occurs more rarely, but has rather the character of an occasional excess from which recovery is easy."[42] But Mahan, too, caught the evangelical fever of the times when he wrote: "Power, force is a faculty of national life; one of the talents committed to nations by God."[43] And that icon of American liberals, the great jurist Oliver Wendell Holmes, Jr., recalled his youthful battle experiences in the Civil War as brutal yet ennobling: "the faith is true and adorable which leads a soldier to throw his life away in obedience to a blindly accepted duty."[44]

With the explosion of the first atomic bomb, the rhetoric was transformed to the point that throughout the Cold War every U.S. and Soviet leader at one time or another observed that nuclear war was "unthinkable," or words to that effect. In that sense, the nuclear age was a watershed: whatever else general war may have been, it could no longer be considered cost-effective. But Chinese Communist Chairman Mao Zedong (one of whose most quoted sayings was that "political power grows out of the barrel of a gun"[45]) also said of the catastrophic effects of nuclear weapons: "when the atomic bomb is exploded, even if one-half of mankind perishes, there will still be one-half left."[46] Some of this talk was bluster based on weakness—a traditional Chinese stratagem. But Mao also followed von Clausewitz (and Lenin) in his conviction that war is a continuation of the political process by military means, an instrumental view of the use of force elaborated by guerrilla theorist Régis Debray to justify revolutionary violence.[47] Mao's point was not necessarily glorification of force, but of what it could achieve, in the spirit of German "Iron Chancellor" Otto von Bismarck who, asked whether he wanted war, is said to have replied: "Certainly not, what I want is victory!"

The better angels of human nature were also at work even before the nuclear era. The two bloodiest wars in history were bracketed by attempts to outlaw war, although with primarily verbal solutions, at the 1899 and 1907 Hague Peace Conferences, and in the League of Nations Covenant and the futile Kellogg-Briand pact of 1928 that "outlawed" war. Other more effective efforts sought to civilize and limit warfare, in particular the several Geneva Conventions. History will judge whether the United Nations has been able to do better than its predecessors.

The Balance Sheet

We have stressed the dark and violent face of humankind as a war-prone species. Even if the human individual (especially the female) is innately peace-loving, there nevertheless appears to be a built-in cultural proclivity toward making war in the name of one's ethnic, religious, linguistic, or national group or ideology, and in the future perhaps for reasons of depleted resources and excess population. Certainly over the past century the peace movement, broadly speaking, has run a poor second to the war makers. The twentieth century, in addition to the two great wars, has also experienced hundreds of "small wars" that killed in the neighborhood of 25 million people. The twenty-first century promises little respite in the killing done in the name of territory, race, religion, ethnic group, or plain power-seeking, in at least some corners of the globe.

In order to tackle a topic that is as deeply felt as war and peace, one needs to keep a balanced perspective. Since the UN Charter was signed in 1945, there has been no general war, thanks mainly to the horror of nuclear weapons, and peace has been made between numerous factions in conflict. Electronic journalism that supplies bloody pictures in real time across the globe gives the impression that the dark side is not only still with us but is in fact winning out. But in actuality, warfare is at a relative minimum, and the dangerous and potentially terrifying nuclear standoff between adversaries in the half-century Cold War struggle has been vastly transformed. Without minimizing the horrors of individual conflict situations, the balance sheet does show at least some items of good news.

Above all, war has become unthinkable between the democracies, and some of the most sanguinary conflicts of the age may burn themselves out.

Forty-five years of warfare between Israel and its hostile Arab neighbors seemed to be drawing to a close by the mid–1990s. But the peace process is fragile, and vulnerable to setbacks that could jeopardize the evolving *modus vivendi.* There is also hope for ending the communal/confessional violence that has escalated in Northern Ireland since the late 1960s; but like the Middle East, the situation in Ulster pits moderates against extremists among both Catholics and Protestants, and is similarly fragile. Lebanon—a political fever swamp since 1975—ended its civil war with its factions quiescent, if not wholly reconciled to coexistence.

Can we speak of progress, of moving however fitfully toward a more peaceful future? Consider the words of John Keegan, one of the world's foremost students of warfare:

> As we contemplate this end-of-the-century world . . . may war at last be recognized as having lost its usefulness and deep attractiveness? War in our time has been not merely a means of resolving inter-state disputes but also a vehicle through which the embittered, the dispossessed, the naked of the earth, the hungry masses yearning to breathe free, express their anger, jealousies and pent-up urge to violence. There are grounds for believing that at last, after five thousand years of recorded war making, cultural and material changes may be working to inhibit man's proclivity to take up arms.[48]

But strategists, like doctors, disagree on the patient's prognosis. Edward Luttwak sees the likelihood of "a new, much less restrained culture of war. . . emerging and spreading."[49] Later chapters will provide an opportunity to see who is right.

A NOTE ABOUT LANGUAGE

Before taking a closer look at the likely agenda for future conflict, it is a good idea to standardize our vocabulary.

"Conflict" is a broad concept that becomes particularly confusing when we use ambiguous language (trade wars, bloody disputes, regional conflicts, etc.) to discuss it. Many people use the word "conflict" to mean any and all differences, quarrels, political struggles, economic or social differences, *coups d'état*—and wars. Like the Red Queen in *Alice in Wonderland,* here words mean what people say they mean. People turn out to have in mind a broad spectrum of differences, starting with simple arguments and ending with wars.

Many analysts define "wars" as conflicts entailing at least 1000 deaths.[50] If we use that criterion, we can point to 41 major conflicts and 70 "minor conflicts" in the late 1980s.[51] Some analysts using the same criterion in the 1990s counted 80 or so—53 major conflicts in 42 countries and another 37 involving political violence, with over 80 percent in the developing regions (only a handful interstate, the rest internal).[52] Others counted 43 "small wars" in 1993.[53] Still

TABLE 1-1
BLOOMFIELD-LEISS DYNAMIC PHASE CONFLICT MODEL

D I S P U T E					
C O N F L I C T					
HOSTILITIES					
Phase 1	Phase 2	Phase 3	Phase 4	Phase 5	Settlement
Dispute	Conflict	Hostilities	Post-Hostilities	Post-Hostilities	
Quarrel about an Issue	Military Option Develops	Fighting between Organized Units	Conflict Remains	Dispute Remains Unsettled	Dispute Settled
Factors ⇒ ⇐	*Factors* ⇐ ⇒	*Factors* ⇐ ⇒	*Factors* ⇐ ⇒	*Factors* ⇐ ⇒	

others use larger numbers that turn out to include skirmishes, bloody *coups d'état,* and the like.

Without belaboring the point, a safe round figure for "small wars" over the past several decades is plus or minus 100. In addition, there were scores of lesser conflicts that never turned into hostilities or generated over 1000 casualties, and in addition there were hundreds of particularly nasty disputes in which the parties never came to serious blows. Our discussion will be a good deal less murky if we use some special definitions that aid us in clearer thinking.[54]

Political differences of any kind invariably start with a *dispute*—a quarrel about something, whether it be borders, race, tribe, language, religion, territory, or who is to govern a specific piece of real estate. A *conflict* begins when one or both or all sides begin to consider settling the dispute with force; that is, one or another party begins to seriously arm, or import offensive weaponry, or employ limited or symbolic forms of violence. It becomes a *conflict* when it starts to feel like something potentially more violent than a simple political difference.

When actual fighting breaks out, we call it *hostilities*. This does not just mean a political assassination, car-bombing incident, or border skirmish, which are frequent features of nonhostilities conflict situations. *Hostilities* imply outright, recognizable warfare involving organized military units and generating significant casualties, whether the number is 1000 or 500 or 1500. The sides probably wear different color uniforms, as in the Persian Gulf, or they may wear black pajamas, as in Vietnam. The point is that a shooting war has started. (Having advanced the necessary cautions about loose usage, in the following discussion we will for convenience occasionally use the word "conflict" generically to save time and the reader's patience.) It might sharpen the picture to look at a picture. Table 1-1 is a simplified depiction of the so-called phase model we at MIT have used as a framework for our research on conflict.

The model connotes a dynamic process composed of the various steps through which conflicts can travel. As the arrows suggest, the conflict's direction is not always forward. In some instances, such as the protracted Arab–Israeli War or the India–Pakistan conflict, the post-hostilities situation can loop back to dispute, and from there back to renewed conflict, or from post-hostilities conflict directly back to renewed warfare. The *factors* symbolized by arrows at the bottom of the picture are the hundreds of facts, personalities, relationships, and events tending to move the situation in either direction. The computerized version of this model known as CASCON is the subject of the third part of this book.

NOTES

[1]Many of the references in this chapter to the scholarly literature, as well as several excellent general works on the causes of war, are elaborated upon in the Bibliography.

[2]*Leviathan,* 1651 (New York: E. P. Dutton, 1950).

[3]*The History of the Peloponnesian War* (Harmondsworth: Penguin, 1954).

[4]*The Prince,* 1520 (New York: Modern Library, 1950).

[5]*American Diplomacy, 1900–1950* (Chicago: University of Chicago Press, 1951).

[6]See, for instance, Lincoln P. Bloomfield's *The United Nations and US Foreign Policy: A New Look at the National Interest* (Boston: Little, Brown, rev. ed., 1968).

[7]*Politics among Nations,* 4th ed. (New York: Alfred A. Knopf, 1967); see also *Scientific Man vs. Power Politics* (Chicago: University of Chicago Press, 1946).

[8]*Moral Man and Immoral Society* (New York: Scribners, 1947).

[9]*Peace and War* (New York: Doubleday, 1966).

[10]"The Systems Approach to International Politics," in Kaplan, ed., *New Approaches to International Relations* (New York: St. Martin's Press, 1968).

[11]*Diplomacy* (New York: Simon and Schuster, 1994), p.21.

[12]*A World Restored—Europe after Napoleon: The Politics of Conservatism in a Revolutionary Age* (New York: Grosset and Dunlap, 1964).

[13]*Man, the State, and War: A Theoretical Analysis* (New York: Columbia University Press, 1954).

[14]*War and Change in World Politics* (Cambridge, England: Cambridge University Press, 1981).

[15]"To Eternal Peace," 1795, in *The Philosophy of Kant,* ed. Carl J. Friedrich (New York: Modern Library, 1949).

[16] *The Spirit of the Laws,* 1748 (Worcester: Isaiah Thomas, 1802).

[17] *The Functional Theory of Politics* (New York: St. Martin's Press, 1975).

[18] "The Moral Equivalent of War," in *Memories and Studies* (New York, 1911).

[19] *Capital, the Communist Manifesto and Other Writings* (New York: Modern Library, 1932).

[20] *Essays in Peace Research* (Copenhagen: Ejlers, 1975).

[21] *Capitalist World-Economy* (Cambridge: Cambridge University Press, 1979). See also his *After Liberalism* (New York: New Press, 1995).

[22] *An Essay on the Principle of Population; and A Summary View of the Principle of Population* (Harmondsworth: Penguin, 1970).

[23] *Population Dynamics and International Violence* (Lexington, Mass.: Lexington Books, 1974).

[24] See the last section of this chapter for the special definitions used throughout the book for "disputes," "conflicts," and other words connoting war and peace that are loosely employed in general usage.

[25] For useful references, see the Bibliography, in particular Seyom Brown, *The Causes and Prevention of War* (New York: St. Martin's Press, 1987); and Anatol Rapaport, *The Origins of Violence: Approaches to the Study of Conflict* (New York: Paragon House, 1989).

[26] An International Series of Open Letters, International Institute of Intellectual Cooperation, League of Nations, 1933, p. 103, cited by Johan Kaufmann in "The Evolving United Nations: Principles and Realities," Academic Council for the UN System, Brown University, 1994, p. 3.

[27] Edward O. Wilson, "Is Humanity Suicidal?", *New York Times Magazine,* May 30, 1993, p. 24. The president of the Carnegie Corporation agrees: "ethnocentrism and prejudice are rooted in our ancient past and were probably once adaptive." David Hamburg, *Annual Report 1994,* New York, p. 6.

[28] Konrad Lorenz, *On Aggression* (New York: Harcourt, Brace, 1963) and Robert Ardrey, *The Territorial Imperative* (New York: Athenaeum, 1966).

[29] Martin Daly and Margo Wilson, quoted by Robert Wright in "The Biology of Violence," *New Yorker,* March 13, 1995, p. 72.

[30] Thomas Hobbes, *Leviathan,* pp. 79, 103, 104.

[31] Jean Jacques Rousseau, *The Social Contract* (1762) (London: J. M. Dent and Sons Ltd., 1938), p. 11.

[32] An International Series of Open Letters.

[33] Barbara W. Tuchman, *The March of Folly: From Troy to Vietnam* (New York: Abacus, 1984), p. 26.

[34] Martin Van Creveld, *The Transformation of War* (New York: Free Press, 1991), p. 221.

[35] John Keegan, *A History of Warfare* (New York: Alfred A. Knopf, 1993), pp. 3, 12.

[36] Carl von Clausewitz, *On War,* edited and translated by Michael Howard and Peter Paret (Princeton, N.J.: Princeton University Press, 1976).

[37] Friedrich von Bernhardi, cited by Bernard Brodie in *War and Politics* (New York: Macmillan, 1973), p. 265.

[38] Letter of December 11, 1880 to Johann K. Bluntschli, cited in *Oxford Book of Quotations,* p. 364.

[39] *Twilight of the Idols or How One Philosophizes with a Hammer,* cited in Henry S. Kariel, ed., *Sources in Twentieth Century Political Thought* (Glencoe, Ill.: Free Press, 1964).

[40] Quoted by William Pfaff in "The Fallen Hero," *The New Yorker,* May 8, 1989, pp. 1–7.

[41] *Diplomacy,* p. 168.

⁴²Cited by F. R. Dulles in *The Imperial Years* (New York: Thomas Y. Crowell, 1956), p. 47.

⁴³Allen Westcott, ed., *Mahan on Naval Warfare* (Boston: Little, Brown, 1920).

⁴⁴"A Fighting Faith: The Civil War," in Max Lerner, ed., *The Mind and Faith of Justice Holmes* (Boston: Little, Brown, 1943), pp. 20, 23.

⁴⁵Quoted by Stuart R. Schram, *The Political Thought of Mao Tse-Tung* (New York: Praeger, 1963), p. 209.

⁴⁶Quoted by Lucian W. Pye, *Mao Tse-tung: The Man in the Leader* (New York: Basic Books, 1976), p. 257.

⁴⁷Régis Debray, *Revolution in the Revolution? Armed Struggle and Political Struggle in Latin America* (New York: Grove, 1967).

⁴⁸*A History of Warfare,* p. 56.

⁴⁹Edward N. Luttwak, "Toward Post-Heroic Warfare," *Foreign Affairs,* May to June 1995, p. 111.

⁵⁰Ruth Sivard in her annual accounting of *World Military and Social Expenditures* defines war as entailing "deaths averaging more than 1,000 per year." Her lists cover most of the conflicts we and others have studied (Leesburg, Va.: WMSE Publications, annually).

⁵¹Karel Lindgren, G. Kenneth Wilson, and Peter Wallensteen, "Armed Conflicts over Government and Territory," in *States in Armed Conflict 1988,* ed. Peter Wallensteen (Uppsala University, Department of Peace and Conflict Research), Report No. 30, July 1989, p. 35.

⁵²*Human Development Report,* UN Development Program (New York: United Nations, June 1994), p. 47. The Report adds that 90 percent of the casualties suffered were civilian.

⁵³*SIPRI Yearbook 1994* (New York: Oxford University Press, 1994).

⁵⁴See Lincoln P. Bloomfield and Amelia C. Leiss, *Controlling Small Wars* (New York: Alfred A. Knopf, 1969). Others have found our definitions and phase model useful (e.g., "we are influenced by [this] classical definition . . . adopted by most conflict specialists"; see Albert Legault, "United Nations Peacekeeping and Peacemaking," in *The State of the United Nations, 1992* [Providence, R.I.: Academic Council on the UN System, 1992], Reports and Papers No. 3, p. 30).

Two ⌒

THE AGE OF LOCAL CONFLICT
A Short History

THE COLD WAR BACKDROP

In Chapter 1 we saw that warfare has been a chronic feature of the human condition, extending as far back as recorded history runs. In the last two centuries, except of course for its victims, war was generally accepted as part of the natural order of things. In the same period, however, a contrary position was developing that war is immoral, an idea that can be traced to the late eighteenth century and Immanuel Kant, whose "categorical imperative" supplied prescriptions for a state of "perpetual peace." By the early twentieth century, an active peace movement was flourishing in the Western world.

It took the insane carnage of World War I to give impetus to a serious norm condemning military aggression. Tragically for another 50 million souls, the dogs of war were again unleashed from 1939 to 1945 in World War II. The Second World War was the product of unjust treaties, economic stresses, malevolent forces in Germany, Italy, and Japan thirsting for revenge and conquest, and a toothless League of Nations led by myopic democracies. The wartime victors—the United States, Britain, and the USSR (and by courtesy France and China)—were not unaware of this history. The United Nations Charter they drafted in 1945 was aimed at avoiding a repetition of the disastrous recent past.

What made all-out war an intolerable prospect was the advent of nuclear weapons in 1945. In the period that ensued, the Soviet Union's menacing behavior under dictator Josef Stalin, opposed by Western democracies under the United States' leadership, gave a third world war every reason for happening in a climate of hostility unmatched since the religious wars of the sixteenth and seventeenth centuries. But only a madman could regard a nuclear exchange as a rational means of gaining political ends. At the apogee of the Cold War, even during hair-raising crises over Berlin in 1961 and Cuba in 1962, the imperative to avoid nuclear war expressed itself in a tacit mutual strategy of caution.

Despite loose talk on both sides, all U.S. presidents and Soviet leaders, along with most sensible people, acknowledged both the uncontrollability of thermonuclear war and the urgent need to deter potential aggressors, or indeed any use of nuclear weapons. The conceptual dilemma was daunting. Nuclear weapons were rationally unusable. At the same time, it was essential that potential aggressors believe that the victim nevertheless just might respond to attack even at the cost of mutual suicide. The implicit message was "one of us has to be rational and it's not going to be me."

The nuclear theologians worked hard to formulate an intellectual basis for the expanding nuclear arsenals, seeking a more believable deterrent posture than the quickly discredited *massive retaliation* prescription of Secretary of State John Foster Dulles. In the late 1950s, American strategists formulated a doctrine of "limited war," meaning less than all-out nuclear clashes between the United States and the Soviet Union. Henry Kissinger, then a junior Harvard professor, delineated its characteristics: limited rather than unlimited objectives, and a strategy aimed at influencing rather than crushing one's opponent.[1] His colleague Thomas Schelling advocated unused force as a tool for tacit communication to bargain, deter, and compel.[2]

During the 1960s, U.S. administrations elaborated nuclear war-fighting doctrines based on the notion of *controlled escalation.* This policy of so-called flexible response was crafted for Europe until, that is, America's European allies noticed that it could mean destroying them in order to save them. As late as 1981, President Ronald Reagan unnerved Europeans with casual comments about a nuclear war limited to Europe. Soviet military planners, for their part, claimed that a nuclear war could be won, precipitating a bitter argument in the United States in the 1970s in which the political right argued that the United States was in "clear and present danger" of being overwhelmed by oversized Soviet rockets. (In the end Reagan turned out to be an impulsive disarmer, and the USSR turned out to be a political-economic basket case.)

War-fighting formulations on both sides contributed to mutual deterrence but happily remained devoid of any but theoretical meaning.[3] As in the United States, the governing leadership in Moscow did not really believe the "nuclears are usable" arguments. Instead, the Kremlin's fundamental analysis was spelled out in a February 1961 speech by Premier Nikita Khrushchev in which he explained Moscow's line on the distinction between good and bad forms of war. Nuclear war was excluded for obvious reasons. Limited nuclear conflict was equally unacceptable because it would doubtless expand and become all-out. But what communists called wars of national liberation were not only good but downright desirable. Khrushchev's third category in fact reflected the reality of conflicts that were actually taking place—the continuing litany of real wars in which real people get killed. The success of mutual strategic nuclear deterrence had little or no effect on a whole universe of conflicts that were— and still are—fought with so-called conventional weapons.

THE AGE OF SMALL WARS

When we began our research project on local and regional conflicts at the Massachusetts Institute of Technology (MIT) in the mid-1960s, we observed that over 95 percent of the "small wars" were taking place in the southern, less developed half of the world. This is still largely true, although the fault lines are creeping northward. For people in the industrialized, developed world, until recently "local" meant a war that was happening somewhere else. In the earlier post–World War II decades, conflicts could be sorted into four major types: colonial, interstate, primarily internal, and internal with significant external involvement.[4] Since the Cold War ended, the last of the four earlier types no longer really exists. However, it remains the case that the *internal* variety of conflict still represents over 95 percent of the total.

Colonial Wars

Within three decades following World War II, all the great Western overseas empires had crumbled in the tidal wave of decolonization that swept the globe, a process both stimulated and overseen by the United Nations. (The one remaining empire—that of the USSR—precipitously dissolved in 1989–91.) The fragmentation of the old nineteenth-century colonial map into independent states left a legacy of national pride, unsettled boundaries, shortages of trained personnel, and often nonviable economies. Decolonization was not always violent, but both its peaceful and warlike aspects dominated the UN agenda during the 1940s and 1950s. The decolonization process, rather than the rhetorical communist version, was the true "liberation movement" of the twentieth century.

Interstate Wars

Wars between states constituted the classic category of warfare. Immediately after the defeat of the Axis in 1945, wars broke out in several areas. The Arab–Israeli conflict was the United Nations' first, and from 1948 to the present involved six major battles. During this period, three bloody outbreaks of war also occurred between India and Pakistan, chiefly over the status of the territory of Jammu and Kashmir. And the inability of Greek and Turkish Cypriots to share their lovely island after the British colonial ruler withdrew brought an ugly war climaxing in an earlier version of "ethnic cleansing" by the Turkish army in 1974. Three decades later, UN peacekeepers were still present at least somewhere in all three conflicts, which remain unsettled in one degree or another.

For a time after the Cold War ended, as more and more struggles took place *within* state boundaries, interstate conflict seemed to have become obsolete. But late in the Cold War period the world began to experience a revival of territorial wars of the old-fashioned variety. Cases in point were the 1980–88 war between Iran and Iraq, at least nominally over the Shatt-al-Arab boundary and the Iranian province of Khuzestan; the 1982–83 war between Britain and Argentina over the Falklands/Malvinas Islands in the south Atlantic; and from 1991 the Serbian attempt to carve a Greater Serbia from parts of Bosnia and Croatia. Conflict broke out in the same period over mineral resources—among Mauritania, Morocco, and Algeria over phosphate-rich Western Sahara; between Libya and Chad over the uranium-bearing Aozou strip; and between China, Vietnam, and others over the potentially oil-rich Spratly Islands in the South China Sea.

Internal Conflicts

The core of the East-West competition during the Cold War lay within turbulent, mainly new countries to the south. Many of these struggles mirrored long-festering ethnic, religious, or linguistic differences, socioeconomic inequities, oppression of minorities, or suppression of human rights. Civil unrest often reflected turbulence in the wake of the decolonization process that produced approximately 90 new states, some of which were constructed with little regard to tribal boundaries. But during the Cold War the most neuralgic problem for great-power relations involved those internal conflicts "with significant outside involvement," as we labeled it.

The internal variety of conflict takes various forms—revolution, civil war, ethnic and communal, insurrection, insurgency, and guerrilla warfare. It accounted for almost half of the post–World War II conflict agendas, and today it dominates the list. (The fashionable American military label for this genre is low-intensity conflict, or LIC.)

The Cold War began to spread to the Third World in the 1950s. Unlike most interstate wars, the proxy battlegrounds for the superpowers were often places where attempts were underway to change, by force if necessary, the dominant socio-political-economic ideology. In the former French Indochina, the new nationalist leadership that took over in North Vietnam after defeating their French imperial masters also happened to be Moscow-trained and oriented. In the Middle East, the Soviet Union's 1954 leapfrog over the so-called northern tier of Western client states (Turkey, Pakistan, and Iran) into Egypt was met by a stepped-up Western strategy of containment led by the United States.

Virtually every political sparrow that fell was recorded on a global box-score and was believed, sometimes correctly and sometimes absurdly, to impact directly on the nervous superpower peace. One of Washington's several alternative arguments for intervening in Vietnam, where the United States' immediate interests were minimal, was that a show of weakness anywhere conveyed a dangerous signal to Moscow. Based on that global logic, for almost three decades the world's two most powerful antagonists embroiled themselves in Cold War battlegrounds in the developing regions stretching from the Caribbean through Central Africa to Southeast Asia, from Korea, Vietnam, Laos, and Cambodia to Angola, Mozambique, Nicaragua, Cuba, and Afghanistan.

The typical political choreography pitted pro-revolutionary Moscow against stability-preferring Washington. In that scenario the United States was permanently cast in a reactive role. In Europe NATO effectively blocked any Soviet territorial or aggressive intentions. But without the same strategic rationale, Washington sometimes seemed to respond in the style of Pavlov's dogs to perceived Soviet, Cuban, or Chinese inroads anywhere in the Third World even where no strategic interest existed.

Sometimes roles were reversed. In Angola and some other parts of Africa, communist China and communist Russia lined up in support of opposing factions. Equally ironically, the allegedly revolutionary Soviet Union acted in the 1956 Hungarian and 1968 Czech uprisings like a traditional status quo power. In another historical paradox, in 1981 Washington began to apply an active insurgency-*fomenting* policy—the so-called Reagan Doctrine—in Third World states supported by Moscow (or Cuba): Angola, Mozambique, Ethiopia, Nicaragua, and Afghanistan. (The sanguinary struggle during the 1980s between Iran and Iraq did not, despite its strategic locale, become a larger war, doubtless because neither Moscow nor Washington could decide which side it was on and generally tried to balance the opposing sides.)

Small Wars and Superpowers

The picture, then, from 1950 to 1990 was a worldwide panorama of local conflicts stemming from many causes, most of them indigenous, but in many cases treated by the major powers as pawns in the global competition. This made abstractions of some situations where bloodshed and suffering put real people at risk. We call these cases small wars and local conflicts, but the human price of a small war can be tremendous in terms of casualties, refugee populations, and grave setbacks in development. In the late 1990s one needed look no further than Bosnia or Rwanda to comprehend the passions involved and the intensity of commitment. What may appear to outsiders like a brush fire may, from the standpoint of the combatants, be a murderous conflagration.

By the same token, the inability of weak states to carry their struggles to the point of annihilation does not necessarily imply a willingness to compromise or settle, other than an armed truce as in Korea, Cyprus, and Kashmir. Indeed, in the early postwar decades some charismatic non-Western leaders acted out classical definitions of imperialism within their own ambits. In the 1950s Gamal Abdel Nasser held aims for Egypt that embraced all the Arab world and at times the African continent. In the same era Sukarno's territorial ambitions for Indonesia extended to wherever the Malay race was found in Southeast Asia. The goals of Ghana's Kwame Nkrumah reflected a near-mystical notion of pan-Africa, and Cuba's Fidel Castro expressed unlimited objectives toward the whole of Latin America and parts of southern Africa. In 1979, the Ayatollah Ruhollah Khomeini's revolutionary Iran proclaimed a universal mission reminiscent of the earlier rhetorical visions of revolutionary America, France, and Russia.

However Moscow and Washington defined their respective roles, many of these situations had little or nothing to do with "socialism" versus "freedom" except as labels to advance the fortunes of contending local power-seekers. Moscow sought as clients such un-Marxist or "bourgeois nationalist" regimes as Egypt, Indonesia, Sudan, Somalia, Mozambique, Angola, Iraq, and Syria, electing them to a kind of honorary Marxist status. Similarly, the United States chose to bed down with autocratic regimes such as those in Portugal, Iran, Guatemala, and South Korea, which often violated deeply held American principles of democracy and human rights, but for strategic reasons were granted honorary membership in the free world.

By the 1960s the superpowers' box-score approach to conflicts in the developing regions began to create serious distortions in the foreign policies of both. Client states often cultivated Moscow or Washington to acquire military weaponry. (Then, as now, Russian surplus arms were widely available, and then as now the United States relied on arms sales to help offset its huge trade imbalances.) But local politics often made a mockery of the superpower quest for enduring influence; for example, in the 1970s Sudan and Egypt expelled Soviet advisers, and Ethiopia and Iran turned on their American patron.

Indeed, rather than being controlled from abroad, some client states employed a kind of political judo to manipulate their superpower backers, whether the United States and Israel or the Soviet Union and Cuba.[5] Sometimes the local leaders switched from one patron to the other, as occurred in Egypt, Somalia, Sudan, and Ethiopia. (It is intriguing to compare that stratagem with the tactics of the newly formed and weak United States of America in the late eighteenth century when it picked its way between the French and British "superpowers"!)

Thanks to mutual deterrence, panic about a surprise nuclear attack eventually abated. But it became the conventional wisdom that World War III was likely to start from a local conflict spinning out of control. The most inflammable spot was the Arab–Israeli conflict, in which the two sides were backed by superpowers whose nuclear-armed forces added a hair-raising dimension to each outbreak. In October 1973, even during the U.S.-Soviet détente, Moscow threatened to send in airborne forces to relieve the pressure on Egypt, and Washington responded with a rarely employed "Defcon3" worldwide nuclear alert.

The accession of Mikhail Gorbachev to power in Moscow in 1988, together with a collapsing Soviet economy, triggered the cascading process of Soviet disengagement from virtually all its forward positions. Moscow dropped support for Cuba and renounced the Brezhnev Doctrine that had rhetorically legitimized military control of Russia's East European and Baltic satellites by claiming that no one, once incorporated into the Soviet orbit, could ever leave it. The USSR retreated from its ill-starred 1979 invasion of Afghanistan as it, like the United States earlier in Vietnam, experienced military and moral exhaustion in a situation of unwinnable guerrilla warfare, mounting popular revulsion at home, and worldwide criticism. A winding down of conflict in Nicaragua, El Salvador,

Angola, and Mozambique became possible once Moscow (and Cuba) curtailed military aid, and Washington in turn became willing to back a Central American peace initiative and involvement by the United Nations and the Organization of American States (OAS).

Some of the secondary effects of the Soviet collapse were equally consequential. The long-frustrated birthing process culminating in 1990 in independence for Namibia (formerly South African-ruled South West Africa) could take place with the United Nations as midwife once Cuban and South African forces withdrew from Angola. Beginning in 1991, Vietnam's occupation forces gradually withdrew from Cambodia under a UN-brokered peace accord. Nuclear self-deterrence, combined with time and common sense, had eroded both Lenin's prescription of global conflict stemming from clashes between "imperialist" powers and the Stalinist doctrine of inevitable warfare between systems.

In the 1990s the conflict map changed dramatically with the breakup of communist rule in Russia and Yugoslavia, which dissolved the brittle glue that for a half-century had kept in place hostile and contentious tribes in the Balkans, the Caucasus, and Southwest Asia. The unintended result was a deadly species of ethnic strife in which the question of governance was not "what ideology governs?" but "what tribe rules?" The newly downsized Russian Federation seemed eager to join the United States in a de facto coalition that enabled the UN Security Council to tamp down local conflicts so that both could focus on their domestic problems.

ARMS AND CONFLICT

The international arms trade has been a controversial topic for many years, going back to denunciations of "merchants of death" in the 1920s. It has been praised on the one hand as a security instrument and moneymaker, and condemned on the other for diverting badly needed development funds and destructively weaponizing local conflicts. Discussions of the spread of conventional arms have been dominated by concerns about the transfer of sophisticated weaponry. Certainly, such weaponry has created casualties, usually civilian, in many conflicts. "Small wars" have killed around 25 million people since 1945.

A parallel concern has been the role of conventional arms transfers in distorting the economies of poor countries engaged in disputes with their neighbors. By the mid-1990s military spending had actually dropped 10 percent even in the face of a record number of small wars.[6] However, that spending had increased three times as fast in poor as in rich countries. It matched total spending on health and education in at least seven developing countries where conflict was endemic or actually raging.[7]

Some argue that arms are the cause of conflict; others say they are the result. The UN Development Program, characterizing the arms trade as reprehensible in exploiting poverty, identified the arms trade as a cause of conflict: "arms dealers continue to ship weapons to potential trouble spots, showing little concern about fanning the flames of conflict," with "more than 40% of the sales of major conventional weapons during the past decade" going to such trouble spots.[8] Pope John Paul II went further, stating that "those who foment war . . . by the arms trade are accomplices in abominable crimes against humanity."[9] The president of the Carnegie Corporation summed it up well: "Weapons themselves do not cause dangerous conflicts, but their availability in large quantities can easily intensify and prolong such conflicts."[10]

During the Cold War, both sides poured weapons into the hands of their proxies in conflict situations ranging from the Middle East to Vietnam, the Horn of Africa, Central America, and the Caribbean. The global arms transfer picture has in fact been moderating, and arms transfers have been declining. But in the late 1990s Russia led exports to the Third World market, while the United States held a greater percent of the overall market than did Britain, Russia, China, and France combined. For Americans the strategic rationale for arms supply remains valid in the Gulf and the Pacific. But that rationale has been increasingly replaced by a primarily commercial motivation in the worldwide quest for export earnings, with the profit motive dominant as small arms and light weaponry have poured into conflict sources like Rwanda, Sudan, Somalia, and Bosnia. Often it has been shady middlemen and international small arms dealers who have fueled a long list of recent conflicts ranging from Afghanistan, Angola, Myanmar (Burma), and Cambodia to Colombia, Ethiopia, Kashmir, Lebanon, Peru, the Philippines, Sri Lanka, and countries of the former Soviet Union.

A policy approach favored by the U.S. government rests on the not illogical premise that by rectifying a regional military imbalance, peace will be furthered in conflict-prone areas. This seemingly commonsense position was the United States' primary justification for arming Israel, Pakistan, Egypt, South Korea, Turkey, Saudi Arabia, Iraq, and Taiwan, all of whom were being menaced in one way or another by a hostile neighbor. Evidence in support of this policy hypothesis is mixed, however, as we have found in our research, and it was even less clear that the policy always brought stability.

An analysis based on our CASCON database (see Part III of this book) led to the provocative inference that importing arms for balancing purposes might have exacerbated rather than pacified a number of local conflicts. Other analysts found that during 1965–85, U.S. arms exports to 42 countries correlated with subsequent occurrences of military coups, armed repression, and insurgencies.[11] Another of our research conclusions was that, while the gradual introduction of offsetting weaponry might help stabilize an out-of-balance regional faceoff, local stability could be dangerously upset by a *high-speed alteration* in the local military balance.

Low-level killing devices are often supplied by outsiders not for war fighting, but for domestic law and order purposes, as a result of which such weaponry is turned on the people it is supposed to protect. In the recent past, a collection of Frankenstein monsters was inadvertently created through training and arming for civic order, for instance, by the United States in El Salvador, Iran, Panama, and Haiti (sometimes circumventing U.S. law banning defense support for domestic police agencies). Israel did the same in Idi Amin's Uganda, as did France in Rwanda and Burundi, and the former Soviet Union in many places. Amnesty International noted that in 1995 the United States bestowed $4.65 billion worth of weapons and military training to 19 countries guilty of flagrant human rights abuses.[12] With the Cold War over, this policy can be explained only by inattention on the part of civilian leadership.

Controlling Arms

Measures to control conventional arms are uncommonly difficult to negotiate, let alone implement, for several reasons: the reluctance of recipient states to accept second-class status; the desire of supplier nations for market share and lucrative profits; and the continued quest for influence by major governments.

Some modest efforts at restraint have been made, as when small or weak contenders have been deprived of access to lethal arms on both humanitarian and economic grounds. Except when a country needs arms to defend against an external threat to its sovereignty or territorial integrity, in a rational world a ban should be negotiated barring the pouring of arms into unstable regions. But over the years, many such attempts, for one reason or another, have been thwarted. For instance, efforts have repeatedly been made to draw a circle around the Arab–Israeli conflict. A 1950 UN resolution notionally prohibited the input of externally supplied arms, but the pressures on arms-supplying countries to win influence or help friends in the region proved too strong. In Latin America in the late 1960s, the U.S. government barred a planned sale to Peru of supersonic military jets, which would have added a new and expensive dimension to regional arms buildups. The only trouble was that within days, salesmen from a French aircraft firm arrived in Lima with glossy pictures of the new Mirages. The same story has prevailed ever since in most parts of the world, driven by both the supply and the demand side. A particularly cynical case has been China's exports of neighbor-threatening missiles to Pakistan and Iran. And both the Chinese and Russians have transferred equipment appropriate for the development of banned weapons of mass destruction, whether nuclear, chemical, or biological.

At least one clear deterrent to supplier restraint has been evident: some decisions to embargo weaponry to areas in conflict have spawned perverse effects. The major such effect has been to stimulate an indigenous arms industry to reduce dependence on paternalistic outside sources, as happened in both India and Israel. In some cases, an arms embargo can even prolong the fighting. The Bosnian war may have been worsened by the unequal impact of the international embargo on arms, with the well-equipped former Yugoslav army helping the Bosnian Serbs to accomplish their noxious ethnic cleansing of Muslims, who received only an illicit trickle from distant Islamic states. In the end, enough illegal weaponry slipped through into Croatia and Bosnia to equalize the contest on the ground (as long as the Yugoslav Serb army stayed out) and helped produce at least the beginnings of a peace based on exhaustion.

The first serious negotiation in the conventional arms realm took place in Mexico City in the late 1970s and foundered on the three grounds listed at the beginning of this section. After decades of debate, the United Nations in December 1991 finally adopted a modest plan for a register of arms transactions that would include some categories of arms imported and exported on a country-to-country basis—a task that the nongovernmental SIPRI (Stockholm Institute for Peace and Research) and the IISS (International Institute for Strategic Studies) had been performing for several years. A particular effort has been made to curb antipersonnel landmines, which still maim thousands of children in post-conflict battlefields ranging from Angola to Afghanistan to Vietnam. But a UN Conference in Geneva in May 1996 stopped short of a total ban, in part because of United States insistence on reserving the right to continue to mine the tense inter-Korean border. (Germany, the Netherlands, and Canada have abolished the use of mines, and 15 former high-ranking American military officers publicly urged President Clinton to sign on to such a ban.)

The arms-reduction quest continues, however haltingly. A 1992 negotiation broke down after the United States agreed to sell Taiwan F-16 fighter planes and China pulled out. In July 1996, thirty countries agreed at Vienna to modest limits on arms to rogue states (a year earlier a group of Nobel Peace Prize winners proposed a code of conduct "to ban weapons exports to countries with repressive governments or at war"[13]). But what we call gun control on the city streets appears to be improbable for the still anarchic international community.

Introducing *nuclear* weaponry into the regional conflict equation could be catastrophic, whether between India and Pakistan in their unresolved dispute over Kashmir, between North and South Korea in their unsettled conflict, or between Iran and Iraq in their quest for regional hegemony. Some important restraints have been supplied by the almost-universal Nuclear Non-Proliferation Treaty, made permanent by 175 countries in 1995; by the Nuclear Suppliers Group that informally restricts commerce in nuclear fuel fabrication; and by the Missile Technology Control Regime, which works to limit potential delivery systems. Diplomatic efforts with North Korea have shown that outside powers take such a potential threat far more seriously than any posed by conventional arms. (A counter-argument is occasionally made that weapons of mass destruction in the hands of both sides of a local conflict might deter them both, as with the United States and the USSR during the Cold War.[14] No one should count on that, however.) The U.N. voted for a total nuclear test ban in 1996.

The principal danger may not be so much the development of full-fledged nuclear arsenals by countries in conflict as it is the dissemination of loose fissile material to potential terrorist groups. The American National Academy of Sciences has made some important efforts to help Russia account for and safeguard the 1200 tons of uranium and 200 tons of plutonium estimated to be around following the fall of the Soviet regime. Obviously, more such help is urgently needed.

Clearly, people determined to savage one another will use whatever weaponry is at hand. Expensive and sophisticated arms can cause major casualties, but civil wars tend to be fought and won with cheap weapons, small-caliber ammunition, light mortars, and machetes. Certainly, any fresh attempts at conventional arms talks must be made in partnership with recipient countries and must meet the issue of financial loss to suppliers. The difficulty of controlling the arms that are employed once a conflict turns violent is another powerful argument that the best policy is to prevent the conflict in the first place.

THE NEW WORLD DISORDER

An Open Moment

The first test of the revitalized international system was Iraq's mugging, trashing, and attempted political extinction of Kuwait in August 1990. However incoherent Washington's policy explanations ("jobs," "democracy," "oil," "collective security," etc.), by openly invading its neighbor, Iraq violated the one rule of international conduct which all states support. Operation Desert Storm was possible because starting in 1991 the two former superpowers agreed on 31 UN Security Council resolutions on Iraq. It was also possible because of the contingent threat to Saudi Arabia and the global oil supply. Success in expelling Iraqi dictator Saddam Hussein from Kuwait, if not from power, seemed to jump-start the process of collective security.

Cross-border aggression was not the main challenge of the 1990s. Instead, the volcano of change spewed forth what Václav Havel called "a lava of post-communist surprises," generating a panorama of turbulence and strategic ambiguity as multinational states broke up and other states simply broke. For left-over conflicts in old Cold War battlefields, UN peacekeeping was the method of choice to monitor cease-fires and help with transitions in Angola, Mozambique, El Salvador, and Nicaragua, along with older trouble spots such as Western Sahara, Namibia, Golan and the Sinai, southern Lebanon, and Cyprus.

The trickiest new threat to the hoped-for harmony in the post–Cold War world was an explosion of mayhem within state borders. Renewed anarchy in Cambodia, man-made starvation in Somalia, assault on the fragile newly won democracy in Haiti, and genocide in Bosnia and Rwanda all violated not so much the "law" as the underlying moral order. Article 2(7) of the UN Charter ostensibly bars the organization from touching such cases because they are "essentially within the domestic jurisdiction of any state." Those new cases would also not have passed the Cold War test of strategic threat. With the fear of superpower escalation gone, however, and with a major assist from world-wide television coverage, they powerfully assailed the global conscience.

Working within a drastically altered strategic landscape, a born-again Security Council began a chapter of law-in-the-making with novel interventionary doctrines intended to justify multilateral intervention to deal with famine-creating anarchy, ethnic cleansing, and deliberate mass creation of refugees. It wasn't exactly peacekeeping as in Cyprus, and certainly not collective security as in the Gulf. It was an unprecedented policing function carrying such provisional labels as peacemaking, humanitarian enforcement, and second-generation operations, with a multilateral-minded United States in the lead. The meaning of the Charter phrase, "threats to the maintenance of international peace and security," became stretched beyond recognition. Despite all the obvious ambiguities, however, the early 1990s seemed to offer an open moment for the dream of a system of global law and order, and one equipped with a heart as well. But the moment was brief.

The Cases from Hell

The new era of multilateral intervention for humanitarian purposes started in Iraq in 1991 when the defeated regime of Saddam Hussein turned savagely on its disaffected Kurdish population in the North (where Baghdad was probably guilty of using chemical weapons to suppress an earlier revolt in 1988). In response to public outrage, the victorious UN/U.S. coalition moved inside Iraqi territory and established no-fly zones in both North and South, along with protected aid channels to "Kurdistan" (although tragically not in the South where the regime was brutally crushing Shi'ite dissidence).

Successive UN resolutions mandated the destruction of long-range ballistic missiles and weapons of mass destruction, along with an unprecedentedly intrusive monitoring of missile testing and other sites. When Baghdad balked at monitoring, UN threats backed by U.S. bombing of selected targets reinforced the Security Council's economic sanctions blocking Iraqi oil revenues. Even then, the UN inspectors could not be sure that the rulers had not hidden stockpiles of illicit biological warfare materials.

Baghdad's partial compliance on one issue after another came only after credible threats of punishment, along with the prospect of lifting the increasingly onerous sanctions. Baghdad responded to the combination of carrots and sticks with a series of "charm offensives" that put hard-line U.S. policy at odds with commerce-minded French, Russian, and Turkish interests. Nevertheless, the U.S.-led UN strategy generally succeeded in greatly reducing an Iraqi threat. It is hard to escape the conclusion that an offending power has to be militarily defeated before the community will actually enforce its norms against unacceptable national behavior.

Several other UN peace enforcement operations did not pose that particular question, but for other reasons brought the trend of peace enforcement to a screeching halt. Soon after the Kurdish rescue operation, the international community was confronted with a string of other interventionary situations including Somalia, Haiti, Rwanda, and Bosnia, all of which lacked the clarity of the collective security enterprise in Iraq. Rapidly mounting controversy about them in the United Nations and in the intervening countries, combined with the massive human suffering on the part of the victims, suggests the appropriateness of the label "Cases from Hell." Chapter 5 elaborates on the issues of peacekeeping and beyond.

In Somalia, where anarchy was generating mass starvation, the United Nations was shamed into action by Secretary General Boutros Boutros-Ghali, and the Council for the first time launched a peacekeeping operation that had not been requested by the "host government" (in this case there was no government at all). The initial American force sent in by President Bush in late 1992 used both diplomacy and military presence to stem the famine, along with some promising steps to create a civil peace. In December 1992 the Security Council authorized the United States, the secretary general, and others to use all necessary means to establish a "secure environment" for humanitarian relief operations in Somalia.

The UN mission became controversial when in a kind of "mission creep" it began to slide from truce-monitoring peacekeeping toward the far more difficult task of reconstructing Somalia's political fabric. Errors and worse were compounded in the local UN operation while a virtually independent U.S. military operation using Ranger forces culminated in a disastrous firefight. U.S. casualties were gruesomely displayed on television, triggering so disproportionate a backlash in the United States that it could be explained only by failure to lay out for the American public the facts of the new international environment. Worse yet, Washington, having itself composed the main Security Council resolutions, tried after the October 1993 firefight "to wash its hands of an operation that it had started and almost entirely directed." As put by one outraged UN official, the United Nations was "seduced and then abandoned" by the United States.[15] The United States withdrew and so, in 1995, did the United Nations, washing its hands of the entire matter. Intervention in the Horn of Africa was an enterprise that, despite its success in stemming mass starvation, showed that both the United Nations and the United States were not ready to take on a purposeful policing job in the presence of anarchy.

Around the same time in the splintered former Yugoslavia, the United Nations undertook another humanitarian mission of aid to hundreds of thousands of people who had been made internal refugees by all sides but primarily by the noxious Serb policy of ethnic cleansing which had uprooted and terrorized Bosnian Muslims. The Security Council authorized use of "all means necessary" to protect aid. However, Britain and France, which, unlike the United States, had several thousand noncombatant peacekeepers on the ground, consistently balked at using proffered NATO airpower to beat back the Serbs. In May 1993 the Council established six "safe havens" for embattled Muslim populations and authorized force to protect the peacekeepers. But for one reason or another all the great powers were unwilling for over three years to back their own norms or their rhetoric. Serb and Croat leaders continued their murderous campaign, as a result of which thousands died and hundreds of thousands were made homeless. It was not until one final massacre that NATO airpower was finally employed to punish the Bosnian Serbs, and serious steps were taken to wind down the war. With a series of new Croat offensives and Muslim victories in 1995 the tide of battle dramatically turned. Through sheer exhaustion, together with intensive American diplomatic efforts in 1995 culminating in the Dayton accord, peace began to take hold, at least for the short term. Almost 60,000 NATO troops, including 20,000 Americans, were in place in 1996 to separate the warring forces. But the long-term survival of Bosnia remained problematic.

In Rwanda a small UN contingent was already on the ground in the capital Kigali when in 1994 the Hutu government launched a horrendous massacre of minority Tutsis, generating hundreds of thousands of corpses and even more refugees. Still another humanitarian disaster unfolded before the world's eyes. But after the high costs and criticism of intervention in Somalia and Bosnia, Washington was determined not to get involved again and joined in the decision to pull out the UN force just as the Hutu massacres began. French forces partially stepped into the breach, and some UN forces were sent back—after genocide had taken place. Then the same scenario involving the same tribes began to recur in neighboring Burundi.

In Haiti the issue was the restoration of democratic rule, supplanting the official thuggery that made poverty-stricken Haiti's internal strife particularly cruel. To do so required at least a believable show of force. But a United States once burned wanted none of that. In October 1993, a U.S. warship, the USS *Harlan County,* carrying a small number of lightly armed international monitors, was scared off from landing at Port-au-Prince by a band of the military junta's thugs, and executed a humiliating retreat. The Security Council remained incapable of enforcing its own decisions (the equally involved OAS, faithfully reflecting Latin America's deep resistance to anything resembling intervention, was not a credible alternative), and only in 1994 did the United States finally decide to act forcefully. A skillfully managed landing and deployment of U.S. forces was peaceful, thanks to former president Jimmy Carter's rather unorthodox good offices, most American troops were replaced by other UN contingents in 1995, and elections were held, but with uncertain permanent results for that poor and historically misruled country.

In diplomacy as in war, success has a hundred fathers but defeat—or even plain bad luck—is an orphan. In Bosnia a European Community suffering from tired blood and historical amnesia for all too long avoided its responsibilities to oppose Serb expansion, and Washington—regrettably, though correctly—declined to act alone. In Somalia and Rwanda humanitarian intervention was overtaken by a bloody endgame between claimants for power, while in Haiti good luck as much as good management facilitated the peaceful restoration of the democratically elected president.

In all these cases from Hell, the Security Council and the UN secretary general made some questionable judgments, and the responsible powers faltered when it came to risking even minor casualties. Waiting in the wings were equally hairy scenarios of tribal warfare in Russia's periphery and, from the evidence of Chechnya, within the multiethnic Russian Federation itself. Human rights outrages continued unchecked from Sudan and Zaïre to Myanmar (Burma) and China.

The United States is the one country that is indispensable to an international law and order function. But the U.S. role became problematic in the face of changing world realities, congressional hostility toward the United Nations, uncertain presidential leadership, and an understandable urge by Americans to turn inward after a half-century of global activism. The other Western democracies exhibited political weakness, Moscow was in chaos, and China's future course was unpredictable. In sum, just when the international community had begun to act like one, its seriousness of purpose and staying power were in serious question.

The lessons of multilateral "overstretch" remain to be fully absorbed. An obvious lesson is that humanitarian aid may well require armed protection if it is to reach its recipients. Another is that peacekeeping and enforcement are different concepts and need to be sharply differentiated. A third lesson is that multilateral field operations must be better coordinated. A thoughtful postmortem of the Somalia experience concluded that given the complex political, bureaucratic, and cultural realities, "the worst of both worlds . . . was to turn over responsibility to the United Nations while maintaining US troops at risk and involving US policymakers so intimately in UN operations."[16] But the fourth lesson is not a new one: preventive measures are best applied before a disease develops. Two billion dollars in band-aids (the cost of UN operations in Somalia) did not get at the deeper roots of conflict. There may be a fifth lesson too: before the first four lessons can be applied, both leadership and public opinion in the major countries will need to catch up with new global realities.

GOOD NEWS/BAD NEWS

This brief history should end on a balanced note, particularly since good news is rare in any discussion of conflict. It helps to remember that the local conflicts of the 1990s, however sanguinary, are not planet-threatening, and the number of casualties they engendered do not come anywhere near the two world wars that smashed whole civilizations.

Some wars do end, and other conflicts never reach the point of violence, thanks to quiet diplomacy, cool heads, or the healing passage of time. The Iran–Iraq war of the 1980s was ended, as were the brutal Mozambique and Angolan wars and the protracted conflict over Namibia. The same period witnessed the internal miracle of statesmanship and tolerance that removed South Africa from the critical list. A relative form of peace began to emerge in two other protracted civil conflicts—Lebanon and Ulster—whose outcome few would have foreseen. And the king of them all—the 45-year Arab–Israeli conflict featuring a half-dozen major outbreaks of hostilities—has perhaps a fifty-fifty chance to become a "cold peace" in the sense of avoiding new major warfare despite extremist elements on both sides.

In September 1995 Greece lifted its trade ban that was crippling neighboring Macedonia in the tinderbox Balkans. The year also saw a glimmer of hope over the contested Spratly Islands when China and the Philippines signed an agreement to settle their disputes through international law. In Tajikistan, with Russia ending its support for the rebels, the president amnestied them. In return, they surrendered their weapons. In Mali few noticed the burning of firearms to mark the end of a five-year conflict between Tuareg nomad rebels and the Malian army. Also in 1996, Saudi Arabia and Qatar agreed to end a border dispute that had strained relations and led to armed clashes.

South America, despite setbacks, was also moving toward regional peace. Chile and Argentina settled their long-standing quarrel over the Beagle Channel, Paraguay and Bolivia made peace, and in the 1990s 22 other border disputes were ended. Even the annual blowup between Peru and Ecuador was perhaps susceptible to solution as the two traditional adversaries agreed to demilitarize their border (if anyone could find it). In Central America externally abetted strife in Nicaragua was tranquilized, even if deep structural problems remained. In neighboring El Salvador, thanks also to an indispensable UN presence, the 1992 agreement ending its bitter civil war has held up. There is at least the hope of completing the crucial land transfers to disenfranchised farmers, given the modest funds necessary to continue the small UN presence. Perhaps most extraordinary, given its grim history of repression in which more than 140,000 have been killed or missing, Guatemala shows signs of moderating its notorious military-led abuse, thanks to pervasive UN monitors to whom abuses could be freely reported. On May 6, 1996, the leftist guerrillas signed a cease-fire agreement with the government that at least offered hope of ending the 35-year war. And 1996 brought a tentative peace accord between Mexico and the Zapatista rebels.

Finally, the breakup of the Soviet empire took place in a more peaceful manner than in many empires of the past. The lukewarm peace that descended between the West and Russia left much to be desired. But it was infinitely preferable to what came before, lifting from civilization's back as it did a grim half-century threat of global nuclear annihilation.

NOTES

[1]Henry A. Kissinger, *Nuclear Weapons and Foreign Policy* (New York: Harper, 1957).

[2]Thomas C. Schelling, *A Strategy of Conflict* (Cambridge, Mass.: Harvard University Press, 1957).

[3]See, for instance, National Security Adviser McGeorge Bundy reporting on how Presidents Kennedy and Johnson decisively rejected the notion of ever actually using nuclear weapons. "To Cap the Volcano," *Foreign Affairs,* October 1969.

⁴For other typologies, see, for example, Raimo Väyrynen, "Domestic Crises and International Wars," in Peter Wallensteen, ed., *Peace Research: Achievements and Challenges* (Boulder, Colo.: Westview Press, 1988).

⁵Ambassador Henry Cabot Lodge reported to President Kennedy from Saigon that "the US has never been able to control any of the very unsatisfactory governments through which we have had to work." Quoted by Richard Reeves, *Kennedy: Profile of Power* (New York: Simon and Schuster, 1994), p. 605.

⁶*Conventional Arms Transfers to Developing Nations,* Congressional Research Service, Washington, D.C., August 4, 1995, pp. 5 ff. See also Ruth Sivard, *World Military and Social Expenditures* (Washington, D.C.: World Priorities), annual.

⁷The seven are Myanmar (Burma), Angola, Mozambique, Somalia, Yemen, Ethiopia, and Pakistan. *The Economist,* June 4, 1994, p. 43.

⁸*Human Development Report 1994,* published for the UN Development Program (New York: Oxford University Press, 1994), p. 54.

⁹Speech in Yaounde, Cameroon, *Boston Globe,* September 13, 1995.

¹⁰David A. Hamburg, "Preventing Contemporary Group Violence," Carnegie Corporation, New York, Annual Report 1993, p. 6.

¹¹Former Defense Department official Robert S. McGarrah, in *Christian Science Monitor,* January 13, 1988.

¹²Amnesty International, "Human Rights and U.S. Security Assistance," 1996, reported in *Boston Globe,* June 7, 1996.

¹³*New York Times,* September 6, 1995.

¹⁴See Kenneth Waltz's argument in Waltz and Scott D. Sagan, *The Spread of Nuclear Weapons: A Debate* (New York: W. W. Norton, 1995).

¹⁵Walter Clarke and Jeffrey Herbt, "Somalia and the Future of Humanitarian Intervention," *Foreign Affairs,* March–April 1996, p. 73.

¹⁶*Hope Restored: Humanitarian Aid in Somalia 1900–94* (Washington, D.C.: Refugee Policy Group, November 1994), pp. 2, 113, 118.

Three ↶

THE CONFLICT MAP
Continuity and Change

THINKING ABOUT THE FUTURE

Someone once wrote that predicting the future is easy and that what's hard is figuring out what's going on now. But forecasting is not easy either. As the prophetic Czech playwright-president Václav Havel has said, "We live in the post-modern world, where everything is possible and almost nothing is certain." We tend to extrapolate the familiar present into the future, but as often as not the results turn out to be wrong, with the most "realistic" projections sometimes yielding the least likely outcomes.

Consider the survey conducted in 1893 that asked 73 prominent Americans to picture the world of 1993. They predicted that first-class mail would drop from 2 cents to a penny, that people would live to 150, and that fewer people would divorce or go to prison (although they did presciently see everyone paying income taxes!).[1] Closer to our concerns, in March of 1963 President John F. Kennedy predicted that by 1970 "there may be ten nuclear powers instead of four, and by 1975, fifteen or twenty . . . or twenty-five."[2]

Kennedy was hardly alone in his forecast; famous scientists as well as the UN secretary general had foreseen even more nuclear weapons proliferators. Yet in 1968 the Non-Proliferation Treaty was signed, and by the second half of the 1990s there were still only the five official nuclear weapons powers (the "Perm5," the permanent members of the UN Security Council) as well as three unofficial possessors (India, Israel, and Pakistan) along with several suspicious "wannabe's" such as North Korea, Iraq, and Iran, all of which were under pressure to take the pledge of nuclear nonproliferation. (South Africa and Brazil had already reversed their programs.)

The 1970s must have been a bad period for good forecasting. In February 1970 a highly respected periodical— *The Economist*—asked, "Will There Be Less Violence"? Sensing at that moment a "curious feeling of relative quiescence," the editorial suggested that with luck "the 1970s may be less violent than the 1960s" because "externally-supported guerrilla wars could gradually become harder to sustain," and because of a predicted decline in "genuinely local move-ments of the revolutionary young" and not so young.[3]

Should the editors have anticipated that a fourth round in the Arab–Israeli war would break out three years later, dragging the nuclear superpowers into a dangerous confrontation? How could the London-based handicappers know that in the late 1970s Moscow would order a massive invasion of Afghanistan because its puppet regime there could no longer survive? Or predict in 1978 Vietnam's military move into Cambodia? For that matter, did anyone anticipate the war in the Persian Gulf following Iraq's 1980 attack on Iran that eventually killed a million or more? Where were the great powers' intelligence services during the mounting storm in Iran that by the end of the 1970s would mobi-lize the "revolutionary young" to overthrow the Shah's regime and with it the Western strategy of Iran as regional peacekeeper? And who foresaw that Pres-ident Reagan would in the early 1980s launch his own "externally supported guerrilla wars" against Soviet or Cuban-supported radical-left regimes—the so-called Reagan Doctrine?

Nevertheless, it was natural for a forecast made in the mid-1990s to extrap-olate the period's notorious "cases from Hell"—Somalia, Bosnia, Haiti, and Rwanda—into a future that would be dominated by ethnic warfare and human-itarian crises arising from domestic anarchy. That forecast would not necessar-ily be wrong. A safe bet is that local conflicts will constitute a growth industry. For one thing, it was never true—as Ronald Reagan asserted in 1980—that "if there was no Soviet Union, there would be no hot spots around the world." For another, since the end of the Cold War, local conflicts have surfaced at a brisk clip. But experience with earlier crystal ball-gazing suggests a little humil-ity, and in what follows it helps to remember that the detailed future is essen-tially unknowable.

What Kind of World?

The next section examines in more depth the likely future conflict map. To set the stage we first look at the larger global environment toward which we seem to be moving. When serious people make guesses about the big picture over the next couple of decades, what do their special lenses show?

Presumably, we should feel encouraged by George Kennan's observation that the absence of great political-military conflicts "is without precedent in the history of recent centuries."[4] This time, however, *The Economist* sees trouble ahead because, according to its logic, the twenty-first century will be more like the multipolar nineteenth century than the twentieth, and a multipower world is more liable to go wrong than a two-power one. (Political scientists have debated for years whether multipolarity or bipolarity produces greater stabil-ity.)[5] Since the coming age is also one of military high-tech as well as post-imperial ethnic ferment, "the 21st century version . . . may yet prove even more hazardous than the 19th century's."[6] Many would challenge the point on the ground that power is safer when diffused than when it is concentrated in a potentially deadly bipolarity.

Bipolarity is not, however, dead, and some are fascinated by the possible line-up in a future global struggle. The Balkan wars of the 1990s gave impetus to the image of a renewed battle between Western Christianity and Mideast Islam. Harvard Professor Samuel Huntington in an influential article argued that "The fault lines between civilizations [are] replacing the political and ideological boundaries of the Cold War as the flash point for crisis and bloodshed." His sobering conclusion was that "conflicts between groups in different civilizations will be more frequent, more sustained and more violent than conflicts between groups in the same civilization; violent conflicts between groups in different civilizations are the most likely and most dangerous source of escalation that could lead to global wars . . . a central focus of conflict in the immediate future will be between the West and several Islamic-Confucian states."[7]

Others imagined various global lineups. The dissolution of the Soviet Union inspired scenarios of major clashes between Slavs and Turks along their long ethnic frontier across Eurasia. Another global faceoff is between economic "haves" and "have-nots." Yale historian Paul Kennedy, after reviewing projections by eco-pessimists such as Lester Brown of Worldwatch Institute and eco-optimists George Gilder and fellow forecasters of ever-increasing global prosperity, concluded that "the gap between rich and poor will steadily widen as we enter the twenty-first century, leading not only to social unrest within developed countries but also to growing North-South tensions, mass migration, and environmental damage from which even the 'winners' might not emerge unscathed."[8] He subsequently upgraded the north-south battle to the status of "The global problem of the early twenty-first century":

> Across our planet a number of what might be termed demographic-technological fault lines are emerging, between fast-growing, adolescent, resource-poor, undercapitalized, and undereducated populations on one side and technologically inventive, demographically moribund and increasingly nervous rich societies on the other. . . . How those on the two sides of these widening regional or intercontinental fissures are to relate to each other early in the next century dwarfs every other issue in global affairs.[9]

Gloomy forecasts are not the monopoly of scholars and journalists. Some political leaders portray a grim future unless better ways are found for dealing with the consequences. Addressing the French National Assembly following the fiftieth anniversary of D-Day in 1994, President Bill Clinton described the future that is in store for the world if Europe and NATO fail to live up to their Cold War achievements. He gave his worst-case scenario:

> Militant nationalism is on the rise, transforming the healthy pride of nations, tribes, religious and ethnic groups into cancerous prejudice, eating away

at states and leaving their people addicted to the political painkillers of violence and demagoguery. . . . We see the signs of this disease from the
purposeful slaughter in Bosnia to the random violence of skinheads in all
our nations. We see it in the incendiary misuses of history, and in the anti-
Semitism and irredentism of some former communist states. And beyond
Europe, we see the dark future of these trends in mass slaughter, unbri-
dled terrorism, devastating poverty and total environmental and social disintegration.[10]

Europeans saw things similarly, but rather than being hypothetical were
starkly descriptive. The 1994 Summit Declaration of the Organization for Security and Cooperation in Europe (OSCE) identified as among the main sources
of crisis, loss of life, and human misery the widespread "plagues of aggressive
nationalism, racism, chauvinism, xenophobia, anti-semitism and ethnic tension
. . . along with social and economic instability."[11]

Others discern a coming threat to the national state system that has been
in place since the Peace of Westphalia in 1648. Ample signs are visible that unfettered national sovereignty is becoming an artifact of the past. But is an age of
nation-building going to give way to an epidemic of nation-busting? "The core
problem," says one expert, "is wars of national debilitation . . . sundering fragile but functioning nation states and gnawing at the well-being of stable
nations."[12] Stanley Hoffmann spells out the implications: "If the world consists
of disintegrating states, then the cooperative processes that are supposed to fuel
harmony . . . are easily overwhelmed by millions of refugees who flee massacres and disasters . . . or call for protection whenever they cannot escape."[13]

A military historian completes the gloomy picture: "In North America and
Western Europe, future war-making entities will probably resemble the Assassins, the group which . . . terrorized the medieval Middle East for two
centuries. . . . Regular armed forces . . . will degenerate into police forces or
. . . mere armed gangs; the day of the condottieri will return."[14]

That scenario is grim enough, with political fanatics competing—or col-
laborating—with the Mafia while drug lords battle over turf (as they do in
present-day Colombia and other source countries, sometimes even seeking help
from the local revolutionaries[15]). A vastly greater nightmare would be the actual
use of nuclear weaponry in the world's conflict-prone regions like the Middle
East, the Balkans, Africa, and South Asia (not to mention New York harbor or
the nation's capital).

Certainly it seems tragically true, as political scientist Kenneth Waltz puts
it, that "war today is the privilege of the poor." A widely cited article by journalist Robert Kaplan extrapolated to the wider world the anarchic chaos of
Africa.[16] In this scenario, the northern rich are flooded with refugees, blamed
for perpetuating the lack of economic progress and for supplying the lethal
weaponry, and charged with supplying the UN Security Council with the funds,
logistics, and much of the manpower needed to police the increasingly lawless
global landscape. "As we approach the turn of the century," according to the

administrator of the UN Development Program, "the social, economic, environmental and political crises that many developing countries confront . . . have taken on an urgency and a magnitude unparalleled in history. Instability and conflict are spreading like a metastasized cancer."[17] One may ponder the fate of the rich man who built his castle in the slums.

The seers who focus on the good news are few and far between. But the logic of the "eco-pessimists" concerning overpopulation, resource scarcity, mass migration, and civic chaos is not unanimous. "Cornucopians" such as Julian Simon argue that technology and human resiliency will combine to discredit the neo-Malthusian disaster scenarios. Indeed, the UN Human Development Report for 1994 showed a substantial *decline* in the proportion of countries suffering in "abysmal human conditions," from around 70 percent in 1960 to 32 percent in 1992: "The share of the world population enjoying fairly satisfactory human development levels . . . increased from 25% in 1960 to 60% in 1992."[18] (But perhaps that increases the chance of conflict, if you believe the remark of Russian philosopher and anarchist Prince Pyotr Kropotkin that "the hopeless don't revolt"—implying that when hope rises, watch out!)

In short, there's also good news and bad news here. Human nature is such that even though there are fewer conflicts today than before and some Third World progress is more encouraging, a kind of Gresham's Law drives out the good in favor of the bad. And the bad could get worse.

What leverage might be used to reduce future conflicts growing out of manmade chaos and violence? A common reply is to change the international system itself to provide greater fairness. Former National Security Adviser Zbigniew Brzezinski suggested that as the crucial variable, "A politically activated world, driven by rising social frustrations, could easily become vulnerable to massive instability and violence in the absence of tangible progress toward an increasingly cooperative and just global system."[19] Russian pessimism, always close to the surface and no longer offset by utopianism, employs similar logic: "The world is experiencing a gradual yet steady erosion of the structure of international relations created after the Second World War . . . the emerging system will be far less stable. Unless they organize themselves better, the West and Russia will have far fewer possibilities to influence this system than they did in the past."[20]

System change won't help, however, if the source of the problem lies deep in the genetic material where our ancestry still burdens us with the "tendency as a species toward prejudice, egocentrism, and ethnocentrism": "Many individuals feel a heightened sense of uncertainty and insecurity. Some react with exaggerated intolerance of the outside world or with violence toward those who are seen as alien and threatening. Political demagogues can readily inflame these feelings.[21] Many believe that the greatest deterrent to conflict is the existence of democracy, based on the premise that democratic forms of government are the least likely to engage in warfare with one another. Is this premise true?

Democracy as a War-Preventive

The UN secretary general, finally liberated from his forced rhetorical neutrality of the Cold War, has observed: "Democracies are likely to be peace-loving and not likely to wage war on other democracies." Even historic adversaries such as Greece and Turkey have stopped short of fighting each other directly.[22] The German philosopher Immanuel Kant prescribed a world of "republics" for a peaceful world, and most modern scholars agree with Michael Doyle's more analytic conclusion that relations between democratic states tend to be harmonious.[23] Freedom House in 1994 reported that of the 353 wars fought since 1819, none has been waged between two established democracies, leading to the conclusion "Democracies do not war against each other."[24]

Some are uncomfortable with this generalization. *The Economist* asserts that even if every state were to become a democracy, "self-interest, irrespective of what sort of government you have, has always caused most wars; and it is as vigorous today as ever it was." (The editors cite as wars between democracies the American Civil War and—less persuasively—the Boer War.)[25] Criticizing *The Economist's* reasoning, Yale political scientist Bruce Russett concludes that over the last 50 years, "pairs of democratic states have been only one-eighth as likely as other kinds of states to threaten to use force against one another, and only one-tenth as likely to carry out these threats." He adds: "Democracies have also been less likely to escalate disputes with one another, and more likely to avail themselves of third-party mediation. . . . In the absence of direct attack, institutionalized checks and balances make democracies' decisions to go to war slow and very public. One need not fear a surprise attack from a democracy."[26]

Obvious exceptions aside, democracies do help create a better international order because their institutionalized checks and balances at best yield *open* societies, in contrast to dictatorships which require control of information and secrecy for monopoly rule. This insight was well understood during the arms control verification debates of the Cold War when Westerners were sure that someone in their country would spill the beans long before a clandestine nuclear program would get very far. Saddam Hussein's Iraq could never have achieved so much secretly if there had been an independent and nosy Iraqi equivalent of America's Federation of Atomic Scientists. In an age when reliable monitoring of nuclear and other arms control agreements can mean war or peace, the argument for democracy is powerful.

Russett's reference to institutions focuses on the essential point. Elections are the condition *sine qua non* for representative government, which in turn is the foundation of political democracy. However, the notion that free elections by themselves produce a democracy is a myth that has been refuted in such places as Haiti and Angola, where civil conflict followed elections in 1990 and 1991, respectively. We are learning the hard way that a functioning democracy embodies not just a participatory framework but also a *process*. It is one that cannot be imposed by fiat.

The process centers on habits of compromise and tolerance in dealing with domestic differences, above all an agreement to disagree. The process usually takes form in a legislature where the majority rules, but where protection also exists for minority positions (as, for example, in the notion of "concurrent majorities" advanced by the nineteenth-century American statesman John Calhoun). The test of a democratic process is the consensus among interest groups and factions within the community that enables the society to function peaceably even in the face of major differences among its constituent parts. Democracy is in that sense what might be called a "second-order agreement."

An even more important characteristic for a true democracy is a skein and network of voluntary groupings, associations, and coalitions that occupy the space between government at the top and the mass of individuals at the bottom. Such intermediating nongovernmental institutions are the basis for the concept of *civil society*. Where it does exist in viable and mature democracies it inhibits not only war-making between similar states, but civil war as well. The principle is illustrated in a compelling way in Alexis de Tocqueville's perceptive observations of society in the youthful United States. In particular, he notes the American tendency to join multiple nongovernmental groups, accomplish things at the local level, and (still valid 165 years later) look on the national government as distant and even irrelevant.[27]

A weak civil society is evident in struggles to the death between factions that share the same space in central Africa and the Balkans, and in the virulent nationalism sweeping parts of the former Soviet Union and Yugoslavia. What is missing in some new states in Africa long ruled by outsiders, as well as in fragments of the old communist empires recently liberated from topside tyranny, is a rich sociopolitical infrastructure that the former masters would have found threatening to their monopoly of power and that they thus prevented from developing. Testimony for the point was unwittingly supplied by Cuban Defense Minister Raul Castro in March 1996 when he complained about allowing some self-employment of workers in his communist society. This, he worried, could create "the basis for organized groupings, associations and actions free of the state" that could "constitute a test tube for the subversive efforts of the enemy."[28]

Civil society is facilitated by structural reforms such as power-sharing in governing coalitions, alternating majorities, or federal and confederal structures, which, as with the U.S. Constitution, leave to constituent parts the powers not specifically assigned to the central government. These all act, as someone put it, like fuel rods that moderate a nuclear reactor, keeping its explosive potential under control. Others suggest decentralization of the economy, which strengthens nongovernmental actors in the society.

However, recent events suggest that, perversely, the *process of democratization* itself can generate civil strife. That process, like the process of westernization, is by its nature revolutionary in upsetting an established social or

political order. Instabilities develop and persist until new ground rules embodying compromise and tolerance are widely accepted. Two scholars of the phenomenon conclude that democratizing states are war-prone because "democratization typically creates a syndrome of weak central authority, unstable
domestic coalitions, and high-energy mass politics."[29] (It should also be remembered that the democratic Weimar Republic held elections that brought the Nazis
to power.)

Another word of caution is in order. Aristotle, in describing the various
forms of rule such as autocracy, aristocracy, and democracy, warned of a malignant version of each form. The negative side of democracy, he stated, is
"mobocracy," in which a popular fever can drive elected officials to extreme
behavior. This characteristic was what the arrogant George Canning, Britain's
early nineteenth-century prime minister, had in mind when he warned of "the
fatal artillery of public excitation." Indeed, de Tocqueville observed that
although democracy finds it hard to begin a war, it also finds it hard to end it.[30]
Two notable Americans, Walter Lippmann and James Reston, agreed and recommended insulating government against the popular will when the people
are bent on war. The nuclear age has sobered up public opinion to the point
where it is still true that democracies do not generally fight one another. More
precisely, however, it is *mature* democracies that are averse to war and inoculated against civil breakdown, whereas immature ones tend to share with
autocracies a proclivity to conflict.

Forces of Integration and Disintegration

The world's cultures may clash head-on, and Africa's chaos could spread
to the rest of the planet. But whether or not this comes to pass—and it may
not—a more general if less dramatic clash is taking place at all levels of human
society. That struggle is between the outward push of economic and technological interdependencies based on cooperation, and the inward pull of the tribe
that tugs people back toward their familiar, manageable home base.[31] Global
society is engaged in a historic, if silent, race between forces tending toward
integration and forces favoring disintegration. That tension is likely to prevail
for a long time.

A profound irony is at work here. The big story of the late twentieth century is the enormous integrating power of economic and financial interdependence combined with cross-border technology. That force in turn fosters the
creation of large multinational entities and boundary-ignoring transnational
communities. The outbreak of ethnic conflict and civil chaos seems an anchro-
nism—an inexplicable phenomenon that reflects the dark side of human nature.
The world's sophisticates celebrate globalization as liberating people by bind-
ing them together benignly in a web of economic and technological connec-
tive tissue.[32] But in a world of impersonal institutions, corrupt governments, and

monster weapons, dependency and loss of autonomy can also be disorienting and generate anomie.

The inward pull of family, tribe, village, provincial, and national communities is, however, a far more natural force than economic and technological interdependence. At its best, cultural diversity is the fount for much of the world's glorious variety and coloration, its miraculous panorama of art, music, literature, and language. But at worst the pathological expression of the roots-seeking impulse is extreme nationalism that can trigger sociopolitical disintegration. It took only the push of a hot button to unleash tribal warfare and ethnic cleansing in the ruins of empire from the former Yugoslavia to Central Asia, or to launch human floodtides across state frontiers in Europe, Asia, and Africa. There is no shortage of incendiary power-seekers to supply the tinder for ethnic conflagrations. Unleashing the virulent strain of nationalism has exposed the helpless to bloody power struggles, moral outrages, religious strife, state-sponsored terrorism, and the horrors of ethnic cleansing, mass refugee-creation, and slow-motion genocide.

A special product of this pernicious process is religious fundamentalism when its exclusivity encourages intolerance, fosters hatred, and at the extreme breeds war. In traditional societies convulsed by a headlong rush toward modernity, clerics claiming a monopoly on truth appear in many guises, from some Shi'a Islamists in Iran and Lebanon to extremists at the fringe of ultra-orthodox Jewry in Israel, evangelical Christianity in America, and Hindu radicalism in India. Religious fundamentalism takes bizarre and even murderous shapes when fanatics use political power to enforce submission to their version of the truth.

Islamic fundamentalism, more correctly labeled Islamism, is driven by a special dynamic that stirs ancient fears in parts of Christian Europe. It should be understood that anti-Western Islamism is reinforced in its dynamism, especially among the young, by the growing penetration of vulgar and violent Western pop culture through film and television. Indeed, the guardians of any religious faith recognize this as a corrupting influence that imperils traditional cultural and spiritual values, as shown in the Israeli election of May 1996 in which a similar backlash was demonstrated.

Another factor that strengthens anti-Western radicalism is the existence of incompetent, corrupt rule in some parts of the Middle East, Latin America, and Africa. Failed public services, official venality, and mass unemployment have been to a degree offset in places such as Gaza, Algiers, and Cairo by radical organizations that accumulate practical support, much as the old-time American party bosses in the cities did with their Thanksgiving baskets and street-corner job markets.

The extreme manifestation of radical fundamentalism is political terrorism. Political terrorists claim to be at war, and they argue that it is unfair to demand nonviolence of people who are deprived of any other recourse. Some cite the

American Declaration of Independence, which states as much. But no grievance can morally justify targeting the innocent,[33] not to mention what sometimes appears to be recreational terrorism among the young in such places as Lebanon, Liberia, and Ulster.

Yet how can we explain why ethnic groups that have managed to get along in the past should suddenly turn on their neighbors, at a minimum demanding a monopoly of political power and at worst engaging in ethnic cleansing?[34] The writer Lawrence Durrell in *Bitter Lemons* drew an unforgettable word picture of tragically sundered ties between neighbors in Cyprus.[35] The former American ambassador to Yugoslavia blames cynical leadership for tearing apart peacefully coexisting (and often intermarrying) Serbs, Croats, and Bosnian Muslims,[36] to the point where the the self-styled Bosnian Serb "foreign minister" could announce that "for us Serbs, collective suicide is better than living together" with Bosnian Muslims.[37] This extreme sentiment cast a deep shadow over the 1995 Bosnian peace agreement. (A Belgrade analyst has noted that ironically ethnic warfare was fiercest where intermarriage was greatest and argues that only imposed rule can sustain coexistence.)[38]

In the Yugoslav case, an earlier civil war may have indeed been prevented by that imposed rule—namely, the Ottoman and Austro-Hungarian empires in their respective Balkan spheres, and later by Marshal Tito's communist rule that deliberately blurred ethnic lines. It is not only in Yugoslavia that a tribal in-group has been capable of acting out its latent pathology. But in some parts of the world in a perverse sense the villain is history itself. Some tribes positively marinate in their past—unlike Americans, of whom historian Barbara Tuchman once commented that "you can't change your grandparents, but you can forget them."

To Iranians fighting Iraq in the 1980s, the seventh-century battles between Persians and Arabs were all too real. To Serbs fighting Bosnian Muslims in the 1990s, their fourteenth-century defeat by the Turks at Kosovo was equally real. Peaceful coexistence requires tolerance, of the industrial-strength variety. But the exclusive claim to the ultimate truth made by political and religious extremists excludes the very process of mutual accommodation that lies at the heart of democracy.

A New World Map?

A single overarching theme—New World Order, End of History, Clash of Civilizations, Imperial Overstretch—may capture a piece of the truth, but single-factor explanations of history (like Lenin's 1916 prediction of the inevitable clash between capitalist states) tend to be at a minimum incomplete.

A different hypothesis about the future suggests itself. It is of course not impossible that forces of extremism and immoderation will coopt entire civilizations, cultures, races, or groupings. But in fact there exist *forces for moderation and reform within virtually all nations, religions, and ethnic groups, within every country, every community, and every religion.*

At the international level, the enemies of peace and security are brethren to the enemies of peace and security at home. Together they form an unwitting transnational coalition that at its extreme paralyzes the political process, undermines education and science, degrades women, and encourages the apocalyptic twin horsemen of civil chaos and international insecurity. The greatest threat to their malign power is not a countervailing sect or belief. It is moderate leadership that preaches tolerance, treats public office as a public trust, and provides for the basic human needs of the citizenry so that they do not have to depend on fanatics for either bread or human aspirations.

The underlying competition in the years ahead will take place between modernizing moderates who favor the compromising process we call democratic, and true believers who cannot concede any of the truth to those who differ, and to whom compromise is downright sinful. The battlefields of that struggle will be the schools, churches, mosques, synagogues, and radio and television stations—wherever truth contends with superstition. That struggle will also be fought wherever women can find their voices. The battle is against ignorance, and the principal weapon is education, whose original meaning is to lead people out of darkness. The motto is from Wilson Mizner, who said faith is fine "but it's doubt that gets you an education."

The moderates may be a silent majority whose potential is obscured by the fanatics and by corrupt leadership that undermines the community's immune system, but in the longer run history is on their side. That is not because progress is inevitable. What is inevitable as never before is the broadening of the bounds of community by the expansion of trade and communications, by education, by the empowerment of women, and by the growing recognition of individual and minority rights.

To capture the complexity of the future toward which we are moving, imagine a kind of supermap. The basic underlying map shows *states,* each occupying its own "sovereign" territory, each run by a government (except those experiencing anarchy—meaning literally, "no rule"). The rest of reality requires a series of transparent overlays that we superimpose on the territorial map.

The first overlay shows *nations* and *tribes*—groups of humans who identify with each other rather than with other groupings. Some of those nations such as Japan and Korea are concentrated within a single state's boundaries and can legitimately be called by that common misnomer "nation-state." Many other nations and tribes cut across state boundaries, whether in the Caucasus, the Balkans, the United Kingdom, Canada, or Africa where scores of postcolonial states inherited the old European-drawn boundaries that ignored tribal realities.

The basic map also shows familiar regions with their chief regional organizations such as the European Union (EU), the Organization of American States (OAS), the Organization of African Unity (OAU), the Arab League, and the North American Free Trade Agreement (NAFTA). A second transparent overlay is needed to show what we might term *noncontiguous regions*. Modern telecommunications and electronics have enabled some nonadjacent groupings of states and nonstates to act as nongeographic regions, so to speak. This overlay shows such entities as the Organization for Economic Cooperation and Development (OECD)—the central research and scientific club of the world's advanced industrial democracies from Australia and Japan to Sweden—the Commonwealth, the Organization for Security and Cooperation in Europe (OSCE), the new Asian and Pacific Economic Cooperation grouping (APEC), the G-7 (informally G-8—Germany, the United States, Italy, France, Great Britain, Canada, Japan, and by invitation, Russia–plus the European Union) who meet regularly to discuss the global economy, the Islamic Conference of 42 states from Malaysia to Morocco, and the Organization of Petroleum Exporting Countries (OPEC), the global cartel that decides on oil production.

Here are also found the networks of transnational actors—multinational corporations, traders, financial networks, telecommunication linkages, religions, professional federations, satellite TV, Internet surfers, drug cartels, and terrorist coalitions—operating across the map and impossible to pin down as being headquartered in any single country.

Political science lives by the question "Who rules?" The future will feature what Harlan Cleveland calls "a world with no one in charge." But growing economic, financial, and technological interdependence can only function within a basically stable political environment. In the final chapters of this book, we confront the policy question this dilemma poses: how to develop a system of minimal law and order in a world that values above all its diversity, autonomy, and individuality?

THE EMERGING CONFLICT AGENDA

In Chapter 2 the conflicts of the period 1945 to the end of the Cold War were divided for convenience into four categories: colonial, interstate, and internal, with the latter subdivided into primarily internal and internal with significant external involvement. The last-named, of course, represented the chief proxy battlefield of the Cold War. Are these the relevant categories as we peer ahead toward the new millennium?

The End of Colonial Warfare

For a time the first category—the colonialism that dominated the UN agenda for two decades after World War II—seemed an artifact of past history, with French-ruled New Caledonia a leftover case. Yes, imperial rule continues in Tibet

and other non-Han regions where Beijing governs, and although not always recognized as such, a kind of "colonial" rule over resistant minority groups exists
in other multiethnic states (see the following section of this chapter).

A new "decolonization" agenda unexpectedly emerged from the Soviet
Union's collapse in 1989–91 and that of communist Yugoslavia shortly thereafter. Both opened the floodgates to resurgent national independence movements in a giant arc stretching from the Baltic through Poland, Hungary, and
Moldova to the Balkans and the Caucasus, and across to central Asia. Has this
latter-day version of the colonial issue spent its force, or does it still belong on
the conflict agenda?

The answer is yes and no. Pieces of the former Soviet Union for the most
part sorted themselves into independent states: three in the Baltic region,
Moldova in the west, Ukraine and Belarus in the center, Armenia, Georgia, and
Azerbaijan in the Caucasus, and Kazakhstan and four other Muslim-dominated
republics to the east. Moscow's former satellite states in Eastern Europe did not
have to fight for independence, which President Mikhail Gorbachev astonish-
ingly restored to them. Elsewhere, however, the revolutionary transformation
stimulated internal struggles for power accompanied by a renewal of old fights
with neighbors. These cases might be labelled "internal colonialism."

Within the Russian Federation itself, non-Russian peoples were suddenly
free to express their resentment of their involuntary incorporation into
nineteenth-century Tsarist Russia, and anticolonial protest appeared. The would-
be breakaway "nations" included the Trans-Dniester region of Moldova,
Ingushetia, Northern Ossetia, and other ethnic groups in the Caucasus, along
with regions most outsiders have never heard of such as Kabardin-Nalkaria and
Karachevo-Cherkassia. The reawakened passions for autonomy were not unlike
those among Western Europe's former African and Asian colonies. This time,
however, in both Russia and Yugoslavia, it was frequently a demagogic power-
seeker who picked at old wounds and deliberately undermined habits of peaceful cohabitation. Some of these situations could replay the Chechnya's bloody
resistance in the 1990s to Moscow's brutal effort to reassert control.

A Chechnya scenario is conceivable for Pathan tribesmen in Pakistan, Muslims in Indian-ruled Kashmir, and Kurdish separatists in Iraq, Turkey, and Iran.
When Ankara sent forces into Cyprus during the 1970s to create a de facto state
for its Turkish Cypriot half-brothers, the minority ethnic Turkish population
pretty much seceded. For a worst-case scenario, consider the 25 million ethnic
Russians in the newly independent states of the former Soviet Union. Or the 2
million Turks resident (but not citizens) in Germany (including 400,000 Kurds)
and an even larger proportion of Algerians in France. Now project on those
areas a hardening of Russian policy, a worsening of the Kurdish war in south-
eastern Turkey, or a victorious Islamist theocracy in North Africa. In North America Canadians must still deal with the linguistic-religious-political-economic
alienation of Quebec, while both Quebec and anglophone Canada face growing autonomy-seeking by native populations of Indians and Inuit.

An autonomy-seeking political movement typically turns into a war when the parent state tries to crush its refractory component instead of offering peaceful solutions such as federation, power-sharing, and protection of minority rights. All the above examples belong on the future roster of potential colonial-type conflicts.

Conflict between States

During the Cold War years, interstate wars seemed to become passé. Today, with the recent focus on civil strife, they are still less noticeable than the internal mayhem that captures the headlines. But plenty of the past quarrels described in Chapter 2 remain unresolved. Of the potential conflict roster, roughly one-third are likely to occur between states. A watch list for the next historic period must prudently include adversarial pairings whose underlying disputes continue to fester.

India and Pakistan have not fought a war since 1971, but their chronic territorial squabble in Kashmir has turned bloody several times in the over 40 years since the United Nations called for a plebiscite. Another war could be catastrophic between two countries that now possess unacknowledged nuclear arsenals.

The Arab–Israeli conflict, the frequent centerpiece of superpower crisis diplomacy during the Cold War, has moderated in important ways but by no means turned into a durable peace. The Israeli–Egyptian peace treaty of 1979 ruled out another major Arab–Israeli war by taking off the board half the troops that had fought on the Arab side for 30 years. The Palestinian–Israeli semi-détente marked by the Rabin-Arafat White House handshake opened the way for neighboring Jordan to make peace in 1994 complete with territorial concessions. However, the Israeli change of government in 1996 created new uncertainties for the peace process; Syria and its satellite Lebanon were still unreconciled with Israel; and Iraq and Iran competed for the title of most zealously anti-Zionist. Some highly combustible material remains in place in the Eastern Mediterranean.

Nor is that all. Saudi Arabia and Yemen have deeply unsettled scores, as do Iraq and Kuwait. Yemen and Eritrea exchanged gunfire in December 1995 over the disputed island of Greater Hanish in the strategic Red Sea. Rivalries in the Arab world will become more acute between monarchies and radical movements, between Sunni and Shi'ite Muslims, and between Iraqi and Syrian Ba'athist movements. Iran, Iraq, Libya, and Sudan may be incapable of seriously damaging their favorite villain, the United States, but state-sponsored terrorism is likely to assume ever uglier shapes.

Equally serious is the tension between Iran and its cross-Gulf Arab adversaries such as the United Arab Emirates, exacerbated by Iran's virtual annexation of the nominally shared island of Abu Musa in the strategically vital Strait of Hormuz along with two of the three Tumbs, and Teheran's continued threat of subversion in Saudi Arabia and Bahrein. New tensions will erupt as Iran seeks to compete with Turkey across the unstable belt of Turkic- and Persian-oriented societies from Afghanistan eastward. And a regional missile race was foreshadowed by Iraq's demonstrated ability in the Gulf War to hit Tel Aviv and Riyadh with Scud missiles, by Saudi and Pakistani possession of Chinese CSS-2s and M-11s, respectively, and by Israel's nuclear-tipped Jericho arsenal.

The absence of clearly demarcated boundaries will remain a source of stress between Algeria and Morocco, Morocco and Mauritania, Nigeria and Cameroon, and Ethiopia and Somalia. India has yet to resolve border differences with China in the Himalayan foothills that generated violence in the 1960s. Historic tensions will persist between Vietnamese and Cambodians, and between Chinese and Malay populations in Southeast Asia. Japan will not sign a peace treaty with Russia until Russia yields up the southern Kurile islands it seized at the end of World War II.

In that region, Vietnam and China were historic enemies even if Washington never understood that during the Vietnam War. The two came to blows in 1979 when the Vietnamese David administered what it called a "bloody nose" to the neighboring Goliath in response to the latter's decision to "teach Vietnam a lesson." The Sino-Vietnamese quarrel over the potentially oil-rich Spratly Islands in the South China Sea (also claimed by the Philippines, Taiwan, Malaysia, and Borneo) sharpened in 1995 when China seized the aptly named Mischief Reef. Tensions are bound to worsen given the high economic stakes (estimates of oil in the South China Sea range from 10 billion to 100 billion barrels). Japanese fighter aircraft have been scrambled against Chinese jets intruding in the East China Sea Senkaku Islands (Diaoyutai in Japanese) claimed by Japan, China, and Taiwan. And Korea experienced riots in February 1996 over Japanese claims to the barren rocks called Tokdo (*Takeshima* in Japanese).

Latin America is a region of particular ambiguity for the forecaster. There the news is not all bad. In 1985 the protracted Beagle Channel dispute between Chile and Argentina was settled, and in the mid-1990s Argentine President Carlos Menem renounced the use of force in the dispute with Britain over the Falkland/Malvinas Islands that produced a shooting war in 1982. The bad news was the revival in the 1990s of nationalist chest-thumping and saber-rattling over unresolved territorial issues in a region that professes deep devotion to international law and the pacific settlement of disputes. In the mid-1990s there were dead and wounded in a particularly nasty border skirmish between Ecuador and Peru—an annual event on the anniversary of the 1942 settlement that Ecuador continues not to recognize, despite its guarantee by the United States, Chile, Argentina, and Brazil, and despite some moderating trends in 1996.

Another half-dozen Latin American territorial issues may bring future conflict. Nicaragua and Colombia are contesting two Caribbean islands, Colombia is challenging the status of a peninsula it shares with Venezuela, Venezuela is disputing its border with Guyana over which they fought in 1970, and Guyana is quarreling with Suriname. Honduras has not accepted the World Court's 1992 ruling in its argument with El Salvador, with both countries challenging Nicaragua's position in the Gulf of Fonseca, and Brazil and Venezuela reject each other's definition of their admittedly ambiguous Amazonian borders.

It is commonly believed that Europe in our era will be mercifully free of the virus that so long dominated its earlier history. On the southern fringe, however, Greece and Turkey are likely to remain alienated over Cyprus and the status of islands in the Aegean Sea such as Imea off the Turkish coast, where the two NATO allies skirmished in February 1996. Turkish and Greek Cypriots show little sign of settling their ancient quarrel three decades after the United Nations sent in peacekeepers. And Italy and ex-Yugoslavia have not entirely given up on their ancient dispute over Trieste that was supposedly settled long ago, in 1954.

As already discussed, the breakup of the Soviet empire unleashed pent-up pressures between states on its periphery that remain to be resolved, particularly in the mountainous and largely Muslim Caucasus. The fateful consequences of the breakup of Soviet and Yugoslav communist rule have by no means played themselves out in other parts of the Balkans and the former Soviet Union. If in the Balkans abuse by Serb overlords of the ethnic Albanian majority in Kosovo is troublesome, expansion of the conflict to neighboring Macedonia with its 2.2 million ethnic Albanians, and then to ethnic Greeks in Albania and Albanians in Greece, would create a far more lethal stew, this time involving Bulgaria, Greece, and Turkey. Perhaps not soon but one day a grim scenario could evolve out of the situation of the 2.3 million ethnic Hungarians in Romanian Transylvania and elsewhere in Central Europe.

A major potential trigger for conflict between states stems from the·dispersion of 25 million ethnic Russians claiming (or actually suffering) mistreatment in pockets of the former Soviet empire from the Baltics through Moldova and Ukraine, across the Caspian to the new Muslim states of southwest Asia. Like the Baltic states and Moldova, all the new southwest Asian Muslim states have Russian minorities of which the largest numbers 6 million in Kazakhstan (which Russia still hopes to bring back into its fold). Thousands of Russian troops remain locked in stalemated warfare in Tajikistan.

The passion of Russians and Serbs for their ethnic brethren (one doesn't often hear of a *sistren* problem) highlighted the generic issue of dispersed fellow-tribesmen seen earlier in both Israeli and Palestinian diasporas. According to a well-known survivor of political change in Russia, "If [Russians in the 'near abroad'] face danger, if their rights are violated, and if as a result they begin a mass exodus to Russia, we will see a virtual explosion of the most militant chauvinism in Russia, which will smash all the modest democratic achievements we have made. Our foreign policy will be radically transformed."[39]

In the wings, ready to exploit that worst-case political nightmare are Russia's ultranationalist factions, typified by Vladimir Zhirinovsky whose lunatic strategizing envisaged a Peter the Great–type southward expansion as part of a Hitlerian "final division of the world. . . . Russian soldiers will wash their boots in the warm waters of the Indian Ocean. . . . We must pacify that region forever."[40]

A less bizarre but serious potential nightmare lurks in the unresolved differences between Russia and Ukraine to whose separation many Russians remain unreconciled. With 12 million ethnic Russians, Ukraine could become destabilized by turmoil, perhaps in the Crimea or along its western borders.

New democracies like Russia and Ukraine are presumably subject to the common maxim that democracies don't fight one another. Maybe a new sensitivity to public opinion and international opprobrium would have a deterrent effect. But realism requires acknowledging that, where recent dictatorial rule still lurks near the surface, the transformation of former dictatorships in Eurasia, Latin America, and Africa into partial democracies may be insufficient to sustain the general rule.

It is obvious that the older categorical distinctions between "colonial," "interstate," and "internal" conflicts can get very blurred. In an age of mass migrations, breakup of multinational states, and renewed nationalist and ethnic passions, some situations will display characteristics of two or even three of the categories. In the Caucasus, the mini-war between Armenia and Azerbaijan over the enclave of Nagorno-Karabakh, and the neighboring Abkhazian revolt in the revived state of Georgia, both featured "anticolonial" sentiments on the part of the ethnic groups in revolt. The first is clearly also an interstate conflict. In the second, Russia was a major player on the Abkhazian side against Georgia.

In a sense, both are also internal conflicts, a category we will now examine. But in doing so, we need to keep in mind that in many of the struggles inside the boundaries of a state, the disaffected minority group also has a big ethnic brother outside who acts in effect as another party to the conflict. We have already noted the extreme case involving 25 million ethnic Russians living in new states on Russia's periphery, as well as egregious instances such as Turkey's invasion of Cyprus in 1974 to help the Turkish Cypriot minority create its own phantom state. Pakistan is obviously the backer of secessionist Kashmiri Muslims, and the Bosnian Serb territory has just as obviously had Belgrade as its silent partner. Are these conflicts internal or interstate? The answer is: both.

Myron Weiner has studied a wide range of other cases in which "suppressed political and ethnic groups . . . turn to their ethnic or religious kinfolk abroad for financial, military and political support," instances that clearly complicate the picture for domestic governance. His examples include radical religious groups such as the Islamic Salvation Front in Algeria, Hamas in the Palestinian "pre-state," and Hizbollah in southern Lebanon. He clearly had in mind the Turks in Germany, Koreans in Japan, and North Africans in France when he wrote, "In an age of terrorism, even a small number of disaffected youth, hostile to the countries in which they live and were born, can become dangerous tools of the regimes and radical groups of the country of their forefathers."[41]

It is against this often ambiguous backdrop that we turn to the internal conflict category.

Conflict within States

With the end of the Cold War, top billing on the future conflict agenda changed dramatically from possible nuclear holocaust to domestic warfare between brothers (or rather cousins) who share space, but who make racial, ethnic, cultural, religious, or linguistic differences the test of friendship or enmity. This genre of conflict brings out the dark side of the world's otherwise glorious diversity. Cynical or fanatical leaders can whip rural or urban masses into a revived xenophobia, while global television coverage makes outsiders aware of crimes against humanity committed in the name of a nation, tribe, or religion.

Civil conflict has many causes and is hardly a new phenomenon. The sometimes violent xenophobia displayed in recent times where refugees and other migrants have clustered in Western Europe was not very different from a riot in London in 1517 known as "Evil May Day," in which a mob of 2000 assaulted foreigners and looted their shops.[42] Much of the recent turmoil took place in newly emerging states which, according to elder statesman George Kennan are as poorly prepared "for the responsibilities of independent statehood" as the emerging states which John Quincy Adams warned Americans in 1823 against trying to shape.[43] Other causes include unrelieved poverty, failed governments and states, demographic and environmental pressures, leftover armaments, lust for power, revenge over real and fancied grievances, poorly held-together multinational states, tyranny at the top, and corruption in the middle.

Still-fragile democratic practices may fail as some have in Eurasia, Latin America, and Africa. Some states accustomed to dictators may revert to anarchy, in the fashion of Haiti in the early 1990s, or to militancy and tribalism as in Somalia, Liberia, or Rwanda, or equally distressing, a Nigeria unable to fulfill its enormous potential. Other Third World regimes that were propped up by competing Cold War supporters could still suffer the chaos that befell Angola and Mozambique as well as Somalia and Afghanistan. Such anarchy will be exacerbated where remaining stocks of weaponry pumped in by outside powers bolster "their" sides. Rwanda has been a special victim of this syndrome. (See the section "Arms and Conflict" in Chapter 2.)

A common denominator is struggle over governance—that is, who is to rule over the piece of territory denominated a state? "Who rules" was the issue in the civil wars that created modern Britain, France, the United States, Russia, and China, several of which were bloodier than today's revolutions. The French Revolution created refugees, those in Russia and China produced tyranny. The American Revolution was both sanguinary and costly. Only the so-called Glorious Revolution in England of 1688 was genuinely benign. Crises will continue to arise over which group is to dominate policy; command the armed forces; control the media and central bank; acquire the presidential palace, planes, and limousines; and send a representative to the United Nations and ambassadors to a hundred countries. In short, who is to have the power?

Competition for power can turn into conflict when the battle is between tribal competitors. Rwanda and Burundi suffer chronic and savage warfare between majority Hutus and minority Tutsis, exacerbated when Belgium and France took sides in the relationship. A comparable struggle is possible elsewhere between ethnically similar clans and subclans where state boundaries were drawn for the convenience of European rulers rather than for the convenience of the people who lived there.

The toughest challenge is to identify those situations where "nothing has really happened yet" but which are potentially spring-loaded under the surface. Examples that readily come to mind are Zaïre and Sudan, where ethnic clashes have internally displaced millions; or Zambia, where despite the natural resource base more than half the population lives in absolute poverty. Big multinational states such as Pakistan and Iran, as well as Russia and China, contain disaffected minorities. They may never break apart the way Yugoslavia did. But they also might break up, with huge consequences for regional and even world security.

The planet contains many minorities that coexist peacefully with a majority culture; where they do not, the mix becomes potentially explosive. In Latin America a socioeconomic struggle continues between the Ladino "haves" and the predominantly Indian "have-nots," with conflict in Guatemala topping most recent critical lists along with the Chiapas revolt in Mexico. In south Asia the fiber of Indian democracy has been tested by Hindu nationalists such as the extremists among the electoral victors in May 1996 who want Muslim, Sikh, and other minorities to accept Hindu primacy. Neighboring Pakistan combats internal Islamic extremists as well as a Pathan independence movement. And Sri Lanka may have still not wholly resolved its bloody war with the Tamil secession movement, while Southeast Asia copes with Chinese-Malay stresses. The Kurdish independence drive will remain suppressed but will constitute a running sore for Turkey and Iraq. Even an integrating Western Europe is no exception, with autonomy-seeking movements, some of which become occasionally violent, among Basques and Catalans in Spain, Bretons and Corsicans in France, and Welsh and Scots in the United Kingdom.

The future agenda for internal conflict will not be immune to the repugnant practice of purposefully targeting or displacing one's own civilian population. The goal of ethnic cleansing, which Stalin experimented with, Hitler mass-produced, and the Bosnian Serbs revived, is to eradicate the unwanted minority from the territory one way or another. Civilian refugees generated by "internal conflicts, internal violence, forced relocation, and other gross violations of human rights"[44] now include so-called internal refugees, displaced within the state's borders and thus imperfectly covered by rules drawn up for persecuted people who have fled their country of origin. Equally repugnant is the use of food as a weapon, particularly where the climate is problematic, resulting in man-made famine, fratricide, and flight.

Czech President Václav Havel has warned that "cultural conflicts are increasing and are more dangerous than at any other time in history,"[45] while a thoughtful journalist believes that "the United States could wake up 10 years from now and discover that the world has diplomatic cancer—a mass of failed states metastasizing in a cycle of violence and underdevelopment and slowly sapping the strength of the international system."[46]

Yet, when viewed in perspective, this distressing panorama of civil strife should still be contrasted with the catastrophic wars fought in the past, and with four decades under the threat of thermonuclear annihilation. It is not preordained that conflicts will be permanent, however ancient the grievances. Nor are chaos and anarchy fated to persist. When one side decisively wins, or when exhaustion yields a settlement, even a Somalia or an Afghanistan could once more become a functioning state in an identifiable political space.

Resource and Environmental Disorders

Most such forecasts of political and territorial conflict, however speculative, at least rest empirically on demonstrable reality. The often-predicted environmental/resources disasters for the most part have not happened yet (which may be why, as *The Economist* put it, "the prophets of doom have a fertile market"[47]). The good news is that sensible policies could mitigate some of their worst effects; the bad news is that this category may turn out to be a pervasive source of future conflict.

The tone was starkly established by Robert Kaplan in an article cited earlier that shook many people, including the president of the United States. Kaplan, in describing "how scarcity, crime, overpopulation, tribalism and disease are rapidly destroying the social fabric of our planet," extrapolated global catastrophe from what he observed in Africa:

> It is time to understand "the environment" for what it is: the national security issue of the early twenty-first century. The political and strategic impact of surging populations, spreading disease, deforestation and soil erosion, water depletion, air pollution, and, possibly, rising sea levels in critical, overcrowded regions—developments that will prompt mass migrations and, in turn, incite group conflicts—will be the core foreign policy challenge from which most others will ultimately emanate.[48]

In a similar vein, environmentalist Norman Myers warned that "If we continue on our road to environmental ruin worldwide, [the environment] will likely become the predominant cause of conflict in the decades ahead."[49]

A more restrained analysis by Canadian scholar Thomas Homer-Dixon spelled out the eco-disaster hypothesis: "as the human population grows and environmental damage progresses, policymakers will have less and less capacity to intervene to keep this damage from producing serious social disruption, including conflict."[50] The World Resources Institute for its part linked the criterion of sustainability to security in foreseeing "the impending surge of the world population and the burdens it will impose on standards of social equity" leading to a widespread breakdown in civil order.[51]

"The conflicts of the future will be over declining environmental *resources* such as fish," according to another Canadian expert: "Human populations are rising, an important food resource is being decimated. Fish have become something seen as worth fighting for."[52] The competition for dwindling natural resources has already generated several "mini-wars" at sea that, given their widely separated geographic adversaries, might be described as "free-floating." Guns have been fired in anger over fishing rights between Britain and Iceland in the so-called Cod War of the 1960s and 1970s, in the mid-1990s between Canada and Spain in overfished international waters off Newfoundland, in the Sea of Okhotsk between Russia and China, and between Argentina and Taiwan in the South Atlantic.

For some rare good news, in the Canadian-Spanish case some watery brinksmanship by normally irenic Canada led to an agreement between Canada and the European Community that could serve as a model for preserving endangered fish stocks around the globe. In addition to the provisions on conservation, the agreement was exceptional in providing for some beefed-up enforcement powers for the 15-member Northwest Atlantic Fisheries Organization that is supposed to oversee the industry but is entirely voluntary.[53]

Farther out into the future, we can envisage conflict arising from environmental degradation that spills across borders and forces mass migration, as well as quarrels in the so-called global commons over the allocation of deep seabed hard minerals (should world prices ever make their extraction again profitable); outer space activities that threaten others in orbit or on the ground; revived Antarctic claims; or disputes over the still-unmanaged Arctic.[54]

The World Bank foresees a severe water crisis over the next decade or two, given that 80 countries with 40 percent of the world's population already suffer water shortages. A Bank vice president put it bluntly: "Many of the wars in this century were about oil, but wars of the next century will be over water."[55] According to Norman Myers, water shortages in the Middle East provide a "flash-point for war."

Myers also warns that with at least 50 million Africans starving, and food riots bringing down several governments in recent years, trouble lies ahead. In Central America broken economies can't deal with eco-disasters that have already sparked "civil disorders and massive migration." And in Africa and Asia global warming could raise the seas and "send 400 million refugees across national borders."[56] An English analyst of the Bosnia disaster argued that economic disparities caused a scramble for dwindling assets as the gulf widened between rich and poor: "Resource wars often have a heightened ethnic character. . . . What appears at a distance to be inexplicable barbaric acts is the systematic purging of one group by another to rob them of their assets."[57] Earlier Belgium and Canada and current Lebanon and Ulster come to mind.

On a lesser scale, conflict could arise from illicit international disposal of toxic and nuclear waste, and from cross-border air and water pollution. This broad array of environmental evils could pose serious threats to the prospects for stable and peaceful relations between and within states.

On a broader scale, conflict seems to be associated with the dynamics of major change generally, whether economic, social, or political. The efforts by extremists in Algeria and Egypt to reverse modernization and Westernization could have consequences that mimic Iran's tempestuous experience in 1978–79. In an age of enormous transitions, turbulence is inherent in both revolution and its backlash. French revolutionary Danton's apothegm that "revolution devours its children" has proved no less true of a Lenin, Mao, Sukarno, or Nkrumah than of a Robespierre, with future victims not hard to discern.

Whether the underlying dispute is about an unsettled border, ethnic cleansing, deep-sea hard mineral mining, overfishing, the flooding of refugees into another country, or water scarcity, a gun is still a gun and a war still a war. Most conflicts will be contested between recognizable entities such as states or other organized communities, and will take such familiar shapes as soldiers wearing uniforms of different colors shooting at each other or gunboats battling on the high seas. They will still be most appropriately dealt with in the larger framework of international law and order—and by strategies of conflict prevention discussed in the next chapter.

NOTES

[1]Reported in the *Boston Globe,* May 26, 1995.
[2]News conference of March 21, 1963, quoted by Richard Reeves, *President Kennedy: Profile of Power* (New York: Simon and Schuster, 1993), p. 477.
[3]*The Economist,* January 10, 1970, various pages.
[4]Inaugural lecture, National Foreign Affairs Training Center, Department of State, Washington, D.C., October 13, 1994.
[5]See "The Nature of the Balance-of-Power System" in the Bibliography.
[6]The *Economist,* January 6, 1995, p. 17.
[7]"The Clash of Civilizations?", *Foreign Affairs,* Vol. 72, No. 3, Summer 1993, pp. 29, 48.
[8]*Preparing for the Twenty-First Century* (New York: Random House, 1993), p. 334.
[9]Matthew Connelly and Paul Kennedy, "Must It Be the Rest Against the West?", *The Atlantic Monthly,* December 1994, pp. 76–77.
[10]White House Press Release, June 7, 1994.

[11]Budapest Summit Declaration, in *Toward a Genuine Partnership in a New Era,* CSCE Budapest Document 1994, p. 1.

[12]Leslie Gelb, "The Teacup Wars," *Foreign Affairs,* November–December 1994, p. 5.

[13]Stanley Hoffmann, "The Crisis of Liberal Internationalism," *Foreign Policy,* Spring 1995, pp. 168–69.

[14]Martin Van Creveld, *The Transformation of War* (New York: Free Press, 1991), pp. 197, 207. (The condottieri were mercenaries in various fourteenth-century Italian wars.)

[15]In March 1995 a Colombian drug trafficker reportedly offered guerrilla leaders a $200,000 bounty for every crop eradication plane or helicopter shot down. Reported by James Brooks in *New York Times,* March 27, 1995.

[16]Robert Kaplan, "The Coming Anarchy," *Atlantic Monthly,* February 1994. See also his *The Ends of the Earth: A Journey at the Dawn of the 21st Century* (New York: Random House, 1995).

[17]James Gustave Speth, address to Council on Foreign Relations, New York, March 22, 1995, p. 2.

[18]*Human Development Report,* UN Development Program (New York: United Nations, June 1994), p. 1. Also note Barrington Moore's conclusion from his massive study of revolution that economic deprivation correlates poorly with a tendency to violence. *Social Origins of Dictatorship and Democracy* (Boston: Beacon Press, 1967), p. 454.

[19]"Power and Morality," *World Monitor,* March 1993, p. 24.

[20]Sergei A. Karaganov in *Damage Limitation or Crisis? Russia and the Outside World,* Robert D. Blackwill and Sergei A. Karaganov, eds. (Washington, D.C.: Brassey's, 1994).

[21]David A. Hamburg, "Preventing Contemporary Intergroup Violence," President's Annual Report for 1993, Carnegie Corporation of New York, p. 5. For a more detailed discussion, see the section "Violence and Human Nature" in Chapter 1 of the present volume.

[22]"Democracy: A Newly-Recognized Imperative," in *Global Governance,* Vol. 1, No. 1, Winter 1995, p. 4.

[23]Most recently, "An International Liberal Community" in Graham Allison and Gregory F. Treverton, eds., *Rethinking American Security: Beyond the Cold War to the New World Order* (New York: W. W. Norton, 1991). James Lee Ray argues that "No conflict between states since 1945 (or before) has ever escalated to war unless at least one of the states was not democratic." See *International Organization,* Vol. 43, No. 3, Summer 1989, p. 439.

[24]Cited in the *Christian Science Monitor,* December 15, 1994, p. 3.

[25]*The Economist,* December 24–January 6, 1995, p. 17.

[26]Bruce Russett, letter to the editor, *The Economist,* April 29, 1995.

[27]Alexis de Tocqueville, *Democracy in America, 1835* (New York: New American Library, 1956).

[28]Quoted in *New York Times,* March 31, 1996.

[29]Edward D. Mansfield and Jack Snyder, "Democratization and War," *Foreign Affairs,* May–June 1995, p. 88.

[30]de Tocqueville, p. 278.

[31]This theme was developed in Harlan Cleveland and Lincoln P. Bloomfield, *Rethinking International Cooperation,* Humphrey Institute, University of Minnesota, 1988.

[32]Stanley Hoffmann suggests that both are expressions of classical liberalism, with the liberal internationalists working toward a "transnational economic society" on the world scene and their liberal isolationist brethren seeking the Rousseauan ideal of "small, self-sufficient and inward-looking democratic communities." See "The Crisis of Liberal Internationalism," in *Foreign Policy,* Spring 1995, p. 160.

[33]Put more elegantly in Umberto Eco's masterpiece of medieval fiction *The Name of the Rose:* "Fear prophets . . . and those prepared to die for the truth, for as a rule they make many others die with them" (New York: Harcourt Brace Jovanovich, 1983), p. 491.

[34]The Bibliography presents a section of useful references on this topic.

[35]New York: E. P. Dutton, 1957.

[36]Warren Zimmerman, "Origins of a Catastrophe: Memoirs of the Last American Ambassador to Yugoslavia," *Foreign Affairs,* March–April 1995.

[37]Reported by Samantha Power in *Boston Globe,* April 6, 1995.

[38]Alexsa Djilas in a communication to the author.

[39]Georgi Arbatov, "Eurasia Letter: A New Cold War?", *Foreign Policy,* No. 95, Summer 1994, p. 98.

[40]Quoted by Jacob W. Kipp in "The Zhirinovsky Threat," *Foreign Affairs,* May–June, 1994, p. 78.

[41]"Nations Without Borders," *Foreign Affairs,* March–April 1996, pp. 133–34.

[42]Recounted by John Hale in *The Civilization of Europe in the Renaissance* (New York: Athenaeum, 1994), p. 56. Also see the Bibliography section, "Sources of Internal and Interstate Conflict."

[43]George F. Kennan, "On American Principles," *Foreign Affairs,* March–April 1995, p. 123.

[44]Francis M. Deng, "Dealing with the Displaced: A Challenge to the International Community," *Global Governance,* Vol. 1, No. 1, Winter 1995, p. 45.

[45]Speech on July 4, 1994 at Independence Hall, Philadelphia; see *New York Times,* July 8, 1994.

[46]Thomas L. Friedman in *New York Times,* October 10, 1994.

[47]July 23, 1994, p. 25.

[48]*The Atlantic Monthly,* February 1994, pp. 44, 58. Emphasis added.

[49]Norman Myers, *Ultimate Security: The Environmental Basis of Political Stability* (New York: W. W. Norton, 1993), p. 17.

[50]Thomas Homer-Dixon, "On the Threshold: Environmental Changes as Causes of Acute Conflict," *International Security,* Vol. 16, No. 2, Fall 1991, pp. 79, 91, 106.

[51]"The 2050 Project," World Resources Institute, Washington, D.C., Vol. 1, No. 2, Spring 1994, pp. 1–3.

[52]Professor Dan Middlemiss, professor of military and strategic studies at Dalhousie University, quoted in *Boston Globe,* March 26, 1995.

[53]*New York Times,* April 17, 1995.

[54]See Lincoln P. Bloomfield, "The Arctic: Last Unmanaged Frontier," *Foreign Affairs,* Fall 1981.

[55]Ismail Serageldon, vice president for Environmentally Sustainable Development, quoted in *New York Times,* August 10, 1995.

[56]*Ultimate Security: The Environmental Basis of Political Stability,* pp. 10, 37 ff.

[57]Mark Duffield of the University of Birmingham, quoted in *New York Times,* August 8, 1994.

Four ∽

HEADING OFF CONFLICTS BEFORE THEY HAPPEN

Early Warning and Preventive Diplomacy

When the Cold War ended, the bipolar world turned multipolar and perhaps even nonpolar. Although the close of the turbulent twentieth century had many familiar features, the patterns of conflict, of U.S. involvement, and of multilateral capabilities, were all undergoing change. The turn of the millennium may or may not be a genuine hinge of history, but it is a particularly good time to reexamine the capacity of the international community and its principal supporters to cope with conflicts that disturb the neighborhood. In the late 1990s the UN peace and security system was in trouble, but what to do about it was by no means clear. Is the problem with the United Nations? Should greater reliance be placed on regional organizations? On do-it-yourself action by individual states, or on what some of us call a "coalition of the willing"? And exactly what peace-maintaining functions are we really talking about?

Intervention in disputes and conflicts[1] can take a wide variety of shapes ranging from quiet diplomacy no one hears about all the way to collective action that looks like a war. Those are the end points of a spectrum of enormous political sensitivity along which lie crucial gradations of intrusiveness and national touchiness. The most modest—and most desirable—rung on the ladder is what might be called prophylactic intervention, that is, attempts to peacefully resolve disputes that otherwise might lead to conflicts, and to prevent conflicts from leading to armed hostilities.

Second best is peacekeeping, which is covered in the next chapter. A distant but vital third best, treated in Chapter 6, is collective security, that is, applying collective community force to punish egregious national or international crimes after they have been committed. The steps along the conflict-control continuum are not abstractions: the choice of means can bring life or death to large numbers of people.

This chapter looks at the most modest—and best—starting point on the dispute settlement continuum: tackling the issues at stake before they escalate.

FIRST BEST: DISPUTE SETTLEMENT AND CONFLICT RESOLUTION

The Roots of Conflict

The core of any conflict is the *underlying dispute* between or within states, whether the issue concerns borders, resources, governance, ethnic differences, or violations of human rights. In a thoroughly rational world, disputes would be tackled at an early stage. How early? The UNESCO Constitution is noted for its preamble, drafted by American poet Archibald MacLeish, which states that "Since wars begin in the minds of men, it is in the minds of men that the defenses of peace must be constructed." This approach is a logical antidote to chronic reliance on reactive crisis management. But realistically, true first causes lie in the mists of history and the depths of the human psyche, and it is unclear how to devise basic alterations to the "mind of man" short of universal brain surgery.

Still, anyone who believes in education cannot give up on other remedies for ignorance. "You've got to be taught to hate," says the song from the musical *South Pacific,* a truth confirmed by first-hand observation of the way children have been indoctrinated to perpetuate grievances and cultural stereotypes in long-term conflicts such as those in Cyprus and the Middle East. The president of the Carnegie Corporation got it right. Pivotal educational institutions such as the family, schools, community-based organizations, and the media, David Hamburg states, have the power to shape attitudes and skills toward decent human relations or toward hatred and violence. If they really wish to be constructive, such organizations need to utilize the findings from research on intergroup relations and conflict resolution.[2]

In the real world, however, a conflict-control policy must also focus on shorter-term strategies aimed at settling disputes or, if that fails, cooling down conflicts and stopping wars. The more immediate causes for many conflicts can be found in festering domestic injustices, such as a majority regime abusing a minority, rulers contemplating a territorial grab, countries deadlocked over a disputed border, a rogue political force threatening to sabotage an agreed solution, or a resentful nation smarting under an unjust treaty. Other targets for a purposeful conflict-prevention strategy include destabilizing weapon developments, scarce resources, and top-level larceny. A number of these issues were addressed in some preventive diplomacy efforts of the 1990s, such as U.S. negotiations with Russia and Ukraine on nuclear weapons disposal and with North Korea on its weapons program, U.S. and European pressures on Zaïre's rebarbative President Mobutu to step down, and multilateral talks over water resources in the Middle East.[3] Others, such as Iraq's war preparations and weapons development, were not.

Other deeper-rooted sources of conflict exist, such as growing pressures arising from overpopulation, environmental degradation that can lead to mass migration, underdevelopment, and poverty. Remedial programs of family planning assistance, prudential crop and forest management, targeted development aid, and reformed structures of governance[4] are important as conflict-prevention policies.

Some pathways to cessation of violence lack idealism but can be objectively effective. Peace of a sort can come from total victory; a less draconian path is what negotiation theorists call a "hurting stalemate"—the kind of moral and physical exhaustion that began to bring about change in the Middle East, Ulster, and the Balkans in the 1990s. Finally, not every dispute requires outside involvement, and a surprising number simply fade away. A secretary of state, reflecting on his experience, wrote: "I think we tended then—and now—to exaggerate the necessity to take action. Given time, many problems work themselves out or disappear."[5]

This may be true, but given the world's dismal record of failure to act in a timely fashion, one hesitates to advocate any more passivity than already exists in the system.

Settling Disputes Peacefully

Peaceful methods of conflict resolution have long been available. Chapter VI of the UN Charter, for example, lists a comprehensive battery of methods for resolving or moderating disputes before they heat up and become small wars. It was never assumed that the United Nations would be responsible for resolving all disputes between, let alone inside, countries. Indeed, Article 33 calls on the parties to any dispute whose continuation could endanger international peace and security to "first of all, seek a solution by negotiation, enquiry, mediation, conciliation, arbitration, judicial settlement" or other peaceful means of their choice. The record of quiet diplomacy to defuse potential crises without turning to the UN Security Council is far from zero, often featuring unsung heroes whose triumphs are rarely trumpeted.

The record of states, however, has not been impressive when we consider formal methods of dispute-settlement such as compulsory arbitration—a method that has become commonplace in labor-management relations (and which the U.N. Law of the Sea Treaty includes as an option for disputes arising under its terms). The use of the International Court of Justice (ICJ) was greatly inhibited as a result of its rejection by the Soviets during the Cold War and by new states' suspicions of the international legal system's perceived Western bias. Nor was it helped by the United States' insistence on clinging to the so-called Connally Amendment of 1945 which led to hobbling the Court by reserving to the United States the decision as to whether or not a dispute was within its "domestic jurisdiction." When U.S.-Russian relations began to improve after 1990, both agreed at least rhetorically to place some contentious matters before the World Court.

The ICJ has had some successes in dealing with primarily legal questions. It has ruled on several boundary disputes between Mali and Burkina Faso in

1986 and between Chad and Libya in 1994. Apart from some nationality, human rights, and treaty issues, however, it has more often failed when the issue was political. Albania's disregard in 1949 of the Court's ruling in the Corfu Channel case was matched 37 years later in the Nicaragua harbor-mining judgment in which the United States, unlike even communist Albania or Qadhaffi's Libya, denied the Court's jurisdiction. In a less anarchic world, international agreements would have built-in recourse to compulsory arbitration and impartial adjudication. But on the big-ticket items, most countries are unwilling to subject their sovereignty to third-party judgment.

The first step beyond low-key bilateral or third-party methods of dispute-resolution is *fact-finding*—the simplest form of multilateral intervention. Even during the Cold War the major powers, bitterly divided over whether the secretary general or the Security Council should direct peacekeeping operations, achieved consensus on what came to be called Peace Observation. It became relatively routine to dispatch to reported trouble spots UN representatives who sometimes used their good offices quietly to mediate or conciliate the dispute. This has happened since 1958 in problem areas ranging from Lebanon and Jordan to Cyprus, Afghanistan, and Western Sahara. The fact-finder may be a single representative of the UN secretary general or of the president of the Security Council. It has become acceptable for the secretary general not only to take the initiative in bringing matters to the Council, as specified in Article 99 of the Charter, but also to dispatch small-scale fact-finding and good-offices missions on his own initiative.

Next along the sensitivity spectrum is the dispatch of an observation group consisting of uniformed or civilian personnel loaned for the purpose by member-states. Over the years since 1945, the United Nations has sent such observers to Kashmir, Palestine, West Irian, Yemen, the Dominican Republic, Iraq, the Sinai, and elsewhere. In the late 1980s UN observers monitored the Soviet withdrawal from Afghanistan, supervised the cease-fire between Iran and Iraq, and oversaw Cuban and South African troop withdrawals in Angola while the UN Transition Assistance Group policed Namibia's move to independence. Humanitarian personnel and human rights monitors have through early deployment encouraged reconciliation and dialogue in El Salvador, Guatemala, and Tajikistan.

For peace observation and monitoring short of intrusive peacekeeping or peacemaking by military units (treated in Chapter 5), it is still important to minimize host-country sensitivity so that it does not hinder constructive conflict prevention. Technological "fixes" are becoming increasingly available that can make a monitoring presence within a state's border less intrusive and therefore more politically acceptable. All-weather radar-imaging satellites are able to detect military concentrations. With adequate funding (and a restored reputation), the United Nations could "rent" access to existing satellites, private or governmental. In an age of privatization, a case can be made for independent monitoring. For instance, several years ago the Carnegie Endowment for International

Peace's Commercial Observation Satellite Project had commercially available French and Soviet satellite photographs evaluated by trained photo-interpreters. More recently, Earthwatch and other space-imaging systems became available.[6] Electronic sensor technology was helpful for the nonintrusive (and thus politically acceptable) U.S.-manned Sinai Field Mission that formed part of the disengagement package in the Middle East in 1973 and again in 1978 following the Camp David Egypt–Israel peace talks. That technology is more modest than the so-called National Means of Verification used in espionage and monitoring arms control agreements (although the capability gap is narrowing). In 1995, after losing an F-16 on a reconnaissance mission over Bosnia, the United States offered drone observation and high-speed SR-71 aircraft for battlefield surveillance. It also offered satellite reconnaissance pictures to support war crime charges, particularly against Serbian offenders. Satellite and other remote observation could be effective in other contentious situations for conflict-reducing elements of reassurance, confidence-building, and insulation from outside interference.

The Value and Limits of Private Diplomacy

There is no rule that only officialdom should mediate disputes. In the Argentine–Chile Beagle Channel dispute at South America's tip, the Pope played a role reminiscent of the monarchs' mediatory role in the nineteenth century. The parties in the protracted Ethiopian–Eritrean conflict were brought together by former President Carter's International Negotiating Network, with financing from sources as diverse as Norway and Japan, leading to a referendum and independence for Eritrea in 1993. Presidents Nelson Mandela and Mugabe mediated in Angola and Mozambique, as did a lay Catholic group called the Community of Saint Egidio in Mozambique in the early 1990s. In addition, many private organizations have tried to bring parties together in what Joseph Montville calls "dual track diplomacy."[7]

Some nongovernmental groups successfully brought together Arabs and Israelis as well as Greek and Turkish Cypriots when relations between them were most acrimonious. Intensive unofficial discussions were organized in out-of-area settings where these hitherto isolated individuals could become acquainted and undemonized. During the Cold War, organizations ranging from the Quakers to the United Nations Association of the USA sponsored similar retreats where U.S. and Soviet experts could maintain contact on issues dividing their countries. The Harvard Negotiating Project exported techniques of conflict resolution based on Professor Roger Fisher's methodology of "getting to yes." And in the early 1990s, when after over 40 years of warfare Palestinian and Israeli officials were finally ready to negotiate, it was a Norwegian research organization (backed by the Norwegian foreign ministry) that supplied the impetus and venue for the initial meetings. All these efforts, to the extent they realistically took account of the fundamental interests at stake, helped move the situations along their long and arduous road to settlement. That settlement can, of course, only be made final by the responsible political authorities.

Unfortunately, however, these are exceptions. Prudential prevention is the essence of diplomacy, but it runs against the grain of short-term political considerations. All too often the underlying issues remain unaddressed until the next bloody outbreak. In the main, modern history is a dismal chronicle of missed opportunities to take effective early steps, followed by later painful costs.

No collective preventive efforts were seriously undertaken prior to the 1982 war between Britain and Argentina over the Falklands/Malvinas, or before the buildup leading to Iraq's September 1980 invasion of Iran. In the Gulf, purposeful disincentives by Washington and London, instead of self-deception and wishful thinking, might have prevented Iraq's invasion of Kuwait in 1990 and brought a less bloody outcome. The glaring example of too little and too late is the genocidal war starting in 1991 in the former Yugoslavia, where Germany insisted on premature recognition of independence for Croatia and Slovenia and, consequently, for Bosnia-Herzegovina, where the Serb minority was clearly unwilling to live under majority Muslim rule. Washington reportedly discouraged an early compromise agreement to partition Bosnia,[8] and for all too long European politicians declined to counter unspeakable behavior on Europe's doorstep.

Even if states were readier to tackle the peace and security agenda in a timely fashion and to agree on the need for cooperative action, there are obvious limits to the ability of even a reformed United Nations to take on expanded diplomatic or policing functions. If the remaining superpower—the United States—correctly declines to act as global policeman, the obvious alternative to deal with destabilizing disorder and intolerable national behavior is to *head it off before it takes place.* Conflict prevention and preventive diplomacy came into vogue in the mid-1990s as a result of U.S. reluctance to intervene. The challenge is to transform those noble sentiments from slogan to policy.

First, however, one caveat is in order. Peacemakers will be more relevant and effective if they overcome the natural tendency to assume that all differences are negotiable. The world has learned the hard way that occasionally a conflict can be genuinely nonnegotiable, as both the UN secretary general and the Russian government found out before they reluctantly decided to support the use of force in January 1991 to eject Iraq from Kuwait. They had literally gone the last mile with Saddam Hussein, only to admit finally that no compromise was possible. The painful lesson is that doctrinal pacifism can sometimes give a green light to aggression and tyranny, whether it be a Hitler planning the conquest of Europe, a Saddam Hussein coveting neighboring states, or the heirs of Yugoslavia's wreckage pursuing murderous dreams of expansion.

If the community lets matters fester to the point of explosion, it will have to choose between doing too little or trying to force compliance through deployment of ships, tanks, and aircraft by powerful states. If the aggressor is a nuclear-armed great power, the system will be back where it was at the height of the Cold War—adding one more reason to focus on conflict prevention.

What else might help to strengthen preventive action beyond the initial steps of conflict-resolution diplomacy?

THREE STRATEGIES OF PREVENTIVE DIPLOMACY

Publicity

If the underlying dispute does not yield to quiet diplomacy, and particularly if one party is the greater offender, the next step is to aim the spotlight on alleged misbehavior in order to confirm charges and to embarrass the wrongdoer or, alternatively, to reassure everyone that it was a false alarm. Publicity in the age of global communications can be a powerful diplomatic instrument to encourage noncoercive compliance through its powers of, so to speak, shame, embarrassment, and ridicule.

Governments are resistant to open discussion of alleged misbehavior, for official candor can be downright embarrassing. This is all the more reason why, when a serious threat is building, impartial, credible information should be diffused in a glare pitiless enough to inhibit aggressive behavior, to keep responsible governments from waffling, and to encourage the offender to back down. (This sequence worked to good effect in policing the aftermath of the 1991 Gulf War.) Sometimes discreet diplomacy is best, but secrecy is all too often an excuse for bureaucratic and diplomatic inaction. The spotlight transforms the quiet fact-finding process into a more visible weapon of deterrence that can help to discourage wrongdoing and encourage compromise.

There is a UN High Commissioner for Human Rights with modest powers of inquiry and reporting. In addition, more of the "spotlight" functions could be allocated to nongovernmental groups that are free of diplomatic hangups, such as the International Press Institute, the World Federation of UN Associations, Freedom House, various Human Rights Watches, and Amnesty International. Intense commercial television coverage stimulated international humanitarian action in Ethiopia in the late 1980s and Somalia in the early 1990s. So that network news editors do not always set the action agenda, UN observer missions should carry camcorders and the United Nations should make the videotapes publicly available at cost.

Deterrence

Deterrence as a strategy lay at the heart of Western nuclear policy during the Cold War. It aimed at creating a conviction—more accurately, an uncertainty—that conventional military aggression on the part of the USSR might produce a wholly unwanted effect in the form of a devastating nuclear riposte. Happily, the policy was never tested.

As an accepted psychological mechanism, however, deterrence can play an important role in the arsenal of conflict prevention and should not remain the monopoly of nuclear strategists. Actual peacekeeping-type units on the ground can send a signal from a menaced border *before* fighting breaks out (as was done on the Macedonian side of the Serbian-Macedonian border). On the larger stage, effective strategies of deterrence could strengthen compliance by would-be nuclear proliferators. Deterrence has to come early rather than late. In 1994, warnings emanating from Rwanda that genocide was starting were loud and clear. Between April and June, the international community—realistically speaking, the United States, Britain, and France—had the information, but they vacillated and weaseled while perhaps 800,000 minority Tutsis were shot, hacked, or clubbed to death in a murderous frenzy by the army and Hutu-dominated militias. The rest of the grisly story is well known, as are the excuses based on disillusionment with humanitarian intervention in Somalia. If there is no system ensuring effective deterrent action in the face of genocide, there is no meaningful community and no real system of law and order.

Even if effective action is ultimately taken, it will not deter violation of basic international norms if it comes late rather than early. If the European powers (or the United States, or even one NATO frigate) as early as 1991 had confronted the latter-day Serb vandals offshore at Dubrovnik, or actively protected relief supplies and UN peacekeepers at Sarajevo airport when they were first fired upon, or had punished open violations of the no-fly zone, events might have turned out differently. If the huffing and puffing in major Western capitals had added up to a believable threat, the radical Balkan expansionists might have been stopped. Serb leaders soon understood that the threats were hollow, and they remained undeterred until, three years later, NATO under U.S. leadership finally started to enforce the UN mandate to protect Sarajevo and other "safe areas" (several of which had already been overrun by the Serbs). The policy prescription is embarrassingly obvious: democratic leaders should follow through on their threats to enforce the "law"; otherwise, undemocratic leaders will make fools and hypocrites of them.

Deterrence is one reason why meaningful sanctions against human rights abuses should be codified. U.S. national legislation has denied some aid to egregious violators, and occasionally reforms have followed. The community's rulebook needs a sharper set of teeth. The UN Genocide Convention, along with the Fourth Geneva Convention and its successors on laws of war, should be expanded to cover "ethnic cleansing" of the Yugoslav variety. Sanctions should be added to the declaration on human rights of minorities which the General Assembly passed in December 1992. Future official torturers and rapists will be carefully calibrating the degree of seriousness displayed by the International War Crimes Tribunals for the former Yugoslavia and for Rwanda created by the United Nations.

Creating mass refugee flows as a deliberate policy is a particularly savage form of official behavior, whether in Bosnia, Rwanda, or anywhere else. Relief agencies don't like to discuss murderous activities by tyrants, and diplomats usually tiptoe around "host government" sensitivities. The consequence has been virtual immunity for those who torment and displace masses of innocents while good people clean up after their crimes. The concept of war crimes, left vague by the Nuremberg trials, should explicitly cover peacetime crimes against humanity such as the deliberate generation of refugees.[9]

Peaceful Change

In the best of all possible worlds, compliance begins with obedience to *law*. The law works in disputes where the parties are prepared to compromise or, if given a fair hearing, to accept an impartial third-party judgment. Except for a Hitler or a Saddam Hussein for whom the only remedy may be counterforce, states generally comply with international law to the extent that the rules are considered fair. The problem arises when the reason for not accepting third-party adjudication or arbitration is either mistrust of the dominant legal system or unvarnished insistence on winning. Disputes that are not "justiciable" require application not so much of existing law as of justice and equity.

One of history's most compelling lessons is the need for a commitment to peaceful change procedures, in the spirit of President John F. Kennedy when he said that "those who make peaceful change impossible make violent change inevitable." When the UN Charter was drafted, the memory of the interwar years was fresh. Providing for peaceful change was understood as essential to minimize violent change.[10] Article 14 of the UN Charter[11] was drafted with the Versailles Treaty's disastrous rigidity in mind, and the United Nations played a major role in the process of decolonization—a de facto peaceful change process. The General Assembly was never intended to acquire "legislative" powers (except when the foreign ministers asked it to decide the disposition of the Italian colonies after World War II), and Article 14 has been invoked only rarely. A rigid commitment to "stability"—France in the interwar years, the United States after 1945 in Iran or Cuba, the Soviets in Eastern Europe—can be a prescription for political disaster.

Perhaps the thorniest challenge for statecraft in the next historical period is that of secessionist movements around the world. The basic formula for governance since the seventeenth century has been the state. Since the nineteenth century, when Germany and Italy each incorporated their many small independent parts into one national state, the "nation-state" has been the common format (even if it incorrectly describes the many multinational states). In the early twentieth-century environment of greater nationalist awareness, pressures for ethnic, religious, or linguistic group autonomy were growing. In the aftermath of World War I, President Woodrow Wilson pressed his ideal of "national self-determination" on the allies, in the conviction that the indigenous people, not foreign rulers, should decide their own political fate. (When it came to the Balkans, however, the "South Slavs"—that is, Yugoslavia—were incorporated into a common kingdom including the Serbs, Croats, and Slovenes.)

In the decades after the Second World War, national self-determination became the motto of the colonial peoples whose move toward independence the United Nations was overseeing. But many multinational states remained in the world. Many were newly independent states where the colonial power had often drawn a line of convenience—its convenience, that is—around a variety of disparate nations and labeled it a state. Some multiethnic states found successful formulas for peaceful coexistence and even integration into a single society, as in the United States. But in the 1990s, pressures for greater autonomy make up much of the crisis agenda.

The tension between equally powerful principles of self-determination and territorial integrity make solutions extraordinarily difficult, particularly when it comes to actually fissioning off pieces of a state. Normally, that should be the last resort of people who cannot exist together peacefully. But Woodrow Wilson's time may have finally come: small states such as Eritrea or Estonia show that size is no longer essential to viability. Under the surface, the nation-state is in fact yielding in some places to what Kenichi Ohmae calls "region states,"[12] creating what Gideon Gottlied labels "soft forms of nationhood."[13]

The status of territories is technically a legal issue. But these are usually highly political matters, with deep emotional content, rather than being justiciable. Earlier in this chapter, we noted a variety of means to deal with such grievances given the will of the parties to find solutions. In addition, the International Court of Justice should dust off its rarely used capacity to deal with disputes in the fashion lawyers call *ex aequo et bono,* meaning applying equity and common sense rather than the letter of law. Small panels of UN Security Council members could be more often charged with working out an equitable resolution of clashing claims before they become full-blown Council debates. Candidates for better peaceful change strategies include the festering situation of majority Muslims in Indian-ruled Kashmir, permanent stalemate in Cyprus that threatens Greek-Turkish relations, suppression of Kurdish minority rights in Turkey and Iraq, and growing militancy over ownership of potentially rich resources in the Spratly Islands squabbled over by half a dozen Asian and Southeast Asian States. There are clearly other possibilities than clinging to a nonviable unitary state: partition into separate political entities à la India and Palestine (Bosnia, Kashmir); dual citizenship (Quebec); shared sovereignty or condominium (Cyprus, Northern Ireland, Iraq, Turkey); power-sharing within the central government à la Belgium and Switzerland (South Africa, Rwanda); cantonization à la Switzerland (India); secession à la Somaliland (South Sudan); autonomous regional self-government à la Catalonia's "country within Spain" (some Russian republics); and independence à la Eritrea (Tibet, Taiwan).

It is not fanciful to guess that genuine autonomy, and possibly even political independence, will someday be granted for such dissident regions as

Kashmir, Kurdistan, Kosovo, East Timor, Quebec, Tibet, and Chechnya. A bright intergalactic visitor might reasonably ask why not do it now before thousands of lives are lost and millions of refugees created. Indeed, some of these regions might not fission off in a violent fashion if accommodation takes place. The nations and their leaders might well adopt as the global motto, and as a realistic definition of peace itself—"The dynamic management of change without war."

EARLY WARNING

One constructive consequence of the so-called Cases from Hell in the 1990s and their residue of disillusionment regarding humanitarian intervention was a surge of attention to *conflict prevention* (usually called preventive diplomacy for one of its parts). In that process, special attention has been devoted to better early warning of developing conflict situations, including proposals for crisis prevention centers and related techniques for alerting governments and international diplomats. Such procedures can be useful to force attention to incipient hot spots that governments may be aware of but tend to ignore. Technology-based systems such as the CASCON program presented in Part III of this book can help busy officials and other consumers of early warning information to remember history and stretch their own imaginations. In that sense, good early warning can be a valuable process for forcing action.

Information barriers to more effective conflict prevention lie not so much at the production as at the consumption end. In our information age the problem is certainly not lack of data concerning events and trends. The available information may be poorly organized, screened, and analyzed, but it is actually torrential. Intelligence services routinely monitor evolving crises in countries around the world, as do private news, banking, and human rights organizations. More systematic conflict analysis systems such as CASCON can help, but they cannot substitute for human judgment as to what is important, or make officialdom act when it does not want to. The heart of the matter is still the pursuit of purposeful policy strategies to head off international and internal warfare before it explodes in one's face.

A serious attack on the early warning issue should also broaden its focus to socioeconomic-sociopolitical indicators of instability within human societies. According to one careful analyst, four factors will underlie conflict in the developing regions: decreased food availability, economic decline, population displacement, and disruption of institutions and social relations.[14] Demographic studies examine the correlations between population pressures and political turmoil. Norman Myers broadened the equation to a direct "connection between population pressures, environmental ruin and constant civil war," citing population-prompted violence between India and Bangladesh, El Salvador and Honduras, Rwanda and Tanzania, and Nigeria vis-à-vis its neighbors.[15] Using a range of measures and indicators, the Population Crisis Committee examined 120 countries and found a possible correlation in 101. The top candidates on their watch list for potential instability were Uganda, Mauritania, Ethiopia, Zaïre, Burundi, Sudan, and Chad. (Those with the highest demographic pressures but not necessarily other key conflict variables were Kenya, Ivory Coast, Saudi Arabia, again Tanzania, Botswana, and Libya.) The possible consequences range from destabilizing mass migrations to terrorism and political instability.[16] It should be remembered that any connection with conflict is still only inferential, but given the demographic numbers, if future history is going to supply the missing empirical evidence, it may be too late then to take the needed remedial action.[17]

An intriguing attempt to quantify the environment–conflict linkage is found in the work of Professor Roy Prosterman, who correlated *land distribution*—or rather *mal*distribution—with revolutionary potential. Prosterman's data suggest "substantial danger of major revolution for any country 30 percent or more of whose total population consisted of landless peasants—and a critical danger where that percentage reached 40."[18] Among his striking examples are pre-1959 Cuba with 39 percent, pre-1961 South Vietnam with up to 58 percent, pre-1975 Ethiopia with 60 percent, pre-1979 Iran with 35 percent, pre-1980 Nicaragua with over 38 percent, and El Salvador with 38 percent. The Worldwatch Institute concluded, "Most land reform struggles have been, and will continue to be, accompanied by violence and political instability. . . . International statistical comparisons show that levels . . . tend to be highest in the countries with the most inequitable land distribution patterns."[19]

What other objective early warning signals might be derived from socioeconomic conditions? The UN Development Program (UNDP) worked up what it termed *operational indicators of human security,* which it believes can constitute an early warning system. Its 1994 Human Development Indicators rank-ordered countries accordingly. Perhaps not surprisingly, most of the countries currently in conflict were bunched at the lowest rungs of that ladder. The UNDP correctly defines some other countries higher up on its development scale as nevertheless in potential crisis—Myanmar (Burma), Sudan, and Zaïre. Conflict prevention also should mean paying attention to other countries on the lowest rungs but not in crisis: Guinea, Burkina Faso, Niger, Mali, Guinea Bissau, Mauritania, Malawi, Benin, Uganda—poor Africa!—and Bhutan. UNDP's analysis also implies that Egypt, South Africa, Nigeria, and Brazil—four exemplars of the new "middle class" of developing countries—could join the list of failed states because of wide income gaps, raising the possibility of disastrous social and political upheavals.[20]

We can argue endlessly about causes and effects. Nonetheless, it probably remains true that, as French writer Jean Paul Sartre wrote three decades ago, "When the rising birth rate brings wider famine in its wake, when those new-comers have life to fear rather more than death, the torrent of violence sweeps away all barriers."[21]

THE PSYCHOLOGICAL BARRIERS TO
CONFLICT PREVENTION

A more purposeful conflict-prevention strategy is inhibited by the decision-making culture that evolved in Washington and other capitals during the fast-paced tense years of the Cold War. Even when adequate early warning of con-flict is in hand, key decision makers often fail to reflect on its potential meaning and relevance. Indeed, as some of them will ruefully confess, there is little if any reflective time on their response-oriented agendas.

Why should this be so? One reason is objective: the unending litany of crises whose short time frame seems to demand an early response or at least the calling of endless meetings. In part, the habit is a leftover of the Cold War years when the United States defined its interests as global, so that every spar-row that fell was *ipso facto* a U.S. crisis. Even at its most leisurely, however, the time horizon of the secretary of state's staff meetings or the sessions in the White House Situation Room is set by the incoming cable and CNN traf-fic. The most long-term discussions at the top typically plan for the next NATO or G-7 summit, or UN General Assembly, or congressional hearing—which are rarely more than six months away. In that culture, for a planner to be rel-evant is to be in on things.[22] The dilemma is that the more relevant the plan-ner, the less it is a planning operation and the more a crisis management sys-tem.

Other reasons for the chronic deficit in preventive activity are subjective. People at the apex of the policy pyramid—senior State Department, Defense Department, and CIA officers, as well as National Security Council staffers—spend most of their time "putting out fires," even if some of the fires turn out to be false alarms or nine-day wonders. It is highly unlikely that the bone-weary officials who finally clear their in-baskets by 8 P.M. or later will cheer-fully submit to a briefing about a situation that, however potentially ominous, is not near the explosion stage. (The fatigue factor is one of the most under-rated elements in national decision making.) The system sometimes works well, but at its worst, a Gresham's Law of official life always gives preference to a "crisis," however fraudulent or unworthy of top-level attention, at the expense of early warning and conflict prevention.

This bureaucratic scenario may seem to trivialize the profound dilemma of those carrying the heaviest responsibilities, but the problem is even worse than described above. For in truth the pace of events at the top of the foreign policy and national security machine is not only exhausting; it is also incomparably stimulating. Without trying to psychoanalyze top officialdom in Washington and New York, London, Paris, Moscow, or Beijing, a certain personality type appears to be attracted by the high tension and drama of life at the top. One National Security adviser commented to the author that "when nothing's happening, I'm bored." By "nothing happening," he meant the momentary absence of exigent crises. Unconsciously, he also meant, "I don't want to waste my time and energy on something uninteresting that may break six months or a year from now—that's not what I do here." The same person may also be capable of producing a thoughtful future-oriented scenario when playing the scholarly role. In short, it's not always the person; most of all it's the system.

The need is less for additional information sources and data centers than it is for better ways to process and refine early warning data to make it more relevant, and preferably irresistible, to officialdom. The central unsolved problem is to get important early warning indicators on the official agenda and into the action process. Precisely the wrong approach to this was the UN secretary general's decision, presumably on economy grounds, to abolish rather than strengthen the recently created UN Office of Coordination of Research and Collection of Information (ORCI), whose mission was to organize and systematize the United Nations' information flow into more usable forms, using high-speed data processing and policy-relevant databases. If early warning performs the old function of the "canary in the coal mine," the planner often suffers the fate of the canary whose inert body confirms the presence of lethal gases.

The news is not all bad. The imperative of avoiding future entanglement in new Somalias, Bosnias, or Rwandas led to a modest official search for targeted ways to employ conflict-prevention strategies. Some of the results were promising: a small but significant tripwire U.S. military unit in blue berets on the Macedonian border referred to earlier; a State Department task force and a National Intelligence officer for early warning; and invigorated diplomatic activity to head off conflicts in the African region, notably through the Greater Horn of Africa Initiative concerned with food, transport, and cash for a quick response to new humanitarian crises, along with early warning systems to anticipate conflicts jeopardizing food security.[23]

Better early warning at the policy level also calls for reforming the policy planning function to integrate it better into decision making. It also entails encouraging greater use of systematic data technologies, whether computerized reminders of history such as CASCON (see Part III of this book) or senior-level political gaming of over-the-horizon problems.[24] It is past time for foreign policy to update its tools and begin to catch up with the state-of-the-art worlds of business and the military. And it is surely past the time to become more serious about the preventive uses of deterrence, publicity, peaceful change, and relevant international law.

NOTES

[1]The reader is reminded of the definitions presented at the end of Chapter 1.

[2]David A. Hamburg, *Education for Conflict Resolution,* Report of the President (New York: Carnegie Corporation, 1994), p. 7.

[3]See Michael S. Lund, "Underrating Preventive Diplomacy," *Foreign Affairs,* July–August 1995, p. 161.

[4]See Kuman Rupesinghe, "Toward a Policy Framework for Advancing Preventive Diplomacy," *International Alert,* London, December 1994, p. 10.

[5]Dean Rusk, *As I Saw It* (New York: W. W. Norton, 1990), p. 137.

[6]Michael Krepon, "Spying from Space," *Foreign Policy,* No. 75, Summer 1989, p. 98, and Bruce D. Berkowitz, "Information Age Intelligence," *Foreign Policy,* Summer 1996.

[7]Joseph V. Montville, ed., *Conflict and Peacemaking in Multiethnic Societies* (Lexington, Mass.: D. C. Heath, 1990).

[8]According to David Binder in *The New York Times,* August 29, 1993, "U.S. Policymakers on Bosnia Admit Errors in Opposing Partition in 1992."

[9]Tom Farer describes UN efforts to develop new legal norms for protecting the internally displaced in "How the International System Copes with Involuntary Migration," in *Threatened Peoples, Threatened Borders: World Migration and US Policy,* Michael S. Teitelbaum and Myron Weiner, eds. (New York: W. W. Norton, 1995), pp. 274–75.

[10]See Bloomfield, *Evolution or Revolution: The UN and the Problem of Peaceful Territorial Change* (Cambridge, Mass.: Harvard University Press, 1958).

[11]"The General Assembly may recommend measures for the peaceful adjustment of any situation deemed likely to impair the general welfare of friendly relations among nations" (except disputes being considered by the Security Council).

[12]"The Rise of the Region State," *Foreign Affairs,* Spring 1993, p. 78.

[13]"Nations Without States," *Foreign Affairs,* May–June 1994, p. 112.

[14]Thomas Homer-Dixon, "On the Threshold: Environmental Changes as Causes of Acute Conflict," *International Security,* Fall 1991.

[15]Norman Myers, *Ultimate Security: The Environmental Basis of Political Stability* (New York: W.W. Norton, 1993), p. 10.

[16]Linda Feldmann, "Study Correlates Population Rise, Political Instability," *The Christian Science Monitor,* June 26, 1989.

[17]See Sharon L. Camp, "Population: The Critical Decade," in *Foreign Policy,* No. 90, Spring 1993, pp. 126ff.

[18]Roy L. Prosterman et al., "Land Reform and the El Salvador Crisis," *International Security,* Vol. 6, No. 1, Summer 1981, p. 54.

[19]Erik Eckholm, *The Dispossessed of the Earth: Land Reform and Sustainable Development,* Worldwatch Paper No. 30, June 1979, pp. 34–35. See more recently *The Guardian of the Land: Indigenous People,* Worldwatch Report No. 112, December 1992.

[20]*Human Development Report 1994* published for the United Nations Development Program (New York: Oxford University Press, 1994), pp. 102–103.

[21]Introduction to Frantz Fanon, *The Wretched of the Earth, 1961* (New York: Grove Press, 1968), p. 20.

[22]I tried to analyze this problem in Bloomfield, "Planning Foreign Policy: Can It Be Done?", *Political Science Quarterly* 93, Fall 1978, updated in *The Foreign Policy Process: A Modern Primer* (Englewood Cliffs, N.J.: Prentice-Hall, 1982).

[23]See the article by J. Brian Attwood, administrator of USAID, "Nation Building and Crisis Prevention in the Post–Cold War Period," *Brown Journal of World Affairs,* Winter 1994, pp. 14–15.

[24]See Bloomfield's "Reflections on Gaming" in "Forum: Political and Military Gaming," *Orbis,* Winter 1984.

Five ⟶

POLICING THE GLOBAL NEIGHBORHOOD

Who Does What?

After the Cold War disappeared from center stage, the global drama centered on a rash of small wars, most of them inside the borders of states and many of those impervious to external ministrations. Chapter 2 sketched the background for the Cases from Hell, Somalia, Bosnia, and Rwanda, and their descent into the bloodletting of unleashed nationalist passions and ethnic savagery. The United Nations' unprecedented attempts to manage conflicts within the borders of states took it beyond the traditional canon of unfettered national sovereignty that, however unrealistic, in principle bars outside intervention. The short-lived New World Order of President George Bush followed a solid victory for collective security in pushing Iraq out of Kuwait in 1991. It was quickly undermined by a series of savage civil wars with which UN peacekeeping as previously conceived was incapable of coping.

With the global nuclear threat tremendously reduced, the likely conflict agenda for the years ahead does not require that all the world's disputes or armed struggles be the concern of outsiders. The law-abiding must oppose a clear-cut act of armed aggression (see Chapter 6). But the agenda features civil wars, anarchy, or abuse of ethnic groups, which are also hard to ignore if a situation meets one of three tests: (1) it impacts international or regional peace and security; (2) it destabilizes the intricate system of interdependencies on which the world economy rests; or (3) it so offends common standards of human decency that humanitarian intervention becomes a moral imperative. These are the criteria for at least some form of community policing designed to maintain a reasonable level of law, order, and civility in the neighborhood. They are also a definition of U.S. and other nations' interests that may be at stake in regional and local conflicts that meet the tests.

The question is, who is to do the policing when the community decides to respond to a 911 call? The answer in the early 1990s was the United Nations, which was created to provide the machinery for dealing with disputes and threats to the peace. However, the Cases from Hell set in motion a backlash in

Washington and some other capitals, which left no assurance that needful action would be taken even when a case met one of the three tests.

Yet in the same period the "demand side" was growing, consistent with the nature of the world's problems. Between 1988 and 1996 the number of disputes and conflicts in which the United Nations was involved rose from 11 to 28, and the United Nations was completing electoral activities in 21 countries compared with 6 four years earlier, and was administering sanctions in 7 countries compared with 1 in 1988 and 2 in 1992. Curiously, given the controversy about multilateral peacekeeping, the American public appeared to have a different view than some of their elected officials on ways of dealing with conflicts that meet the specified test, even allowing for a certain degree of disillusionment. Surveys conducted in December 1995 and April 1996 by the Wirthlin Group reported 49 percent saying in 1996 that the United Nations is doing "a good job," compared with 45 percent one year after the Gulf War, but with 54 percent the previous December. In 1996, a total of 63 percent wanted U.S. units in a UN force to remain under American command, compared with 42 percent in 1995. However, in 1996, a total of 71 percent were not likely to vote for a candidate seeking to weaken the United Nations, and 64 percent (compared with 60 percent in 1989) believed the United States should pay its dues rather than withhold funds to pressure the organization.[1]

Fundamental defects in the system turned 1990s peacekeeping into Mission Impossible. UN peacekeepers were given mandates that included using force when necessary, but except for the endgame in Bosnia in 1995–96, they were not given the means to do so and were unable to protect either themselves or the civilians they were trying to help. In the light of harsh experience, it is urgent to rethink the linked concept of armed peacekeeping and humanitarian intervention.

THE UNITED NATIONS AS CONFLICT MANAGER

Creation of the UN system in the mid-1940s was premised on several propositions, some of which proved questionable: the frightfulness of war would create a universal imperative sufficient to override the inward pull of nationalism; memories of the 1930s would ensure an effective system of universal collective security; legislative-type institutions could be reincarnated at the intergovernmental level; economic programs should work toward equilibrium rather than equity; and states were the only relevant world actors. The founders were realistic for their time and place, but underlying their approach was a leftover eighteenth- and nineteenth-century conviction that, with the right machinery in place, progress was inevitable and humans perfectible.[2]

Multilateral peacekeeping as we know it was created in the midst of a pair of horrendous crises in late October 1956: Hungary, where the international community was impotent in the face of a brutal Soviet invasion, and Suez, where inventive diplomats devised a way to put lightly armed soldiers between two sides to guard a truce. There was no provision for it in the UN Charter, but as a practical matter, an urgent need was identified and acted upon, establishing a new halfway house—Chapter Six and a Half, as it were—between the pacific settlement of disputes specified in Chapter 6 and Chapter 7's stalled provisions for collective military enforcement against aggression.

The idea was not totally new in the world's history. A chronicler of the Middle Ages reports a fascinating multilateral peacekeeping organization created in 1455 in Italy, not just to settle wars but to maintain the peace (which it did for 50 years).[3] Yet over five hundred years later, international society, compared with familiar political communities, remains essentially a voluntary self-help realm where numerical majorities have only symbolic meaning when it comes to real power. A major exception is found in some programs in nonsecurity elements of the UN system which do not make the headlines but have in fact changed the world. Successful UN system programs range from the prospective eradication of smallpox, control of the Ebola virus, and care of the world's refugees to allocation of radio frequencies and inspection of nuclear plants to prevent proliferation. All of these programs require some diminution of national freedom of action. Arguments about national sovereignty are not often heard, however, when it comes to cooperative monitoring of global weather or fixing rules for the world's air and sea travel, or many other functions where sovereignty is not surrendered but is pooled to achieve practical results no nation can reach alone.

Still, for many the touchstone of success is effectiveness in coping with security threats old and new, and when we consider a *police* function—which is what international security means today—a nerve-end is felt, and assertions of national sovereignty become strident. The task ahead for responsible national leaders is to resolve that dilemma in ways that improve the capacity of the international community not only to "peacekeep" between consenting states, but also to respond to anarchy or mayhem within countries that threaten the larger peace or represent a moral imperative.

Peacekeeping Successes

Multilateral peacekeeping underwent a revival in the late 1980s as Moscow retreated from decades of exploitation of Third World instability, matched by invariable U.S. support for whatever status quo was under assault. In the mid-1990s the United Nations deployed almost 75,000 military personnel along with 4200 civilian and others, compared with a grand total of 11,000 in 1988. That revival underwent some rocky times. In the prior period, however, multilateral peacekeeping was the means of choice to avoid the necessity of U.S. intervention as well as to insulate a local conflict from possible superpower involvement. That background is worth a brief summary here.

During the Cold War the United Nations' capacity to deal with disputes was sharply limited by the Soviet Union's distrust of an institution it could not control. For two decades the United States commanded a majority and was relatively open to use of UN mechanisms—although not for its most sensitive actions such as the Vietnam War, which were not winning majority support.

The key characteristics of traditional UN peacekeeping between 1956 and the late 1980s were as follows.

1. Uniformed soldiers, usually in battalion strength, wearing both national and UN insignia, lightly armed, and loaned by countries that were either neutral in the Cold War or generally trusted (e.g., Canada and the Scandinavians).

2. The advance consent of all the fighting parties.

3. A noncombat role except in limited self-defense.

4. A primary mission of "interposition," meaning getting between the sides after a cease-fire was achieved and the parties had stopped shooting at each other.

The ground rules changed somewhat after UNEF I—the first United Nations Emergency Force in Egypt—melted away in the face of Egyptian President Nasser's threats that led to the June 1967 Middle East war. A modest political barrier was crossed with a new rule that a UN force could not be removed without the consent of the United Nations body that had dispatched it. Another change was the inclusion of major alliance members in the forces, starting with Poland in UNEF II and later France in UNIFIL—the UN Interim Force in Lebanon placed in southern Lebanon after the 1978 Israeli invasion. The most fundamental transformation was symbolized by the Soviet Union's decision to pay up; together with France the Soviet Union had refused to pay its assessed contributions for UN peacekeeping forces in the Middle East and the Congo. This destructive precedent was later followed when the United States withheld its contribution when things went badly in Somalia and elsewhere.

Peacekeeping was a UN success story from the 1950s on. Lightly armed and politically neutral battalions contributed by member countries were placed between Arabs and Israelis, Congolese factions, Greek and Turkish Cypriots, and Indians and Pakistanis. In the 1960s and early 1970s, a tedious argument was waged in the United Nations Committee of 33 as to whether the secretary general or the Security Council had primacy in peacekeeping. The issue became moot when Moscow decided not to oppose the UN force in Cyprus, called for UN interposition when Egypt was losing the 1973 Middle East war, voted for UNIFIL in southern Lebanon, and in 1987 and 1988 under President Mikhail Gorbachev proposed expanding the United Nations' powers.

Multilateral peacekeeping was revived as the winding down of several small wars coincided with Soviet retreat from four decades of exploitation of Third World conflicts. Thenceforth both the United States and Russia contributed military observers to UN units. When Moscow abandoned its bloody Afghan adventure, UN observers monitored the General Accord outlining a settlement and supervised withdrawal of Soviet troops as part of the UN Good Offices Mission for Afghanistan (UNGOMAP). (Unfortunately, this did not end tribal and religious warfare in that devastated country.)

By the late 1990s there were 17 UN missions in place. Although some were peacekeepers in the traditional sense, calls multiplied for outside intervention in civil mayhem, famine, or sheer anarchy. Thus some peacekeeping missions crossed a fateful boundary line into peace enforcement, which, as we have seen, became highly controversial and for a time threatened to derail the whole concept of multilateral peacekeeping. Other new and unfamiliar tasks were added, such as monitoring elections in newly released territories along with disarming the war's losers.

Still functioning as old-fashioned peacekeepers were UNTSO (the 220-person United Nations Truce Supervision Organization in the Middle East); UNMOGIP (the token UN Military Observer Group in India and Pakistan); UNFICYP (the not-so-token UN Peacekeeping Force in Cyprus); UNDOF (the UN Disengagement Observer Force in the still-uncertain truce between Israel and Syria); and UNIFIL, which was still in the no-man's land of southern Lebanon. Iran and Iraq's mutual exhaustion in their bloody 1980s war enabled 350 UN observers to supervise their cease-fire under another acronym—UNIMOG (UN Iran-Iraq Military Observer Group). In 1991 UNIKOM (UN Iraq-Kuwait Observer Mission) moved into Kuwait.

New kinds of peacekeeping missions were organized when 35 countries asked the United Nations to provide electoral help and to monitor the disarming of the sides in leftover civil wars such as those abandoned by their U.S. or Soviet-Cuban supporters in Angola (UNAVEM II—UN Angola Verification Mission II) and Mozambique (ONUMOZ—UN Operation in Mozambique).

A UN mission monitored elections aimed at democratic governance in El Salvador (ONUSAL—UN Observer Mission in El Salvador) and observed a referendum in disputed—and phosphate-rich—Western Sahara (MINURSO). UN monitoring bodies consisting of both civilians and protective units (UNTAG) helped to peacefully transform South African-ruled South West Africa into independent Namibia. A small UN unit (UNOMIG) observed the tenuous cease-fire in Georgia's civil war.

The UN missions in Angola, Mozambique, and Cambodia achieved success against unfavorable odds in helping to re-knit political systems that had been severely mutilated by war and worse. In Somalia the UN peacekeepers discovered how extraordinarily difficult it was to add to their task what is called nation-building, a process that required extensive intrusion into the domestic processes of the country concerned. UNTAC (United Nations Transitional Authority for Cambodia) in 1992–93 was in fact engaged in nation-building in the same period. Although the ultimate results may not be known for years, on balance the contribution of 22,000 UN soldiers and administrators furnished by 30 countries was positive in the long road of bringing peace to that tragic land. Although the murderous Khmer Rouge faction was not eliminated, the UN mission ended a war that for a decade had decimated the country, brought 300,000 refugees home, created one of Asia's most democratic constitutions, set up elections in which 90 percent voted, and helped raise the country's GNP by 5 percent. When we consider the frustrations over peace enforcement and the insistence on instant results or instant withdrawal, we should recall that the Paris agreement on which the Cambodian arrangements were based took five years just to negotiate.

In 1988 the UN peacekeeping function received the Nobel Peace Prize. By 1995, a total of 162 UN peacekeepers had been killed and 1420 injured.

Peacekeeping Controversies

The end of the Cold War, together with the success of enforcement in Operation Desert Storm, encouraged President George Bush and other leaders to believe the time had come for more proactive use of multilateral machinery to deal with the emerging conflict agenda inside national borders. Then, as we have seen, the early 1990s brought controversial escalation from the accepted rules and premises of peacekeeping toward an uncharted gray zone variously labeled peace enforcement, humanitarian intervention, or peacekeeping plus that threatened to bring the whole concept to a screeching halt.

Actually, the same dilemma had faced the UN operation (ONUC) in the Congo (now Zaïre) in the early 1960s and had generated bitter controversies between the United Nations, the Soviets, and the right-wing supporters of mineral-rich Katanga Province. The operation was successful in leaving a legacy of a unified Zaïre. But in the process UN Secretary-General Dag Hammarskjold was killed in a suspicious plane crash while en route to Katanga. Savage anti–United Nations propaganda was waged by critics from both the U.S.S.R. and the Western far right. The difficulty in emplacing such a force in a strife-torn country was also experienced by UNIFIL, whose ultimately untenable mission between pro- and anti-Israeli forces in southern Lebanon brought substantial casualties to virtually unarmed UN peacekeepers from Fiji and other contributors.

Another fundamental question raised by the Somalia experience was whether the blue berets were there to feed the starving, observe a cease-fire, or monitor an election. Or in a case of anarchy, are the peacekeepers to create or restore a viable government—the function of "nation building"—tried successfully in Cambodia and disastrously in Somalia? (The decision in late 1995 to launch a major air strike and deploy 60,000 NATO troops to police a Bosnian peace agreement symbolized recognition of the need for robust military forces when peacekeeping turns violent. But assurances were given that there was to be no "nation-building," which virtually guaranteed that new controversies would arise when the parties violated the Dayton accord.)

Another major issue grows out of the UN system of voluntary cooperation of financing peacekeeping operations. A controversy arose in budget-conscious capitals over the surge of peacekeeping costs from $230 million in 1988 to $1.69 billion in 1992 and $3.61 billion in 1994. How can international arrangements adequate for a new century be financed without producing an annual bankruptcy crisis?

Numerous suggestions have been made over the years that will help develop new revenue streams to sustain peacekeeping operations, most involving a small surcharge on transnational transactions such as communications, air travel, and space activities.[4] Any such reform would require the largest contributors' conviction, now lacking, that the "policing" of aggressive or genocidal national behavior, which they often demand and then criticize, is genuinely in their interests and politically cost-effective. The inherent difficulty of voluntary contributions for peacekeeping is illustrated by the failure of the United States Congress to appropriate sufficient funds to pay the American share, even after reforms demanded by the Reagan administration had been implemented. That Americans pay only approximately $7 per capita for all the activities of the UN combined, from peacekeeping to smallpox control and radio frequency allocation, suggests that the problem is not cost alone. When the responsible powers have the will to conduct a peacekeeping operation, they are likely to find ways of paying their dues, as France and the Soviet Union did after withholding payment for earlier Middle East peacekeeping.

Some ad hoc peacekeeping or observation operations have been formed outside the United Nations under the label of "multinational." Some have been successful and noncontroversial, notably the United States Field Support Mission as part of the post–1973 Middle East disengagement package. The U.S., and ultimately the allied, reflagging of Kuwaiti tankers in the Gulf in 1987 after Iran mined the shipping lanes was originally controversial but eventually achieved a successful outcome. Other ventures have been less successful, mainly because they are not recognizably neutral (for example, the four-power Western intervention in Lebanon in 1982–83 that proved disastrous when the United States seemed to take sides).

Some countries have borrowed the peacekeeping label in order to legitimize unilateral intervention. In the early twentieth century, the United States frequently intervened in Caribbean and Central American countries, in the spirit of President Theodore Roosevelt's famous rationale for "exercising an international police power."[5] Washington again undertook unilateral "peacekeeping" in 1965 in the Dominican Republic (subsequently calling in the OAS), in 1982 in Grenada, and in 1989 in Panama. After the United Nations passed resolutions calling for democracy in Haiti, the United States sent troops in 1994, later yielding to a UN force. India labeled as peacekeepers its troops in Sri Lanka's civil war, as Syria has in Lebanon. France has intervened unilaterally in a dozen of its former African colonies from Dakar in 1962 to the Comoros in 1989. In 1994 France unilaterally "peacekept" by creating its own safe haven inside war-torn Rwanda.

Russia, not wishing to look like either Stalin or his tsarist predecessors, has found peacekeeping a useful label to legitimize the policing of dissension and secession pressures within its Russian Federation (although the mask slipped badly in Chechnya in the bloody warfare that began in 1994). The same is true along its often chaotic fringes in the so-called near-abroad of newly independent republics, where Russia stations around 130,000 troops with the republics' agreement and lists about a quarter as engaged in peacekeeping duties. In the late 1990s, there were 25,000 "peace keepers" in conflict-ridden Tajikistan.

Another issue has been peacekeeping's occasional tendency to continue indefinitely without real progress in peacemaking. In the Arab–Israeli conflict, there was positive value in fielding a succession of UN peacekeeping missions trying to fence off the conflict to avoid escalation in the strategic Middle East while efforts continued to seek solutions. But a periodically renewed UN mandate in Cyprus has lessened the pressure on the parties there to settle.

In 1995 the UN secretary general proposed to make peacekeeping more efficient, calling for a rapid reaction force, permanent UN missions with up to 50 observers in tense countries, and more UN control over nationally contributed troops.[6] This proposal seemed to run counter to the mood of backlash, although it actually backed away from his earlier proposals for peace enforcement in his 1992 *Agenda for Peace*. In May 1996, he asked that member states form a multinational force in Burundi, saying such a mission was beyond the present capacity of the UN.[7]

Others have made proposals for better coordination between headquarters and field, a mobile military headquarters unit, and privatizing some or all of UN peacekeeping.

For decades the four Scandinavian governments have bypassed official short-sightedness by operating peacekeeping training programs, as has the nonprofit International Peace Academy in New York and more recently the Pearson Peacekeeping Center organized by Canadians in Cornwallis, Nova Scotia. It would make sense to officially sanction and help finance those enlightened do-it-yourself arrangements.

The use of force when necessary in peacekeeping raises a question domestic police agencies have confronted. The United Nations should urgently research the rapidly growing armamentarium of nonlethal technologies ranging from inhibiting foams and nets to electromagnetic means of disabling hostile power grids.[8] But mainly, a sound strategic concept is needed.

THE REGIONAL APPROACH: A POSSIBLE SOLUTION?

In view of the overload at the global center, calls are being heard to beef up regional and subregional organizations so that they will carry more of the peacekeeping burden and perhaps even armed "peacemaking." The drafters of the UN Charter thought of regional organizations as the legs on which the organization would rest. President Franklin D. Roosevelt, with the Inter-American system in mind, was the chief proponent. Under Chapter 8, regional organizations were supposed to be the international "police" of first resort in trying to settle disputes. As it turned out, the only effective regional grouping following World War II was the North Atlantic Treaty Organization—NATO—which was not a Chapter 8 body but succeeded because it had a concrete mission—to deter and if necessary repel Soviet military moves on Western Europe—and also because its members were democracies that shared both political values and commitment to the mission.

The regional organizations that did qualify under Chapter 8 of the Charter (what became the Organization of American States, the Organization of African Unity, and the Arab League) have until now proven to be poor law-and-order agents for the community, either because a major regional country was battling the rest (Cuba in Latin America, Israel in the Middle East, South Africa in Africa) or because they lacked resources and leadership. They have only rarely acted as they were supposed to. The OAS donated a fig leaf to the United States' invasion of the Dominican Republic in 1965, the OAU sent a force into Chad in the early 1980s, and the Arab League replaced British forces in Kuwait in 1961 and more recently "legitimized" Syrian forces in Lebanon. Some subregional organizations have had greater successes, for instance, the so-called Contadora Group in helping close out the Central American wars of the 1980s, and a West African grouping that at least for a time tried to bring peace to Liberia.

With changes in the Middle East and African regions, and with the United Nations so overextended, the time has come to explore ways to place greater reliance on regional organizations. Such an attempt would be consistent with the more general trend toward decentralization of functions in both public and private sectors, but the regional organizations will have to change significantly if they are to share the peacemaker's burden. Assuming that such changes are at least theoretically possible, what would a modestly improved system look like?

In June 1996, NATO agreed to become a regional peacekeeper and troubleshooter in Bosnia (after being left impotent by its members for three years in the face of aggression and genocide in Europe itself). The ill-conceived plan to expand NATO eastward to Poland, Hungary, and the Czech Republic could get in the way of its new role by strengthening the paranoid streak in Russian nationalism. And of course, NATO will still retain its historic mission of deterring any would-be hegemonic Eurasian power (implicitly Russia, with Germany again as subtext). It might help NATO's transition into a reshaped future role by explicitly reconstituting it as a regional organization under Chapter 8, building on experience with IFOR (NATO Implementation Force) in Bosnia.

Another regional option for Europe is the Organization for Security and Cooperation in Europe (OSCE). This 53-member group under its former title of Conference on Security and Cooperation in Europe played a politically useful, if unexpected, role by holding the crumbling Soviet Union to an agreed regional human rights standard. CSCE proved no better than any other agent in facing up to the Bosnian disaster, but it has played a mediatory role in the Baltics and Central Europe, and in addition, in disputed Nagorno-Karabakh. Like NATO, OSCE also agreed to supply peacekeeping troops to the United Nations and maintained an observer mission in Macedonia. It has declared itself a regional organization, but the downside is that it had to withdraw its observers from Kosovo. Moreover, 10 of its 53 members were involved in shooting wars, and it has no real power. Its Budapest Declaration of December 1994 did, however, imply new hope for Europeanizing at least some of Europe's disorders.

In Latin America, under the Bogota Pact and Rio Treaty, the Organization of American States is equipped, at least on paper, with a wide spectrum of functions ranging from conflict resolution to collective security. OAS peacekeepers served in the Dominican Republic (following U.S. intervention). The organization has had modest success in fact-finding and dispute-settlement, as have subregional groupings such as the Contadora Group in Central America, but the organization has been notably allergic to anything resembling intervention (or U.S. domination).

Freed of Cold War hangups that entangled the United States in Cuba, Nicaragua, and El Salvador, the OAS has taken some modest steps away from its rigid noninterventionism, thanks to hemispheric progress toward democracy. In June 1991, in what became known as the Santiago Commitment, the foreign ministers pledged to adopt "timely and expeditious procedures to ensure the promotion and defense of democracy." Establishing a new cost to overthrowing a democratic government may have stayed the hand of would-be military coup leaders in 1992, and the next year helped keep the president of Guatemala from becoming dictator.[9] Considering Latin America's oversize military establishments as well as the U.S. military's role in inadvertently promoting some of the region's most obnoxious military figures, regional military training should change its focus to preparing hemispheric peacekeeping units for ready deployment on call of the OAS, much as Scandinavia has trained its peacekeepers.

The same applies to the African region—not tomorrow, since the OAU has been irrelevant to most African conflicts, but perhaps the day after. The Organization of African Unity has had some successes in interstate conflicts such as Somalia–Kenya, Mali–Burkina Faso, Morocco–Algeria, and Congo–Zaïre, and actually sent peacekeepers to Chad in 1981. It has not been as helpful in internal conflicts in places such as Benin and Mali.

Individual countries have sometimes acted as subregional cop—for instance, Tanzania in Uganda. Ethiopia's leaders played an impressive role in trying to bring peace to Somalia. A West African Military Observer Group in Liberia (ECOMOG), organized by the Economic Community for West Africa (ECOWAS), enjoyed some initial success in trying to overcoming anarchy in Liberia with peacekeeping troops from five countries, but was eventually charged with criminal behavior in the midst of that country's agony. The OAU secretary general has also attempted to mediate in several looming crises—a daunting and full-time chore in that troubled continent.

In the Pacific region the Asia-Pacific Economic Cooperation forum has made a start, and the Association of South East Asian Nations (ASEAN) has created a Southeast Asian Nations Regional Forum (ARF). It is too early to envisage a regional security or peacemaking role in the region, and for the foreseeable future there seems to be no substitute for a U.S. role as strategic makeweight and steadying influence while China, Japan, Russia, the Koreas, and Southeast Asia readjust their changing relationships.

It is clear that the existing international machinery, whether global or regional, suffers from major weaknesses—the United Nations because in particular the United States wants someone else to take over peacekeeping and peace enforcement, but is reluctant to pay for it; and the regional organizations because they have never acquired the infrastructure, the resources, or the political will to play a responsible policing role in their own neighborhoods. Yet if at the turn of the century both the national interest and the general interest call for a more reliable system of international law and order so that the main business of society can take place, the large questions of international peace and security will require serious rethinking not unlike that which shaped the present system more than half a century ago.

NOTES

[1] Reported in *The Interdependent,* United Nations Association of the USA, New York, Winter 1995–96 and Spring 1996. Comparable findings in a national Gallup poll of both mass and leader opinion were reported in "American Public Opinion and U.S. Foreign Policy," ed. John Rielly, Chicago Council on Foreign Relations, 1995, pp. 7, 27.

[2] Harlan Cleveland and Lincoln P. Bloomfield, *Rethinking International Cooperation* (Minneapolis, MN: Humphrey Institute, University of Minnesota, 1988), pp. 13–19.

[3] John Hale, *The Civilization of Europe in the Renaissance* (New York: Athenaeum, 1994), pp. 132–33.

[4] An outstanding treatment of the whole issue of UN financing is contained in Jeffrey Laurenti, *National Taxpayers, International Organizations: Sharing the Burden of Financing the United Nations,* (New York: United Nations Association of the USA, 1995).

[5] President Theodore Roosevelt in the so-called Roosevelt Corollary to the Monroe Doctrine stated that "Chronic wrongdoing, or an impotence which results in a general loosening of the ties of civilized society, may . . . ultimately require intervention by some civilized nation, and in the Western Hemisphere the adherence of the United States to the Monroe Doctrine may force the United States, however reluctantly, in flagrant cases of such wrongdoing or impotence, to the exercise of an international police power."

[6] *An Agenda for Peace 1995* (New York: UN Publications, 1995).

[7] *New York Times,* May 9, 1996.

[8] *Non-Lethal Technologies: Military Options and Implications,* Report of an Independent Task Force (New York: Council on Foreign Relations, 1995), p. 3.

[9] Richard J. Bloomfield, "Making the Western Hemisphere Safe for Democracy? The OAS Defense-of-Democracy Regime," in Carl Kaysen, Robert A. Pastor, Laura W. Reed, eds., *Collective Responses to Regional Problems* (Cambridge, Mass.: American Academy of Arts and Sciences, 1994), pp. 16, 26.

Six ᕫ
THE QUEST FOR SECURITY
Ideals and Reality

ENFORCEMENT IN AN IMPERFECT COMMUNITY

The concept of collective security goes to the heart of the twentieth century's efforts to create an entity resembling a world community. Collective security requires that countries combine their national military forces in a coalition aimed at punishing acts of armed aggression. Such a coalition was usually understood to mean "universal" in contrast to more limited military alliances. The League of Nations tried to make collective security real in 1935 when Italian dictator Benito Mussolini invaded Ethiopia. The League applied some sanctions, but none that really hurt. The Hoare-Laval pact was a disgraceful cave-in that prompted British Foreign Secretary Anthony Eden to resign, and it marked a watershed between the hopes for a peaceful world and the subsequent carnage of World War II.

Past failures inspired the founders of the United Nations, meeting in San Francisco in 1945, to create what they hoped would be an effective collective security system. But for 45 years of great-power stalemate and worse, Chapter 7 of the UN Charter prescribing enforcement powers remained on hold. In the 1991 Gulf War, collective security seemed to come alive, but in a few short years its future was again uncertain. Is the concept of universal or near-universal collective security an unrealistic political fantasy? Why is it so hard to build into the international system enforceable rules that add up to the kind of "law and order" most nations crave?

Most people know what compliance and enforcement mean in their familiar local settings. They also know the cost of breaking the law and give considerable credibility to likely enforcement action, whether by cops on the beat, sheriffs, tax collectors, or armies. In a democracy, active participation in the process strengthens their commitment. "Community" implies a fundamental agreement on enforceable rules, within a framework that supplies incentives to compliance and disincentives to misbehavior. Government works because people have a presumptive self-interest in abiding by the rules and are aware that there is a penalty for noncompliance.

At the international level, world society is a partial and imperfect community that lacks the essential qualities of sovereignty and power that are so familiar at the national level. It simulates government but cannot really act like one, although the UN Charter confers legitimacy on organized collective action. In an increasingly close-knit world economy, the peace, security, and welfare of all nations logically require improved arrangements for international "governance" (which by the way does *not* mean government). But the limiting realities are the community's infinite variety, decentralized power centers, fragments of structure and organization, primary reliance on self-help with only a contingent possibility of community "police" assistance when threatened, and no real tradition of pooled sovereignty. All these limitations are likely to continue.

COLLECTIVE SECURITY AGAINST AGGRESSION

The Record

Historically, the international security system has been one of self-help, defined by strong traditions of national sovereignty. The security provisions of the League of Nations Covenant, contained in Article 10, required unanimity, but in any event were repudiated by the U.S. Senate before they were ever tried. During World War II, America renewed its commitment to responsible involvement in world affairs, and with the other victorious powers accepted historically unprecedented enforcement provisions in the new security system. Indeed, the prime purpose of the United Nations was to prevent a repetition of the carnage of World Wars I and II by opposing and, better yet, preventing armed aggression. Chapter 7 of the Charter for the first time required states to comply even if they did not deem it to be in their interest to do so or had taken no part in the decision making.

For the next 45 years, the United Nations' enforcement provisions were vitiated by conflict between the major powers. The designated regional agencies — the OAS, OAU, and Arab League — proved ineffective as regional policemen. The Cold War generated an ad hoc system of alliances, above all NATO, which substituted for universal collective security. This system provided the principal deterrent and, if necessary, enforcement of the agreed rules against aggression or its threat.

Until 1991, with the exception of North Korea's invasion of South Korea in 1950, the global system failed to enforce its own rules when confronted with cross-border military aggression. The international community repeatedly failed to respond to cross-border armed attacks: Egypt, Syria, and Jordan against Israel; Israel against Lebanon; Turkey in Cyprus; North Vietnam against its neighbors; both Algeria and Morocco in Western Sahara; China in India and Vietnam; South Africa on its borders; the USSR in Eastern Europe and Afghanistan; Iraq in Iran; Libya in Chad; Iran in the Gulf islands; and Argentina in the Falklands/Malvinas. Some would add to that list the United States' mining of Nicaraguan harbors in the early 1980s and invasion of Panama in 1989. Others would vigorously affirm that these actions were legitimately defensive.

Compliance measures were never seriously invoked against India, which ignored the United Nations' call in 1948 for a plebiscite on Kashmir, or against Greece and Turkey when each sabotaged agreements on Cyprus. Cold War paralysis and antiquated notions of international law kept the powers from acting against the Khmer Rouge's genocide in Cambodia in the 1970s, and against atrocities in Uganda, East Timor, and the Central African Republic.

The concept of universal collective security rests on a commitment to join against any act that all permanent Security Council members call aggression. But once that is said, many shadings appear. Some conflicts are ambiguous in both origin and conduct. Instead of soldiers crossing an international border to shoot at other soldiers wearing different colored uniforms, the sides might wear camouflage or even suits. Even when an aggressor can be clearly identified, a UN majority has usually preferred not to label it so.

Frequently, it is far from clear whose side is in the right. Iraq was the attacker against Iran in 1980, but Iran had been fomenting dissidence among Iraqi Shi'ites. In June 1967 Israel struck preemptively—after Egypt threw out the UN peacekeeping force and mobilized along with Syria. In 1979, Tanzania and Vietnam moved troops into Uganda and Cambodia, respectively; but in the eyes of some these "invasions" countered a greater evil of indigenous genocide, even if that was not their motivation.

When the community does not function as such, sometimes individual states engage in do-it-yourself enforcement. For example, Iran repulsed Iraq's attack in 1980, and in 1982 the British repelled the Argentine invasion of the Falkland Islands. Even preventive enforcement may be possible, as when Israel attacked Iraq's Osiris nuclear reactor in 1981 and when the United States cooled off Libyan leader Colonel Quadaffi's international adventurism with a bombing raid in April 1986. In 1983 the United States ousted a Marxist regime in Grenada that threatened American medical students and in 1989 invaded Panama to arrest President Manuel Noriega for drug crimes.

The one UN action during the Cold War that was close to universal occurred in June 1950 when, with the United States in the lead, an international coalition went to war to repel North Korean armed aggression against South Korea only five years after the Allied victory over the Axis. It was not universal, nor technically even Chapter 7 enforcement, because the Soviets had walked out of the Security Council over the issue of Chinese representation. A 16-nation coalition under the UN banner, led by the United States as the Security Council's "executive agent," achieved the limited objective of expelling the aggressor. (But, as in Iraq in 1991, the offending leadership was left in power.) The price of total victory in Korea might well have been war with the Soviet Union, and General Douglas MacArthur's reckless march to the Yalu River did provoke China into war with mainly U.S. forces.

With the exception of Korea, the incubus of superpower rivalry lay like a stone on international decision making for collective security until the late 1980s. The majority of states declined to choose between the giant antagonists, and acts of international criminality went largely unpunished. With that burden finally lifted, the Security Council acted in August and September 1990 as its founders intended, with the members voting without dissent to condemn Iraq's assault on and attempted extinction of neighboring Kuwait, applying punishing sanctions, and in January–February 1991 pushing Iraq out of Kuwait.

The Security Council's unprecedented invocation of Chapter 7 enforcement powers in 1991 revived the long-dormant concept of collective security. Cross-border aggression was unambiguous, a UN member state was visibly mugging and ravishing another, and the global petroleum jugular vein was imperiled. The previous inhibition of U.S.-Soviet stalemate and dangerous escalation was no longer blocking collective enforcement of this fundamental rule.

In Iraq, as in Korea 40 years earlier, the United States, under the UN banner, was the chief enforcer. In both instances the United Nations was, to mix metaphors, both umbrella (to broaden participation) and figleaf (to supply legitimacy to an action the United States favored but could not or would not take on alone). In fact, 35 countries contributed manpower, arms, or funds; 28 supplied military forces. Operations Desert Shield and Desert Storm were deemed highly successful UN/U.S. coalition operations to restore peace.

As we have seen, the political atmosphere deteriorated shortly thereafter to the point where so-called humanitarian enforcement and even traditional peacekeeping were less likely to be employed. But it would be extremely dangerous if the United States, burned by its experiences in the Cases from Hell, were to emulate Mark Twain's cat, which wouldn't sit on a hot stove again, but wouldn't sit on a cold one either.

Sanctions

Under the UN Charter's Chapter 7, nonmilitary sanctions were always available as a first step to secure compliance, including such measures as trade, arms, and financial embargos; expulsion from international organizations and from cultural and sports events; suspension of technical assistance and severance of postal and communications services; and war crimes indictments.

Sanctions have been increasingly invoked but with mixed results. Economic sanctions on Rhodesia (now Zimbabwe) in 1965 for its (white) unilateral breakaway from Britain were ineffective. A mandatory arms embargo against South Africa for *apartheid* in 1977 was more influential because it was generally observed by the major trading powers and undergirded by bilateral economic sanctions. More recent sanctions against Iraq have been generally successful, doubtless because they banned all transactions with the outside world except imports of food and medicine (some oil sales were permitted in the spring of 1996). Some deterrent effects could be attributed to sanctions on international airlines plus an arms embargo voted against Libya in 1992 and 1993, as well as UN–OAS sanctions against Haiti aimed at restoring a democratically elected government. Arms embargoes have been voted on Rwanda, parts of Angola, Somalia, and Libya. Even leaky sanctions against Serbia for backing the murderous conquests of its Bosnian brethren appeared to be somewhat effective in temporarily transforming the criminally expansionist Milosevic into partner-in-peacemaking Milosevic. In April 1996, the Security Council voted mild sanctions against Sudan for refusing to hand over would-be assassins of Egyptian President Hosni Mubarak.

A recent study by the Institute of International Economics has concluded that if sanctions seek to reverse an aggression or disable an outlaw state's military potential, the chances of success are low. The odds improve when the goals are modest, the target is small and highly dependent on the outside, and an active internal opposition exists. To make sanctions effective they should be universal, with compensation provided for those otherwise tempted to cheat, along with positive incentives for the violator to behave.[1]

In the Haitian case a combination of carrots—the June 1993 Security Council offer of $1 billion aid—and sticks—a beefed-up worldwide arms and oil embargo and freeze of Haitian assets—facilitated the agreement to restore President Jean-Bertrand Aristide, which Washington subsequently brokered. In Haiti and elsewhere, however, the burden of sanctions falls primarily on the innocent because sanctions are imposed on abstractions called Haiti or Iraq as a form of collective punishment, implied probation, and hoped-for deterrence.

A more humane approach would punish the criminal leadership directly, with innovative sanctions targeted on leadership and its assets, as was done belatedly in Haiti. An understandable squeamishness concerning political assassination that altered U.S. policy in the 1970s should be rethought against the far greater immorality of punishing large numbers of noncombatant women, children, and elderly for the crimes of the few.

As we have seen, the trouble arose in the 1990s when peacekeeping by nonfighting units encountered aggressive behavior, and began to spill over into what looked like *enforcement,* and in particular enforcement *within* the borders of states. Enforcement means applying sanctions (the first steps under UN Charter Chapter 7) and ultimately using force if necessary to punish aggressors and other transgressors of the community's ground rules. The previous chapter traced the blurring of the line that traditionally separated peacekeeping from enforcement, starting with the Somali famine in 1992 in parallel with the Bosnian civil war, and soon thereafter the massacres in Rwanda. As we saw, these multilateral operations turned into a kind of halfway house that wasn't quite peacekeeping but not quite collective security either, and in which the initial peacekeeping purpose developed "mission creep" as the mandate expanded to the use of force if necessary to protect delivery of humanitarian assistance.

For a while that seemed a logical feature of the post–Cold War world, with the United Nations implementing a new sort of "common law" to cope forcibly if necessary with humanitarian crises brought on by internal strife.

However, peacekeeping's rules of engagement limited the UN units to self-defense, so the peacekeepers and aid-deliverers wound up unable to protect either civilian populations or themselves. In short, it became "mission impossible."

To make matters worse, the notion of any kind of UN intervention *inside* national borders, whether to end famine or to protect people from civil war or anarchy, also lacked a conceptual framework or even a vocabulary. When the Security Council decided to create a secure environment in Somalia and set up protected areas in Bosnia, UN peacekeepers suddenly had the choice of fighting back and calling for air strikes or proving ineffectual. UN Secretary General Boutros Boutros-Ghali's suggestion of peace enforcement in his 1992 *Agenda for Peace* seemed an oxymoron and was later modified after it encountered intense governmental skepticism. Both the taking of sides and the use of force to carry out a humanitarian mandate were the direct antithesis of peacekeeping, and represented a good definition of collective enforcement envisaged by Chapter 7.

The transition from the accepted function of peacekeeping to the *terra incognita* of humanitarian enforcement might have worked if the nations of the world had constituted a genuine community, in the sense of shared values and the usual powers of policing, taxation, and the rest. However, there was no agreement on such increased powers for the United Nations. Even if the UN structures were to be reformed, it cannot be overlooked that the Security Council's decisions are decisions by the major governments, primarily the United States. In the Cases from Hell, those governments shrank from the implications of their own decisions and helped to provoke a sequence of fiascos that rendered intensely controversial the whole notion of multilateral policing under the United Nations. When the United States returned to Haiti, it was under its own command, later replaced by UN units. When action finally was taken in Bosnia, the force was predominantly American, under NATO, not UN, command.

There are alternatives to using the United Nations in cases of future aggression and other international criminality. One is to use a group of militarily capable member states acting under a UN mandate, as in Korea in 1950 and the Gulf in 1991–92—what some have termed a "coalition of the willing." Another possibility, explored in Chapter 5, is to expand the powers and roles of at least some regional organizations.

In a wide variety of situations, however, the United Nations has a role others cannot readily fill. Despite the paranoid nightmares of some, the United Nations has no forces of its own or any military power independent of the major states and in particular the United States. We should not forget that in Somalia a ghastly famine that tore at people's heartstrings was ended, and in Bosnia the United Nations helped several million souls survive amidst ethnic carnage.

OTHER INTERNATIONAL CRIMES AND MISDEMEANORS

Apart from overt naked aggression, enforcing the "law" presents other problems, such as barring the proliferation of nuclear, chemical, and biological weapons of mass destruction and intermediate or intercontinental range missiles while the great powers presently in possession find safe ways to end their own monopoly.

North Korea's threat in 1993 to renounce the Nuclear Non-Proliferation Treaty (NPT) triggered a potentially destabilizing nuclear and missile threat in Asia, reopening long-tabooed nuclear questions in Japan. Compliance arrangements under the International Atomic Energy Agency (IAEA) are indirect, in that the IAEA can turn to the UN Security Council, which under Article 24 has "primary responsibility for the maintenance of international peace and security." Some clandestine weaponeering can appear so threatening that states may not wait for the stately UN processes of what Harlan Cleveland calls a "committee-of-sovereigns-with-a-staff."[2] The Israeli Air Force engaged in do-it-yourself enforcement in 1981 to abort nuclear progress in Iraq's Osirak reactor, and for over a decade the United States acted unilaterally—and unsuccessfully—to deter Pakistan from developing nuclear weapons capabilities.

In the North Korean case, the IAEA took the extraordinary step of demanding "special inspections" of two suspected nuclear waste sites and a suspected reprocessing facility, as well as continuous monitoring at other places, all of which Pyongyang refused. The United States, acting for the NPT and UN community, then improvised a combination of threats and inducements. In October 1994 after months of intense negotiation, the United States and Pyongyang announced agreement, which seemed to be holding despite ups and downs.

Carrots and sticks constitute the essence of counter-proliferation diplomacy. It was central to the intensive American diplomacy aimed at curbing the North Korean threat, and earlier it reportedly helped turn Argentina and Brazil away from nuclear weapons programs. Penalties and rewards should be visible to nuclear cheaters, as should inducements to other have-nots to take the pledge. For example, in drafting the NPT it was necessary to embody assurances that signers would not miss out on relevant technology.

The technical and political ambiguities of enforcement arrangements became evident when Libya was charged with building a clandestine chemical warfare plant that it insisted was for pharmaceutical or fertilizer production. Similar ambiguities surfaced when UN inspectors tried to track down suspected secret Iraqi facilities. The line between licit and illicit activities will become even fuzzier when proposals for limiting production of fissionable materials are negotiated.

A particularly ugly threat is that of biological warfare in forms that a ruthless regime could employ for terrorist purposes. Allied forces in the Gulf

War would have been virtually powerless to respond to use by Iraq of its stock of bioweaponry. The Japanese Aum Shinrikyo cult's actual use of sarin gas and its production of clostridium spores for terrorist use constituted a wakeup call. But society still has no real idea about how to deal with, for example, an attack using anthrax or with microbes such as those causing Ebola fever.[3]

State-sponsored terrorism poses a sufficiently transnational threat to give the international community presumptive jurisdiction. A model for a regime is the one created by General Assembly actions in 1972 to deal with airplane hijacking which followed a rash of actual hijackings. That broad consensus, backed by widespread technical search routines, now greatly inhibits the crime. But norms regarding terrorism and hostage-taking are blurred by their partisans' claims that kidnappers are "freedom fighters" and hostages are "guests." The UN General Assembly should define an unequivocal norm that holding innocent civilians for political purposes is an unacceptable violation of fundamental human rights which the international community has a legitimate right to rectify, and should formulate rules that deny potential terrorists access to airports and to cooperation by banks (on the model adopted for drug trafficking).

Some novel multilateral enforcement tasks that require new thinking and action are posed by other less familiar international crimes, such as electronic sabotage of transnational networks, and illicit traffic in nuclear or toxic wastes. International regimes involving imaginative monitoring and reporting systems will be needed to help maintain the integrity of the ubiquitous transborder "electronic environment" against criminal interference and against use of computer viruses or other forms of electronic sabotage of the electronic networks on which trade and finance depend.

A STRATEGY FOR THE FUTURE

As America heads toward the new millennium, its world role is still in flux. The process of redefining American interests toward conflicts abroad has had a roller-coaster ride. The end of the Cold War produced euphoria and a sense of renewed purpose in Washington, captured by President George Bush's declaration of a New World Order along with the revival of collective security in the 1991 Gulf War. By the mid-1990s, pessimism took over as a handful of civil conflicts in the Balkans and Africa with little intrinsic strategic importance but great humanitarian pull transformed peacekeeping into unplanned—and highly controversial—"humanitarian enforcement."

The definition of U.S. vital interests became downsized, if only rhetorically, in the wake of disillusionment over the pain and confusion of peacekeeping efforts in Somalia and Bosnia. The unintended consequences of "peacekeeping plus" inspired Washington to announce a policy toward UN peacekeeping on May 5, 1994,[4] which stressed the primarily war-fighting task of the U.S. armed forces. It stated that when conflicts did not "touch our core national interests" the United States would seek collective rather than unilateral action. It spelled out the criteria for U.S. approval of peace enforcement missions, including support of Congress, available funds, and an exit strategy. It made clear some rather self-evident principles as a form of damage-limitation to appease irate members of Congress: the United Nations would have no standing army, Americans would not be made to serve under foreign generals, minimum risks would be taken, and so forth.

In fact, no persuasive proposals exist for a UN "standing army," although a good case can be made for a modest standby unit to avoid delays when the United States and others in the Security Council decide on action. And Americans do frequently serve under foreign officers, in NATO as well as in some UN units, although they are always subject to ultimate U.S. decisions. Unfortunately, any forceful intervention decided on by the United States, whether unilateral or multilateral, puts soldiers in harm's way. In fact, in late 1995 the United States returned to active involvement by belatedly taking over the Bosnian peace process and contributing a third of NATO's peace-policing force.

The final returns are still not in, and the United States needs a coherent strategy to deal with the changed nature of conflict. Single themes such as New World Order, End of History, and Clash of Civilizations are attention-getting, but, like all sound bites, they are too simplistic. Bismarck could have had some official U.S. attitudes in mind when he observed that indignation is not a policy. How can a workable basis be found for policy toward the small wars and internal implosions that dominate our times?

REDEFINING U.S. INTERESTS

A rational policy for conflict management should be based on three fundamental national interests. One primordial interest is America's global economic position, which requires a reasonable level of political stability around the shrunken globe. The United States' worldwide interests are negatively affected by turbulence that creates dangerous whirlpools in international relationships. Global economic interests cannot be maintained with a laissez-faire policy toward political and military conflict.

A second interest grows out of Americans' 200-year preference to show a humane external face to the world along with their commercial wares. (George Washington's Farewell Address prescribed enhanced trade and a benign countenance to all.) As one historian writes, "America remains an idealistic and moralizing society, which cannot stand idly by when gross wickedness is taking place anywhere in the world."[5] Given the power of television and the growing role of whistle-blowing private groups, demands for human rights or political

justice can never be dismissed as a sideshow that the United States can optionally avoid.

The third relevant U.S. interest is the most problematic. It stems from core
values of political democracy and free enterprise, and it raises anew the 200-
year-old argument between active U.S. proselytizing abroad versus presenting
the world an ideal model—in Henry Clay's words keeping "the lamp burning
brightly on this western shore, as a light to all nations."

This issue has come to the fore in U.S. relations with China and with Ara-
bian/Persian Gulf, Southeast Asian, and other "allies" who repress democratic
forces at home while soliciting American support. It will recur as relations with
embryonic new democracies in Eurasia come under strain. As discussed in Chapter 3, history tells us that democracies keep the peace better than tyrannies.
Where a recognizable democratic process is throttled by its enemies, it should
engage U.S. interests.

The policy objective flowing from these three basic interests is not complicated. It is to work toward a threshold level of law and order in the international community that enhances U.S. global purposes by working toward both
conflict limitation and justice. The question "Should America be the world's
policeman" is not the right one to ask. Even if a president sought that role, it
would not long be tolerated by other countries, not to mention the Congress
and the American people. If the United States will not support forceful intervention in situations that do not clearly threaten vital interests, the rational alternative is a far more focused effort to prevent conflicts.

Aside from armed forces, there is much else that the United States can contribute. The United States continues to have worldwide interests and activities
that are multiplying, whatever the passing mood of the Congress. It is self-
evident that the United States is concerned about a stable world environment
in which to conduct trade, international finance, and a thousand other activities beyond its borders. U.S. interests call for reshaping the instruments of conflict prevention and policing in order that those instruments can perform coher-
ently and efficaciously when action is needed. And it hardly needs repeating
that the United States must pay up its delinquent UN dues as it expects other
countries to do, even when they disagree with some UN activities.

The predominant role of the United States in the end-of-the-century
renewed quest for security will arouse concern on the part of other countries
that want autonomy along with access to American markets and American protection. This ambivalence is an understandable natural feature of an unequal
relationship. At the same time, successful functioning of the global system is
realistically dependent on the one power capable of ensuring global free
trade—or of launching a massive logistical effort such as the Gulf War when
a clear threat arises to the larger peace. Equally, U.S. attempts to withdraw from
its external responsibilities could be fatal for international peace and security.
As Secretary of State Dean Rusk put it, America is the fat boy in the canoe, and
when we roll, everyone rolls with us.

FRAGMENTS OF COMMUNITY: A REALISTIC PRESCRIPTION

The post–Cold War era could still be a time of constructive reforms in the international system. The Cases from Hell should be a learning experience rather than an excuse for backing away from the long-established American goal of an effective regime of international law from which everyone but outlaws will benefit. Multilateral peacekeeping is a proven tool for minimizing conflict, and humanitarian assistance is the charge morality lays on the world's comfortable. Neither aid nor peacekeeping, however, can succeed in a hostile environment without physical protection and the means to respond to harassment. The belated resort to NATO in Bosnia helped to correct the earlier impression of Western political unsteadiness and moral weakness when peacekeepers and populace alike were abused with impunity in Somalia, Bosnia, and elsewhere. It is imperative that cynics and fanatics waiting in the wings to advance their virulent nationalism be persuaded that earlier failure to enforce the community's rules did not flash a green light for arson in other ethnic tinderboxes.

One of the obvious weaknesses of the international community as enforcer of its rules is inconsistency. The Security Council was active in enforcing its no-fly zones against Iraq in its north but not its south; in forcibly protecting famine relief in Somalia but not Sudan; in defending Kuwait but not Azerbaijan. The people of East Timor, for the most part Roman Catholic, have suffered grievously at the hands of Muslim Indonesia, which defied the United Nations and grabbed that territory in 1976. Slow-motion genocide there, though no less murderous than in Bosnia, was treated with kid gloves to avoid irritating Jakarta. China abuses the Tibetans, baring its teeth when outsiders criticize, but the great trading nations, including the United States, set a higher priority on trade. The same major countries limited their protests to Moscow over Chechnya to avoid weakening the Yeltsin regime.

Consistent law enforcement toward all offensive behavior between and within states cannot reasonably be expected in our kind of world. As with the rest of human life, consistency cannot always be the litmus test for success. It is not cynical but realistic to acknowledge that the world is fortunate if the large matters—blatant aggression, the ozone layer, nuclear spread, mass famine—are tackled even while some lesser crimes go unpunished.

Some believe that empowering the United Nations to take independent action in new crises will remedy the situation. A standing UN force might make the law enforcement process more automatic (and some might be surprised to learn that President Ronald Reagan in December 1992 said that "we must work toward a standing UN force—an army of conscience—that is fully prepared to carve out human sanctuaries through force if necessary"). Realistically, however, such a force, even with the great power veto over its use, is not a likely prospect in the aftermath of the Cases from Hell.

The same goal can be sought with improved standardization and training of standby national units on the widest possible basis, as well as the earmarking of adequate logistical support by the United States and other high-tech countries. The aim should be to ensure that another time when the Security Council—always including the United States—calls for intervention in a situation of genocide or anarchy, trained personnel for emergency military policing duties will be available from contributing states for immediate deployment, armed units will be on alert to protect them, and funds will be available to pay the bill. Equally important is the ready availability of observation and conflict-prevention units for deployment before a crisis.

Peaceful resolution of disputes through compromise remains the peacemaker's primary charge, but history has painfully demonstrated the importance of opposing aggression and genocide, even within state borders. Unfortunately, some demands turn out to be nonnegotiable, and doctrinal pacifism can still be a prescription for aggression and tyranny. Historians agree that Allied failure to react to German reoccupation of the Rhineland in 1936 lit a small fuse that eventually exploded in 50 million graves. Thucydides said of the Athenians that they were "born into the world to take no rest themselves and to give none to others." It may be a Hitler seeking conquest of Europe, a North Vietnamese Communist party planning dominion over all of Indochina, a Saddam Hussein plotting conquest of neighboring UN member states, or a Milosevich or Karadzic pressing Serbian expansion. Pacifist prescriptions are useless when confronted with the occasional would-be conqueror, whether dressed as a German brownshirt, communist agitprop, Japanese militarist, Iranian fundamentalist, or Iraqi general. All were nonbargainers.

A blatant attack across recognized international borders is rare, but the response by the law-abiding remains the ultimate test of the system. Munich is not always the correct historical analogy, but neither is Vietnam or Somalia. The experience in Somalia and Bosnia makes it unlikely that effort to revive the dormant provisions under Article 43 for earmarked fighting forces can succeed. Still, another case as clear-cut as Iraq's invasion and attempted political extinction of Kuwait, endangering a resource on which much of the world depends, must evoke a collective response.

The United Nations is based on the principle of universal membership, with a rule of one-country-one-vote in the General Assembly. This is as it should be, particularly given that the General Assembly has only the power to recommend, not act. Certainly, all voices should be heard in the great global debates on universal norms and guidelines, and on creation of international programs in which all share, such as the 175 states that agreed in 1995 to extend indefinitely the Nuclear Non-Proliferation Treaty. Similarly, the chemical and biological weapons treaties can work only if they engage virtually all states.

When it comes to *action* programs, however, the purpose is not equity but effectiveness. The idea of using "coalitions of the willing" to carry out vital functions if the community fails to act might seem to run counter to the principle/fiction of sovereign equality. In peacekeeping and even enforcement, the token contribution of small and medium states is important to symbolize community will and involvement. Realistically, however, no more than 40 states are presently in a position to give leadership based on advanced technology, capital, and educated, trained, and equipped armed forces. The so-called United Nations that fought and won World War II against global forces of tyranny and conquest consisted of 26 countries. Sixteen and 40 countries, respectively, formed the U.S.-led UN Korean and Gulf War forces, and 18 are sufficient to make reasonably effective the international Missile Technology Control Regime agreed to in 1987 by the major countries involved.

Enforcement action will always require the most serious consideration before collective action is agreed to. Even if enforcement action were more automatic, however, there would still be cases where the standard treaty escape hatch of "supreme national interests" would have to be invoked. Abolition of the great-power veto on actions under UN Charter Chapter 6 for peacefully settling disputes makes sense. But the great-power veto in Chapter 7 on military enforcement remains the condition for participation by countries such as the United States, France, Russia, and China, and its elimination is no more likely (or desirable) now than it was in 1945.

Some analysts advocate revising the UN Charter in order to cure the organization's perceived weaknesses. Some reforms are needed, such as eliminating obsolete UN bodies like the Trusteeship Council, streamlining General Assembly practices, and making better provisions for rapid response to crises. There is nothing wrong, however, with the basic norms and ground rules contained in the present UN Charter, which still add up to an excellent statement of American purposes and principles. The United Nations provides ample machinery for prevention, deterrence, and enforcement—once the members decide to use it.

In the real world, peace cannot be synonymous with utopia or nirvana. Indeed, we should remember the words of Winston Churchill: "The UN was set up not to get us to Heaven but to keep us from Hell." Human nature has two sides, as observed in the first chapter of this book: One side is benign and pacific, the other is egotistical, quarrelsome, and sometimes belligerent. Progress itself is dynamic, not static, and the road to both democracy and well-being is bumpy. Conflicts between and within states will break out. And while compliance with the international community's norms is best achieved through voluntary rather than coercive means, at the end of the day what counts is the will to keep the peace.

As is stressed throughout this book, the most intelligent and cost-effective way for the community to deal with the conflicts that unsettle regional stability or afflict the community's conscience is through strategies of prevention and peaceful change. Both are essential if there is to be peace with justice. If a mission statement for the next era can be captured in a phrase, that phrase is "the effective management of dynamic change without war."

The debate is not over, and the likely future conflict agenda will pose crucial choices to the United States and other states. New actors abound on the world stage, including potent "nongovernments" ranging from religious movements and multinational corporations to transnational communities of scientists and intellectuals and a whole congeries of nongovernmental organizations that play an increasing role in international life from relief to human rights monitoring. Still, a notional "international will" must in the final analysis mean the policies of states.[6] That in turn depends on political leadership that interprets national interests through a wide lens and eschews the "Principle of the Dangerous Precedent," which prescribes that nothing should ever be done for the first time.[7]

International leadership can sometimes come from small and middle powers who can often combine their political flexibility with moral strength. However, a genuine community of nations can sustain itself only if it also has the powerful in its service. The American people will still be moved by humanitarian appeals as well as direct security threats, and on the record will support more multilateral cooperation than will some of their political leaders. At the same time, fresh disasters abroad such as famines, failed states, or tribal/ethnic warfare, however grim for the people at risk, may not pass the threshold test for U.S. military involvement, will seem less threatening for international peace and security, and will confront an overloaded and still imperfect UN conflict-management system.

Historical perspective might be helpful here. There is extraordinary relevance today of words spoken almost a century ago by a president of the United States no one ever accused of softheadedness: "The increasing interdependence and complexity of international political and economic relations renders it incumbent on all civilized and orderly powers to insist on the proper policing of the world."[8]

International law and order may have meant to Theodore Roosevelt something akin to the nineteenth-century Holy Alliance that maintained the conservative status quo. For our world it means something quite different, implying not only essential stability but also such nonconservative goals as punishing tyrannical or murderous rule so that our planet is morally tolerable, and enforcing those environmental rules without which it could in future become physically uninhabitable.

Whether or not we like it, the notion of preserving international peace and security is inextricably linked to U.S. involvement. That was true when the League of Nations failed, and it was true when the world's powers created and implemented a new system under the United Nations. There is still no substitute for American backing if collective action to preserve or restore peace is to succeed. Nor is there any substitute for political imagination and moral authority on the part of American and other democratic leaders, without which there can be no effective United Nations, no law, and no order.

NOTES

[1]As reported by Mark Sommer in "Sanctions Are Becoming 'Weapons of Choice,' " in the *Christian Science Monitor,* August 3, 1993.

[2]Harlan Cleveland, *Birth of a New World* (San Francisco: Jossey-Bass, 1993), p. 66.

[3]Laurie Garrett, "The Return of Infectious Diseases," *Foreign Affairs,* January–February 1996, pp. 75–76. (The author correctly notes the potential value of a civil society that might restrain such evil preparations, a point made in Chapter 3.)

[4]The Clinton Administration's Policy on Reforming Multilateral Peace Operations, *Department of State Publication 10161,* Washington, D.C., May 1994.

[5]Paul Johnson, "The Myth of American Isolationism," *Foreign Affairs,* May–June 1995, p. 164.

[6]As historian Paul Kennedy concluded from his look ahead, "even if the autonomy and functions of the state have been eroded by transnational trends, no adequate substitute has emerged to replace it as the key unit in responding to global change." *Preparing for the Twenty-First Century* (New York: Random House, 1993), p. 134.

[7]F. M. Cormforth, quoted by Reverend Peter J. Gomes in *New York Times,* May 22, 1993.

[8]President Theodore Roosevelt to Congress in 1902, quoted by Henry A. Kissinger in *Diplomacy* (New York: Simon & Schuster, 1994), p. 39.

Seven ⌒

THE ANATOMY OF
CONFLICT[1]

Toward a Theory of Conflict Prevention

I n the late 1990s scholars and others who campaigned over the years for a strategy of conflict anticipation could take satisfaction from the widespread interest in preventive diplomacy and early warning. Unfortunately, aborting conflicts before they happen is one of the hardest things for politicians and diplomats to do. It is equally difficult for them to draw appropriate lessons from the past or, for that matter, to remember relevant history.

To be sure, the wrong lessons can be drawn from history, and each conflict case is distinctive—but not entirely. A better strategy for dealing with future conflict situations requires paying more attention to the lessons of history than has been customary in the era of the sound bite. Harder still is to overcome the tunnel vision that keeps regional or country specialists from occasionally ranging across the map for lessons about the nature of conflict as a sometimes universal phenomenon.

This is by no means to put down the expert. No computer can ever substitute for first-hand professional or even journalistic experience. Long before high-speed data processing, analysts using traditional methods could learn a great deal about the processes of war and peace. Some scholars broke new ground in analyzing the phenomenon of conflict by developing hypotheses, amassing data on multiple cases, and searching for instructive correlations.[2]

Busy professionals and overscheduled students operate under pressures that beg for aids to both the memory and the imagination. A better tool for understanding the internal dynamics of conflict needs to take into account not just data on specifics, but also conceptual elements such as structure, pressures that drive the process, and ways in which those pressures can be controlled. That kind of analysis, grounded in historical evidence, can assist in *early warning* of situations that may explode into warfare. In turn, it can help to demystify the essential elements in the process of *conflict prevention*. Such an analysis requires a workable concept of the anatomy of conflict—not of any specific situation, but of conflict as a generic phenomenon.

THE DYNAMICS OF CONFLICT

The first step in revealing that anatomy is recognition of the fact that conflict is a dynamic process and not a single, unchanging state of affairs. People refer to the Arab–Israeli conflict or the India–Pakistan conflict or the Falkland–Malvinas conflict as convenient shorthand for a complex sequence of quarrels, wars, and armed truces that can persist over decades—or be over in a week. The analytical task is not made easier by widespread imprecision in the language people employ to talk about a wide range of adversarial situations. Phrases such as war, conflict, dispute, and escalation are used interchangeably—for example, trade war, escalating rhetoric, the conflict between Allies and Axis in World War II, and so on. One situation might feature bellicose language and still be a fairly peaceful scene. Another, however, might involve saber-rattling using real sabers. And clearly, a profoundly different event takes place when organized military formations start shooting at each other.

A more coherent concept starts with a fundamental premise that *conflict is dynamic in the sense of passing through some or all of a sequence of distinctive and identifiable stages,* or *phases.* Within each phase can be found a variety of conditions, personalities, actions, events, and perceptions. Some of these can reasonably be assumed to generate pressures moving the situation toward "worsening," that is, of increased violence or its threat; or conversely, pressures to move the situation in a more benign direction, that is, away from violence. These influential elements are conveniently described as *factors.* These "factors" can be hypothesized as combining their relative strength in a way that determines whether or not the conflict worsens, that is, crosses a *threshold* between phases in the direction of greater or less violence.

To sum up: within each *phase* certain *factors* interact in such a way as to influence the movement of the conflict toward or away from violence. The transition of a conflict across *thresholds* between phases is a result of the interaction of the factors in the previous phase. Avoiding or minimizing violence may not always be the policy objective if a greater evil must be opposed. We chose it as the criterion both because it is a paramount policy objective of civilized states and because it is morally right.

The Phases: Dispute, Conflict, Hostilities

A conflictual situation invariably arises out of a substantive quarrel about something—territory, borders, resources, legitimacy of rulers, political ideology, ethnic differences based on race or religion, or whatever. This quarrel about something we label a *dispute*—Phase 1 of the conflict model. It is not a "war," or in our terms even a conflict, although it can lead to both. It is an argument about something two or more parties value. The argument or quarrel may be waged at the polls, in the courtroom, the bazaar, the boardroom, economically through trade or finance, politically through diplomacy, or psychologically in the media or the streets.

If the quarrel is not resolved, a dispute may (and all too often does) turn in a military direction when the use of force seems plausible. That is why such deep-rooted differences as those between Arabs and Israelis or Indians and Pakistanis have had the capacity to generate new rounds of bloodshed. A dispute over an issue is not always military, but usually has that potential unless and until the underlying essential substantive differences between the parties are dealt with.

If one or more parties to a dispute transforms the situation in ways that look military—produces or imports arms that provide it an option to press its demands by force, or makes threatening noises, or conducts provocative military maneuvers, or decides that force already possessed is adequate to a test of arms—in short, introduces a military option or has people thinking in terms of force—then a *conflict* has been generated.

The introduction of a military option moves a dispute to the *conflict* phase—Phase 2 in our model. This does not necessarily mean that hostilities have occurred or even that they are inevitable, but just that they have become more likely. The conflict is still in a pre-hostilities stage. Purposeful use of arms is now a possibility, however, and the peace-minded need new vigilance to head off the worst. If significant fighting does break out, whether intended or accidental, a third phase begins which (since the word "war" is too vague) we call *hostilities*, meaning actual combat by organized military units, regular or irregular, generating significant casualties. (Some analyses define war or serious hostilities as entailing at least 1000 casualties.)[3]

This definition of hostilities does not include lesser violent incidents such as a border skirmish with a relative handful of casualties or a *coup d'état* change of regime that includes some head-breaking. War, with limited or unlimited objectives harnessed to force, is too important a breakdown of the social order to be confused with the occasional violence of politics at its worst. Some conflict analysts do count such minor bloodletting and thus come out with considerably larger numbers of cases than we do. We believe that this practice understates and even blurs the crucial line that is crossed with the move from peacetime, however turbulent, to actual warfare.

During the *hostilities* phase, fighting may spread to wider geographic areas; additional parties may become engaged; small-scale skirmishes may blossom into pitched battles; or a war begun with small arms may develop into one in which the full panoply of weapons in the adversaries' inventories is hurled against opposing forces, and perhaps civilian and economic targets as well. In short, intensification (sometimes called escalation) takes place.

If hostilities are terminated, another threshold is crossed to a fourth phase, in which the conflict (and thus the underlying dispute) continues, but without fighting. The conflict remains if at least one party continues to view the quarrel in potentially military terms. The conflict ceases when the dispute is no longer perceived significantly in military terms, real or potential.

A fifth phase may thus be entered if, after the military option is discarded, the conflict simply peters out, although the dispute remains unresolved. When, finally, the parties manage to resolve their underlying quarrel, or cease to care about it, the dispute is settled and with it the "case" is ended. Diplomacy can move on to the next crisis.

To sum up: Phase 1 is the *dispute* stage in which a divisive issue exists but has not yet been cast by either disputant in terms in which military power becomes significantly relevant. Phase 2 is the pre-hostilities *conflict* phase in which no serious shooting takes place, but it begins to "look like war" as a military buildup starts, or an arms race develops, or military forces are deployed with serious intent to use them at some point and people view the situation in potentially military terms. Phase 3, the *hostilities* phase, occurs when the disputants have crossed the fateful threshold to actual fighting. Phase 4, *the cessation of hostilities* phase, is an armed truce, so to speak, but with no end to the conflict, let alone a settlement of the underlying dispute. Phase 5 is a phase *beyond conflict,* in which the situation is no longer perceived in military terms, but the dispute persists. Finally, there is the ultimate *settlement* stage in which the underlying dispute and, consequently, the conflict, are settled. A simplified depiction of the dynamic phase model is shown here again for convenience (Table 7-1).

This model of phased conflict also implies a feedback mechanism, not illustrated here, whereby a post-hostilities situation (Phase 4) can loop back into Phase 3—hostilities—return to Phase 4, and revert to open warfare again and again. This in fact was the story of the Arab–Israeli conflict (1947, 1956, 1967, 1970, 1973, 1982) and is that of the India–Pakistan series of wars (1948, 1965, 1971).

The notion of *thresholds* separating different phases of conflict needs some explanation. These moments of execution might be considered the crucial elements of the dynamic situation and the points of leverage for conflict control. But exact moments of transition from one threshold to another are often difficult to identify precisely. In addition, they suggest, misleadingly, that if one is looking for policy handles, the important moment of change comes when an event becomes visible—when hostilities break out, an arms deal is publicly consummated, negotiations succeed, and so on. The moment of conception may be more significant than the transitional moment of birth; it is at the time of conception that events are, so to speak, foreordained.

Violence-producing and violence-minimizing factors interact dynamically *during* phases rather than at the exact moment of transition. Thus, although thresholds are convenient points of demarcation at which to separate phases, the event of transition is itself a product of forces that have been at work during the phase.

Fortunately, some cases of conflict never cross the threshold of outbreak of hostilities. Others stay for a mercifully brief time in the hostilities phase and then are either pacified while moving through Phase 4, where the conflict is

TABLE 7-1

BLOOMFIELD-LEISS DYNAMIC PHASE CONFLICT MODEL

D I S P U T E					
C O N F L I C T					
HOSTILITIES					
Phase 1	Phase 2	Phase 3	Phase 4	Phase 5	Settlement
Dispute	Conflict	Hostilities	Post-Hostilities	Post-Hostilities	
Quarrel about an Issue	Military Option Develops	Fighting between Organized Units	Conflict Remains	Dispute Remains Unsettled	Dispute Settled
Factors ⇒ ⇐	*Factors* ⇐ ⇒	*Factors* ⇐ ⇒	*Factors* ⇐ ⇒	*Factors* ⇐ ⇒	

still sharp but not openly violent, or perhaps go through Phase 5, where there is no longer any intention to resolve the dispute by military means, and go on to settlement. Some cases may even go directly from the battlefield to settlement if the results of battle are decisive enough, although what happened to Carthage hardly qualifies as a satisfactory avoidance of Phases 4 and 5. Another less apocalyptic example would be the end of a resistance movement in occupied territory when occupation forces surrender or withdraw. A depressing number of conflicts linger in the hostilities phase, moving through subphases representing intensification of hostilities (escalation), or perhaps resting in a tenuous, cease-fire "peace" (Phase 4) until—with renewed wind and limb—hostilities resume.

Furthermore, there is no time limit on any single phase. The Cold War was in effect a half-century-long Phase 2 conflict that remained pre-hostilities thanks to mutual deterrence. In 1947 the Kashmir conflict between India and Pakistan remained in Phase 2 only a matter of days before plunging into open hostilities, which recurred twice more and could still return, this time with nuclear weapons in both Hindu and Muslim hands.

Choice of Relevant Factors

The notion of a dynamic phase model presupposes the presence of factors that could be identified as bearing on the way the conflict developed—that is, on the transitions to new phases. The CASCON approach has been to search for factors in the form of actual data embodied in the histories of local conflicts. Unlike most previous analyses of conflict data, CASCON's database was developed *inductively,* drawing not on available encyclopedic information about conflicts and states, but rather on *what in fact happened in post–World-War II conflict situations.*[4] When the historians, armed with our dynamic phase model, analyzed the first 16 cases within our structured framework, data emerged about the personalities of leaders, action within disputed areas, help or opposition from outsiders, and economic and other forces working to affect the situation—in short, statements about a variety of things that actually took place in "their" conflict.

From this plethora of case-specific "things," we drew out several hundred generic propositions, each directly traceable to one or more factors within the cases researched. To illustrate, a factor specific to the India–China case was: "Chinese advances in the Northeast Frontier Agency threatened the Assam oil fields and menaced Indian control of the neck of land that connects Assam to the rest of India." From this and similar factors, we derived a single generalized factor: "Advances by one side threaten important economic resource areas of the other side." Those propositions became CASCON's database of 571 factors, covering the first three phases of our dynamic model.

With regard to the scope of the factors, we wanted to escape the confines of the strategists and war-gamers who during the Cold War years tended to focus only on politico-military considerations. Instead, we sought a wide-angle lens embracing conflict-relevant factors in categories ranging from strategic to economic, psychological, and ethnocultural.

Organizing Conflict-Relevant Factors

One can organize a picture of the conflict process in many ways. The utility of each depends on the kinds of questions it is best suited to illustrate. Since our interest has been in all kinds of conflicts short of a now-improbable all-out thermonuclear war, we elected to construct a model that seemed applicable to a wide range and that promised to illuminate the policy problem of conflict control.

Factors sought in this way tend to be combined in logical categories, covering what we considered the influential variables. The 10 categories are: previous or general relations between sides; great-power or allied involvement; general external relations; military-strategic; international organization (UN, legal, public opinion); ethnic (refugees, minorities); economic/resources;

internal politics of the sides; communication and information; and actions in a disputed area.

The process of arriving at these logical "boxes" in which to categorize factors involved posing questions based on general knowledge, within common-sense parameters:

DEGREE OF COMMITMENT.   What proportion of available military force is used? Are the strategies being pursued more modest than either party is capable of pursuing? How widespread or restricted is the issue at stake? For example, does it involve only points on the border or certain sections of the country? Or is the issue one of national survival? Are the populations of the parties united behind their leaders in the conflict?

AUTONOMY OF ACTION.   What factors affect the degree to which the parties to local conflicts are subject to outside influences constraining their freedom of action? Factors concerning general dependence on external military or economic aid and political assistance, as well as on specific material support in the conflict, are included here. Also included are the controversies that can arise among allies and coalitions as to how the conflict should be conducted.

ENVIRONMENT.   The physical nature of the locale can profoundly influence the way in which a conflict unfolds. The actions of the parties themselves are influenced by the ease with which each of them can project power and influence into the critical area. For this reason, geographic and weather factors are important, as are roads, railroads, airports, rivers, and harbors. Whether the country is flat and open, mountainous or jungle, and whether borders are defined and controllable, can also be significant. These factors also affect the accessibility of the area to those external powers—other states or international organizations—that might contemplate intervention.

INFORMATION.   The speed and accuracy with which information about developments within a conflict reaches the parties and interested outside powers can have a major bearing on the conflict. The channels of communications—how and from whom information is received—can help determine whether or not information is to be believed. Included, therefore, are factors relating to reliable reports on immediate events as well as to long-range assessments of capabilities and intentions.

TIME.   In many conflicts, pressures are generated by time constraints. Is there time to await clarification, or are events moving so rapidly that action must be taken immediately if it is to be taken at all? Does the future appear to hold promise of an improvement or a deterioration in the relative balance of power between the parties? Are there specific anticipated events that may affect the prospects of one or both parties, such as an election, the arrival of arms, actions taken by international organizations, interventions by external powers? Such time factors have a bearing on the way in which parties to a local conflict behave and, hence, on the course the conflict takes.

MILITARY RELATIONSHIP.   Perceptions of the present and future military power of the parties to the conflict and of the military balance between them can be just as critical as the actual facts. It may determine decisions about when, and how vigorously, to take action. Included in this grouping are factors relating to the numbers in the armed forces, how much and what kinds of equipment they have, how well they are trained, how rapidly they can be moved about to meet new challenges or capitalize on new opportunities, and how many threats they must be prepared to meet simultaneously. Related to all these issues are the kinds of strategy and tactics both sides are employing and whether the military doctrines of the parties are suitable to the challenges they face.

INTERNAL COHESION.   The stability and unity of the people of a country or region are prime factors in internal conflicts. (By definition, the absence of such stability and unity makes internal strife possible.) There are also a number of ways in which the internal cohesion can influence the course of interstate conflict. Pressures from powerful groups in a divided nation can constrain its leaders' freedom of action. Foreign adventures are a classic way in which weak leaders seek to unite their followers and distract them from problems at home. The degree of internal cohesion also helps determine each side's perceptions of the other's "staying power" and can reveal the existence of active or potential "allies" within the enemy camp.

INTERNAL CONTROL.   The authority of central leadership over segments of its nominal following is often weak or absent in internal conflict. In both internal and interstate conflicts, however, factors may be found within opposing camps that reflect the degree of leadership—including knowledge of the level of authority that can be exercised over local activists, both civilian and military.

ETHNIC RELATIONSHIPS.   Both within each side to a local conflict and between the sides, a variety of factors can at times be found that reflect basic racial, tribal, religious, or linguistic factors. Post–Cold War history vividly shows how such factors can produce a volatile situation when the issues in the conflict take shape along ethnic lines.

IDEOLOGY.   Ideologies are still a potent element affecting the course of local conflict if one considers nationalism (including self-determination), democracy, socialism, traditionalism, and religious fundamentalism. All can be banners behind which political forces rally, and thus all qualify as factors conditioning peoples' perceptions and expectations.

PAST RELATIONSHIPS.   Many of the issues between local adversaries have their genesis in long-standing disputes over boundaries, irredentist claims, and other historic animosities. This source of factors includes not only the memories that conflicting parties carry with them into their new quarrel, but also the manner in which each will interpret or perceive the other's words, deeds, and intentions. Furthermore, actions that the parties have taken in earlier phases of the conflict can help condition their own, their supporters', and their adversaries' present outlooks and expectations. People may learn from history, but sometimes they learn the wrong lessons.

ACTIONS OF INTERNATIONAL ORGANIZATIONS.   Since the states of the world have at least some instruments for keeping the peace, it is not surprising that a large number of factors found to be operating within conflicts involve these organizations in some way. Included in this category are the United Nations, of course, but also regional arrangements such as the Organization of American States, the Arab League, and the Organization of African Unity. Factors here relate to past actions the organizations have taken—the kinds of action, the speed and harmony with which they proceeded, the success they had—and to the parties' expectations about the role these bodies might play in the unfolding conflict.

GREAT-POWER INTERESTS, COMMITMENTS, AND ACTIONS.   This major cluster of factors encompasses the variety of impacts major powers can have—or have had—on the course of local conflicts. Many have acquired obligations toward developing countries or regions that color the assessment of their stake in the outcomes of local quarrels, as well as local expectations about the role the great power will play. Ideological ties, formal treaty commitments, historic spheres of interest or responsibility, base rights, and economic interests can all affect local conflicts. Whether conflicts are sparked by competitive great-power interests (as was increasingly the case in the waning Cold War) or whether local adversaries seek to draw in a friendly superpower, time and again the great powers play critical roles, whether acting in concert or in competition.

IMPLICATIONS OF THEORY

Several intriguing hypotheses about the nature and course of conflicts are implicit in the picture so far:

> Conflicts have a general, common structure: some fundamental features of conflict are common not just to some but to the entire universe of conflicts in the modern world.

> All cases can be subsumed within part or all of a "life-cycle" model": all go through a preliminary dispute phase and may also go through one or more hostilities and post-hostilities phases.

In each phase, identifiable factors generate pressures that may influence the course of the case toward the next threshold and transition into another phase. These factors may be offset by other influential factors that tend toward the prevention of that transition.

Acceptance of these three hypotheses generated others that also undergirded the development of CASCON:

Changes in the relationship among factors will affect the likelihood of a conflict's undergoing transition from one phase to another.

Policy measures appropriate for the phase in question and aimed at reinforcing violence-minimizing factors and offsetting violence-generating factors can alter significantly the course of the conflict. (Certainly there are other valid policy considerations than the minimization of violence. But this was the test that we chose for defining "worse" or "better," and that later gave CASCON its detailed bone structure.)

New or incipient crises and conflicts can benefit from comparison with some or all of relevant history to learn more about their prospects and about ways to keep them from worsening.

A systematic method of conflict analysis can help to offset the chronic priority of crisis management over prevention.

A model, of course, does only part of the job of identifying causal elements. Portraying a complex phenomenon schematically does not mean that all operative elements can be identified or that cause-effect relationships can be clearly understood. However, enough of the cause-effect relationships must be understood for a user to be confident that a given policy activity will likely reinforce or offset any given combination of factors. But can historic causes ever be identified, with real confidence, as the basis for later effects?

This question poses anew some of the vexing philosophic problems inherent in the search for causes of war. (See Chapter 1.) The beginnings of a conflict stretch back into time, originating from causes that are only imperfectly knowable. Various situations, occurrences, and constellations of pressures can be identified along the route toward a conflict—some of them obviously "causes." It is equally true that a conflict may have exploded into hostilities because of some hitherto undetected situation or because a new condition was suddenly introduced.

Not all pressures along the time-space continuum are man-made, or visible at the time, or "always there." Some even represent gathered momentum,[5] just as some barriers to intensification represent inertia rather than purposeful policy. The analyst will probably always have to be content with proximate causes, with no assurance that the basic forces generating conflict are fully revealed. A related intellectual hazard is believing that all conflicts are "determined," in the sense that, given the appropriate ingredients, they will proceed in certain inevitable ways. But within a combination of environmental situations,

TABLE 7-2
Structure of Local Conflict Control

Phase of Conflict	Threshold of Transition between Phases	Description of Phase or Transition	Crucial Factors Bearing on Transition		Conflict-Control Policy Objectives
			Toward Conflict Control (Away from violence)	Away from Conflict Control (Toward Violence)	
P-I		Dispute, not perceived in military terms by either party	• Tending to keep dispute nonmilitary • Tending toward settlement	• Tending to introduce military option • Tending away from settlement	• Keeping dispute nonmilitary • Settling the dispute
	I-II	Introduction of military option by one or both parties	(Factors operating during Phase I have combined to push the dispute across the threshold to Phase II, making it a conflict)		
P-II		Conflict, perceived in military terms by one or both parties	• Inhibiting the outbreak of hostilities • Restricting the scale/scope of potential hostilities • Tending toward settlement	• Promoting the outbreak of hostilities • Expanding the scale/scope of potential hostilities • Tending away from settlement	• Preventing the outbreak of hostilities • Restricting the scale/scope of potential hostilities • Settling the dispute
	II-III	Outbreak of hostilities	(Factors operating during Phase II have combined to push conflict across the threshold of Phase III, generating hostilities)		
P-III		Hostilities	• Moderating hostilities • Terminating hostilities • Tending toward settlement	• Intensifying hostilities • Continuing hostilities • Tending away from settlement	• Moderating hostilities • Terminating hostilities • Settling the dispute

Pre-Dispute — DISPUTE — CONFLICT — PRE-HOSTILITIES — HOSTILITIES

POST-HOSTILITIES

CONFLICT

DISPUTE

→ Dispute Settled

III-IV Termination of hostilities

(Factors operating during Phase III have combined to push conflict across threshold to Phase IV, terminating actual fighting)

- Inhibiting the resumption of hostilities
- Restricting the scale/scope of potential hostilities
- Tending toward settlement

- Promoting the resumption of hostilities
- Expanding the scale/scope of potential hostilities
- Tending away from settlement

- Preventing the resumption of hostilities
- Restricting the scale/scope of potential hostilities
- Settling the dispute

IV

P-IV Post-hostilities but conflict still perceived in potentially military terms by at least one party

IV-V End of conflict

(Factors operating during previous phases have combined to remove the military option of both adversaries, but the underlying dispute remains)

- Tending to keep dispute nonmilitary
- Tending toward settlement

- Tending to introduce military option
- Tending away from settlement

- Keeping dispute nonmilitary
- Settling the dispute

V

P-V Dispute, not perceived in military terms by either party

S Settlement of dispute

(Factors operating during previous phases—or factors unrelated to conflict itself—have combined to bring underlying dispute to settlement)

willful intentions, and triggering events, all reaching critical mass at the point a conflict becomes acute, some probable cause-effect relationships can be discerned.

One basis for this is simple historical correlation. In one sense, every significant correlation between a given set of circumstances and a given action may be interpreted as embodying either an explanation or a prediction about probable cause and effect. In our own conflict model, correlations between transitions and the factors in the pre-transition stage imply cause and effect in a limited but important sense. With similar caveats medical scientists implicate specified "risk factors" in coronary artery disease. The factors present during the identifiable phases of a conflict correlate with transitions, but only in this sense do they add up to causation.

Ideally, all factors should be identified in order that all elements of probable causality may be translated into relevant conflict-control measures. The further one tracks a dispute back in time, the more difficult becomes the process of identification and correlation. An important root cause of internal conflict is implied, as we have seen, in the correlation of revolution with the degree to which land is held by a certain proportion of the population (i.e., ownership of most arable land in El Salvador in the 1980s by a tiny percentage of *latifundista* was a sure-fire prescription for the revolution there, aided and abetted of course by people with their own agenda). Direct connections have also become evident between the stresses of the modernization process and the incidence of conflict.

Just as conflict is a dynamic process and not a single state of affairs, so also conflict control entails related but distinct objectives that differ from phase to phase. One control objective is common to every phase: *to settle the underlying dispute.* Failing that, there are additional objectives that should be targeted. Initially, the objective is to *keep a dispute nonmilitary* (Phase 1). Once a military option has been introduced (Phase 2), the objective is to *prevent the outbreak of hostilities.* If hostilities break out (Phase 3), the objective is to *contain (i.e., moderate) or terminate them.*

If hostilities are terminated by a truce (Phase 4), policy should aim at preventing their resumption and at restricting their scale if they are resumed. If, after fighting is stopped, the situation is tranquilized to a point where neither party any longer seeks a military solution (Phase 5), the objective is to keep it that way. Table 7-2 depicts the structured reasoning involved in the basic research we undertook that culminated in the CASCON program. Genuine conflict resolution can only mean resolving the underlying dispute. Phase 1, the dispute phase in which a quarrel has started about something in contention, is of vital importance for preventing the transition from dispute to conflict, that is, to Phase 2, and above all for preventing it from going to Phase 3, hostilities.

A few examples make the point. Social justice in Cuba during the pre-Castro years might have prevented guerrilla warfare from developing and perhaps obviated the Bay of Pigs fiasco and the terrifying Cuban Missile Crisis. More attention to human rights might have eased the violent 1978 transformation in Iran. A policy of religious and ethnic autonomy or separation would perhaps have averted the strife over the status of Kashmir and the protracted conflicts in Palestine and Cyprus. More determined diplomacy backed by force might have averted the wars in the 1980s over the Falklands/Malvinas and between Iran and Iraq, and in the early 1990s within the former Yugoslavia.

In principle, preventive diplomacy ought to be employed as early as possible in the life of a dispute. Realistically, however, the world is fortunate when policy focuses on conflicts in their Phase 2 stage, when hostilities have become more likely but have not yet actually broken out.

SOME POLICY INFERENCES FROM THEORY

If identifying conflict-relevant factors in a policy-useful way is a daunting task, identifying policy measures that will move those factors toward or away from violence is even more challenging. Yet it is the task facing the growing number of both officials and scholars who are now trying to become specific about early warning and preventive diplomacy.

Conflict-controlling measures applied mechanistically could of course be counterproductive or even immoral. No single factor will always exert pressure in one direction only, toward or away from violence. For example, in the Soviet-Iranian conflict in the late 1940s, the relative weakness of the Iranian central government was, during pre-hostilities (Phase 2), a factor tending to encourage the Soviet Union and its Azerbaijani separatist cohorts to resort to force to wrest Azerbaijan province from Iranian control. At a comparable stage in the Bay of Pigs crisis, the supposed weakness of Castro's control—evidenced by the mass exodus from Cuba of his early supporters and by continued anti-Castro guerrilla activities in Cuba—misled the United States into believing that a very low-level use of force could topple the government. The real or apparent weakness of the central government, in both cases at this phase, was a factor tending toward violence.

Once hostilities had broken out in Iran in 1945, however, such weakness had a perverse effect in the short term, permitting a rapid and relatively bloodless Azerbaijani-Soviet victory that quickly terminated hostilities. (In the longer run, the outcome was reversed.) In Cuba, the presumed weakness turned out to be an illusion, facing the United States with either defeat of its proxy or intensifying the hostilities.

A SUGGESTIVE EXPERIMENT

A modest early experiment with a representative sample of cases developed for our conflict research surfaced some suggestive policy implications for action. The way the factors were "coded" (explained in Chapter 9) indicated the opinion of experts as to whether in a given case a particular factor in retrospect was conflict-minimizing or tended toward violence. The interesting result was that over one-third—36 percent—of factors coded as conflict-minimizing occurred in the first, or dispute phase (Phase 1). That is to say, over one-third of available violence-minimizing policy activity was logically applicable *before* a dispute turned into a conflict.

As a dispute became a Phase 2 conflict, the total number of available conflict-control measures declined. In our small sample, although 149 possible countermeasures were at least theoretically available in Phase 1, by contrast only 94 were identified for Phase 2. As the situation worsened, the number grew smaller still: 83 for the first round of hostilities (Phase 3), 75 for Phase 4, and 24 for a resumed hostilities phase. What obviously happened was something we should have already known empirically: the range and variety of peace-aiming measures declines as options begin to close, attitudes harden, and perceptions increasingly narrow down to a preoccupation with the violent bands of the spectrum. Worse yet, even if guns are silenced, the task of moving toward a lasting solution is usually far more difficult than before the guns have spoken.

The research method placed no special weight on any particular phase. But the process of deriving conflict-control measures from factors yielded fewer and fewer steps that policymakers might take to avert violence as conflict progressed along its path to bloodshed.

Breaking down the factors in question and their associated measures, we found that by far the largest number (34 percent of the total) were peacemaking and peacekeeping diplomatic measures by international organizations, especially the use of the machinery of the United Nations or such regional organizations as the Organization of American States and the Organization of African Unity. Measures in this category ranged from assistance in local efforts to resettle or control refugees to active peacekeeping efforts in the form of border patrols and interposed forces. Even more impressive conflict prevention was implied if improved capabilities had existed such as readily available (and adequately financed) standing, or at least quick-reaction, peacekeeping and "humanitarian enforcement" units able to be dispatched quickly to areas of trouble, and supported by military aircraft and other military technology capable of making their presence most effective.

To sum up: in that "multilateral" category, almost twice the number of factors and inferred policy measures were available in Phase 1 as in Phase 2, and far more than the number after fighting broke out—the stage where most real-world actual policy activity is focused.

The availability in an early stage of the category of measures we call internal-political, which involved building sound socioeconomic bases for effective governance, outnumbered later possibilities by a significant margin. Except for out-and-out repression, which a strong government can apply any time (and a weak one can attempt, usually expediting its own demise), the best time to carry on nation-building is clearly before the nation is engaged in a serious quarrel with another nation or a civil war. Somalia in the early 1990s was a glaring illustration of this maxim.

The availability of external-political measures was also inferentially greatest in the dispute phase and next greatest in Phase 2. Military-strategic policy followed the same pattern, with the largest proportions of suggested measures in Phases 1 and 2, centering around deterrence postures. The same was true of economic and technological measures. (Not surprisingly, "great-power" influence continued to be relevant during hostilities and after.)

Also not surprisingly, a substantial set of potential measures could be inferred from the coding of factors (20 percent) relating to great powers, allies, and neighboring states, that is, outsiders. Ironically, although meddling by outside powers can be a particularly pernicious conflict-promoting force, external powers emerge time and again as crucial potential sources of pressure for conflict control. Policy inferences from this category of measures ranged from insulating the conflict from great-power conflicts to using available leverage to encourage local forces toward moderation and accommodation. In the post–Cold War period, the sudden indifference of a previously involved external power was often a major influence toward settlement.

Theoretically available control measures involving military forces and strategy (14 percent) ranged from improved command and control within the local armed forces to great-power military strategies minimizing the need for overseas bases and deterring others from fostering local dissidence. Internal political measures included those affecting the cohesiveness and stability of the government, civilian control of the military establishment, clarity of objectives, and rationality of decision making.

Potential arms and hardware measures (6.8 percent) appeared to have more applications early in the conflict process. Specific opportunities for measures of arms control were more numerous in Phase 2, when arms buildups were underway, than in any other phase. However, some later research cast a rather different light on policies relating to the supply of arms and other materiel to be used in the conflicts (see Chapter 2).

Another 6 percent of potential measures could be grouped as economic and technical. Here were found such basic measures as economic and technical assistance, as well as lessening external reliance on local bases (e.g., by developing long-range airlift capabilities) and thereby reducing the impact of such vested interests on the outcomes of local quarrels.

A last category relating to communication and information, small to begin with in the factor database, yielded a numerically small number of instances (4 percent) but were far from unimportant. Better facilities for rapid and secure communication between adversaries might, in some instances, have prevented hasty responses based on misperception. In fact, they helped quickly end the 1965 India–Pakistan battle. More adequate intelligence as to the facts might, at other times, have prevented one side from plunging into a situation, only to find that a much greater commitment of force was required in order to protect its initial modest commitment (would you believe the United States in Vietnam?). And a more accurate long-term assessment of the capabilities of a quarrelsome neighbor could have helped alleviate exaggerated and sometimes unjustified fears that set off spiraling arms races.

A profound political irony is thrown into sharp relief when these theoretical opportunities for conflict control are compared with the opportunities actually seized in these same cases. Although our figures have no profound statistical value, it surely is no coincidence that the *number of measures that we know in retrospect were actually taken in these cases was roughly in inverse proportion to those that, with the benefit of hindsight, might have been taken in pursuit of a purposeful conflict-control strategy.*

In Phase 1, 9 out of 149 possible measures, and in Phase 2, 9 out of a possible 94, were taken. Only when violence broke out in Phase 3 were there real signs of conflict-control activity: 31 measures out of 83 "possible" were taken. But when hostilities ceased in Phase 4, interest began to flag: 14 measures were taken out of 75 which we saw as possible; and where hostilities were resumed, 11 out of 25 identified as relevant were taken.

When we looked at *types* of control measures that were actually taken, by far the most numerous were those in the realms of military and strategic action and UN consideration (18 and 20 instances each). Not surprisingly, both peaked after hostilities actually broke out. Next was external-political action (16 instances), which also focused heavily on the hostilities phases. Some conflict-suppressing activity (such as acts of repression by the Portuguese authorities in Angola) were of a kind that in the longer run seemed certain to produce even more severe conflict.

The bottom line from a review of both parts of the experiment on conflict-controlling activity showed that policy activity stood in virtually inverse proportion to realistic chances of influencing events preventively. This finding confirmed our sobering intuition that, despite rhetoric about preventive diplomacy, much official effort to control conflicts is undertaken after things become too volatile to ignore and tragically late to affect events constructively.

The modest but suggestive research results reported in this chapter have a clear relevance to policy. Chapter 4 on heading off conflicts elaborates the depressing tendency of officialdom to live in the very short term and short change policy planning in favor of operational tactics in response to immediate stimuli. But Chapter 4 also spells out some practical categories of conflict prevention that make use of early warning to transform rhetoric into genuine preventive diplomacy.

NOTES

[1]The work of Bloomfield's former long-time associate Amelia C. Leiss contributed importantly to the arguments and findings in this chapter.

[2]See the Bibliography for relevant contributions.

[3]See the definitions at the end of Chapter 1.

[4]The conceptual foundation of CASCON's database was part of and yet different from a growing body of systematic analysis by political scientists seeking to understand the causes of conflict. Some outstanding scholars who studied conflict developed an information base that might be termed *deductive*—that is, drawn from available sources of data. Such early pioneers as Quincy Wright, Lewis Richardson, and Professor J. David Singer have inventoried wars between (and sometimes within) states over various historic periods, seeking to correlate outbreak and intensity with variables such as population, wealth, trade, UN action or inaction, regime type, and the like. Significant research contributions have also been made by Rudolf Rummel, Ted Gurr, Hayward Alker, Nazli Choucri, and others cited in the Bibliography.

[5]For evidence of the presence at critical choice points of nonrational factors of pressures, acceleration, and a sense of fatality, a classic example may be the World War I case. See Barbara W. Tuchman, *The Guns of August* (New York: Macmillan, 1962).

Eight
THEORY INTO PRACTICE
The Evolution of CASCON

C ASCON—Computer Aided System for Analysis of Conflicts—developed from the empirical and theoretical work at MIT on the Bloomfield-Leiss conflict model discussed in Chapter 7. MIT has a long-standing tradition of respect for both fundamental scientific research and its pragmatic application in engineering practice. CASCON is a systematic method of conflict analysis as well as a computer program and database designed to support that analysis.

CASCON provides a unique analytical tool for the student or scholar studying conflict, and for the government and international organization official concerned with early warning, conflict prevention, and crisis management. The CASCON software included with this book contains a database of 85 modern conflicts, each coded for 571 specific conditions or elements, called factors, that experts consider to have been influential in pushing those situations across a threshold in the direction of either war or peace. Accompanying each case is a short history, called a precis. The database may be augmented by incorporating additional cases prepared by the user or obtained from other researchers.

The latest version of CASCON operates under the Microsoft Windows™ operating system available on tens of millions of personal computers around the world. In contrast, the first version of CASCON ran only on a one-of-a-kind computer time-sharing system at MIT (the CTSS system). For much of the 1970s and 1980s, the second version of CASCON ran on MIT's Multics system, which was somewhat more accessible to the outside world. In 1988, an experimental third version of CASCON became available on IBM-style personal computers under DOS. The DOS version won an award for educational software and received distribution to scores of researchers, teachers, and professionals.

In one sense CASCON's history is an illustrative example of the bureaucratic and institutional vagaries of three decades of rising and falling government and foundation support for social science research. CASCON falls somewhere between theory-building (which is of problematic interest to government and foundations) and short-fuse, mission-oriented projects (which are usually inappropriate for empirical research).

CASCON is a computerized spinoff from a long-term research project on arms control and local conflict directed by Professor Lincoln Bloomfield at the

MIT Center for International Studies starting in the mid-1960s. The MIT Arms Control project was motivated to undertake a broad study of conflicts in the developing regions of the world, based on the conviction that there must be a better way than lurching from crisis to crisis. That had been Bloomfield's experience in 11 years in the U.S. State Department and subsequently in the National Security Council, and it continues today. Disillusionment following U.S. involvement in Vietnam and concern in the 1990s about intervention in "small wars" all reinforce the need to devise improved methods for analyzing crises before they explode, and for encouraging earlier preventive policy action. The end of the Cold War brought this topic to the fore.

In seeking to improve the art of preventive diplomacy and conflict prevention well before it became a growth industry and with Bloomfield's former State Department colleagues in mind, we developed a prototype computerized conflict-analysis system that we called CASCON. We were less concerned about being encyclopedic or excessively rigorous than about suiting the computer tools to the conflict-analysis task. If CASCON were to be actually used by students as well as by people in the political and diplomatic trenches, the product had to be attuned to the requirements and lifestyles not only of expert scholars but also of real-world users.

THE U.S. GOVERNMENT FLIRTS WITH CASCON

The MIT Arms Control Project, though financed by a number of sources, was sponsored primarily by the U.S. Arms Control and Disarmament Agency (ACDA). In 1967 we presented detailed findings to ACDA and others in the State Department regarding the nature of small wars and the flow and control of conventional arms. We recommended conflict-control policies for the wars that were then breaking out in the developing regions at a rate of something like 1.5 per year. Following that briefing, the imaginative associate director of ACDA, Lieutenant General John Davis, challenged us to try our hands at "computerizing" our conflict model and the accompanying data. CASCON was a direct outgrowth of our acceptance of that challenge. We built our local conflict model along with the case studies into an experimental computer program on MIT's CTSS time-sharing computer system. In 1969, we tried out the early CASCON in the CONEX-IV political game with promising results.[1] This game broke new ground by including two similarly composed U.S. teams, concealed from one another, both responding to the same stimuli but distinguished by the key experimental variable of CASCON support for one team.[2]

Even before the computerization task was completed, we were able during the 1967 June war in the Middle East to respond to an inquiry from a White House task force about the relative merit of various kinds of cease-fires agreed to during hostilities. With the benefit of our structured database, we reported that out of five instances of cease-fires, fighting broke out again in all the cases when troops remained in place. But hostilities did *not* break out again in the majority of cases where the cease-fire was accompanied by troop withdrawals. Results were perhaps inconclusive, doubtless unscientific, but not uninteresting.

CASCON was one small part of an extraordinary amount of experimental social science research that civilian agencies of government such as ACDA and State funded in the 1960s. By the mid-1970s, an enhanced version of CASCON had been enthusiastically received by several U.S. government agencies and adopted as a project by the UN Institute for Training and Research (UNITAR). It was also under active consideration for further development by government agencies and private foundations. As a secondary benefit CASCON, even in its experimental form, was found to be of research value to scholars studying conflict, as well as an exciting educational tool for students to learn about both world politics and computers. Yet the effort, despite its early promise, stalled in its tracks, and development ceased for a decade.

Elliot Richardson's brief but stimulating tenure in the State Department's number two spot made 1969 an early high water mark of official openness to possibilities of applying new technologies to substantive policy. In his famous letter to President Franklin D. Roosevelt advising him about nuclear fission research, Albert Einstein implied that scholarship and research, to have an effect on policy, must receive the same access, network, and attention to hierarchy as other sectors.[3]

Deputy Secretary Richardson gave the CASCON experiment an indispensable cachet by personally exposing it to a computer user's committee he had formed representing all bureaus. After a Bloomfield briefing on CASCON, Richardson directed the committee to "volunteer" to undertake a third, confidence-check coding of our then 52 cases by experts within the bureaus. Richardson, who shortly thereafter left State to become secretary of the Department of Health, Education and Welfare, later wrote: "Even in its pilot form, the CASCON system showed great promise as a way of comparing a newly emerging conflict with past episodes of conflict, thus pointing to measures that might be helpful in limiting or containing the new conflict."[4]

The State Department's Bureau of Intelligence and Research (INR) subsequently detailed three regional specialists to acquire hands-on experience with the pilot CASCON system. They suggested matching future conflict cases against prototypical clusters of factors that tended toward or away from violence. That suggestion we have implemented with several so-called profile cases that are discussed in the next chapter. Unfortunately, the INR specialists' exclusive focus on cases in "their" region tilted the learning experience more toward the realm of bureaucratic subcultures than to generic characteristics of conflict.

During the same time frame as the State Department exploration of CASCON, Allen Moulton undertook the complete redesign and reconstruction of the CASCON computer software using MIT's new Multics time-sharing system. CASCON II became available in 1970–71 at MIT and by phone dial-up to other academic and government users. The technology of the day was limited to slow, clackity teletypes and other printing terminals. Users interacted with the computer using "commands" composed in an arcane CASCON language, with sentences like "list cases in region A having 1-73 T1." In addition to the limitations of the technology, the bureaucratic process of obtaining access to a computer terminal with phone dial-up capability was itself so complicated that visiting MIT was often more straightforward than using CASCON in Washington or New York.

In February 1973 Bloomfield was asked to demonstrate CASCON to a group of INR officers assembled by Dr. E. Raymond Platig, Director of the Office of External Research. INR's reactions were mixed. Some analysts who had experimented with the CASCON method thought that, with its potentially rich database, it could contribute empirically to theory about conflict and, if broken down into more detail, become operationally useful. Others who take the view that each new historical event is *sui generis* saw little or no utility for their work except as a convenient method of document retrieval. In 1976 the Deputy Director of External Research, stressing actual crisis potential, wrote: "I think I reflect the views of others when I say that CASCON continues to be a most promising experiment in harnessing advanced technology and social science methodologies to the substantive needs of officers in foreign affairs agencies under tense or even crisis circumstances."[5]

In the late 1970s, the U.S. Arms Control and Disarmament Agency, which had financed virtually all of our MIT conflict research including CASCON, invited Bloomfield to brief the director and his deputies on CASCON as well as "other interesting developments in the field," with special emphasis on arms control questions. In order to be able to illustrate some practical result from ACDA's substantial research investment, a quick exploration of CASCON's arms control-relevant factors produced an unexpected result—one that the conventional wisdom would not have predicted. ACDA subsequently called to express enthusiastic interest and to register its intention to begin using CASCON internally.

That intention was short-lived. Our always-cautious ACDA project officer later summed up the position. CASCON, he wrote, "has real value as a training device and as an instrument for theory-building [but] much more work on the system would be required in order to determine if it could be usable as an aid in the policy-making process."[6] He was, of course, partly right, although his following statement that ACDA research funds were being directed "toward higher priority projects" meant there would be no support for CASCON's developmental phase and for the kind of early warning techniques the government would be begging for by the mid-1990s.

In the same period, the National Security Council staff also experimented with CASCON. It concluded that CASCON should be able to report which if any of the remedial "measures" had in fact been taken in a particular case. We have not had the resources to undertake this substantial piece of additional research and development.

THE UNITED NATIONS TAKES THE PLUNGE

We had insisted from the outset that all our project research, including CAS-CON, be done on an open basis. The pilot version of CASCON was thus available to international organizations, scholars, and anyone else with an interest in conflicts (above all, to students at MIT). Not surprisingly, the most active interest came from the United Nations.

In early 1971, Chief Adebo and Dr. Oscar Schachter, Director and Deputy Director of the United Nations Institute for Training and Research (UNITAR), respectively, invited Bloomfield to brief a gathering of UN and mission officials in New York. In February 1973, UNITAR sent three senior Fellows (from India, Ethiopia, and Chile) to visit MIT in order to become familiar with CASCON.

Their report to UNITAR sensibly suggested that, since CASCON had been developed under U.S. government auspices, for UN use, "it would be useful to keep a constant review of the database through fresh coding by people with different perspectives, including some from countries that are parties to the disputes in question." Their conclusion was as follows: "We believe an expanded CASCON System can be of enormous assistance to the UN and its researchers. The premise on which Professor Bloomfield developed this system is a sound one and deserves full attention and support from the United Nations."[7]

In September 1973, CASCON was adopted as part of the UNITAR program of work for the subsequent year. It spelled out the potential value of CASCON's data for UNITAR research and training programs in peaceful settlement of disputes and, possibly, as an aid to UN officials in analyzing by analogy trends in current conflict situations and exploring possibilities for remedial action. UNITAR thus proposed "to collaborate with MIT in improving, adapting and testing the system for possible uses within the United Nations."[8] Soon thereafter, as in Washington, the UN project was suspended for lack of funding.[9]

By that time, in the mid-1970s, U.S. government agencies were demanding short-term payoffs, while the major U.S. foundations were abruptly curtailing their support for international relations studies. U.S. involvement in Vietnam had also made CIA money unwelcome on campus. Only the Defense Department had the money and the inclination to pay for social science conflict research—and that only fitfully and limited by the Mansfield amendment requiring direct military application.

In retrospect, it would probably have been out of character during that turbulent period for either government or foundations to provide such support. It was, after all, a time when decades of social science research were indicted by the radical left, particularly on campuses (for the most part unfairly), for contributing to Vietnam and indeed to U.S. foreign policy failures in general. Indeed, for a time some particularly hysterical students singled out CASCON on the MIT campus as a malevolent scheme to crush peasant revolutions. (On one riotous occasion when Bloomfield described CASCON's war-minimizing purpose, one particularly incendiary faculty mentor ordered his troops to drown out the speaker who was "getting too reasonable.")

CASCON IN THE UNIVERSITY

Even as its institutional sponsors veered off in different directions, CASCON lived on as a part-time labor of love in the belief that it represented an embryonic research and teaching tool of potential value, a conviction encouraged by early experiences. To the extent that a computerized data system can go into hibernation, CASCON slept fitfully for a decade, roused only by students and the occasional researcher, until MIT's Project Athena came along in the mid-1980s and administered what poetically might be called the magic kiss that stimulated further development.

In the spring of 1970, having been retained to advise the government of Guyana concerning a means of settling its dispute with neighboring Venezuela, Bloomfield experimented with the use of the primitive pilot CASCON to analyze the conflict. His conclusions became, as they say, academic, when without warning the two foreign ministers decided to get together and resolve the matter!

MIT Professor Nazli Choucri used 45 CASCON cases in her *Population Dynamics and International Violence,* in which she examined the relationship in developing countries between conflict behavior and underlying factors of population, resources, and technology. She concluded that CASCON "can . . . be employed as an early warning system for detecting the development of conflict situations based on pattern recognition . . . in order to assess potential consequences."[10]

A former State Department colleague, reporting in 1976 from the Johns Hopkins School of Advanced International Studies, used CASCON "to discover the conditions and motivations in a local conflict situation that impel toward the introduction of UN peacekeeping forces." His findings showed a provocative correlation between intervention by international organizations and the presence of great power involvement.[11]

The most unequivocal results came from using CASCON as a teaching tool that combined computer familiarization with experience in researching conflicts (plus a little badly needed geography and history). At MIT Professor Choucri used CASCON in her "Causes of War" course, and Professor Hayward Alker included CASCON in his graduate seminars (which he has repeated in 1996 at the University of Southern California).

In Bloomfield's yearly freshman seminars, students independently researched conflict situations of their choice—past, present, or even future— entered their codings in CASCON, and shared their findings and insights with the class. Several hundred MIT students had this experience, to which they have reacted with the kind of enthusiasm that makes teaching worthwhile. As the years passed, the 1971-vintage CASCON program, originally designed for tele-types, began to look strange to new generations of students accustomed to video screens. The program, after all, was almost as old as the students!

Beginning in 1984, MIT's Project Athena, as part of its mission to advance the use of computer technology in education and research, provided support to extend CASCON's database and to reconstruct the software on personal computers. The database was expanded to 66 cases. The factor list was thoroughly reviewed, reorganized, clarified, and expanded based on the suggestions of users over the years. In 1988, the new third version of CASCON running on PC's under the DOS operating system was completed and made available at cost through the MIT Center for International Studies. A subsequent grant from the U.S. Institute of Peace enabled us to expand the database to 85 cases. In 1988, the DOS version of CASCON received the Distinguished Software Award in Political Science from EDUCOM/NCRIPTAL (the National Center for Research to Improve Post-Secondary Teaching and Learning).

RENEWED PROFESSIONAL INTEREST

Shortly before the DOS version of CASCON was completed, new interest arose in the professional community. A decade after UNITAR voted to adopt CAS-CON but failed to follow through, an extraordinary unofficial initiative helped to nudge the United Nations into action on the kind of early warning and conflict-prevention activity promised by the Secretary General's 1982 annual report. The actors were two bright young UN Secretariat employees, David Biggs of the United States and Tapio Kanninen of Finland. At the time, neither carried assigned responsibilities in this substantive area. Both were convinced that the time was ripe for the United Nations to move ahead.

On their own, they visited MIT in October 1984 in order "to identify the academic research in political science which could be of use in the short- or long-term in the context of the Secretary General's current effort to upgrade UN information systems and move more actively toward preventive diplomacy." Their "operational goal" was to find "ways to transform the research results to practical 'policy advice packages.'"[12]

As a direct result of their efforts, Bloomfield had the curious experience of repeating in New York in early 1986 essentially the same briefing given at the United Nations 13 years before. In the same period, the United Nations created an innovative planning and information unit, the Office of Research and Coordination of Information (ORCI), headed by James Jonah (who had studied with Bloomfield at MIT). Charged with exploring new sources of conflict-anticipating data and analysis, ORCI adopted the test version of CASCON and began some interesting experiments such as multinational case coding. Unfortunately, ORCI was abolished as an economy measure after only a few years.

New interest also began to appear in Washington. In the mid-1980s, amid an air of discovery and daring experimentation, a new effort was begun to bring computer technology into the State Department to expose policy analysts "to some of the new analytical tools available for foreign policy research." The headline in the State newsletter of January 1986 read: "It's the 'Spirit of '86' as personal computers gain a foothold at State." The story by three enthusiastic computer neophytes starts with this paragraph: "The three of us are true believers in a revolution that is certainly coming to the State Department. . . . we'd like to share our exciting adventure with the rest of you in the Department . . . we're discovering even better and more sophisticated uses of this magnificent tool."[13] One can only wish that the real revolutions that take government by surprise would arrive at such a stately pace.

Since then, in addition to the scores of teachers and researchers in the United States and abroad who have experimented with the earlier CASCON, a number of U.S. government agencies, primarily military and intelligence, have requested the DOS version from MIT (perhaps they were the only ones that could afford the $25 charge.) Unfortunately, there has never been the means to follow up on intentions at the one department we originally had in mind to help—the U.S. Department of State. This is a shame and ironic as well. A "memory hole" still exists in a system in which career personnel are rotated every few years under the direction of political appointees who are themselves likely to disappear in an even shorter time span. In a crisis-prone world, the United States remains a central actor in the drama, and the top tier of officialdom always seems to give precedence to today's crisis over tomorrow's potential disasters. Only in the late 1990s were serious attempts made to become more systematic about early warning and conflict prevention (see Chapter 4).

We should not be too hard on diplomats who, while the technology was still primitive, were scornful of the idea that a computer had any potential for their work. Perhaps now that innovative computer use is standard in virtually all other lines of work, systems such as the new CASCON may play a more useful supplemental role in both the teaching and practice of foreign affairs.

CASCON AS A LECTURE TOOL AND "LAB" EXERCISE

CASCON is a teaching and learning tool of proven effectiveness. It supplies a ready-made "lab" exercise for undergraduate students in college courses in international relations, foreign affairs, conflict studies, and history. It can be used as the basis for an entire segment of a course. It is a potentially rich research tool at the graduate level for international relations or history students, either as a "lab experiment" or as an adjunct to course or thesis research. It can serve at the high school advanced placement level in history or social studies as an introduction to library research and computer application—and as a challenging way to enjoy studying.

In a typical lecture course in international relations, each week the students may listen to two or three hours of lecture, have an hour or more of section discussion, and read perhaps a hundred pages of text. To enliven the educational process, the student's mind should be engaged by something over and above the usual listening and note-taking. There are several alternatives to bring life into that familiar but unimaginative format, as well as to drive home the essential core material.

CASCON has proven an excellent vehicle to overcome these weaknesses in the educational process. In addition, two other methods are useful to build into the curriculum. One method that has become familiar is a simulation ("political game" of the type developed at MIT by Professor Bloomfield) in which, at some point in the course, students role-play various countries or national decision makers, interacting dynamically over a crisis or other policy problem. Political gaming is a tried-and-true success in the classroom and can be particularly interesting when CASCON is added as a supportive element. A second method is the use of videotape, CD-ROMs, and film to bring to life otherwise abstract current and recent historical events. When used with a video projection device, CASCON has also shown considerable value as a supplement to lectures.

The disciplines of law, medicine, business, engineering, and natural sciences employ the laboratory exercise or case study as a means of elucidating complex material to students. In the field of international relations, it has always been difficult to give students practical experience in the kinds of work and thought processes used by professionals. At MIT we have found that CASCON is a highly effective means for providing a disciplined and focused exercise in conflict analysis. Each student, or team of students, selects a particular conflict situation to investigate. The instructor may assign cases or help students in their choices. Depending on the instructor's purpose and the student's interest, several different types of cases may be selected:

► *A current international or civil war situation.* It can be something blowing up right now, or still building up toward a crisis. Pick a situation in the current TV news that is adequately covered by available newspaper and news magazine files in the college library—for example, a threatening situation between fragments of the former Soviet Union.

► *A historical dispute.* Some recent cases are still well covered, such as the UN/Coalition action against Iraq after it invaded Kuwait in 1990. Or, depending on student interest, a case could center on the earlier colonial struggle of an African country, an ethnic conflict in the 1990s, or something more recondite such as the Scottish nationalist movement for independence from Great Britain.

► *An older conflict.* When adequate resources are available, a dedicated student might research, for example, the American Revolution or Sparta versus Athens.

▶ *An imaginary conflict.* In the right circumstances, some students can construct and analyze a scenario that has not yet appeared on the horizon—with the caveat that, to bring it off, it has to be done really well!

The project starts with a reading assignment explaining CASCON and its context, namely, this book. A classroom session follows, based on the reading, with a discussion of the nature of conflict, the CASCON dynamic phase model and definitions, and the procedures the students are to follow in doing their "lab" project. The students will have the book in hand, but may not yet have used the CASCON software.

If a computer is available in the classroom, the system can be demonstrated to the students. The instructor might print a CASCON database precis as a class handout so that students can use it as a model for the write-up of their chosen case.

Students then begin work on their cases. The first step is to read up on that case in the library, on CD-ROM, or on-line on the Internet. Notes should be organized in terms of Phases in the fashion of the CASCON database precis. To locate places where events take place, it is helpful to consult an atlas, an encyclopedia on CD-ROM, or the Internet. The objective is to identify the *essential facts* of the case, not in great depth but sufficiently to identify

▶ case title and dates

▶ region and conflict type

▶ status quo and non-status quo sides

▶ issue or issues in dispute

▶ phases and threshold dates

▶ other parties to the cases, for example, great powers

▶ the essential events and circumstances in each phase that helped "push" the case toward or away from the next threshold of conflict

After drafting a crude but factually accurate precis, based on the essential facts they have uncovered, students should study Chapters 9 and 10, and then familiarize themselves with CASCON's operations, including the on-line HELP screens. Students enter their case in the Case Detail window, and they enter factor codings on-line.

Finally, students use the Compare facility of CASCON to investigate patterns of similarity and dissimilarity with other cases. A brief report for the class should include a precis of the case, a map location, and findings about the other cases that appear "similar." Based on analogy to other similar cases, the report should then examine the most significant factors that the student case has in common in a given phase with database cases, conclusions about the likelihood of "escalation," and recommendations of conflict-minimizing measures implied in the comparison results of significant factors.

NOTES

[1]Lincoln P. Bloomfield, and Cornelius J. Gearin, "Games Foreign Policy Experts Play: The Political Exercise Comes of Age," *Orbis,* Winter 1973.

[2]Lincoln P. Bloomfield, "Reflections on Gaming," *Orbis,* Winter 1984.

[3]This issue is spelled out in Lincoln P. Bloomfield, "Imagination and Responsibility: Dilemmas in Translating Creative Ideas into Action," in Earl Foell and Richard Nenneman, eds., *How Peace Came to the World* (Cambridge, Mass.: MIT Press, 1986).

[4]Letter to Bloomfield dated January 3, 1983.

[5]Letter to Bloomfield dated May 19, 1976.

[6]Letter to Bloomfield dated January 5, 1983.

[7]*Report on UNITAR Fellows' visit to MIT concerning the possible uses of CASCON-II System for United Nations purposes.* Document U/RE 100(14-2), undated.

[8]UN document UNITAR/EX/R.47, August 7, 1973.

[9]Letter to Bloomfield from Dr. Robert S. Jordan dated May 7, 1976.

[10]*Population Dynamics and International Violence* (Lexington, Mass.: Lexington Books, 1974), p. 91.

[11]N. A. Pelcovits and Kevin L. Kramer, "Local Conflict and UN Peacekeeping," *International Studies Quarterly,* December 1976, p. 533.

[12]Letter to Bloomfield from Tapio Kanninen dated October 15, 1984.

[13]Corazon Sandoval Foley, William R. McPherson, and Kenneth E. Roberts, *STATE,* January 1986, p. 2.

Nine ~

CONFLICT ANALYSIS
WITH CASCON

T he CASCON database and computer software were designed to assist officials responsible for policy, as well as students and scholarly researchers studying international conflict.[1] CASCON implements the Bloomfield-Leiss Dynamic Phase Model[2] discussed in Chapter 7. By structuring information about a conflict and its history, CASCON facilitates the process of reasoning about the future course of events using historical analogy.

There are many circumstances in which government officials and business executives must deal with a conflict situation as it develops. Governments need to assess how a conflict will impact their interests and decide if action is warranted. The United Nations and other international organizations may need to act in areas of their responsibilities. Humanitarian agencies may face an urgent need for assistance. Businesses may have concerns about the safety of employees and their families, as well as financial impacts.

CASCON's developers were motivated to help officialdom—whether in governments or in international organizations such as the United Nations—to become more systematic in dealing with one of their chief preoccupations, that of coping with international and internal conflicts, with the benefit of early warning so that preventive diplomacy and other forms of conflict prevention can be initiated. Experimental use of CASCON in the United Nations and government agencies has already shown CASCON's possibilities as a collateral analytical tool to supplement the judgment and experience of the professional.[3]

CASCON was also developed for students and researchers studying international relations, history, or political science. For the student, CASCON provides a compact, structured historical resource on conflict in the post–World War II era. With the help of a computer, students can also experience the same kinds of analytic reasoning processes used by expert professionals. For the scholar researching conflict, CASCON contains a rich vein of data for testing hypotheses and theory building.

WHAT KINDS OF QUESTIONS
CAN CASCON HELP ANSWER?

CASCON is a decision-support system. The computer does not make policy decisions or predict the future. CASCON is a sophisticated, yet flexible, system for
storing and manipulating information about conflicts. As is true of any computerized system, the thinking has to be done by the user. What it can do is
make available on a desktop or laptop computer a handy tool for learning or
analysis, along with a rich store of usable information. Given some purpose on
the user's part, CASCON can help to answer questions the user has formulated
and to reach conclusions about the dynamics of conflict. Here are some of the
kinds of questions one might have in mind when using CASCON:

▶ *What happened in the Falklands/Malvinas war of 1982?* CASCON contains an on-line mini-history, called a precis, for each database case.

▶ *I am concerned about possible conflicts breaking out in Latin America.
  Can I study the cases there that did not become wars and get some clues
  as to the reasons?* CASCON can isolate the Western Hemisphere cases
  that did not go on to hostilities so that the patterns of factor codings can
  be studied.

▶ *I am studying a dispute that is currently brewing in Asia. Can I match it
  against other cases at a similar stage to make some informed guesses as
  to what might happen?* The new case can be entered into CASCON and
  compared against some or all of the other cases in the same phase to
  seek common patterns. CASCON does not make predictions about the
  way a new conflict will unfold, but it will help identify situations that
  appear to be most like it at this particular stage, and outline what happened in those cases.

▶ *Can I invent a conflict situation of my own design—a kind of imaginary
  "future history"—and use it to study the larger universe of conflict?* Just
  as with a real case, a hypothetical case can be coded, entered into CAS-
  CON, and used in the same fashion as real cases.

▶ *Can I completely ignore regional boundaries in coming up with some suggestive indicators for early warning?* CASCON can limit cases to a region
  or not as the user determines.

▶ *Can I test hypotheses regarding correlations between various elements of
  conflicts in order to generate suggestions for further research or for policy purposes?* CASCON offers users a wide variety of tools that can be
  used in combinations of their own devising. For instance, what other
  groupings of cases have factors coded in certain ways? What groupings
  of factors were coded a certain way in some or all cases?

▶ *Can CASCON help me to abstract "ideal types" of conflict situations based
  on observed patterns that might make for a sort of "template" for checking against unfolding disputes—rather like an airline's "hijacker profile?"*

Although every conflict is unique in its actors, locale, conditions, and history, there are common features that often cut across regions and types. CASCON provides several synthetic "profile" cases that can be compared to new user cases. Users can construct additional synthetic "profile" cases based on their own conclusions. (See the section "Finding Patterns in CASCON.")

Remember that, however intriguing a computerized system, it will always be less sophisticated than the complex models and histories that reside inside the heads of experienced professionals. CASCON can help point out features and directions, but in the end analytical results rely on the user's understanding and skill.

WHAT DOES CASCON DO?

The critical questions facing the conflict analyst in an ongoing situation require predicting the future course of events. How will the situation develop if left alone? What will happen if various actions are taken? In many areas of human knowledge, mathematical models provide a reliable guide for prediction. Measurements can be taken from the present situation, combined with values for inputs to be applied, and calculations made for navigating a space ship, operating a television set, or setting dosage for a drug treatment regimen. Some have tried their hand at mathematical models of international conflict.[4] No such model has yet proved capable of prediction that can be relied on for decision. The CASCON approach is to turn to history—the history of events and circumstances of the situation at hand—and the history of other conflicts. CASCON assists in reasoning by historical analogy. Organizing knowledge about every case in the same structure helps to identify similar fact patterns among historical cases at the same stage of development—that is, in the same phase—as the current case. The outcomes of these analogous cases can then be examined for evidence of the future.

Simon's classic paradigm of decision making involves three stages: intelligence, design, and choice. Intelligence is the process of surveying the horizon, collecting information, storing and arranging that information in a useful way, and evaluating the meaning of the cumulative body of information gathered. Design is the process of inventing and exploring the consequences of possible courses of action. Choice is the process of selecting among those alternatives.[5] CASCON does not presume to make decisions or tell experienced professionals what action to take. CASCON, as a decision-support system,[6] focuses on assisting the human analyst in the intelligence and design stages. CASCON assists the student or professional analyst by serving as an aid to the memory and as an aid to the imagination.

CASCON *aids the memory* of the analyst by storing in readily accessible form an inventory of historic facts that might be relevant to an incipient or

Table 9-1
Cascon Database Cases

	Interstate	Internal with Significant External Involvement	Primarily Internal	Colonial
AFRICA	**ALGERIA-MOROCCO 1962–63** Guinea-Ivory Coast 1966–67 **GUINEA-PORTUGUESE GUINEA 1970** GHANA-UPPER VOLTA 1964–66 MOROCCO-MAURITANIA 1957–70 SOMALIA-ETHIOPIA (OGADEN) 1977–88 Somalia-Ethiopia-Kenya 1960–64	**Angola Civil War 1974–** **CHAD 1979–94** **CONGO (KATANGA) 1960–63** **MOZAMBIQUE CIVIL WAR 1975–94** **Western Sahara 1973–**	**Burundi 1965** **ETHIOPIA-ERITREA 1974–93** **NIGERIA (BIAFRA) 1967–70**	**ALGERIA 1954–62** **ANGOLAN INDEPENDENCE 1961–74** **MOROCCO-SPAIN 1956–75** **NAMIBIAN INDEPENDENCE 1947–90** **ZIMBABWE INDEPENDENCE 1965–80**
WESTERN HEMISPHERE	**Bay of Pigs 1961** BELIZE-GUATEMALA 1948–91 CHILE-ARGENTINA 1977–85 Dominican Republic-Haiti 1963 **EL SALVADOR-HONDURAS 1969** Ecuador-U.S.A. 1963–75 **Falklands/Malvinas 1982–** Guyana-Venezuela 1970 **NICARAGUA-COSTA RICA 1955–56** **NICARAGUA-HONDURAS 1957–60** PANAMA 1964 U.S.-MEXICO BORDER 1895–1963	**Bolivia 1967** **DOMINICAN REPUBLIC 1965–66** **EL SALVADOR 1980–92** **GRENADA 1983** **Guatemala 1954** **NICARAGUA 1980–90** Venezuela 1960–63	**Colombia (M19) 1974–90** **CUBA 1952–59**	

Region			
MIDDLE EAST	**Arab-Israeli War 1967** **IRAN-IRAQ 1980–90** Kuwait-Iraq 1961–63 **Middle East War 1973** **Palestine 1947–49** **SOVIET-IRAN 1945–46** **SUEZ 1956** **Sinai 1956** Syria-Turkey 1956–57 TABA STRIP 1982–89 Yarmuk/Jordan Waters 1948–94	**Iraq (Kurds) 1958–63** **Lebanon 1957–58** **LEBANON CIVIL WAR 1975–90** **Muscat and Oman 1957–70** **Yemen 1962–70**	ADEN (SOUTH YEMEN) 1963–67 BAHRAIN 1970
PACIFIC, EAST, AND SOUTHEAST ASIA	**China-Vietnam 1979–** **India-China Border 1954–62** **INDONESIA-MALAYSIA 1963–65** **Quemoy-Matsu 1954–58** Spratly Islands 1974–	Cambodia 1979– **MALAYSIA EMERGENCY** **1948–60**	**Laos 1959–62** **Philippines (Huks) 1946–54**	**INDONESIAN** **INDEPENDENCE** **1945–49** New Caledonia 1984– **WEST IRIAN 1962–63**
SOUTH AND SOUTHWEST ASIA	**BANGLADESH 1971** **India-Pakistan 1965–** **Kashmir 1947–**	**AFGHANISTAN 1979–88**	**Sri Lanka 1948–**	
EUROPE	Gibraltar 1778– SOUTH TYROL 1957–69 TRIESTE 1945–54	**Cyprus (communal) 1963–** **GREEK CIVIL WAR 1944–49**	CZECHOSLOVAKIA REVOLUTION 1989 Spain-Basque 1968– **Ulster 1968–**	**Cyprus (Enosis)** **1954–59**

bold=hostilities CAPS=dispute settled

exploding conflict situation, rather than just those remembered by distracted crisis managers (or students) in the middle of the night, or bounded by a regional expert's specialized mental map. It is not that officials are not well informed; on the contrary, they are frequently extraordinarily so. Rather, bureaucrats and diplomats typically pass in and out of their assignments every three years or so, resulting in official historic memory that is often problematic.

CASCON *aids the imagination* of the analyst by providing an organized way to add information on an incipient or actual conflict into the system, and to regularly update the data as new information and intelligence are received. It helps the user compare a case at any time with violence-generating or violence-minimizing factors in database cases, thus supplying clues to suggestive repetitious patterns. Its factors can serve as a list of important questions to ask about a new case—questions that have proven to be significant in the past. Gaps in the information about a case can be revealed by listing factors coded as "no information," creating a checklist of intelligence requirements, so to speak.

CASCON contains a database of 85 representative conflicts since 1945. Table 9-1 shows a table of the cases in the CASCON database, arranged by region and type, and indicating whether hostilities occurred and also whether the case was settled. Each case is coded for up to 571 specific conditions or elements, called factors, that experts consider to have been influential in pushing those situations across a threshold in the direction of either war or peace. It also contains a short history, called a precis, for each database case. Users can compare cases and find suggestive patterns of similarity for educational, research, or early warning purposes. Users can also interact with CASCON by adding new cases and working with them as temporary parts of the database. The more cases added, the more useful the database can be in comparing cases.

To sum up, CASCON can help enhance understanding and analysis of conflicts between and within countries in four ways:

▶ Providing a convenient way to study 85 representative conflicts that took place since World War II, ranging from full-scale warfare to nonmilitary disputes about territories or resources that never grew into wars.

▶ Providing a structure for organizing and working with information about cases of interest to the user, coded to reflect the user's own viewpoint.

▶ Facilitating comparisons between cases and highlighting specific aspects in which cases are similar or different.

▶ Supplying a basis for early warning about quarrels between or inside countries which may turn into armed conflicts, along with implied remedial policy measures.

At the end of Chapter 8 we discussed how students can benefit from CASCON. Here is a hypothetical scenario illustrating how official policy can benefit.

A BUREAUCRATIC SCENARIO

Suppose for a moment that the U.S. State Department's country director for the hypothetical African country of "Azania" has been routinely monitoring a border dispute between Azania and its northern neighbor that flared up six months ago, with both countries moving troops to the common border. Ever since, as she scans the customary daily intake of newspapers, mail, and cables originating in the U.S. Embassy in the capital city of Kwazutu, rather than just filing items of interest in the three-drawer locked file cabinet, she has done something unusual.

She has put to one side today's more important pieces of paper such as the sobering news in the Priority cable from the field reporting the regime's latest arms purchase, and a SITREP (situation report) from the CIA reporting that one faction within the Azanian government would like to dump the incumbent president and cut a deal with that troublesome neighboring country to the north. She also clips out a story in the *Washington Post* reporting that the African regional organization, the Organization of African Unity (OAU), has again failed to come to grips with the dispute because of a quarrel over Libya's role in the OAU (whose name was sometimes privately modified to Organization of African Disunity).

In addition to her usual work, she also "enters" those snippets of political information into an intriguing MIT-developed computer program called CASCON on her desktop computer. Every few days, for each incoming item she deems of interest, she takes a moment to see if there is a corresponding CASCON "factor." She routinely enters on-line her judgment as to whether each such factor seems to be heading "her case" toward open warfare or, alternatively, toward a peaceful resolution.

A true child of the computer age, our heroine uses CASCON's database as an additional resource for "early warning" of a potential trouble spot in her subregion. Some—but not all—senior colleagues take her seriously.

Three months later, she is awakened at 5:45 A.M. by a call from the State Department Operations Center informing her that a FLASH cable has arrived from the American Embassy in Kwazutu reporting an imminent outbreak of fighting. She picks up the phone and calls her boss, in this case the Deputy Assistant Secretary of State for African Affairs, who was just suiting up for his morning jog. He "tasks" her to bring the information as well as her recommendation for U.S. government action to the regular 9:30 staff meeting of the Assistant Secretary for African Affairs (to which she is not normally invited).

Arriving at Foggy Bottom before the rush hour, she reads the FLASH cable and the longer followup Embassy messages. After reading the latest intelligence and the press office's overnight roundup of wire service reports, she turns to her desktop computer and brings up CASCON. Using the codings she has already put in and adding some new ones reflecting the new events, she runs a quick "Compare" routine.

The instantaneous result of CASCON's similarity algorithm appears on screen as a simple bar graph. She quickly scans the mini-histories (precis) of the six cases CASCON suggests are in varying degrees "similar" at a comparable phase. She recognizes among them four conflict cases of recent vintage that not only had lurched on to the hostilities stage but that also, she now recalled, shared some other similar features to her case, even though some were outside her region.

Using the summary diagram of the comparison, she looks quickly at the side-by-side codings of factors similarly coded as "Toward" intensification/worsening/escalation. What she sees intrigues her. In the four cases that look rather similar, she notices that the experts who coded them put particular stress on a couple of matters that had in fact been bothering her about the Azanian situation. These included a crackdown that recently sent the ruling party's doves into hiding and also a hastily accelerated airlift into a small provincial city of enough sophisticated weaponry to make for real trouble.

That is not all she spots. In the couple of similar cases that did not cross the hostilities threshold, several factors seemed equally suggestive. At roughly the same phase in those two cases, a major outside power had become sufficiently concerned to start up some preventive diplomacy with neighboring countries where its foreign assistance programs gave it some clout. Also, in those cases one side was badly deficient in certain economic resources and thus open to financial pressure.

Checking the precis of those two cases, she sees that both had been at least temporarily tranquilized through multilateral diplomacy—in one instance the United Nations, in the other the Organization of American States (OAS). The second instance was a Latin American case that was not normally of interest to people in the Africa bureau. She doesn't regard the CASCON data as adding up to a prediction, which it is not. But she has this information clearly in mind as she quickly drafts her report, recognizing it as potentially valuable backup for such policy recommendations as

▶ Getting to the United Nations fast, where the case might conceivably be talked to death before anyone starts shooting.

▶ Urging the Treasury Department to push the World Bank toward speedy release of a long-planned low-interest loan for a joint hydro-dam and conservation project on the boundary river between Azania and its northern neighbor.

▶ Having her boss ask the Under Secretary of State for Political Affairs to sign off on an urgent cable pressuring a particular NATO ally to back off from a deal it was planning that would have introduced into that volatile region supersonic jet fighters armed with heat-seeking missiles.

At the Assistant Secretary's meeting, our heroine is asked by her boss to report, and she modestly but cogently presents her analysis and policy recommendations. She plays down what some old-style diplomats might consider the outlandish notion of consulting "computerized history" for policy insights (and, even worse, using information about conflicts that took place in areas dealt with by other regional bureaus!). Nevertheless, with congratulations for her fine analysis and action proposals, the package now goes forward to the Seventh Floor, where the policy receives top-level approval.

STRUCTURING CONFLICT HISTORY FOR CASCON ANALYSIS

CASCON provides a systematic approach to gathering, storing, and organizing information about a conflict situation in a structure suited to historical analogizing. The first step in approaching a new case is to identify the parties, the locale, the issues in dispute, and the dates that mark the thresholds between phases. All of these items are shown on the Case Detail window in the computer. To get an idea of how to prepare a new case, it is often helpful to browse through the historical cases in CASCON's database looking at Case Detail and Precis windows. (See Chapter 10 for how to do this.)

CASE TITLE.   The case title (or name) is a short phrase that identifies the case in the midst of a list. In the CASCON historical database, titles are generally composed of the principal countries involved, the territory or issue disputed, or a familiar name, such as "Middle East War." The historical database also includes the year when significant events began and, if settled, the year of settlement. Cases that remain unresolved generally have a dash at the end of the title to indicate that the matter was still open as of the time the database was published.

CASE CODE.   In addition to a title, every case in CASCON must be assigned a three- or four-letter code. Case codes are used as a short abbreviation to identify the case in the computer. Every case code must be distinct from the codes for all other cases. When a new case is imported or entered into the computer, CASCON checks the code for uniqueness and recommends an alternative if a duplicate code is found.

SIDES.   CASCON treats each case as having two sides, called the status quo side and the non-status quo side, referring not to ideology, but in the neutral sense of which party seeks to initiate a change in the existing situation. The status quo side wants to keep matters as they are; the non-status quo side wants to change the situation. There may be more than one entity involved on each side. The principal actors in the dispute, which make the decisions as to whether the dispute will continue or will be resolved, should be included in the status quo and non-status quo sides in the Case Detail window. Other entities, which play an important though essentially supportive role, should be classified as allies or supporters of one side or the other and mentioned in the precis for the case during the phase where they play a role.

REGION.   CASCON divides the world into six regions. The region refers to the location of the dispute itself, particularly for contested territory, rather than the contesting parties. Region is entered in the Case Detail window. The regions are:

► Africa—the whole continent and neighboring islands, with the exception of Egypt.

► Europe—the continent and adjacent islands, including Russia and Turkey.

► Middle East—the ancient fertile crescent from Egypt across to Iran.

► Pacific, East Asia, and Southeast Asia—the western edge of the great Pacific basin, including the islands, Australia, and New Zealand.

► South and Southwest Asia—the Indian subcontinent and the mountainous and steppe areas to its north.

► Western Hemisphere—North, Central, and South America and nearby islands.

CONFLICT TYPE.   CASCON also classifies cases into four conflict types, which describe the general character of the conflict and the parties involved. Conflict type is entered in the Case Detail window. The conflict types are:

► Interstate—conflict between two or more identifiable states.

► Primarily internal—civil war or insurgency mainly between domestic factions, whether ethnic, linguistic, religious, or so on.

► External intervention—internal conflict with significant external involvement, that is, civil war with outside participation as a major element.

► Colonial—colony versus administering power, entailing a struggle for political independence by indigenous forces against the foreign administering or otherwise ruling power.

ISSUES.   Issues are what the conflict is about. Put another way, issues are matters that, if resolved, would end the conflict. There may, in fact, be more than one issue. Issues are shown in CASCON in two ways. A broad classification appears in the Case Detail window, and a description of the specifics is included in the precis. The classifications are:

► Ethnic—disputes arising out of ethnic differences, including religion and language.

▶ Governance—efforts to change the party or faction in power, or to change the form of government, as well as disputes centering on ideology.

▶ Independence—efforts to throw off the yoke of a foreign colonial power, as well as secession movements of a region presently administered as part of a state.

▶ Resources—disputes arising over control of natural resources or economic power.

▶ Strategic—attempts to gain geopolitical or economic advantage or to fend off a strategic move by another.

▶ Territory—disputes over the control of a contested area.

IDENTIFYING PHASES

PHASE DATES. The heart of CASCON is the notion that all conflictual situations go through one or more identifiable phases. Phases were developed empirically by closely examining a sample of conflicts to identify significant transitions or sharp changes that would distinguish the different phases hypothesized in the model. At what point was a military option introduced into a dispute, giving it a new character of conflict? When, if at all, did hostilities break out? Were there distinct points at which the hostilities intensified or moderated? When did they cease?

Although CASCON's factors focus only on the first three phases of the Bloomfield-Leiss model, the subsequent history of the conflict is outlined in the Case Detail window and described in the precis. The beginning dates for phases and the date of settlement are shown in the Case Detail window and as headings for sections of the case precis. The date for a phase may appear as a specific date (e.g., 11/15/48) or a broader range of time, such as a month, a year, a decade, or a century (e.g., 10/95, 1492, 1870s, or 1700s). From the phase dates in the Case Detail window CASCON determines the *highest level of intensity* (dispute, conflict, or hostilities) and the *latest phase* (phase 1–5, or settlement) for the case.

Some of the cases in the historical database show several cycles of recurring intensification. These are included to document the subsequent history after the initial cycle analyzed with the factors. For user cases only a single cycle is available. To continue CASCON analysis for a potential renewed cycle of violence, it is best to start a new case, linking the two together by cross-references at the end of the first and the beginning of the second. To reuse work from the original case, it can be exported, its name and code modified, and imported back into CASCON as a separate case for further work. The descriptive data and codings from the original cases will need to be reevaluated to reflect changes in the evolution of the situation.

PRECIS.   The basic facts of the case are summarized in a short history, organized by phase. Each section starts with the name of the phase and the threshold date (as recorded in the Case Detail window), followed by a paragraph giving the essential facts, events, names, and places concerning the course of the conflict. The precis can serve as a quick synopsis of the case and as a basis for further research in printed or electronic reference sources.

When laying out the phase structure of a ongoing situation, it is often effective to start at the present. The latest phase depends on the level of intensity of the case: Phase 1 for dispute, Phase 2 for conflict, Phase 3 for hostilities. The case history can then be reviewed, working from the present backward to find the beginning dates of the current phase and prior phases back to Phase 1.

CODING FACTORS

Once phases have been identified, specific *factors* may exert an influence over the dynamics of the situation by "pushing" it either toward or away from the threshold of the next phase. Factors represent economic, political, ethnic, military, social, or psychological events, conditions, or perceptions that could reasonably be shown to have exerted pressures, in varying degree, on the course of a conflict. CASCON's factors were developed empirically from case histories. Factors derive from one or more specific statements about particular post–World War II conflict situations, representing elements deemed relevant in real life by historians, diplomats, or other experts on those conflicts. These specific statements were then inductively combined and generalized into CASCON factors, by replacing specific names and places with generic phrases and by merging similar statements into common factors. The factors encompass the influential variables available from this special form of theorizing about the dynamics of local conflict.

There are 571 factors in CASCON with 176 factors in Phase 1, 189 in Phase 2, and 206 in Phase 3. Within each phase, factors are grouped into 10 categories by subject matter. Factors are assigned a *factor number* beginning with the phase number and category letter code and then a two-digit number within that group. For example, factor "3M-06" is the sixth factor in the military-strategic category in Phase 3. Note that a factor applies only to a single phase. If the same condition is relevant in another phase, there will be a separate factor with a different factor number. The factor categories are:

▶ R   Previous or general relations between sides
▶ G   Great power and allied involvement
▶ X   General external relations
▶ U   International organization (UN, regional, legal, public opinion)
▶ N   Ethnic (refugees, minorities)

- ▶ M   Military-strategic
- ▶ E   Economic/resources
- ▶ P   Internal politics of the sides
- ▶ C   Communication and information
- ▶ D   Actions in disputed area

CASCON provides a standard list of factors for all cases. For each case, a factor *coding* is used to indicate whether a factor is present and, if present, what effect it has. Each of the cases in the CASCON database was coded by three experts, usually one or two scholarly authorities, perhaps a former diplomat, military officer, or UN mediator who had been associated with the case, as well as by one in-house coder at MIT. Where codings diverged, most were reconciled through a set of decision rules, with remaining instances being resolved collegially by the staff.

The factors can be thought of as a checklist of questions to ask about the case. Every factor has been significant in some past case, but it may or may not be relevant to the case at hand. In going through the factors for a phase, the first decision is whether each factor was present or absent at that phase. If present, a factor may have a neutral effect, or it may influence the situation toward or away from "worsening" or "escalation," that is, from the use of violence. For factors identified as present and influential, the degree of influence is rated on three levels. The nine choices for factor codings are:

- ▶ T3   Much influence toward use of military force
- ▶ T2   Some influence toward use of military force
- ▶ T1   Little influence toward use of military force
- ▶ N   No influence in either direction, but present in the case
- ▶ A1   Little influence away from use of force
- ▶ A2   Some influence away from use of force
- ▶ A3   Much influence away from use of force
- ▶ F   Factor false or not present in the case
- ▶ --   No information available about factor

When a new case is opened, all factors are marked as "no information." In coding a case some factors can be skipped over altogether. For example, for a case in Phase 2, none of the Phase 3 factors is applicable. Similarly, if there is no disputed territory, category D can be ignored entirely. For the rest, the "no information" coding is an indication of additional aspects of the case that may need further investigation. CASCON's grouping or filtering capabilities can be used to quickly identify "no information" factors. The coding tool also has a button that skips to the next uncoded factor.

One technique for coding a case is to go through the factor list twice. On the first pass, only the presence or absence of a factor is considered. Factors are marked N for present or F for not present. On the second pass, all the factors marked N are evaluated for influence on the case. Generally, the "much" codings T3 and A3 should be used sparingly to indicate the most salient forces driving the case. Other factors that tilt in one direction or the other can be marked as "little" or "some" depending on the user's judgment of their degree of influence.

HISTORICAL ANALOGY

Once a case is entered into the computer, CASCON's analytic tools can help search for historical analogs. The history of other cases in the same phase with similar factor codings can be suggestive of the outcome of the case being considered. CASCON provides several techniques for matching a subject case, called the *base case,* against other cases in a given phase. When analogous cases are identified, their history can be examined using the precis, expert knowledge, and other resources for indications of the future course of the base case.

One way to look for patterns of similarity or difference is to line up two cases and scan through the factors looking at the codings side by side. The Factors window can be arranged with matched codings to help do this. Cases can be grouped together by region, conflict type, issues, highest level of intensity, or whether settlement was reached. Factors can be arranged by category, by coding, and by the combination of codings in the base case and another case. Using filters, users can combine criteria based on characteristics of cases and factors to explore hypotheses.

CASCON can also match the base case against some or all of the other cases using an automated *compare* feature. A rank-ordered graph of comparability of the base case in the current phase shows the cases with highest comparability at the top. At the other end of the list are cases that have the most dissimilar factor patterns. Case groups can be used to limit the cases considered in the comparison.

When CASCON does its comparison, it matches the codings of each factor in the base case and the other case using a *weighting* table. The standard weighting table takes account of the influence of factors as well as their presence or absence. CASCON also provides a weighting table that ignores influence and focuses just on the presence of factors. Weightings can also be customized to suit user preferences.

Sometimes differences in codings can be indicative. For example, a number of cases involving cease-fires were examined. Those with a cease-fire in place were found to be more likely to resume hostilities than those with a cease-fire with withdrawal. Factors can also be varied experimentally to test the effect of proposed actions.

FINDING PATTERNS IN CASCON

One of the most interesting things the user can do with CASCON is to look for *patterns* in the database. The CASCON factor list is a set of 571 generalized propositions derived from the specifics of a sample group of real-life conflict cases. That original group of cases was not drawn from any one region, nor was it representative of any one type of case such as "interstate." Rather, the database is global in scope and draws on the conflicts from 1945 to the present to illustrate the various conflict types and issues in dispute.

There is, of course, no reason why CASCON cannot be employed to analyze conflicts *within* a single region or type. It is a simple matter for the user to limit to a desired subset the analysis of cases and the results achieved by the comparison routine. One basic premise of CASCON is that, although regional and other characteristics are distinctive, there nevertheless exist some common across-the-board features of conflicts that can help illuminate both the general phenomenon of conflict and the dynamics of any single case.

There are many ways to search CASCON's database for suggestive generalities about conflict, limited only by the user's inventiveness. The user can start out with an hypothesis about conflict—for example, "Situations involving both poor communications and important economic resources are likely to lead to 'worsening.'" The user can then make a special list of the relevant factors and examine what happened in cases where those factors were present and coded as significant.

Another kind of analysis would seek to develop an "ideal model" case based on factors of particular interest. CASCON includes several "Profile" cases developed from factor codings to identify factors that are most closely associated with conflict resolution or its opposite. The user can code other synthetic cases for selected factors and use them as a kind of template against which to compare some or all of the other cases.

Bloomfield developed several profile cases illustrating a method for others to follow. The objective was to identify CASCON factors whose presence history suggests are associated with a specified trend. The inquiry looked for factors that were empirically demonstrated to be favorable to three kinds of situations: First, profile case PRO1 models situations in the Conflict phase (Phase 2) moving *away* from the next phase (Hostilities) and in the direction of Settlement; second, profile case PRO2 models Phase 2 situations moving from the Conflict phase *toward* the Hostilities phase (and thus away from peaceful resolution); and third, profile case PRO3 models Phase 3 war situations moving away from continuing in the Hostilities phase and toward cease-fire and/or conflict resolution. The factors were chosen from the CASCON database on the basis of the way coders scored them. It will be recalled that the CASCON database embodies multiple expert judgments about the dynamic direction in which real-life factors tend to "push" real-life historical cases.

PROFILE CASE PRO1

Profile case PRO1 sought to epitomize a situation in the Conflict phase (Phase 2) that was moving away from the next phase (Hostilities) and in the direction of Settlement. A set of cases was selected whose known history in Phase 2 emphasized these trends. The cases were those in which the Case Detail window showed both subsequent Settlement and whose highest level of intensity had been Conflict (and thus never went to Hostilities).

Using CASCON's Case Filter search method to list all cases meeting the user-specified criteria, five cases were selected and made into a marked case list. They were Aden-South Yemen (ADY), Morocco-Mauritania (MOM), Panama (PAN), South Tyrol (STY), and Trieste (TRI). As a confidence check, one additional user-created case was added (Iraq-US/Coalition/Kuwait whose Phase 2 was August 2, 1990–January 17, 1991).

All the Phase 2 factor codings of "Away" in those cases were tabulated. In addition, the CASCON comparison weightings were altered to assign values as follows: 1 for Little Away (A1), 2 for Some Away (A2), and 3 for Much Away (A3). The Away codings that appeared in at least two cases were tabulated except where a factor in one case was coded Much Away (A3), which was counted as having appeared twice.

The list produced 54 factors, of which 24 scored 5 or better and were thus deemed significant. The factors were sorted, and the result was the rank-ordered list of the 24 highest scoring factors shown in Table 9-2. This list is significant in three ways: First, it presents a data-based conclusion as to highly important elements in conflict cases whose presence gives promise of moving away from fighting and toward settlement. Related is the possibility of inferring from these salient factors conflict-minimizing policies and strategies. Third, it serves as a special Profile case adjoined to the CASCON database with which users can test their User Case with CASCON's Compare capability.

PROFILE CASE PRO2

Profile case PRO2 goes in the opposite direction. The goal is a selected listing of factors that a significant number of coders rated as moving "their" case toward the Hostilities phase and away from peaceful resolution. A new marked case list was created of cases in Phase 2 that went on to Hostilities, in retrospect were serious small wars, and were at least arguably preventable.

Table 9-2.
Profile Case PRO1: Phase 2 Factors Associated with Settlement

2R-02	One side agrees to participate in negotiation.
2P-02	The "status-quo" side believes it can win through political means.
2C-01	Sides have open and accessible means of communication.
2X-05	A third party in a position to influence both sides attempts to restrain one side.
2P-27	The "status quo" side is concerned over world opinion.
2R-08	Representatives of each side agree to arrange a meeting of leaders.
2R-01	Direct negotiations take place between the sides.
2D-08	The "status quo" side has military superiority in the disputed area.
2M-01	The military balance is sharply in favor of the "status quo" side.
2P-36	Opposition parties in the "status quo" side urge concession to the "non-status quo" side's demands.
2R-07	The leaders of one side approach the other side's leader for a *modus vivendi.*
2U-05	The regional organization takes action.
2U-04	One side and the allies of the other are parties to international agreements that prohibit intervention in the affairs of the other side.
2P-01	The "non-status quo" side believes it can win through political means.
2M-03	The military technology of one side is significantly superior to that of the other.
2D-22	Strategic concerns require avoiding events in the disputed area that would disturb great power relationships.
2D-13	The "status quo" side reinforces its garrison in the disputed area.
2G-05	The United States urges direct talks to settle the dispute.
2E-07	The area of conflict is adjacent to or contains an important ground or sea trade route.
2D-01	The "status quo" side is in unchallenged control of the disputed area.
2G-07	Other superpower(s) are impartial at this stage.
2E-09	The "non-status quo" side is dependent on external economic aid.
2D-31	The proximity of one side to the disputed area and its greater power give it great influence.
2D-36	Accurate information is available to the sides in the disputed area.

Out of 63 cases that went to Hostilities, 6 were chosen as meeting the other criteria (as well as being representative of different regions and types). They were Afghanistan (AFG), Iran-Iraq (IRI), El Salvador (ELS), Nigeria (NIG), Falklands/Malvinas (FAM), and Kashmir (KAS). Factor coding summaries were examined for each case, and the factors were tabulated in terms of Toward codings, weighted as above. The result was a somewhat longer rank-ordered list of 73 factors shown in Table 9-3.

PROFILE CASE PRO3

Profile case PRO3 represents a conflict situation in Phase 3 that moves away from the continuation in the Hostilities phase and toward cease-fire or conflict resolution. A new Case Filter was created to select cases that went to Phase 3 (Hostilities) and whose history indicated that they quickly were settled thereafter.

Table 9-3.
Profile Case PRO2: Phase 2 Factors Tending toward Hostilities

2P-05	One side's policy increases in militancy.
2P-34	The "non-status quo" side calculates that its action will be successful.
2R-21	Public opinion in one side is aroused by action of the other side.
2R-20	The "non-status quo" side believes the other side will never yield to its demands.
2D-07	The "non-status quo" side's strategic interest in the disputed area increases.
2R-17	Police or military measures taken by one side increase the momentum for change.
2R-16	One side fails to influence the other by nonmilitary means.
2P-26	One side fears that if planned action is reversed those involved will proceed without restraint.
2R-19	The "status quo" side takes strong measures against the "non-status quo" side and its supporters.
2P-17	Public opinion hardens against the other side.
2P-14	One side fears that yielding to the other side's demands will lead others to make similar demands.
2P-12	One side believes prompt action is needed to forestall more extreme action.
2P-08	One side hardens its position and will negotiate only if its claim is accepted.
2R-09	A deep ideological split develops between the sides.
2P-04	The leaders of one side believe that limited violence will give weight and urgency to diplomatic efforts.
2M-08	One side has limited control over its military forces.
2P-33	The "status quo" side calculates that its action will be successful.
2D-34	Incidents in disputed area increase in seriousness and number.
2D-11	One side sends troops to the disputed area.
2D-10	One side increases its capability to deploy military forces in the disputed area.
2D-29	One side uses its military presence in the disputed area to pursue long-held ideological, political, economic, and strategic goals.
2N-01	The religions of the sides differ.
2P-16	The domestic political situation of one side heightens public attention to the conflict.
2D-28	One side follows a policy of repression against political groups in the disputed area.
2D-13	The "status quo" side reinforces its garrison in the disputed area.
2P-24	The "non-status quo" side develops a strategy that was successful elsewhere.
2P-32	Members of one side are agitated by political developments in other areas of the region.
2P-07	One side shifts from downgrading the dispute to exaggerating it.
2P-09	Opposition parties in one side urge firmer policy toward the other side.
2D-09	The "non-status quo" side has military superiority in the disputed area.
2D-14	There is a weak countervailing military force near the disputed area.
2R-18	Time decreases in which an opportunity can be exploited.
2D-12	Both sides strengthen their military forces in the disputed area.
2R-14	One side charges the other with fomenting revolt within its territory.
2D-30	One side engages in fomenting and encouraging rebellious groups in the area.
2X-10	The success of similar groups elsewhere offers a model for the "non-status quo" side.
2M-04	One side's military strength is growing.
2P-03	Neither side believes it can win through political means.
2M-03	The military technology of one side is significantly superior to the other.
2P-23	Individuals with a personal stake in the status quo are involved in inflammatory incidents.
2P-21	The "non-status quo" side has the experience and capacity to carry on hostilities.
2M-06	One side seeks foreign military aid to redress the military balance in the area.
2P-10	The opposition parties in one side want to achieve their ends more rapidly.
2N-05	One ethnic group has more political/economic power than another.

2D-03	The economic value to both sides of the disputed area increases.
2G-01	One side discounts the threat of intervention by the other side's ally.
2P-11	The opposition parties in one side urge use of force to achieve their goals.
2G-14	The United States is impartial at this stage.
2M-01	The military balance favors the "status quo" side.
2R-13	One side accuses the other of using allies to subvert government.
2D-16	One or both sides establish military posts in territory claimed by the other.
2P-31	One side obtains a proxy force to carry out its policy.
2P-25	The "status quo" side adopts a strategy that was successful elsewhere.
2N-12	There is a sudden influx of population into the area.
2N-10	There is a substantial flow of refugees.
2N-02	One side sees its ethnic troubles as inspired by the other side.
2N-06	Clashes increase between one side and a dissident ethnic group.
2R-06	The sides do not share a common heritage.
2D-25	In the disputed area, popular sentiment overwhelmingly favors change.
2U-03	The United Nations fails to take action.
2D-15	One or both sides build border posts in territory claimed by the other.
2D-18	Both sides to the dispute reinforce their border garrisons.
2E-05	The area contains internationally significant strategic resources.
2E-07	The area of conflict is adjacent to or contains an important ground or sea trade route.
2N-09	Many on one side are linked ethnically with a neighboring group that achieved the same goal.
2E-13	The "non-status quo" side has been experiencing depressed economic conditions.
2E-01	The economic policy of one side is exploitative.
2P-06	Government policy vis-à-vis the other side encounters political opposition.
2D-31	The proximity of one side to the disputed area and its greater power give it great influence.
2X-01	Splits within one side are exacerbated by nearby ideological struggles.
2C-03	Normal diplomatic channels between the two sides are disrupted.
2P-29	Aid to one side portends its use as a base for political action in the region.
2X-07	A third party in a position to influence both sides makes no attempt to restrain one side.

Three database cases met the most stringent interpretation of the criteria — Cuba (BOP), Grenada (GRE), and Indonesia-Malaysia (IMC). Three additional Phase 3 cases also, according to their histories, went relatively promptly to Settlement, via (briefly) Phase 4 or Phase 5. These were Algeria (ALG), Bangladesh (BAN), and Congo Katanga (CON).

By using the Summary of Factors Comparison and choosing Phase 3, factors coded "Away" were tabulated for the 6 cases and factors were weighted similarly to the PRO1 profile case. Of 66 qualifying factors, 25 scored 5 or better and were thus considered significant. The highest-scoring factors are shown in Table 9-4.

IMPLICATIONS FOR CONFLICT MANAGEMENT

The three Profile cases underscore the presence and influence of conflict-minimizing or conflict-maximizing factors. They can be compared with a new case that requires an educated guess as to its likely predisposition toward or

Table 9-4.
Profile Case PRO3: Phase 3 Factors Associated with Settlement

3G-16	A great power indicates interest in terminating hostilities and negotiating a settlement.
3M-39	New military effectiveness on one side discourages the other side from belief in a military victory.
3G-15	A great power urges one side to avoid provoking a full-scale war.
3M-43	The reasons for initial intervention by one side remain, but the forces committed are inadequate.
3R-13	The sides are negotiating.
3G-08	Arrival of arms in one side raises the prospect of a wider war.
3M-03	The military balance remains heavily in favor of one side.
3M-30	External pressures for terminating develop almost as soon as fighting starts.
3R-08	The "non-status quo" side achieves its primary goals.
3M-29	One side is unable to cut off arms supply to the other side.
3X-03	Use of force by one side alienates potential allies.
3X-09	Countries on whom the "non-status quo" side is dependent are unable or unwilling to give further support.
3P-29	Prolongation of hostilities erodes the resources of one side.
3R-16	The leader of one side announces a cease-fire.
3R-11	The sides and their supporters are willing to negotiate a settlement.
3P-11	The "status quo" side counters violence by arrests and strong reprisals.
3M-20	The "non-status quo" side has few and primitive arms, as well as weak training and organization.
3M-01	The "status quo" side has the military advantage.
3M-06	One side maintains overwhelming military preponderance in the area.
3M-07	One side has very weak military forces.
3M-36	The commander in chief of one side's army advises against more military activity.
3G-04	A superpower fears growth of conflict into a wider war.
3G-13	The great power supporter of the "status quo" side contemplates intervention.
3E-02	The "non-status quo" side faces economic problems as a result of hostilities.
3D-14	Practical geographical limits in the disputed area make extended operations difficult.

away from "escalation." They can also serve as a model for users in developing other profiles or idealized cases to use for their own research and heuristic purposes.

For example, what does our third list say about forces that influence a trend toward settlement of a conflict after some hostilities? The key answers appear to include the role of relevant great powers and other outsiders, the military balance, and the availability of some opportunities for peaceful resolution (better described as "peaceful change") to achieve the "non-status quo" side's objectives and grievances. The development of conflict-minimizing strategies with the help of this analysis is the ultimate challenge to the user of CASCON.

NOTES

[1]For the original CASCON concept, see Lincoln P. Bloomfield and Robert Beattie, "Computers and Policy-Making: The CASCON Experiment," *Journal of Conflict Resolution,* Spring 1971.

[2]Lincoln P. Bloomfield, and Amelia C. Leiss, *Controlling Small Wars* (New York: Alfred A. Knopf, 1969).

[3]Lincoln P. Bloomfield, "Computerizing Conflicts," *Foreign Service Journal,* June 1988.

[4]See, for example, Kenneth E. Boulding, *Conflict and Defense: A General Theory* (New York: Harper and Row, 1962), especially Chapters 12 and 13.

[5]Herbert A. Simon, *The New Science of Management Decision* (New York: Harper and Row, 1960).

[6]Peter G.W. Keen and Michael S. Scott Morton, *Decision Support Systems: An Organizational Perspective* (Reading, Mass.: Addison-Wesley, 1978).

Ten ∞

The CASCON User's Guide

CONTENTS

READ THIS FIRST

It is often tempting to jump into computer software without reading the documentation. With CASCON you will be well served to spend a bit of time reading before starting. Chapters 7 and 9 provide the necessary background to understand the conflict model and methodology implemented in CASCON. The database included with the software has 85 post–World War II conflict cases, selected to constitute a representative sample of regions of the world and types of conflict. The database is protected against modification. If you want to work with your own version of a database case, use the technique explained in this chapter for exporting a database case and bring it back in under a new name.

The version of CASCON packaged with this book runs under the Microsoft Windows™ operating system. You can use standard techniques for re-sizing windows and moving them on the screen. The easiest way to use the software is with a mouse or other pointing device. There are keyboard alternatives for most functions, following the usual Windows conventions, but a mouse helps considerably. Note that CASCON uses both the right and left buttons on the mouse. The right button generally brings up a menu of options appropriate to the place where the mouse cursor is pointing.

Starting a CASCON Session

When you start the CASCON program, you will first see the copyright screen, which also shows the name and organization of the licensee of the software. At the time you install CASCON or run it for the first time, the system will prompt you for the licensee name. Thereafter, that name will be shown on the copyright screen. The copyright screen will automatically disappear after a few seconds. You may also click on it or press a key to hasten its disappearance. After the copyright screen is removed, the Welcome screen appears

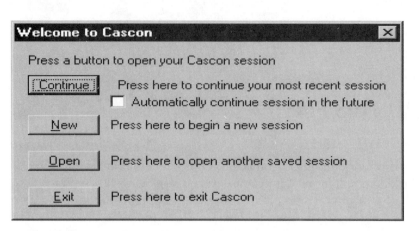

Figure 10.1

with four buttons: three choices for beginning your CASCON session, and Exit to quit without starting a session. (See Figure 10.1.) If you check the box for "automatically continue session in the future," CASCON will automatically continue your session without showing the Welcome screen again. Click on one of the first three buttons to begin your session, or click on Exit to quit:

Continue: Press this button to pick up where you left off last time. Under this item there is a small check box that can be clicked to automatically resume your last session each time you enter CASCON without showing the Welcome box.

New: Press this button to start a new session initially called "Untitled."

Open: Press this button to bring up a list of saved CASCON Session files to select from. CASCON session files have a DOS extension of "CSF" (which stands for CASCON Session File).

Exit: Press this button to quit CASCON.

After you choose, your session will open with a Session window (Figure 10.2). If not already shown, you can enter your name in the space provided. The Session window also has a box for your initials (or any other combination of up to four letters and numbers), which are used to construct file names when a case is exported as described below. You can also indicate your preferred style for presentation of dates (U.S. or European). The small check box marked "Automatically continue session" performs the same function as the similar box on the Welcome screen. This "automatically continue" check box is

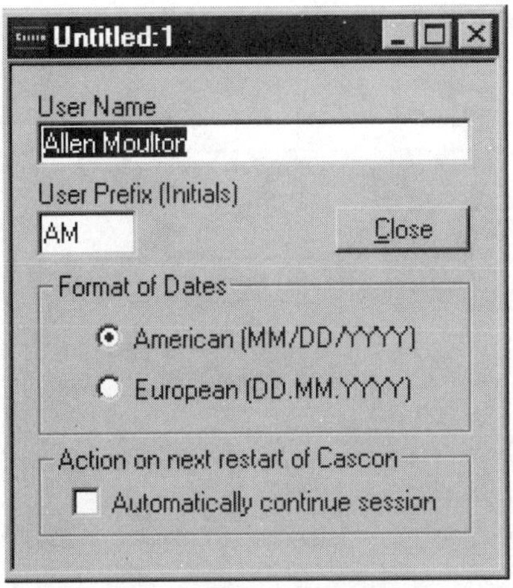

Figure 10.2 Session Window

another way to control whether CASCON will show you the Welcome screen the next time you start the program.

When you start a new session it is called "Untitled." After you enter your name and fill out the rest of the items in the Session window, it is a good idea to give your session a name by saving it to the disk. To save your session, select File and Save As from the menu, or click on the save button on the tool bar. You will be prompted to enter a name for the session file and to choose a directory or folder where the file will be stored. When you reopen a session on restarting CASCON, you will not have to reenter any of the information in the Session window. Your name and preferences, along with any User Cases, lists, filters, and other information, will be reloaded from the session file on the disk. You may wish to keep several CASCON sessions, for example, with different User Cases or filters.

The Session window appears at the beginning of a session. You can close the window by pressing the Close button or using the usual Windows controls in the title bar at the top of the window. To reopen the Session window, select File and Session Preferences from the menu bar.

Behind the Session window you will see the Cases and Factors windows which are explained below (see Figure 10.3). At the top of the CASCON window are a menu and a tool bar with a row of buttons. At the bottom, the status bar shows status or a command explanation on the left and the number of cases and factors on the

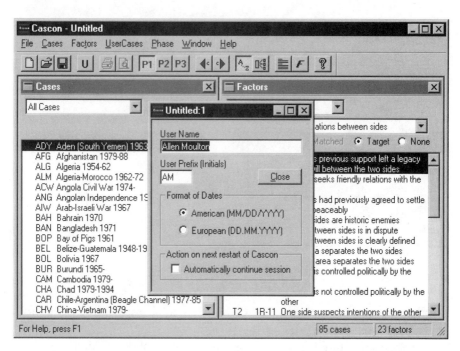

Figure 10.3 Cascon Session Begins

right. When you first start CASCON, take a moment to browse through the menus and tool bar buttons. Note that when you point the mouse at a tool bar button and let it rest for a moment, a small yellow box will appear telling you briefly what that button does. The status line at the bottom also provides a longer explanation of the action for a button or menu item. The menus and tool bar buttons will be described in the discussion that follows. The Windows menu allows you to remove or restore both the tool bar and the status bar from the screen.

When you quit CASCON, you may be asked if you wish to save your work. If your session is still "Untitled," you will be shown a "Save as" screen. Choose a name for your session. A DOS extension of CSF (CASCON Session File) will be added by the system. You will be able to resume your work on that session each time you return to CASCON by automatically continuing your session or choosing "Open" and selecting the name of the session file. To start an entirely different session, click on "New" in the Welcome screen. To start a new session while in CASCON, click on "New" under File on the top menu or the New tool bar button (the leftmost button).

Looking at the Database: Cases

When you start CASCON, the Cases window appears on the left side with an alphabetical list of CASCON's 85 database cases. Next to each case is its three- or four-letter case code (Figure 10.4). Any special Profile cases you have imported or user cases you have added to your session (as described hereafter) will also be included in the list of cases in alphabetical order by the full name of the case. The total number of cases shown in the Cases window appears on the status bar in the lower right-hand corner of your screen. The Cases window can be restored to the screen at any time by clicking on "Cases" and "Names alphabetically" or pressing the "A . . . Z" button.

CASCON stores information by conflict case. You can use the Cases window to control access to that information. One case is highlighted in the window. This case is called the "target case" and is the implicit subject of many other operations. When the number of cases exceeds the space on the screen, the target case may sometimes be scrolled out of view. Nevertheless, the target case remains highlighted. Even when the Cases window is closed, the target case is still remembered.

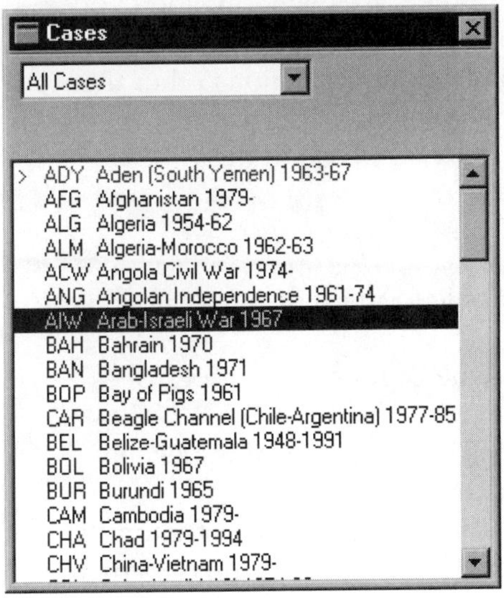

```
┌─ Cases ──────────────────────[X]
│ [All Cases                  ▼]
│
│ > ADY  Aden (South Yemen) 1963-67      ▲
│   AFG  Afghanistan 1979-
│   ALG  Algeria 1954-62
│   ALM  Algeria-Morocco 1962-63
│   ACW  Angola Civil War 1974-
│   ANG  Angolan Independence 1961-74
│   AIW  Arab-Israeli War 1967
│   BAH  Bahrain 1970
│   BAN  Bangladesh 1971
│   BOP  Bay of Pigs 1961
│   CAR  Beagle Channel (Chile-Argentina) 1977-85
│   BEL  Belize-Guatemala 1948-1991
│   BOL  Bolivia 1967
│   BUR  Burundi 1965
│   CAM  Cambodia 1979-
│   CHA  Chad 1979-1994
│   CHV  China-Vietnam 1979-             ▼
```

Figure 10.4 The Cases Window

You can change the case highlighted as the target case by using the arrow keys or by clicking on a case with the mouse. You can also move sequentially through the cases in the window using the sideways green arrow buttons in the tool bar. These buttons move the highlight from one case to the next or previous one even when the Cases window is invisible.

There are four ways to access information in and from the Cases window. First, the header area at the top of the Cases window contains controls for grouping and limiting the cases shown in the window. Second, the menu bar at the top has a "Cases" selection that drops down a menu of actions. Third, the same menu can be popped up by clicking the *right* mouse button while the mouse is in the Cases window. Clicking the right mouse button also changes the highlighted case to the one where the mouse was pointing. Lastly, some frequently used actions are available in the tool bar. To see the meaning of tool bar buttons, move the mouse over any button. A short description of its action will appear in the status bar at the bottom of the screen. Also, if you let the mouse rest on the button for a second or two, a brief explanation box will appear just below the mouse cursor.

LIMITING THE CASE LIST

To limit the case list shown to a particular group of cases, click on the downward scroll arrow at the top of the Cases window and choose "All Cases" or one of the eight other grouping choices listed below. When you choose one of the eight grouping selections other than "All Cases," another box will appear to allow you to select which particular group in that category you wish to see in the Cases window. The choices in the top box are

All Cases: Include all cases.

Grouped by Region: Geographic location in one of six regions of the world.

Grouped by Conflict Type: One of four major types of conflict.

Grouped by Issue Disputed: The fundamental issues that underlie the quarrel, argument, or controversy.

Grouped by Highest Level: The highest degree of intensity reached by the case in terms of the CASCON phase structure.

Grouped by Latest Phase: Indicates whether the case was settled or remains in CASCON phase from 1 to 5.

Grouped by Source of Case: Distinguishes between the list of 85 CASCON historical database cases and the User Cases created by the user or imported.

List of Marked Cases: Cases the user has marked and saved as a named list of cases.

Filtered by Criteria: A set of cases filtered by the user according to user-specified criteria.

The six "Grouped by" options (region, conflict type, issue disputed, highest level, latest phase, and source) refer to the characteristics of each case. The final two options represent especially powerful methods for forming your own case groupings as explained below under Making User Case Groups.

To illustrate restricting the cases appearing in the Cases window, click on "Grouped by Region" and then click on "Africa" in the box just below "Region." The 20 cases from the Africa region will appear. The number of cases being displayed will always appear on the status bar in the lower right-hand corner of the screen. If you have added other African cases, the number will be larger.

CASE DETAILS

To examine the characteristics of an individual case, double-click on the case in the Cases window. The Case Detail window will open, showing the attributes of the case (Figure 10.5). You can also use the menu to open the Case Detail window by clicking on "Descriptive Details" under Cases in the menu bar or in the right mouse button pop-up menu. The case appearing in the Case Detail window will change as you move the target case in the Cases window. Try sliding the Case Detail to the side and watch all the data change (along with the Precis and Factors windows) as you move up and down the case list.

Case code and full name. Each case is assigned a three- or four-letter code for unique identification among the cases in your session. The historical database cases have three-letter codes. When you create your own cases or import cases, you may assign your own case codes. The full name of the case usually combines a descriptive phrase (such as "Middle East War") or the names of the parties ("India-Pakistan") with a range of significant years. When events are ongoing, an initial year is shown with a hyphen and no ending year. The dates used in the case name highlight the major features of the

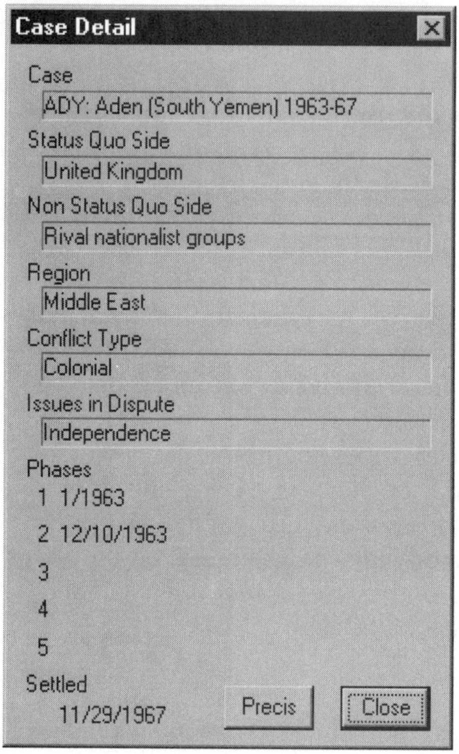

Figure 10.5 Case Detail Window

case and need not correspond precisely with the earliest or latest dates of phases which will be described below.

Sides. Every case is structured into two sides. The Status Quo Side holds the power, territory, or whatever is disputed, and the Non Status Quo Side seeks to alter the situation in its favor. The principal parties to the conflict are listed as sides. Allies and supporters are described in the precis. CASCON uses the generic phrases "Status Quo Side" and "Non Status Quo Side" so that generalized statements (the factors) can be used to compare cases.

Region. Geographic location in one of six regions of the world.

Conflict Type. One of four types of conflict.

Issues in Dispute. The fundamental issue or issues underlying the quarrel, argument, or controversy. Up to three "issues" may be assigned to a case.

Phases: The dates on which each relevant phase started for the case in question, including subsequent recurrences of hostilities and post-hostilities as recorded in the case precis. (CASCON factors cover Phases 1, 2, and 3.) The phases are

Phase 1. Dispute: Quarrel with no military aspects. A quarrel or disputed issue separates the sides, but force is not being considered.

Phase 2. Conflict: Military preparations or deployments but no hostilities. One or both sides are preparing for or threatening military force.

Phase 3. Hostilities: Organized armed conflict. Fighting involving organized armed units.

Phase 4. Post-hostilities with the conflict and the threat of military action continuing.

Phase 5. Post-hostilities with only the dispute continuing.

Settlement: The dispute is ended.

CASE PRECIS

Each CASCON case is accompanied by a short mini-history, called a *precis,* written by an historian and organized by phase. To see the precis for a case, click on the Precis button in the Case Detail window or the Precis button in the tool bar. You can also select "Precis of Case History" from the Cases menu, or the right mouse button pop-up menu in the Cases window. You can change the case for which the precis is shown by changing the target case as described above. To move through the history in the Precis window, use the PgUp and PgDn keys, the scroll bar on the right, or click on a phase number in the header bar. (See Figure 10.6.)

Although the factors coded in CASCON (see Factors) cover only the first three phases (dispute, conflict, hostilities), the precis for a database case describes events in all phases (1 through 5 and, where relevant, Settlement). Similarly, the Case Detail window shows dates for the entire history of the case. Some long-running conflicts have recurring cycles, shown in Precis and Case Detail as, for example, Phase 3–2, meaning the second round of hostilities in that case. Precis and Case Detail also show separately coded but related cases (e.g., PAL, SIN, AIW, MEW) for which precis are all available.

An individual CASCON case does not necessarily cover the entire life cycle of a given conflict. For instance, the 45-year-long Arab-Israeli and India-Pakistani conflicts are not treated as single cases. Rather, they are separated into individual cases (such as the Arab-Israeli War 1967 and the Middle East War 1973, or Kashmir 1947–49 and India-Pakistan 1965–66). This arrangement is used because over an extended

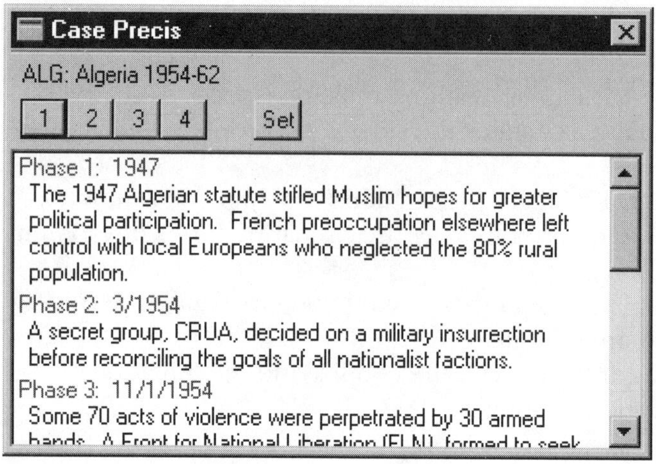

Case Precis

ALG: Algeria 1954-62

| 1 | 2 | 3 | 4 | Set |

Phase 1: 1947
The 1947 Algerian statute stifled Muslim hopes for greater political participation. French preoccupation elsewhere left control with local Europeans who neglected the 80% rural population.
Phase 2: 3/1954
A secret group, CRUA, decided on a military insurrection before reconciling the goals of all nationalist factions.
Phase 3: 11/1/1954
Some 70 acts of violence were perpetrated by 30 armed bands. A Front for National Liberation (FLN) formed to seek

Figure 10.6 Case Precis Window

period with possibly several cycles of violence, the circumstances, actors, and intervenors change greatly. CASCON focuses on the factors that influence the process by which a dispute grows into, or stops short of, warfare. The prior history of the conflict is encapsulated in the factors of each case. By breaking a long-running conflict into separate cases, it is possible to compare the configuration of factors across different locales and time periods with other cases. *CASCON's on-line Help provides a glossary of terms used in the precis.*

Making User Case Groups

You can create your own customized groups of cases in either of two ways. One way is by marking cases in the Cases window and then saving those marks as a case list. The other way is to use a case filter to select cases that match criteria you specify. Both types of customized groups can be used to control the selection of cases shown in the Cases window. They can also be used (as described in the following section) to make additional case and factor filters.

LISTS OF MARKED CASES
This procedure is used when you want to pick some specific cases from the total case list and work with them as a group. You may want to focus attention on a particular group of cases to learn more about

them, perhaps compare them with one another, and look at the factor codings they have in common.

Highlight a case—say, Burundi 1965—and hit the space bar. A mark will appear alongside the case code. The highlight will automatically move to the next case in the window. When a case is already marked, the space bar will remove the mark. You can also use the Cases menu or right mouse button to "toggle" the mark on or off by clicking on "Mark/Unmark Case."

The marks that you set in the Cases window will stay until you turn them off or until you close the session or exit from CASCON. To collect the group of cases you have marked into a list that can be saved for future sessions, use the "Lists of Marked Cases" dialog box to name and save the list (Figure 10.7). Choose Lists of Marked Cases in the menu to bring up the dialog box. The Marked Lists dialog box stays on the screen until you close it. You can continue to perform other operations—even marking cases in the Cases window—while the Marked Lists dialog box is visible.

There are three sections in the Marked Lists dialog box. The top section shows the names of saved lists already created. A special entry for "New list" can be used to create another list. When you click on a list name, the name will appear in the "New name" box directly below the list of names. You can use this box to change the name of the list. When you select "<<New list>>" in the top box, a numbered name is proposed. To change the name, highlight all or part of the name with the mouse, and then type your changes in the "New name" box.

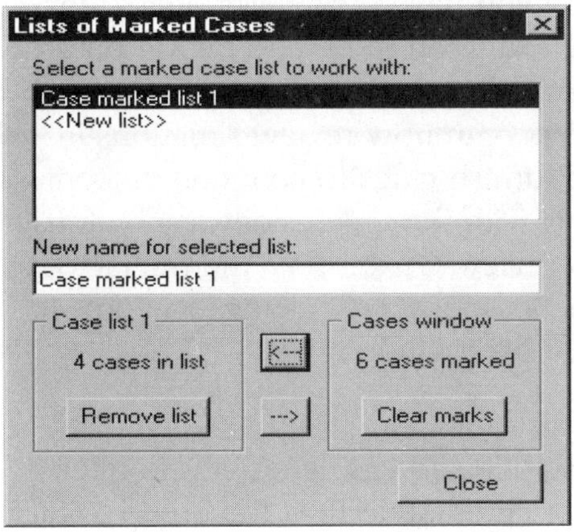

Figure 10.7 Lists of Marked Cases Window

When you select a list from the top section, the number of cases marked will be shown in the Case list section on the lower left. On the lower right is the Cases window section, which shows the number of cases marked in the Cases window. As you mark and unmark cases in the Cases window, the number shown on the lower right will change.

The arrow buttons in between the two lower sections can be used to copy the marks in either direction. To save the marks from the Cases window, press the leftward arrow. The number of cases in the Case list section will then be adjusted to include the new cases you have added to the list. There are also buttons to clear all the marks from the Cases window and to remove a case list. You can restore marks to the Cases window from the Case list by using the rightward arrow. When you restore marks to the Cases window, they are added to the marks already present.

A new list is created as soon as you place marked cases in it. All of your saved lists can be used henceforth until you remove them. You do not have to close the Marked Lists dialog box to have your saved lists available to you. You can bring up the list in the Cases window with "Grouped by Marked List" and by choosing the named list you want to work with. The number of cases in the group will appear in the lower right corner of the screen.

Suppose you want to explore information about certain specific cases in a convenient fashion. One way to do this is to mark those cases in the Cases window, and then create a Marked List as described above. By selecting List of Marked Cases and your new list in the controls at the top of the Cases window, you can restrict the cases in the Cases window to those you have picked out. Read the precis for each of those cases by clicking on the Precis button on the button bar (or "Precis of case history" with the right mouse button or under "Cases" on the top menu). You can now review situations in various relevant phases that might furnish clues to common outcomes. Move through the list of case precis with the green sideways buttons on the tool bar. Similarly, you can review Case Detail and the factor codings of your selected cases. Each window will change as you move through your case list in the Cases window.

CASE FILTER CRITERIA

The second method for making user-created case groups is to filter the overall case list through a set of criteria that limit the group to fit your purposes. A similar factor filter mechanism is described below.

The choice of criteria is under your control. Note that too many or too restrictive criteria in combination can result in few cases, or sometimes no cases, accepted by the filter. Unless you are endeavoring to disprove a hypothesis, such a result may not be helpful.

Filtering for case grouping can be particularly useful in narrowing the case list to a special-purpose group—for example, interstate conflicts in Africa, South Asia, and the Middle East that did not go all the way to hostilities. (This will show seven cases.)

From the Cases menu (or the right mouse button pop-up) click on "Filter criteria." A dialog window will appear with the name of the current filter at the top (see Figure 10.8). The Name box can be used to change the name of the filter or to select a different filter to work on. To change the name, click in the Name box, and type your changes. To select a different filter, press the downward arrow at the end of the box, and select a filter from the list that appears. The filter name and the criteria you previously saved will appear. To begin a new filter, press the "New filter" button next to the name. To remove a filter, press "Clear criteria" and then OK. When you are finished with your changes, press OK to have your changes take effect.

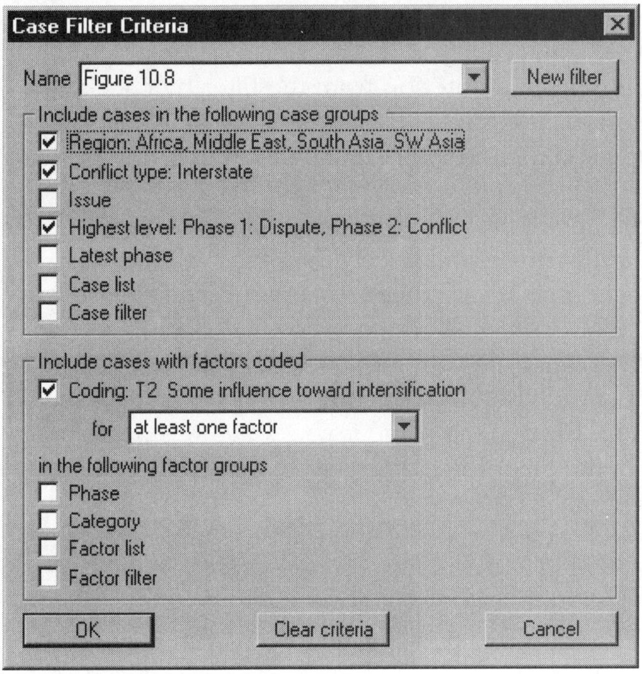

Figure 10.8 Case Filter Criteria

Below the filter name are two sections with criteria you may include in your filter: groups ("Include cases in the following groups") and codings ("Include cases with factors coded").

The case group criteria in the upper section are the same as the choices used for restricting the scope of the Cases window. The first three criteria *(region, conflict type,* and *issue disputed)* are case characteristics which can also be viewed in the Case Detail window. *Highest level* refers to the most intense level of conflict (Phase 1, 2, or 3) appearing among the phases shown in Case Detail and the Precis window. *Latest phase* specifies either settlement or the last phase appearing in Case Detail and the Precis window. *Case list* is used to include cases in a marked list of cases you have saved. *Case filter* lets you use other case filters you have previously prepared. The last two case group criteria remain inactive and grayed out until you save a case list or create a case filter, respectively. In contrast to grouping in the Cases window, a filter allows you to use as many different criteria, and within each criterion as many selections, as you wish. A case must meet all criteria to be accepted by the filter.

To add or remove criteria, click on one of the criteria (say, region) that is not grayed out. You will then see a list of choices for that criterion. Click on each item you wish to include (e.g., Africa, Middle East). Press OK to accept your choices. You may also use the pop-up box to eliminate a criterion from the filter by checking the "ignore this criterion" box below the list of choices. After pressing OK, the items you chose will be shown on the line for that criterion.

To complete the above example, after selecting the three regions, click on "Conflict type" and select "Interstate." Press OK. Click on "Highest level" and select "Phase 1: Dispute" and "Phase 2: Conflict." Press OK. Your criteria should be shown in the top section of the Filter Criteria screen. If they are not correct, click on whichever criterion is incorrect and revise the selections. Note the name of the filter shown at the top. Change the name if you want. When you are satisfied, press OK in the Filter Criteria screen. In the Cases window, select "Filtered by criteria" in the top box and your filter name in the lower box. You should see seven cases in the Cases window. Pull up the Case Detail screen, and step through the cases to see that all meet your criteria.

The coding criteria section titled "Include cases with factors coded" allows you to limit the case search to cases in which certain factors were coded in certain ways (e.g., Phase 1 category R factors coded T1, T2, or T3). Factors and codings are described in the next section. The first thing you must do is restrict the codings in the filter. You can choose any combination of codings. If you select all coding possibilities, any case will pass the filter and the whole section will be effectively eliminated. Once you have restricted the allowable coding, other criteria will light up below.

The next step is to decide whether you want to require "at least one" or "every" factor to match your coding selections. "At least one" means that a case is included if any factor is coded as you want. "Every" is much more restrictive: every single factor must be coded as you specify. Clearly, requiring that every factor have the same coding can easily result in no cases at all. However, if you follow the procedure below to limit the factors considered, and also allow many coding possibilities, you are more likely to find cases that match. For an example of the use of "Every," see Sample run 2 below.

After entering your coding restrictions and selecting "for at least one factor" or "for every factor," use the section labeled "in the following groups" to limit the search to factors of interest. You can use one or more of each of the following kinds of factor groupings:

Phase: The factors for one or more of CASCON's phases. Generally, it is best to choose just a single phase.

Category: The factors in one or more of the 10 categories that organize the factors by subject matter.

Factor list: Specific factors that you have marked and saved as a list.

Factor filter: Factors found by one or more of the factor filters you have prepared.

After pressing OK to save the case filter you have designed, you can bring up the group of matching cases in the Cases window by choosing "Filtered by Criteria" and then selecting the name of your filter. The cases found by the filter will appear in the window, and the number of cases in the group will appear in the lower right corner of the screen.

The preceding example resulted in seven interstate cases in Africa, the Middle East, or South Asia that did not go all the way to hostilities. Suppose you want to further restrict your analysis to cases where military factors were highly influential in Phase 2. Bring up your case filter by selecting "Filter criteria" in the Cases menu (or right mouse button pop-up). Click on "Coding," select T3 and A3, and then press OK. Choose "for at least one factor." Proceed to "Phase," click on "Phase 2," and press OK. Then click on "Category," select "M Military-strategic," and press OK. Check over the criteria, make corrections as needed, and then press OK. If the Cases window is still "Filtered by criteria" and your group, you should see the number of cases drop to three as soon as you press OK. If you have changed the grouping, bring up your filter using the control as previously described. Three cases will remain in the Cases window.

Looking at the Database: Factors

The second major view into the CASCON database is the Factors window (Figure 10.9). Factors are statements describing relevant events, conditions, or facts drawn from actual histories and then generalized for comparability across cases. There are 571 factors covering the first three conflict phases: 176 in Phase 1, 189 in Phase 2, and 206 in Phase 3. Although factor statements do not vary from case

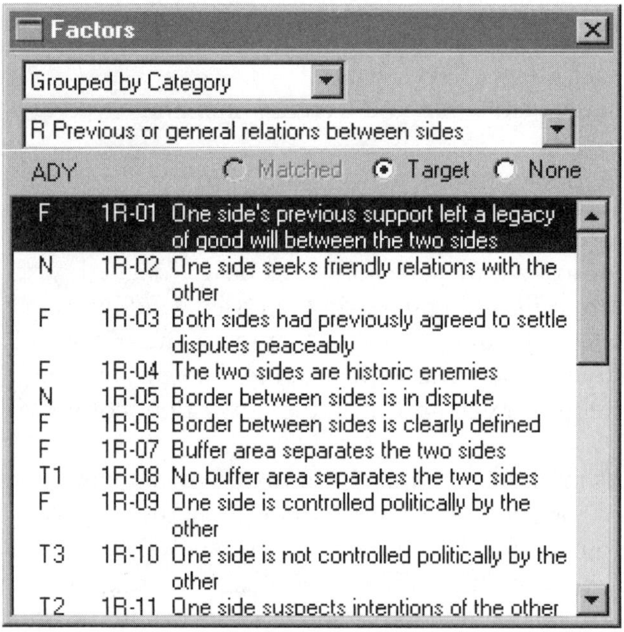

```
┌─ Factors ──────────────────────────────────[X]─┐
│ ┌─────────────────────────────────────┐        │
│ │ Grouped by Category              ▼  │        │
│ └─────────────────────────────────────┘        │
│ ┌─────────────────────────────────────┐        │
│ │ R Previous or general relations between sides ▼ │ │
│ └─────────────────────────────────────┘        │
│  ADY          ○ Matched  ⦿ Target  ○ None      │
│ ┌──────────────────────────────────────────┐   │
│ │ F    1R-01 One side's previous support left a legacy ▲ │
│ │            of good will between the two sides        │
│ │ N    1R-02 One side seeks friendly relations with the │
│ │            other                                     │
│ │ F    1R-03 Both sides had previously agreed to settle │
│ │            disputes peaceably                        │
│ │ F    1R-04 The two sides are historic enemies        │
│ │ N    1R-05 Border between sides is in dispute        │
│ │ F    1R-06 Border between sides is clearly defined   │
│ │ F    1R-07 Buffer area separates the two sides       │
│ │ T1   1R-08 No buffer area separates the two sides    │
│ │ F    1R-09 One side is controlled politically by the │
│ │            other                                     │
│ │ T3   1R-10 One side is not controlled politically by the │
│ │            other                                     │
│ │ T2   1R-11 One side suspects intentions of the other ▼ │
│ └──────────────────────────────────────────┘   │
└─────────────────────────────────────────────────┘
```

Figure 10.9 Factors Window

to case, the relevance and role of each factor in a case are specified by its "coding." In the historical database supplied with CASCON, the factors were coded by diplomatic and academic experts in the history of each case. Because the same generalized statements are used in every case, factors provide a common basis for comparing one case to another.

Factors are organized and numbered by phase and by category. A factor number consists of the phase number, a letter code for the category, and a two-digit number within the category for a phase. Categories classify factors by subject matter. There are 10 categories:

R   Previous or general relations between sides
G   Great power or allied involvement
X   General external relations
U   International organization (UN, regional, legal, public opinion)
N   Ethnic (refugees, minorities)
M   Military-strategic
E   Economic/resources
P   Internal politics of the sides
C   Communication and information
D   Actions in disputed area

Each factor is coded in one of nine possible ways:

T3   Much influence toward use of military force
T2   Some influence toward use of military force
T1   Little influence toward use of military force
N   No influence in either direction but present in the case
A1   Little influence away from use of force
A2   Some influence away from use of force
A3   Much influence away from use of force
F   Factor false or not present in the case
—   No information available about factor

"No information" means that no judgment as to presence or absence of the factor can be made because too little is known to draw a conclusion. When you create a case, all factors are coded "no information" until you enter a definitive coding. A coding of "False" (F) means that the factor statement is inapplicable or contrary to the facts in the case. In other words, the factor is "not present" in the case. The remaining seven codings are for factors that are present in the case. These codings describe a range of effect of the factor in influencing the conflict toward or away from hostilities. The two end points on the scale (T3 and A3) are used for factors critically influential toward or away, respectively, from violence. The midpoint (N) is used for factors that are present in the case but do not influence the course of events in either direction. The remaining codings (T2, T1, A1, and A2) are used to describe lesser gradations of influence in either direction.

The Factors window appears to the right of the Cases window on the screen when CASCON first starts. If you cannot see it, you can make the factors window visible by clicking on the "F" button on the tool bar or by selecting "Windows" and then "Factors" from the main menu. Factors are shown for a single phase at a time. Note that the factors *are not the same* for each of CASCON's three phases. Select the desired phase by using the Phases menu or the P1, P2, or P3 buttons in the tool bar.

To see factor codings for a target case, highlight the case in the Cases window and choose "Factors with target case coding" from the Factors menu. Just as in the Cases window, you can access the Factors menu by clicking on the right mouse button while the mouse is in the Factors window. The three- or four-letter code for the target case will appear in the Factors window above its codings. To see the factor list without case codings, click on "Factor list without codings" from the Factors menu.

When you have set a base case for comparison in the Cases window, you can display factors with matched codings for the base case as well as the target case. Select "Factors with base & target codings" in the Factors menu. You can switch between target codings and matched codings using the radio buttons at the top of the Factors window. When viewing matched codings, the case codes for each case are shown above the respective columns of codings. The base case coding is always the leftmost column. The target case is always adjacent to the factor number.

FACTOR CODING SUMMARY

To see a summary table of case factor codings, select "Summary of codings" from the Cases menu (or right mouse button pop-up). The Summary of Case Factor Codings window (Figure 10.10) shows the number of factors in the current phase coded for each of the nine possibilities described in the previous section. The summary is presented for a single phase. To change the phase, use the "P"

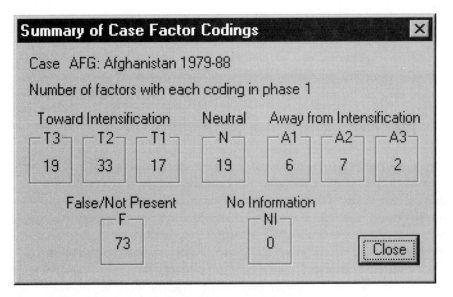

Figure 10.10 Summary of Case Factor Codings Window

buttons on the tool bar or the Phase menu. The numbers will change appropriately as you move through the case list or change the phase. (If case codings are shown in the Factors window, they will also change.)

GROUPING FACTORS

When you start a CASCON session, the Factors window presents factors grouped by category with the first category (R) on the screen. You can re-size the window or move it as you wish. The text for each category will be adjusted to appear within the size you determine. If a group requires more than one screen, a scroll bar will appear on the right. You can also use the scroll bar—or the keyboard up and down arrows and page up and down keys—to move through the factors in the category or other group on the screen. When you reach the top or bottom of a group, the page up and down keys, respectively, will move to the next group of the same type. For example, at the bottom of category R, the page down key will bring up the top of category G. At the top of category R, the page up key moves to the bottom of category D.

As with cases, you can determine the organization of factors presented using the control boxes at the head of the Factors window. Factors are always presented for a single phase at a time. There are five ways to group factors. To see the alternative ways of organizing factors, click on the top control box in the Factors window. The following choices are presented:

Grouped by category
Grouped by case coding
Grouped by matched coding
Lists of marked factors
Filtered by criteria

Grouping factors *by category* organizes factors by subject matter. Case coding and matched coding organize factors by their coding in one or two cases. When grouped *by case coding,* all factors in the phase coded in each of the nine possible ways are grouped together. You can use this grouping, for example, to explore the factors that are most influential on the case. Each group corresponds to one box in the "Summary of Case Factor Codings" window.

Factors grouped *by matched coding* use the combination of base case and target case codings. Although there are 81 possible combinations of codings, nine groups are most useful. The first four groups present factors with similar codings in both cases. The next four groups have factors with dissimilar codings. The last group has all the remaining factors that could not be compared because information was missing in one or both cases. See the section "Matched Coding Analysis" for a description of the matched coding groups.

ORDERING FACTORS
CASCON will present factor groups in a standard order that is generally useful. If you wish to use a different ordering rule, two choices are provided in the Factors menu (or right mouse button pop-up). The first order is by factor number, which means by phase, category, and number within category; the second is by coding value or combined codings. When a single target coding is shown in the Factors window, ordering by coding value uses the target coding. When matched codings appear, a combined value first by base coding and then in reverse by target coding is used.

GROUP CODING PATTERN
When you want to explore the pattern of codings for factors among a group of cases, you can select "Group coding pattern" from the Factors menu. The Group Coding Pattern window (Figure 10.11)

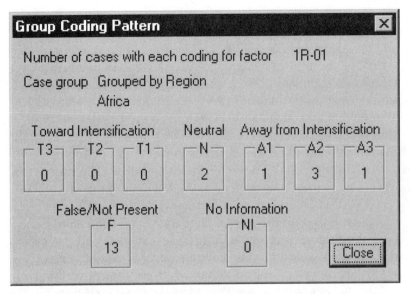

Figure 10.11 Group Coding Pattern Window

counts the number of cases in the current case group in the Cases window that are coded in each of the nine possibilities. By stepping through factors, you can see how the pattern of codings changes for the cases displayed in the Cases window. This can be a very useful tool for research on conflict.

Making User Factor Groups

You can create customized factor groups in the same fashion as case groups explained above. One way is to mark factors in the Factors window and then save those marks as a factor list; the other way is to construct a filter to select factors based on criteria you specify. Both customized types of groups can be used to control the selection of factors shown in the Factors window and can be used as criteria for case and factor filters.

LISTS OF MARKED FACTORS

Choose a phase, highlight a factor, and hit the space bar. A mark will appear alongside the factor. Move the cursor to other factors, and hit the space bar. Moving the space bar in sequence marks each factor encountered. Click the right button, and select Lists of Marked Factors. A box will appear called Lists of Marked Factors. For a new list, select "<<New list>>", and in the "New name for selected list" window, either accept "Factor marked list 1" or type in a more meaningful name. In the lower right under the Factors window, the number of factors you have marked will appear. Return to the Factors window by clicking on it. Use the space bar to mark or unmark some factors. Note how the number of factors changes in the "Lists" dialog box.

To save your list, click on the left-pointing arrow. The number of factors you have marked will appear in the left side of the box under "Factor list 1." You can add marked factors while the Lists box is open, and the number on the right will change. You can clear all the marks from the Factors window with the "Clear marks" button, but the marks you have saved in a list will remain until you eliminate them with the Remove list button. *When you press the left-pointing arrow button, the new list has been saved and can be used henceforth until you remove it.* You can bring up your list in the Factors window by selecting Lists of Marked Factors and choosing the named list you want to work with in the window header. The number of factors in the group will appear in the lower right corner of the screen.

FACTOR FILTER CRITERIA

The second method for making user-created factor groups is to filter the overall factor list through a set of criteria that limits the group to fit your purposes. Specifying the criteria for filtering factors is similar to selecting criteria for cases described above. Although the screens look almost identical, the action is different. Case criteria use factors to select cases, whereas factor criteria use cases to select factors.

The choice of filter criteria is optional. Too many criteria can result in too short a group of factors—or none at all. Filtering factors can be particularly useful in, for example, finding the factors of an internal political nature in a group of cases that were coded as tending toward "escalation." That short list of factors can then be examined to see which, if any, were particularly salient and suggestive of a pattern of causality.

Click the right mouse button in the Factors window and then "Filter Criteria." A dialog box will appear (see Figure 10.12). Either accept the numbered name ("Factor filter criteria set 1"), or give it a more meaningful name. To select a different filter, follow the procedure described on page 165.

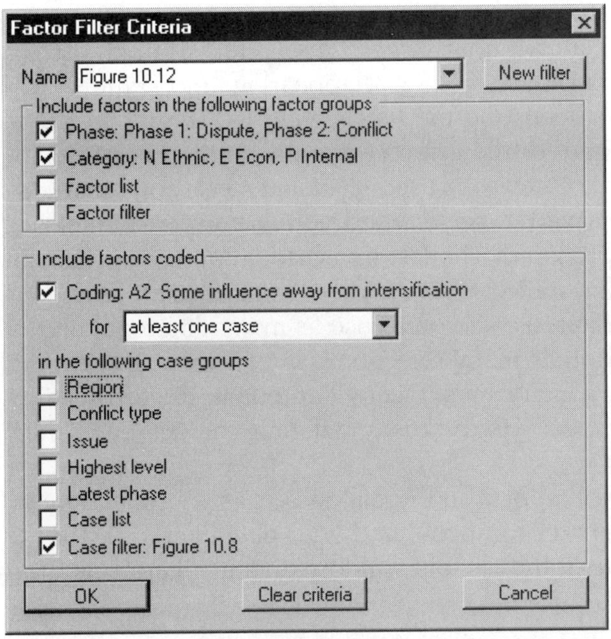

Factor Filter Criteria ✕

Name │Figure 10.12   ▼│   │New filter│

┌─ Include factors in the following factor groups ─
☑ Phase: Phase 1: Dispute, Phase 2: Conflict
☑ Category: N Ethnic, E Econ, P Internal
☐ Factor list
☐ Factor filter

┌─ Include factors coded ─
☑ Coding: A2 Some influence away from intensification

    for │at least one case   ▼│

in the following case groups
☐ Region
☐ Conflict type
☐ Issue
☐ Highest level
☐ Latest phase
☐ Case list
☑ Case filter: Figure 10.8

│   OK   │   │ Clear criteria │   │ Cancel │

Figure 10.12 Factor Filter Criteria Window

Of four criteria in the top section, set the desired phase. Then optionally choose one or several factor categories, and any previously created factor lists or factor filters you wish.

Under "Include factors coded," choose one or more codings; then decide whether to limit the result to factors which in at least one case or in every case were coded in that way. It is unlikely that you can come up with a set of factors coded the same way in every case, unless you are exploring a very short list of cases. Generally, it is best to choose "for at least one case," and then use CASCON's easy method for "eyeballing" comparative factor codings by scanning the Factors windows.

Choose optionally to further limit the search to factors in cases meeting any of seven further criteria: When you have selected the codings to include, the lower section of the screen will light up. You may then use the lower criteria to limit the cases examined in searching for factors coded in the way you have just specified. You may use any of the case group criteria that appear in the upper section of the case filter screen described on page 166. These case group criteria are also the same as the choices used for restricting the scope of the Cases window. The first three criteria *(region, conflict type*, and *issue disputed*) are case characteristics which can also be viewed in the Case Detail window. *Highest level* refers to the most intense level of conflict (Phase 1, 2, or 3) appearing among the phases shown in Case Detail and the Precis window. *Latest phase* specifies either settlement or the last phase appearing in Case Detail and the Precis window. *Case list* is used to include cases in a marked list of cases you have saved. *Case filter* lets you use any case filters you have previously prepared. The last two case group criteria remain inactive and grayed out until you save a case list or create a case filter, respectively. A filter allows you to use as many different criteria, and within each criterion as many selections, as you wish. To be accepted by the filter, a factor must meet all criteria in the top section and be coded as you specify in the cases matching the criteria in the lower section.

Your selections will appear in the dialog box as you make them. Press OK (or Clear criteria or Cancel), and your new filtered factor group will be available in the Factors window under "Filtered by Criteria."

Comparing Cases

COMPARING TWO CASES

A fundamental part of conflict analysis is comparing cases to determine similarities and differences. The CASCON model structures analysis by dividing the history of each case into phases: Phase 1 when a dispute exists between the parties without the threat of military action, Phase 2 when one or both parties are considering the use of force, and Phase 3 when hostilities are taking place. The parties to the conflict are also structured into two sides: the Status Quo side, which wishes to preserve the preexisting situation, and the Non-Status Quo side, which wishes to cause change. Chapter 9 explains the phases and sides at greater length.

Factors are generalized statements about the specifics of the case. Every factor has been drawn from research concerning the significant influences on cases in the past, but restated using generalized terminology that permits comparison across cases in different places and times. For example, instead of mentioning the name of a specific country, terms like "status quo side" or "regional power" are used. Factors in each phase depict the configuration of facts, events, actions, and circumstances present (or absent) in the case during a given phase. Factors present in the case are also coded to show the degree of influence toward or away from violence in the opinion of expert coders.

In CASCON, comparing *two* cases involves lining up the factors in a given phase and looking for patterns of similarity or differences in the codings. The simplest way to do this is to put the codings side by side in the Factors window (see Figure 10.13). To see the codings for two cases, do the following.

Select a case as the subject for comparison. Highlight that case in the Cases window using the mouse or arrow keys. From the Cases menu, select "Set base case." This case will be the base case for comparison until you change it. You may also set the base case using the Compare button on the tool bar. The base case is also saved when you save your session so that you can continue your analysis over several sessions.

In the Factors window, select "Factors with base & target coding" from the menu (or the right mouse button menu). The Factors window will now show two columns of codings for each factor. If you do this immediately after setting the base, the two columns should be identical, since the same case is both base and target at that moment.

Change the target case by moving the highlight in the Cases window or using the green sideways arrows on the tool bar. The left column of codings for the base case will stay the same. The right column will change to the new target case. At the same time, the case codes shown at the tops of the columns will change.

You can now move through the factors and phases, looking at the match-up of factors between the base case and whichever case is currently the target. Alternatively, you can keep the same factors on the screen and move through cases using the green sideways arrows. The base case will stay the same, with the target case column changing each time.

MATCHED CODING ANALYSIS

To see a summary of the coding similarities and differences for a pair of cases, make one case the base and the other the target, and then select "Factor comparison summary" from the Cases menu. The box that appears shows the number of factors in the current phase grouped in nine combinations (see Figure 10.13).

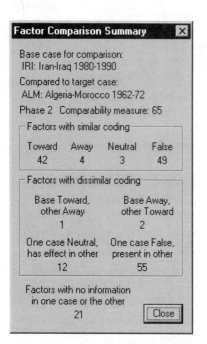

Figure 10.13 Factor Comparison Summary Window

Factors with Similar Coding
Toward in both cases
Away in both cases
Neutral in both cases
False in both cases

Factors with Dissimilar Coding
Base toward, other away
Base away, other toward
One case neutral, has effect in other
One case false, present in other

Coding Cannot Be Matched
Factors with no information in one case or the other

To see the factors grouped in the same way as the summary counts them, select "Grouped by matched coding" in the top control box in the Factors window. Each of the nine groups just described will be available as a selection in the lower box.

Example. Select a case, say, "IRI: Iran-Iraq 1980–90," by highlighting it. Choose a Phase, say "P2," with the button at the top. From the Cases menu, click on "Set base case." A side arrow will appear alongside the case code. The Phase 2 codings for IRI will appear in the Factors window. Move the highlight to "ALM: Algeria-Morocco 1962–63." Click on the "Matched" button in the Factors window header (or select "Factors with base & target codings" from the Factors menu). ALM Phase 2 codings will appear in the second column alongside those of IRI. The codings in the Factors window are grouped and displayed as controlled by the top box inside the Factors window. You can see comparative codings in all 10 categories by using PgUp and PgDn keys.

You can also organize the factors according to the way they were coded. One way is according to "Case Coding," which groups factors according to the nine possibilities of coding (much toward, some toward, little away, no information, etc.). The other way is according to "Matched Coding," which groups factors by the combination of the pair of codings for the base comparison case and the current target highlighted case (see Figure 10.14). For example, you can break out the factors that were coded "Away in both cases," or were coded "Away in base, toward in the other." The comparison between the two cases can also be seen in summary form using the Factor Comparison Summary window described above.

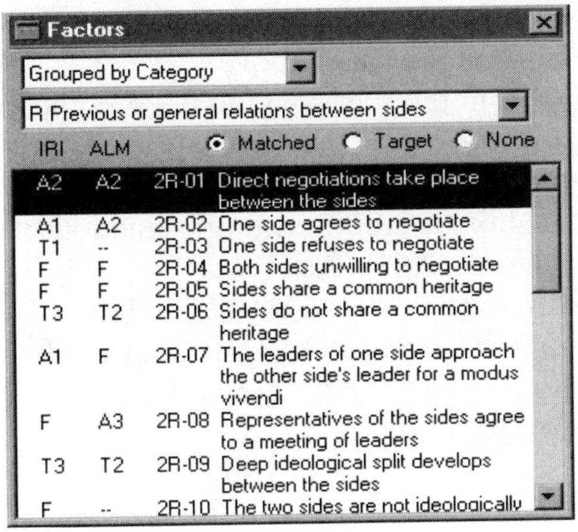

Figure 10.14 Factors with matched codings

COMPARING A CASE TO SEVERAL OTHERS

One of CASCON's major functions is to help you find the cases most similar or most dissimilar to your case in a given phase. To assist you in doing this, CASCON calculates a weighted "comparability measure" that summarizes similarities in factor codings from the point of view of the base case, based on weightings you can control. The comparability measure is not on an absolute scale, but is intended to sort cases in rough order of similarity to the base case. Frequently, the best use of the measure is to identify the half-dozen or so most comparable and most dissimilar cases from the list of cases in which you have an interest.

The comparability measure runs from 100 (meaning an exact match to the base case) down to zero (meaning nothing in common). Factors marked "no information" in either case are ignored in the calculation. For all other factors, a total weighted "distance" is computed. The results are then scaled in a 1- to 100-point range based on the codings of the base case. Since different cases may have different missing factors coded "no information," the measure is not precisely reflexive. For example, the Phase 2 comparability measure for PAL based on CON is 70, but for CON based on PAL it is 69. The more missing factors there are, the more likely the measures will differ somewhat when roles are reversed.

Select Phase 1, 2, or 3 for your comparison using the Phase menu or the P1, P2, P3 buttons on the tool bar. You can change the phase at any time by pressing a different Phase button.

Select the case you wish to make the "base case," that is, the subject of comparison, by highlighting a case in the Cases window. Use any of the techniques described under Cases above.

Ask for a comparison bar graph in the Cases window. Press the Compare button on the tool bar or select "Compare to other cases" in the Cases pull-down or pop-up menus.

The Cases window will now show a graphical representation of the comparability measure (see Figure 10.15). Cases will appear in descending order by comparability measure, which will be shown on the left of the case code. Your base case has "comparability" of 100 with itself. A case that exactly matches the base case for all common factors will also have comparability of 100. Other cases will be arrayed below the base case with the most comparable at the top. At the bottom of the list may be some cases with dashes instead of a comparability measure. These cases have no common

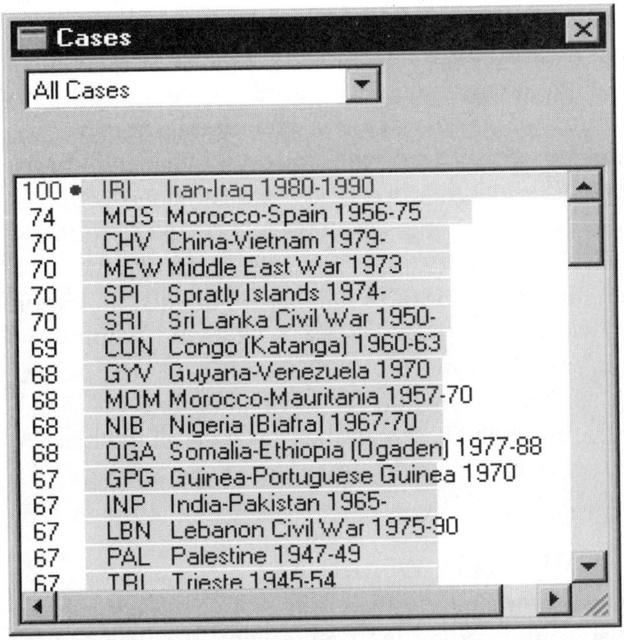

Figure 10.15 Comparison Graph

factors for comparison, usually because they lack the comparison phase.

If you want to restore the case list to alphabetical order, select "Names alphabetical" from the Cases menu or press the "A . . . Z" button on the tool bar. To show the graph again, select "Graph of comparison" from the Cases menu. You can also change the base case at any time by highlighting a case and selecting "Set as base case" from the Cases menu.

LIMITING CASES COMPARED

If you want to limit the group of cases to be compared to your base case, use the Cases window's grouping mechanisms described above. For example, to see comparisons to the Middle East cases, select "Grouped by region" and "Middle East" in the control boxes at the top of the Cases window. When you look at the graph, only the Middle East cases will be shown. Note that the base case does not need to be in the group shown.

LIMITING FACTORS USED IN COMPARISON

CASCON's comparison measure uses all factors in a phase that are coded in the base case and a case being compared. In other words, any factor coded "No information" in *either* case is excluded from the comparison. To limit factors considered, you must remove factors from the base case. The Profile cases described below are designed with only significant factors coded. Only those factors will be used when you compare a Profile case to other cases. You cannot change the coding of a case in the historical CASCON database, but you can export a case and import it back under a different case code (see "Exporting Cases" and "Importing Cases" below). You can then re-code the factors you wish to eliminate as "No information" (see "Creating and Revising User Cases" below). The modified case can then be used as the base case for comparison with only the factors you want to consider.

USING DIFFERENT COMPARISON WEIGHTINGS

CASCON compares cases by matching the coding of each factor in a phase for the base case to the coding in another case. If either coding is "No information," the factor is ignored. If both codings are the same, CASCON uses a zero weight. For all other combinations, CASCON uses a weighting table that you can change to suit your needs. The weighting table can differentiate factor codings either by effect or by whether present. Initially, the table will be based on weighting the toward/away effect (see the accompanying table).

STANDARD WEIGHTING TABLE BASED ON TOWARD/AWAY EFFECT

	T3	T2	T1	N	A1	A2	A3
Factor present in both cases	3	2	1	0	−1	−2	−3
Factor present in one case, not present in other	6	4	2	1	2	4	6

The top row is used when a factor is coded present in both the base and the compared case. "Present" includes any of the seven codings for Toward (T3, T2, T1), Neutral, or Away (A1, A2, A3), which represent the gradations of effect of a factor that is true in a case in its tendency to move toward intensification. In the first mode, when a factor is present in both cases, the absolute difference between the values in the first row is used as the weighting. For example, if a factor is T2 in the base case and A1 in the other case, a weighting of 3 is used. When either case is coded false for a particular factor, the bottom row in the weighting table is used. The non-false, or present, factor coding is used to select a value. For example, if a factor is coded T3 in the base case, but false in the other case, a weighting of 9 is used. To calculate the comparison measure, weightings for all factors in the phase are summed and then converted to a 0–100 scale, with 100 meaning an exact match to the base case.

You can change the values in the Weighting Table used by the CASCON comparison procedure. Select "Weights for compare" from the Cases menu (pull-down or pop-up). The "Comparison Weighting" box will appear with the two rows of weightings as above. Fill in the values you wish to use, or press one of the two "standard" buttons. Press OK to accept your new weightings. The comparison measure for every case will change to reflect your new weightings.

CASCON provides a second "standard" table for weighting factors based on their presence or absence. The left button sets the weightings to the "toward/away effect" table shown above. The right button sets the weightings to the "present/false" weightings shown below. Using "present/false" eliminates the distinction between different codings for present factors. Using the accompanying weighting table, you can explore similarities among cases based purely on the configuration of factors present.

STANDARD WEIGHTING TABLE BASED ON PRESENT/FALSE ONLY

	T3	T2	T1	N	A1	A2	A3
Factor present in both cases	0	0	0	0	0	0	0
Factor present in one case, not present in other	1	1	1	1	1	1	1

COMPARISON EXAMPLE 1

Try comparing IRI with all database cases in Phase 1. Note that the "closest" comparison is with CHV (China-Vietnam, 1979) followed by OGA and MOS. Check out the precis of those cases by clicking on the

Precis button on the tool bar (or with the right mouse button on "Precis of case history"). Size the window as appropriate, and then move the highlight down the list of cases, and the precis will change to each.

Look at the Phase 2 comparison by clicking on the P2 button. Note that in that phase the "closest" are MOS, CHV, MEW, SPI, and SRI. Some of the "closest" cases will obviously not be good cases to compare to, but others will clearly be suggestive. Review the factors that IRI and CHV had in common. Note in particular the factors coded as toward and away in both cases. Consider what conflict-control policies might be appropriate in similar situations to offset conflict-tending factors and to reinforce conflict-averting factors.

COMPARISON EXAMPLE 2

Try using the compare routine with the Profile cases. For instance, import the PRO1 Profile case (based on rank-ordered P-2 factors associated with settlement). Compare it in Phase 2 with the database cases. Look at the precis of the "closest" cases, and you will find that the top three (PAN, STY and EUS), and six of the first eight, never went beyond Phase 2. This should give you confidence in comparing a new User Case in Phase 2 with PRO1, which as you have just seen compares most closely with cases that did not go to hostilities.

Creating and Revising User Cases

There are two ways to incorporate additional cases into CASCON for use alongside the 85 database cases:
1. use the on-line case entry procedure, and
2. import a case from a file prepared off-line or previously exported from CASCON.

When you have prepared a case that you wish to share with another CASCON user, you can use "Export Case" to write the case to a text file that can be easily transferred electronically.

To access CASCON's user case functions, select "User Cases" from the menu bar to see a pull-down menu of six options. Alternatively, you can perform the same functions from the User Cases dialog box, which can be brought up by clicking on the "U" button on the tool bar. If you are working with more than one case or want to see the file names for imported cases, the dialog box may be more convenient. Both the pull-down menu and the dialog box perform the same functions.

CREATING A USER CASE ON-LINE

The first step in preparing your own case is to determine the basic outline of the case's characteristics and history to date. These details are entered on the "Case Detail & Precis" entry screen (Figure 10.16). To start a new case, choose "New Case" from the User Cases menu or from the User Cases dialog box. Give your new case a code made up of three or four letters and numbers. Use the tab key or the mouse to move to the Name box and fill in a descriptive name for the case. The case code and name will appear in the Cases window when you click on OK. If you want to change any of the details or precis for a case after pressing OK, you can bring the Case Detail & Precis screen back up with "Modify Details" in the User Cases pull-down menu or dialog box.

After entering your case name, enter the Status Quo Side and Non Status Quo Side in the dispute. It is important to clarify the principal parties to the dispute here. CASCON facilitates historical analogy by abstracting and structuring each case according to a

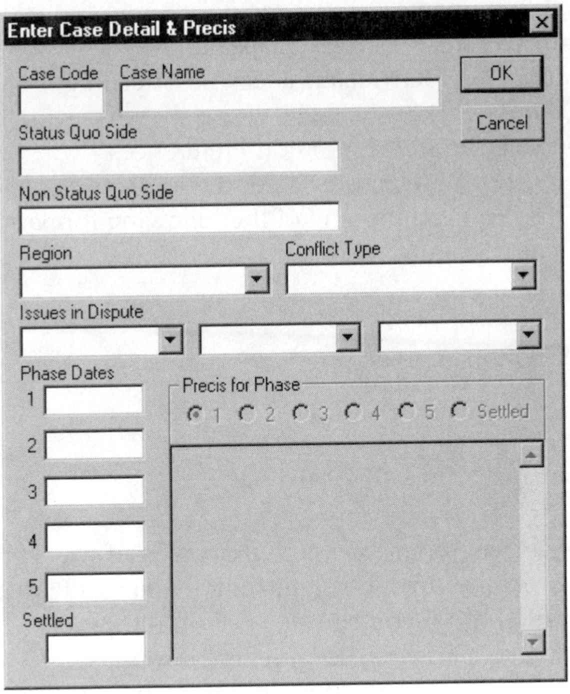

Figure 10.16 Case Detail and Precis Screen

conflict model with two sides—the status quo side which wishes to preserve the preexisting situation, and the non–status quo side which wishes to change matters. If more than one country or organization is joined together on a side, you need to decide which are principals to the dispute and which are allies. The principal parties are entered in the Side boxes. Allies and intervenors are mentioned in the precis for each phase.

Having entered the sides, proceed to select a Region. Use the small button to the right of the box to see a list of choices. When you click on a choice, it will appear in the box. Similarly, select a Conflict Type and up to three Issues. The definitions of these terms are explained in Chapter 9.

The next step is to break down the history of the case to date into phases. Enter the starting date for each phase in the box provided. *You must enter a phase date for CASCON to know that the phase exists.* CASCON will not accept codings for factors for phases without a date. CASCON also determines the Latest Phase and Highest Level from the phase dates. *Enter a date here even if you do not know the exact date when an event happened.*

CASCON can accept a month, year, decade, or even a century as a starting date for a phase. When entering a specific date, you can use either the standard "month/day/year" or the European "day.month.year" convention. CASCON determines your meaning from the punctuation in the date. Dates will always be shown to you using the convention you selected in the "Session Preferences" window (discussed previously). Years abbreviated to two digits are assumed to be in the 1900s. You can use any of the following formats for phase dates:

- ▶ month, day, year (e.g., 12/24/96 or 24.12.96)
- ▶ month and year (e.g., 3/1996 or 3.1996)
- ▶ year (e.g., 1996)
- ▶ decade (e.g., 1990s)
- ▶ century (e.g., 1800s)

The final step in describing your case is to enter a brief precis of its history divided into phases. Include significant events and additional actors in the conflict. Also, you can mention in the precis any connections to other cases. To enter the precis for a phase, click on the phase number radio button above the large box in the lower right-hand corner of the screen. Enter your precis for the phase in the box. A precis is normally a single paragraph per phase. Do not press the enter key, since that will activate the OK button and close the box. Words will automatically wrap at the edge of the box. If your text is longer than the box, continue typing and the box will scroll down. You can edit the text using standard Windows methods, including cut and paste keys and the right mouse button.

To complete your case, press the OK button. Your new case will appear in the Cases window according to the characteristics you have entered. If you wish to revise the precis or any case details after closing the entry window, click on "Modify Details" in the User Cases menu or dialog box.

If your case seems to be missing from the case list, check whether your case belongs in the group selected at the top of the Cases window. For example, if you enter Europe as the region for your case while Africa is selected in the Cases window, your case should not appear. Change the Cases window to "Grouped by source of case" and "User Cases" to see just the cases you have entered or imported. Your case should always appear in this group. If the case seems to be out of order, remember that cases are alphabetized by case name, not case code. For example, a case with code "AAAA" and name "New Case" would be listed under N.

FACTOR CODING ON-LINE

Having entered Case Details and filled in Phase Dates for each phase, you are ready to code your case for the factors that are relevant. When you finish entering a new case and press OK, the Factors window will be brought to the front with blank codings for your new case as the target case. The Coding Tool will also appear on the right side of the screen (Figure 10.17). Use the Coding Tool together with the Factors window to code your case as follows:

Press a Phase button on the button bar that corresponds to the

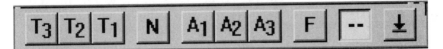

Figure 10.17 Coding Tool

first phase to be coded. *If a Phase button is pressed for a phase which has not been given a date in the user Case Detail, it cannot be coded.*

Make sure the code for your case is shown at the head of the rightmost column of codings in the Factors window. If not, go to the Cases window and highlight your case, then return to the Factors window.

Be sure the Factors window is "Grouped by category," unless you have a preference for a different arrangement.

Select the first factor to be coded by clicking on it.

Use the Coding Tool to code the factor by clicking on the desired coding (e.g., A2). The coding will appear next to the factor, and the highlight will automatically move to the next factor. At the end of a group, the highlight will move to the first factor in the next group.

When you finish a Phase, use the Phase buttons in the tool bar to select another.

The Coding Tool has a button for each of the nine possible codings, plus an extra button that skips to the next uncoded factor in the current phase. The skip button is handy for adding more codings after you have partially completed a case.

The Coding Tool can be hidden or brought up again by clicking on "Coding Tool" under "Window" in the main menu. You can also move the Coding Tool by grabbing an edge with the mouse and dragging it around. It will change shape and either float in the middle of the screen or dock to any edge. When a CASCON database case is active, the Coding Tool will be disabled with the buttons grayed out.

EXPORTING CASES

CASCON can export a case to an ASCII file containing all the case details, precis, and codings. The CASCON historical database is kept internally and cannot be modified. You may, however, export either a database case or a user case to a file. If you would like to bring that case, possibly modified, into CASCON, you should be sure to give it a new "case code." The case code is three or four uppercase letters and numbers that are used to uniquely identify the case.

Highlight a case, and click on User Cases on the top menu and Export Case. The Save As box gives the case a file name constructed from its CASCON case code and your user prefix, and lets you say where it should be saved (normally your CASCON directory or folder). For cases you have previously imported, the file name will be retained from import. Before saving any cases, be sure you have filled in the ID box that came up when CASCON first started. Your three-letter prefix is combined with the case code to make up the name of the file. Press Save to save the file. If you wish to export additional cases, use the Cases window to highlight the case desired, then press the Export Case button again.

IMPORTING CASES
To import a case into CASCON, use the User Cases dialog box or pull-down menu, and press the Import Case button. You will be asked to locate the case file and accept your choice by pressing OK. This is how you bring in the three Profile cases (PRO1, PRO2, and PRO3) as well as the sample user case (SAMP). CASCON will read the file and check it for errors. If errors are found, CASCON will tell you about them. If there are no errors, the case will appear in the Cases window.

PREPARING OR REVISING A CASE FILE OFF-LINE
In addition to entering and revising a case on-line, you may also prepare or revise a case using an ASCII file off-line. A CASCON case file must follow a strict format. When you export a case, it is stored in this format. You may also create a new case in a file following the same rules. The easiest way to prepare a new case off-line is to make a copy of the file called "USERFORM.CAS," which is included with CASCON (see Figure 10.18). This file contains explanations to help you to understand the file format and learn how to prepare your own cases off-line. The user form file should be located where you store your CASCON files. CASCON uses a special symbol ("//") to separate explanatory "comments" from case data.

To work on a case off-line, make a copy of USERFORM.CAS (or an exported case) and open it with NOTEPAD, WORDPAD, or any word processor. Follow the form strictly, filling in or changing information on case code, case name, sides, type, region, issue, phase dates, and precis as indicated. Note that the precis for a phase immediately follows the line with the phase date. Then enter the codings for the factors you wish to code. Be sure to save the file under a different name, such as your initials combined with the case code you have chosen. If you are using a word processor, make sure to save the file as ASCII text (rather than the native format of the word processor program). Give the file a DOS extension of "CAS" so that CASCON can find it easily.

Back in CASCON, under User Cases, click on Import. Select the case you have just worked on and click on Open. The case will

Figure 10.18

```
USERFORM.CAS
//   This file is a sample for entering a CASCON user case offline
//      It provides a sample form and guidance on using the form
//
//   enter a unique four-letter CODE and the name for the case in the line below
>case CODE User Case 1995-

//   enter the status quo side on the line below
-SQS: StatusQuo Side

//   enter the non status quo side on the line below
-NSQ: NonStatusQuo Side

//   enter the region key letter below, using the following choices
//      A Africa
//      E Europe
//      M Middle East
//      P Pacific, East Asia, & SE Asia
//      S South Asia, & SW Asia
//      W Western Hemisphere
-Region: S

//   enter the conflict type key letter below, using the following choices
//      S Interstate
//      I Primarily Internal
//      X Intervention
//      C Colonial
-Type: S

//   enter up to three words for issues in dispute, using the following choices
//      Ethnic
//      Governance
//      Independence
//      Resources
//      Strategic
//      Territory
-Issues: Ethnic Independence

//   For each phase, enter beginning date on the appropriate line, then add
//      a paragraph of text to summarize the history of the case in that phase.
//      Note: the historical precis is optional.
//
//   Phase numbers are Arabic numerals from 1–5,
//      or the letter S (Settlement)
//
//   Dates may be entered in either American format (MM/DD/YYYY)
//      or European format (DD.MM.YYYY)
//
//      the year (YYYY) must be fully specified
//   For dates which are not specified exactly to the day, you
//      may use one of the following forms:
//      MM/YYYY or MM/YYYY—for a month
//      YYYY—for a year
```

continued

```
//     YYY0s—for a decade
//     YY00s—for a century
//
//   If a phase is not present in your case, remove the lines from the file below
//       referring to that phase.
//
-Phase 1: 1800s
Precis for Phase 1

-Phase 2: 1960s
Precis for Phase 2

-Phase 3: 3/26/1971
Precis for Phase 3

-Phase 4: 16.12.1971
Precis for Phase 4

-Phase 5: 1973
Precis for Phase 5

-Phase S: 22.2.1974
Precis for Phase S (Settlement)

//   enter codings for each factor, grouped by phase and category
//   use the following symbols for codings
//       T3 Much toward intensification
//       T2 Some toward intensification
//       T1 Little toward intensification
//       N Present or true in the case, but neutral in effect
//       A1 Little away from intensification
//       A2 Some away from intensification
//       A3 Much away from intensification
//       F False or not present in the case
//       —No information about presence or effect known
//
//   All factors left uncoded will be marked as "no information"
//   Each line below begins with a period, the phase number (1–3),
//   and then the key letter for the factor category, using the following
//       R Previous or general relations between sides
//       G Great power or allied involvement
//       X General external relations
//       M Military-strategic
//       U International organization (UN, legal, public opinion)
//       N Ethnic (refugees, minorities)
//       E Economic/resources
//       P Internal politics of the sides
//       C Communication and information
//       D Actions in disputed area
//
//   If you are coding the first factor of a phase/category, begin entering
//       the codings after leaving at least one space following the category letter.
//       Note that there are no spaces allowed between the period, the phase number,
//       and the category letter.
//
```

continued

```
//   If you want to begin a line with a factor number other than the first,
//      follow the category letter with a hyphen ("-") and a two-digit factor
//      number. No spaces are allowed between the category letter and the
//      hyphen or between the hyphen and the factor number. Following the
//      initial factor number, begin coding as above.
//
//   You may code successive factors in the same phase/category by leaving a space
//      and continuing on the same line. You must begin a new line for another
//      phase or category.
//
//   If a line has no codings, it should be deleted.
-Codings:
.1R A2 A2 A2 T2 F T1 A3 F A2 F T2 T2 N T1 F N T2 T1 F A2 F N F
```

now appear in the case list and will remain there if you save your work. Any cases imported into your CASCON session or created on-line will be saved in your session file on the disk when you exit.

Using Profile Cases

Profile cases are synthetic cases constructed of CASCON factors, which research has shown to be most closely associated historically with either "escalation" or "deescalation." The research technique is explained in Chapter 9. These cases are included with CASCON as case files that can be imported as described above. Profile cases can be helpful in isolating fact patterns that research has shown to be highly significant. The three Profile cases are these:

Profile case number 1—PRO1: consists of the 24 highest-ranked factors in Phase 2 that experts coded as much or some "Away" in a representative sample of cases that never went beyond Phase 2 and were in fact settled.

Profile case number 2—PRO2: consists of the 73 highest-scoring factors in Phase 2 that expert coders judged to have significantly moved the situation toward the Hostilities Phase 3, that is, coded as "Toward."

Profile case number 3—PRO3: consists of the 25 highest-ranked factors in Phase 3—Hostilities—that in the view of experts moved the case toward cease-fires and other forms of conflict resolution, that is, coded as "Away."

To bring one or more of the Profile cases into CASCON to use along with the database and User Cases, click on "User Cases" in the top menu, and then "Import." A dialog box entitled "Open" will appear. In its top window, find the location where you keep CASCON and its associated files.

Click on the Profile case you wish to import into your session, and click the Open button. The case will appear on the alphabetical case list on your screen. The imported case(s) will remain on your case list as long as you save your session file and open the same session when you return to CASCON.

After importing one or more Profile cases, you can use CASCON's "Compare" facilities (described previously) to match the profile against your own case or historical database cases.

Printing

If you wish to print out a copy of some of your work in CASCON, you can use Windows Print Screen or CASCON's Print commands. To use Windows Print Screen, press the Print Screen or Alt-Print Screen key, then paste the image into WORDPAD, NOTEPAD, or any other word processor, and use the Print command in that software to print your results. This technique will work for any image on the screen.

CASCON also can print out the list of cases in the Cases window, the list of factors in the Factors window, and the current case in the Precis window. Use the Print command under File in the main menu or the Print button on the tool bar. You can also preview output using the Print Preview command under File or the Preview button on the tool bar.

To change the print font and the margins on the printed page, use the Page Layout command under File in the main menu. The Page Layout dialog box lets you choose a font and point size. You can also adjust top, bottom, left, and right margins to suit your needs. Note that margins are expressed in inches. Press the OK button to accept your changes.

Some Examples of Analysis with CASCON

Warm-Up: First look over the database—bring up Cases, Precis, Factors, and codings, as well as Case Detail and Summary of Codings, moving and re-sizing or tiling the windows until most are partly visible. Now run down the case list and watch the data change in every window. Then try some sample "runs" through CASCON.

SAMPLE RUN 1: ETHNIC AND MINORITY CONFLICT

Open CASCON. In the Cases window, choose "Group by issue disputed" and select "Ethnic." There will be 25 cases in the window, with the number shown in the lower right corner. Bring up "Precis" with the Precis button on the tool bar (the one with the red and black horizontal lines). Re-size the Precis window to suit. Briefly review the precis of the 25 cases using the sideways arrows on the tool bar. Scroll down to see the Phase 2 for each case. Some cases are not as relevant as others, but note the recurrent theme of growing stress between majority and minority groupings as well as the buildup of threats or actual violence. Go back through the cases looking at Phase 1 to get a sense of some of the roots and sources of subsequent conflict.

Now narrow the list to cases that are internal (both Primarily internal and External intervention) and ethnic, using a case filter. While the mouse is in the Cases window, click the right mouse button to see the pop-up Cases menu. Select "Filter criteria." In the "Case Filter Criteria" dialog box, click on "Conflict type" and select both "Primarily internal" and "External intervention." Press OK in the selection box. Click on "Issue," select "Ethnic," and press OK. Check to see that the criteria displayed are what you have chosen. In the Name box at the top, highlight the whole text, and type "Internal ethnic." Now press OK to save your case filter criteria set. To see your new group, click on the top "group by" box in the header for the Cases window, and select "Filtered by criteria." If your new "Internal ethnic" case group is not already selected, use the lower box in the header to choose it. You will get 11 cases in the Cases window.

A quick scan of the precis suggests that five of the eleven cases seem to be particularly dramatic forms of ethnic conflict. Highlight cases BUR, CYC, IRK, NIB, and SRI and press the space bar on each. A check mark will appear beside each. With the right button, choose "Lists of marked cases." When the dialog box appears, name new list "ethnic internal top 5," and using the left-pointing arrow button, create a marked case list. Close the lists box. Make your marked "ethnic internal top 5" list the current case group by selecting it under "List of Marked Cases" in the Cases window header. The five cases will appear in the case window (and the number 5 in the lower right).

Now look at some of the factors coded in various ways for your list of cases, in both Phase 1 and Phase 2. Click in the Factors window (or bring it to the top with Factors under Windows in the main menu or the "F" button on the tool bar). In the Factors window, choose "Grouped by Category" and then "N Ethnic (refugees, minorities)." Size the window for best use, if necessary. Use the sideways arrows on the tool bar to scan the factor codings for each case in your list, noting some factors coded as T3 or T2 (much or some toward "worsening"). Also note the dearth of "A's" (away from hostilities).

Now you are ready to make a group of relevant factors for your list of five ethnically salient cases. From the Factors menu, select "Filter Criteria." Click on Phase, select "Phase 2: Conflict," and press OK. Click on Category, select ethnic (N) and economic (E), and press OK. Click on "Coding," select all three degrees of Toward (T3, T2, and T1), and press OK. Note that the case criteria light up when you have constrained codings. Select "for every case." Skip region, type, issues, highest level, and last phase. Click in "Case list," select your "ethnic internal top 5" marked list, and then press OK. You have now created "Factor filter criteria set 1."

In the Factors window, choose "Filtered by Criteria," choose "Factor filter criteria set 1," make sure you are in P2, and you should see just one factor which is coded Toward in all five cases:

2N-05 One ethnic group has more political/economic power than another

Now revise the filter to show factors that are coded Toward in one or more of the cases. In the Factors menu, select "Filter criteria" again. If "Factor filter criteria set 1" is not shown, use "Pick" to select it. Below codings, click on "for at least one case" and press OK. Now you will see 27 factors. Make the Case window "active" and move the cursor down the case list, looking at the different codings of the 27 factors in the Factors window. Make your own analysis of the results. The easiest way with a relatively small number of cases or factors is to have both windows open adjacent to one another, with the target case coding showing the Factors window.

Highlight a factor, and move up and down the case list for that factor with the sideways arrows on the tool bar. To reorder the factors by coding within each case, select "Order by coding value" in the Factors menu. You will see the Toward factors at the top and the Away factors near the bottom of the list, followed by factors false or not present in the case. As you shift from case to case, the factors will be reordered so that the Toward factors stay at the top. Use the scroll bar or the arrow and page up and down keys to review the factors for each case. To get a quick picture of the influence of a given factor, select "Group coding pattern" to bring up a box showing how many cases were coded in each way. Step through the factors and see how the pattern changes.

We have found 27 factors pushing some or all of these cases toward hostilities in Phase 2. Now let us look at the countervailing factors pushing away from violence by constructing a similar filter using codings of A3, A2, and A1. Click on "Filter criteria" in the Factors menu to open the Factor Filter Criteria window. Press the "New filter" button. Follow the same procedure to fill in criteria, except select A3, A2, and A1 in Codings, and be sure to select "for at least one case." After pressing OK to save your new "Factor filter criteria set 2," return to the Factors window and use the lower control box in the header to select your new filter. You will see a list of just nine factors working against violence.

Those interested in remedial conflict-prevention measures will recognize that the areas most likely to be involved in ethnic conflict will realistically be restrained in the short run (after all, we are now in Phase 2) by negative constraints such as external dependency (including that imposed by international sanctions) rather than more positive indigenous success. In theory, more positive opportunities might be found in Phase 1, where a dispute exists but is not yet a conflict (i.e., situation perceived in likely military terms). Apply the same techniques to examine factors tending toward and away from violence in Phase 1. You can then endeavor to deduce from the most salient factors some policy measures that should be relevant to offsetting the factors that are coded as "bad," and to reinforce those coded as "good."

SAMPLE RUN 2: COMPARING A USER-CREATED CASE

Make a new User Case for a hypothetical case in the Horn of Africa in which two religious groups are undergoing a worsening low-level insurgency, with the minority group feeling left out of the political process in the national capital and trying to enlist foreign support and import arms for defense (and perhaps offense). "User cases" from the main menu and "Import case." When the file import dialog appears, select "sample.cas" for importing.

Press P2 in the tool bar to see Phase 2. Press the Compare button to compare SAMP in Phase 2 with all cases. Note that despite the global case list, SAMP compares closely with an unusual number of ethnic/minority cases. Prepare a list of the 13 closest cases using the

Lists box to count for you. In the Cases menu, select "Lists of Marked Cases." Move the box so that you can see the Cases window as well. In the Cases window, highlight the case closest to SAMP (i.e., BUR). Press the space bar until the Lists box shows 13 cases marked. Under "New name for selected list," rename your list to "Top 13," and press the left-pointing arrow to make a list of cases. Of the 13 "closest" cases, eight—BUR, SRI, KAS, BAN, LBN, SPB, NIB, and PAL—share those qualities in some measure. Look at the Phase 2 precis of the cases with the top sideways arrow, and observe comparable phenomena.

Do a "Factor comparison summary," moving down the 13 cases, and note the high number of "T" and "A" factors that many of them have in common with SAMP. Return to the Factors window, and press "Matched" to see matched codings. Then "eyeball" the similar codings, using the top sideways arrow buttons. Check the striking persistence of similar T3 and T2 codings for factors 2R-20 and 2P-05, and of "A" codings for 2R-02 and 2P-27. These are important indicators of causality.

Make a Marked list of the eight cases, and Group by that marked list. Bring up the precis, and note that all but one went on to hostilities. Look more closely at the P-2 precis to review things that in retrospect we can see helped "push" that case across the next threshold.

Make a filtered case list, and specify factors coded as "A." Note the factor list that comes up when you change the Factors window to your filter. Look at other CASCON cases in which those factors were similarly coded and see their histories. Use your imagination to infer from "A" and "T" factors some appropriate policy measures aimed at offsetting T factors and reinforcing those coded A.

SAMPLE RUN 3: MIDDLE EAST CASES AND FACTORS
CASCON can help you to explore significant elements of regional and local conflicts, for example, in the conflict-prone Middle East. The user can group cases in various ways and then probe the factors that experts deem significant under a variety of headings. First, look at CASCON's Middle East cases that went to Hostilities (i.e., became shooting wars).

Group cases by Region and Middle East. Eighteen cases will appear (numbers are at the lower right corner of the screen). In the Case Filter Criteria dialog box, select for Case Criteria Set 1 (or whatever you name it) the Middle East under Region and Hostilities under Highest level. When you group by Filtered by Criteria and choose your new case filter, the Cases window should show 12 cases.

Make a more refined search of those Middle East cases that were conflict type Interstate, coded T1, T2, or T3 for Phase 2 factors in the Economic and Ethnic factor categories. Your subsequent cases screen will show seven cases: AIW, IRI, MEW, PAL, SIN, SOI, and SUE.

A more sophisticated search for relevant factors can be made by asking what factors in the four Arab-Israeli wars (AIW, MEW, PAL, SIN) that were coded "Away" were held in common, in the categories of "Great power and allied involvement" and "international organizations," in Phase 2.

In the Factors menu select "Filter criteria" to open the Factor Filter Criteria dialog box. Use the filter criteria set offered at the top, or choose another one. Change the criteria set name if you like. Select Phase 2 and Categories G and U. Select Coding of A1, A2, and A3 for at least one case. The case groups below will then light up. Select Case list, and click on the name that you gave your group of four Arab-Israeli wars above. Press OK to close the criteria box. At the top of the Factors window, select "Filtered by Criteria", and choose your new filter criteria set from the lower box. The status bar in the lower right corner should show 12 factors.

Be sure the Target case coding appears in the Factors window, and scroll through the four-case Marked case list you have created and named. Note that several of the four cases have recurrent "Away" codings, such as 2U-01: "The United Nations urges both sides to negotiate a settlement."

Next, let us look at other cases in the database that have factor 2U-01 coded Away in Phase 2. We will use a case filter to isolate those cases. To do so, we need a factor list with just 2U-01 in it. Make sure 2U-01 is visible in the Factors window. With the right mouse button, choose "Lists of marked factors" to open the dialog box. If the box is covering up the Factors window, move it out of the way by grabbing its title bar with the mouse and dragging it. Look at the lower right-hand section of the box entitled "Factors window." If the number of marks shown is more than zero, clear them by pressing the "Clear marks" button just below. Now that all the marks have been removed, return to the Factors window, click on 2U-01, and press the space bar. A check mark should appear next to the factor number, and the number of marks counted in the dialog box should now be one. Highlight all the text under "New name for selected list," and type in "2U01 only" over what was there. Press the left-pointing arrow just below to record the single mark in the saved factor list. Press "close" to remove the dialog box.

Now we are ready to build our case filter. In the Cases window, click the right mouse button, and select "Filter criteria" from the menu to bring up the case filter dialog box. If the case filter has already been used, use "New filter" to get a new one or press "Clear criteria" to clean out all the old criteria. Click on "Coding," select all the A's (A1, A2, A3), and press OK. Check that all three levels of A appear in the criteria box. From the factor groups that light up below, click on "Factor list," select your "2U01 only" list in the pop-up box, and press OK. Go to the "Name" box, and enter a name for your new case criteria set. Press OK to save the new criteria.

In the grouping box at the top of the Cases window, select "Filtered by Criteria" and then choose your new criteria set from the lower box. The Cases window should now show 23 cases with the number recorded on the status bar in the lower right-hand corner.

To further narrow the focus of analysis, let us examine just those cases out of the 23 just found that went all the way to hostilities (Phase 3). Reopen the criteria dialog box as above. The criteria you entered before should be unchanged. Now click on "Highest level," select "Phase 3—Hostilities," and press OK. Press OK again after visually checking the criteria. CASCON should immediately adjust the Cases window to show the 18 cases meeting the tighter criteria. For these cases, the UN's urging of negotiation did not succeed.

You can now proceed to look for patterns in the other factors influencing these cases. Bring up "Group Coding Pattern" from the Factors menu, and step through the factors with the mouse or arrow keys. With so many factors it may be helpful to narrow the list using a factor filter, perhaps to look for factors coded Away in at least one of the 18 cases. You can refer to the case filter you prepared above to limit cases to just those 18 cases. If you then make further changes to the case filter, CASCON will immediately adjust the dependent factor filter accordingly.

A SELECTIVE ANNOTATED BIBLIOGRAPHY ON CONFLICT

Brian Burgoon

T he bibliography is divided into two parts: sources of conflict and conflict resolution. Each is subdivided according to controversies that structure the literature. Within these categories, the bibliography briefly summarizes some of the most important classic and recent writings. It excludes many important articles and books in the literature, such as works that focus exclusively on great-power conflicts, on international economic rather than political conflicts, or on a particular region.

The bibliography is divided into two general categories: sources of internal and interstate conflict; and conflict resolution. Each is in turn divided into appropriate sub-categories.

SOURCES OF INTERNAL AND INTERSTATE CONFLICT

The Nature of the Balance-of-Power System

Blainey, Geoffrey. *The Causes of War* (New York: Free Press, 1973). In its third edition, the book provides an analysis of international wars since 1700 and critiques various theories on the causes of war. The author argues that the causes of war can best be understood by analyzing the causes of peace. These causes, he states, have remained constant throughout time and are still the same in the nuclear age. Blainey gives pride of place to conflicting or consensual perceptions of relative military capability and prospects for victory.

Bueno de Mesquita, Bruce. "An Expected Utility Theory of International Conflict," *American Political Science Review,* Vol. 74, 1980. *The War Trap* (New Haven, Conn.:

Yale University Press, 1981). "The War Trap Revisited: A Revised Expected Utility Model," *American Political Science Review,* Vol. 79, 1985. This body of work develops a theory of international conflict that focuses on a state's expected utility in entering or avoiding conflict. Treating the state as a rational-utility-maximizing agent, Bueno de Mesquita contends that positive expected utility on the part of leaders is a necessary, though not sufficient, condition for conflict; that is, states will go to war if the expected cost/benefit ratio of doing so is more favorable than the ratio of the status quo. The factors going into expected utility are many, including international power distribution, uncertainty, and the leaders' propensity to take risks. The author's arguments are formal (that is, expressed through mathematical proofs) and tested empirically through quantitative analysis of a large body of cases (including the *Correlates of War* database).

Bull, Hedley. *The Anarchical Society: A Study of Order in World Politics* (New York: Columbia University Press, 1977). Bull's *magnum opus,* this book considers three questions in three corresponding sections: "What is order in world politics? How is order maintained in the contemporary states system? And what alternative paths to world order are desirable and feasible?" He argues that, contrary to conventional wisdom, territorial state sovereignty is not in decline and that such sovereignty does not mean an absence of order but is in fact an important basis of order, through the balance of power, international law, diplomacy, and the threat of war. In part a treatise on international conflict resolution, the book provides a series of arguments for how balance-of-power statecraft and international law can promote peace in an anarchical society of states.

Deutsch, Karl, and J. David Singer. "Multipolar Power Systems and International Stability," *World Politics,* Vol. 16, 1964. Deutsch and Singer develop and test the old idea in classic balance-of-power theory that the stability of the international system increases as the number of actors increases. In their view, the existence of more interaction opportunities lowers tensions, and the involvement of more states lowers the amount of attention and worry associated with any one state. Such an argument conflicts with Waltz's later claim that fewer poles are generally better than many. Using quantitative evidence to investigate this conventional wisdom, Deutsch and Singer find support for the hypothesis.

Gilpin, Robert. *War and Change in World Politics* (Cambridge: Cambridge University Press, 1981). In this book Gilpin develops a theory of war and great-power change in the international system. His theory is one of cyclical hegemonic rise and decline. Hegemons, in his view, always rise to power using their military, technological, and economic advantages. Such states then tend to become decadent and inefficient, and to spend too many resources trying to protect their position at the periphery of the system. In the last stage of the cycle, a challenging state that has been growing in power for autonomous reasons dethrones the old hegemon, usually through wars. Therein the cycle begins again. Gilpin's theory marries the liberal tradition of peaceful incremental change with the Marxist tradition of dialectical change: a particular balance-of-power system facilitates changes in the balance of power of states, thereby sowing the seeds of its own transformation through explosive conflict.

Jervis, Robert. "Cooperation Under the Security Dilemma," *World Politics,* Vol. 30, 1978. According to this seminal article, the condition of anarchy in the international system, combined with difficulties in distinguishing offensive from defensive military preparations, often gives rise to a security dilemma: statesmen seeking to enhance their state's security by developing military defenses may actually degrade their security by being perceived as threatening to other states, whose leaders seek only to preserve their own states' security. This dilemma is more or less acute depending in part on the policies, actions, and technologies statesmen employ in their defense. For instance, where military preparations meant primarily for the defense of territory are difficult to distinguish from military technologies useful for offensive attacks on territory, attempts to improve defensive security will more easily be seen as threatening to other states. Conversely, any technology, strategy, information, or action that distinguishes offensive from defensive military preparations mitigates the security dilemma.

Mearsheimer, John. "Back to the Future: Instability in Europe After the Cold War," *International Security*, Vol. 15, No. 1, 1990. Mearsheimer maintains that the end of bipolarity and the dissolution of the Soviet Union that marked the ending of the Cold War are likely to lead to increasing conflict among nations in Europe. In an eloquent, if pessimistic, application of structural realist theory of conflict (see Waltz, 1979), Mearsheimer affirms that ideational changes in European attitudes, the development of economic interdependence and of international institutions regulating relations and promoting peace, and the advent of democratic rule are not sufficient conditions for peace. His focus is on the perils of multipolarity and power inequality in a condition of basic anarchy; multipolarity is more dangerous than bipolarity, he says, because in multipolarity potential aggressors confront uncertain alliances and are thereby less deterred. Preserving the peace, in Mearsheimer's view, requires continued U.S. commitment to European security and limited proliferation of nuclear weapons (except for Germany), as well as active steps to lower "hypernationalism."

Morgenthau, Hans J. *Politics Among Nations,* 4th edition (New York: Alfred A. Knopf, 1967). One of the most influential realist tracts, Morgenthau's work seeks to study the world as it actually is, which to him is a world of opposing interests resulting from forces inherent in human nature. Humans seek to maximize power, and, as a consequence, moral principles can never be fully realized. War emerges from these innate forces, and the avoidance of war requires statesmen to seek balances of power consistent with pessimistic assumptions of human nature. Of the many hypotheses about war developed in the volume, two are the most important and controversial: multipolarity is more stable and peaceful than bipolarity, and balances of power are desirable rather than inevitable.

Walt, Stephen M. *The Origins of Alliances* (Ithaca, N.Y.: Cornell University Press, 1987). Walt focuses on the formation of alliances among countries, explaining when countries decide to balance power by joining a weaker state or collection of states in opposition to some more powerful state or collectivity, and when they opt to "bandwagon" by joining with the stronger side. To explain when and with whom countries will balance and when they will bandwagon, Walt focuses on threats rather than either ideological affinities or power alone. Four key factors affect a state's calculation of another state's threat: aggregate power; geographic proximity; offensive capabilities; and offensive intentions. Three of these four factors are, of course, common to traditional states. Walt uses this fact to support his argument about threat-balancing. He concludes that balancing is much more common than bandwagoning, because balancing is more likely to ensure autonomous security. Bandwagoning is likely under some conditions, however, such as between two countries that are geographically proximate and that have large disparities in their aggregate power.

Waltz, Kenneth N. *Man, the State, and War: A Theoretical Analysis* (New York: Columbia University Press, 1954). This seminal work draws insights from modern political theorists, including Spinoza, Kant, and Rousseau, as well as the many scholars influenced by their ideas, to understand the causes of war and to define the conditions under which war can be controlled or eliminated. Waltz's analysis develops the famous distinction between different levels of analysis, or images, in which the core causes of war are said to reside. These images correspond to different aggregations of people. He draws on Spinoza's writings to consider the argument that man's intrinsic nature and behavior, such as a lust for power or a death wish, account for war. He draws on Kant to begin analysis of the view that the character of states, their form of governance or economic structure, explains the incidence of war. Finally, he draws on Rousseau to consider the view that properties of the international system, in particular its anarchic character, explain war. In analyzing the arguments of the classics and their successors in debates over the causes of war and its prevention, Waltz is most sympathetic to the view that the international system, the third image, explains the persistence of war. He thereby foreshadows his much more theoretically parsimonious, if less readable, *Theory of International Politics,* written 25 years later.

Waltz's *Theory of International Politics* (Reading, Mass.: Addison-Wesley, 1979) is probably realism's most influential statement on the causes of war. It argues that some of the most powerful and enduring causes of war between countries are due to structural characteristics of the international system rather than the internal characteristics of nations which are the units within that system. The ordering principle of the international system is anarchy—the absence of superintendent authority vested with coercive power. Anarchy causes states that value their own survival to seek sources of coercive force and to balance the power, or capabilities, of other states in the system. The other characteristic of the international system is the distribution of capabilities, the most important distinction being between multipolar distributions and bipolar distributions. Through these characteristics of international structure, Waltz provides partial explanations for, among other things, alliance patterns, grand strategy, economic policies, and war.

Wendt, Alexander. "Anarchy Is What States Make of It: The Social Construction of Power Politics," *International Organization,* Vol. 46, No. 2 (Spring 1992). This article is written in opposition to the structural realist view that the anarchical character of the international system necessarily conditions states to believe it is a self-help system in which countries must rely only on their own safeguards for security and cannot depend on other states or international institutions. Wendt contends that this realist view treats the interests and identities of states as unchanging, not acknowledging that the self-help system and the balance-of-power system condition the identities of states and the meaning of anarchy. Such institutions, Wendt states, are themselves manipulable constructs of human interaction. Thus he sees the balance-of-power system as historically constructed and subject to transformation by practices of sovereignty, by an evolution of cooperation, and by critical strategic practice.

Economic and Environmental Stresses

Ashley, Richard K. *The Political Economy of War and Peace* (London: Frances Pinter, 1980). Ashley's first book is an ambitious application of the lateral pressure theory (see Choucri and North below) to explain the emergence of balance-of-power politics. It looks at the triad of the United States, the Soviet Union, and China to show how the rivalry spawned by growth led to a system characterized by aggressive power-balancing. Ashley extends the focus of lateral pressure analysis from unilateral and bilateral actions between states to multilateral, systemic processes. Using sophisticated models and empirical analysis, the book tries to bring systemic realism into lateral pressure theory, while at the same time criticizing realism in view of the historical contingency of power politics.

Brewer, Anthony. *Marxist Theories of Imperialism: A Critical Survey* (London: Frances Pinter, 1980). Brewer's book surveys and assesses Marxist theories of imperialism, from Marx's writings and those of early Marxists like Lenin, Bukharin, and Luxembourg to those of present-day scholars, including Wallerstein, Galtung, and others. What these writers have in common is their view that the capitalist economy, defined as a logic of market exchange either within one country or as an international system, leads to hierarchical relations among classes and nations, including imperialism. Many of these theorists also see capitalist exchange as underlying wars between countries, such as

Lenin's prediction that capitalist countries competing for resources and sources of demand in other countries will eventually clash. The book provides a sympathetic but critical analysis of the conceptual quality and empirical strength of these writings.

Choucri, Nazli, and Robert C. North. *Nations in Conflict* (San Francisco: Freeman, 1975) "Lateral Pressure Theory in International Relations: Concept and Theory," in Manus I. Midlarsky, *Handbook of War Studies* (Boston: Unwin Hyman, 1989). Both *Nations in Conflict* and the research agenda it initiated (summarized in the subsequent article) develop a theory of international conflict and interaction that focuses on lateral pressure, "the extension of a country's behavior and interests outside of its territorial boundaries." Lateral pressure is not synonymous with war, although the theory explains how wars often result from such pressure. The core source of lateral pressure is the interaction of the "demands" and "capabilities" of nations. These demands and capabilities, in turn, depend crucially on three "master variables": population, including all demographic features of a territory; technology, encompassing "both mechanical and organization knowledge and skills"; and resources, including water supplies, arable land, fuels, and other raw materials. These variables emphasize the interaction of political and economic factors at a variety of levels of analysis, and the dependence of politics on the natural environment. The original formulation of this theory in *Nations in Conflict* was applied to explain war, particularly World War I. Later applications, discussed in the article, have developed elaborate and empirically ambitious profiles of countries based on their population, technology, and resource attributes in order to explain alliance patterns, international migration, and power-balancing.

Galtung, Johan. "A Structural Theory of Aggression," *Journal of Peace Research,* Vol. 1, 1964, pp. 95–119. In this influential article, Galtung develops a theory of individual, group, and state aggression that focuses on social structure. He criticizes prevailing theories for either removing individual decisions from their social context or focusing on the basic suffering caused by that context. Galtung's theory emphasizes a more inclusive conception of social context that combines the idea of frustration with the idea of perceiving aggression as a possible way out of the frustrating situation.

Gleick, Peter. "Water and Conflict: Fresh Water Resources and International Security," *International Security,* Vol. 18 (Summer 1993). Gleick describes ways in which water resources have historically been the objectives of interstate conflict and how they have been used as instruments of war. He suggests that maldistribution of fresh water, together with population and development trends, will make water an increasingly important issue in world politics and conflict. Gleick also develops quantitative indices for measuring the vulnerability of states to water-related conflict, and he outlines advances in international legal principles for managing internationally shared water resources.

Homer-Dixon, Thomas. "On the Threshold: Environmental Changes as Causes of Acute Conflict," *International Security,* Vol. 16 (Fall 1991). This article argues that emerging environmental challenges may cause armed conflicts, especially within and between developing countries. Environmental degradation in the Third World—including atmospheric, terrestrial, and aquatic environmental problems—may reduce agricultural production, retard economic growth, displace populations, and disrupt "regular and legitimized" social relations. These consequences may, in turn, "cause several specific types of acute conflict, including scarcity disputes between countries, clashes between ethnic groups, and civil strife and insurgency." The author considers whether market mechanisms will permit countries to address the security impacts of environmental degradation, but concludes that policymakers will be less and less able to do so as the environmental problems become more acute. Although more prophetic than explanatory, Homer-Dixon concludes with a plea for more empirical research into his various hypotheses.

Mathews, Jessica Tuchman. "The Environment and International Security," *Foreign Affairs,* Vol. 68, no. 2, 1989. Mathews states that environmental stresses are becoming important determinants of national security and may increasingly fuel international conflict. She focuses on two such stresses: resource degradation associated with population growth, such as soil degradation and deforestation; and global climatic effects associated with modernity, such as acid rain and ozone depletion. She points out how resource degradation, in particular, already directly fuels conflicts, such as over shared water resources, and indirectly does so by undermining economic performance and political stability. The problem is that countries tend to overlook or ignore the environmental bases of some conflicts and insecurity, focusing instead on economic and political symptoms. She suggests a variety of institutional, political, and technical innovations that could improve attention to these problems in the future.

Identity Politics: Ethnicity and Ideology

Deutsch, Karl W. *Nationalism and Social Communication: An Inquiry into the Foundations of Nationality* (Cambridge, Mass.: MIT Press, 1966). Deutsch explores the objective, subjective, and quantitative aspects of nationality and the long-run trends of national assimilation and differentiation. Clusters of settlement, nodes of transportation, centers of culture, areas and centers of language, divisions of caste and class, barriers between markets, sharp regional differences in wealth and interdependence, and the uneven impact of historical events and social institutions all act together to produce a highly differentiated world of regions, nations, and peoples.

Gellner, Ernest. *Nations and Nationalism* (Ithaca, N.Y.: Cornell University Press, 1983). Gellner's influential study of nationalism argues that the roots of nationalism lie in the industrial and social organization of a territoriality. He states that the relationship between culture and the state depends on a variety of such factors as: innovation, occupational mobility, the effectiveness of the mass media, universal literacy, and an all-embracing educational system "based on a standard idiom." The more present these factors are, Gellner maintains, the more harmoniously connected the state and its culture. In turn, the more these are connected, the more affluent and growing a nation. Political units that do not "conform to the principle 'one state, one culture' feel the strain in the form of nationalistic activity."

Gurr, Ted Robert. "Why Minorities Rebel: A Global Analysis of Communal Mobilization and Conflict Since 1945," *International Political Science Review,* Vol. 14, 1993. *Minorities at Risk: A Global View of Ethno-political Conflicts* (Washington, D.C.: United States Institute of Peace Press, 1993). Both the article and the book consider why ethnic minorities rebel against majority groups and their governments, and what can be done to settle ethno-political disputes. The findings are based on a survey of 233 different minority groups around the world. The survey identifies these groups' geographical distribution and their economic, political, and cultural situations.

Horowitz, Donald. *Ethnic Groups in Conflict* (Berkeley: University of California Press, 1991). This book compares conflict in societies divided along ethnic, religious, racial, or communal lines. Horowitz tries to identify common political patterns in such divided societies through a detailed analysis of ethnic group mobilization and political organization. Along the way, he develops a model of democratic political organization to reduce ethnic conflict. This model takes the form of a political system comprising electoral patterns and federal structures that strengthen centrist-oriented forces to marginalize ethnic extremists.

Huntington, Samuel P. "The Clash of Civilizations?" *Foreign Affairs* (Summer 1993). Huntington maintains that world politics is entering a new phase of history in which the fundamental basis of international conflict will be neither economic, power-political, nor ideological, but instead a clash of civilizations. Taking "civilizations" to be the world's highest cultural/identity unit (often above nations and nation-states), he argues that civilizations will increasingly clash because differences among civilizations are many and deep; interactions among different peoples are increasing; social and economic modernizations are separating people from local identities; cultural characteristics are less mutable than political or economic ones; and economic regionalism is increasing.

Kohn, Hans. *Nationalism: Its Meaning and History* (Princeton, N.J.: D. Van Nostrand Company, 1955). An influential scholar of the origins and nature of nationalism, Kohn divides his book into two parts. The first is an extended essay on the eighteenth-century origins of Western European nationalism and its spread to Asia, the Americas, and Africa. Arguing that there is no one nationalism, Kohn claims that nationalism "is a historical phenomenon and thus determined by the political ideas and the social structure of the various lands where it takes root." The second part of the book includes readings from 24 thinkers and practitioners important to the development of and insightful about nationalism. These include passages from the writings of Machiavelli, Hegel, Napoleon, Wagner, Mussolini, Dostoevsky, and Nehru.

Montville, Joseph V., ed. *Conflict and Peacemaking in Multiethnic Societies* (Lexington, Mass.: Lexington Books, 1991). This edited book includes a range of essays on the nature of ethnic conflict, on different methods for studying conflict, and on conflict management and resolution. Three countries receive the most prominent attention (Northern Ireland, Sri Lanka, and Sudan), but the volume also includes essays on Nigeria and Zimbabwe. The contributors include psychologists, sociologists, and political scientists, and as a result the authors offer different methodologies and claims about ethnic conflict and its amelioration.

Posen, Barry. "Nationalism, the Mass Army, and Military Power," *International Security,* Vol. 18, No. 2 (Fall 1993). Posen argues that nationalism increases the intensity of warfare by enhancing the ability of states "to mobilize the creative energies and the spirit of self-sacrifice of millions of soldiers." He also explains how some aspects of nationalism are caused or intensified by the task of preparation for warfare, mainly through deliberate action by state leaders. As a plausibility probe, he applies these arguments to French and Prussian/German relations between the Seven Years' War (1756–63) and the eve of World War I.

Posen, Barry. "The Security Dilemma and Ethnic Conflict," *Survival,* Vol. 35 (Spring 1993). Posen assesses the degree to which the security dilemma—the phenomenon by which one group's efforts to defend itself actually lowers its security by threatening another group—in conflicts arises from proximate groups of people suddenly finding themselves responsible for their own security. He argues that ethnic conflicts having this character tend to exacerbate the general existence of the security dilemma, because they tend to make offensive and defensive preparations indistinguishable and to treat offensive strategies for enhancing security as superior to defensive ones. He develops these arguments with application to the breakup of Yugoslavia and relations between Russia and Ukraine.

Van Evera, S. "Hypotheses on Nationalism and War," *International Security,* Vol. 18, No. 4 (Spring 1994). Pointing out that the literatures on war and on nationalism have said plenty about the causes of each but little on how nationalism can lead to war, Van Evera develops a series of hypotheses on the war effects of nationalism. He focuses on the kinds of nationalism most likely to lead to war and on the conditions under which any given nationalism is most dangerous. He doesn't try to test these hypotheses empirically.

Walt, Stephen. *Revolution and War* (Ithaca, N.Y.: Cornell University Press, 1996). Walt examines the role of revolution as a cause of interstate war, arguing that revolutions frequently lead to war as a result of two parallel myths often held by a revolution-laden country and other countries: "The belief that the revolution will spread rapidly if it is not crushed immediately, and the belief that a reversal of the revolution will be easy to accomplish." Both beliefs support offense-oriented strategies that, in turn, contribute to the outbreak of war.

Welch, David A. *Justice and the Genesis of War* (New York: Cambridge University Press, 1993). This book rejects the view that wars between countries are caused by conflict over power and interest alone, where arguments about justice are mere justifications for pursuit of interest. Through detailed case studies on the origins of five major international conflicts, Welch contends that in all but one of these conflicts "moral claims played a key role in moving the parties to war." Thus he seeks to expand the realist view of state leaders as simply selfish and fearful toward a view that leaders care deeply about right and wrong in their statecraft.

Wolfers, Arnold. "Statesmanship and Moral Choice" *World Politics* (January 1949). Wolfers argues against the position that international relations is fundamentally different from other human behavior, and that no moral judgment can be made about the decisions of statesmen. He maintains that in international relations, as in the behavior of individuals, choices are moral when they maximize moral value. All actions by statesmen can and should be seen as morally relevant rather than as pursuant to the "necessities of state." He distinguishes ethical perfectionists, who judge actions according to absolutist principles, from ethical nonperfectionists, who believe that men must make the best moral choice that circumstances and judgments of consequences permit. The latter pragmatic standards, he states, are most appropriate for judging both state and individual action. Wolfers claims that human and state interactions can be defined according to degree of shared morality and sense of community, with complete enmity and amity representing the extreme conditions. The more international relations are characterized by a state of enmity, the greater the likelihood of war.

Governance Forms

Chan, S. "Mirror, Mirror on the Wall: Are the Freer Countries More Pacific?," *Journal of Conflict Resolution,* Vol. 28, 1984, pp. 617–48. Chan analyzes the Singer/Small Correlates of War database of international wars between 1816 and 1980 in order to test R. J. Rummel's proposition that "the more libertarian a state, the less its foreign violence." Chan finds that several tests do not support the hypothesis. Only if the focus is "country-diachronic" or if one focuses on the period between 1973 and 1980 is there support for the claim. He also finds modest support for the idea that free countries are less likely than less free countries to fight on the side of the initiator of war. His findings are consistent with M. W. Doyle's focus on democracy and war, but Chan does not test to see how frequently free countries fight one another.

Doyle, M. W. "Kant, Liberal Legacies, and Foreign Affairs: Part 1," *Philosophy and Public Affairs,* Vol. 12, 1983a, pp. 205–35. "Kant, Liberal Legacies, and Foreign Affairs: Part 2," *Philosophy and Public Affairs,* Vol. 12, 1983b, pp. 323–53. In both articles, Doyle explores the reasoning and empirical basis for Kant's argument that republican regimes (characterized by a constitutional and representative government and a separation of powers) are more peaceful than nonrepublican regimes. Working with cases that go back to the eighteenth century, he makes the core conclusion contrary to Kant's thesis, that democratic countries are not appreciably more peaceful than nondemocratic countries but that democratic countries almost never fight each other. The cases are so clear on this latter question that a number of scholars point out that the conclusion that democratic states don't fight each other comes as close to an empirical law as any conclusion in the social sciences.

Huntington, Samuel P. *The Third Wave: Democratization in the Late Twentieth Century* (Oklahoma: University of Oklahoma Press, 1991). Huntington's study is premised on the claim that a recent spate of democratizations (some 30 countries between 1974 and 1990) constitutes a third wave of democratization. The first two waves were (1) the extension of suffrage in the United States in 1820 and its spread to other countries until some 29 democracies existed in 1920; and (2), after a "reverse wave" in the interwar period, the extension of democracy to encompass some 36 countries following the Allied triumph in World War II. Huntington's focus is mainly on explaining the third wave, as opposed to any particular country's shift to democracy. He gives special attention to five major factors: the deepening legitimacy problems of authoritarian regimes in a world where democratic values are widely accepted; the unprecedented global economic growth of the 1960s; a shift in the doctrine and activities of the Catholic Church from defender to opponent of authoritarianism; changes in the policies of external actors like the United States, the Soviet Union, and the European Community; and "snowballing," the demonstration effect of democratization on other countries.

Karl, Terry, and Philippe Schmitter. "Democratization Around the Globe: Its Opportunities and Risks," in M. Klare and D. Thomas, eds., *World Security: Challenges for a New Century* (New York: St. Martin's Press, 1991). Karl and Schmitter consider the nature and origins of what they term a fourth wave of democratization to sweep the globe, and they assess the durability of this wave and its implications for the international system. They emphasize that this recent wave of democratization differs from the previous three in that it has not followed some exogenous cataclysmic event (like World Wars I and II) and has been much more global in reach. Their explanation focuses on the diffusion effects of democratization, such as through examples transmitted by the international media, and on the related increasing influence of formal nongovernmental organizations and informal informational networks devoted to the promotion of human rights, the protection of minorities, and democracy. They distinguish different kinds of democracy according to their points of departure (e.g., differences in development, literacy, urbanization), modes of transition (e.g., elite-led and unilateral versus mass-based and negotiated), the role of external actors, and the sequence of transformations. After explaining why there are some strong forces making the wave relatively durable, the authors claim that the most important implication for the international system is to force major changes in the military and aid programs of leading democracies like the United States.

Rupesinghe, Kumar. "Democratization Processes and Their Implications for International Security," in UNESCO, *Peace and Conflict Issues After the Cold War,* 1992. Given the well-documented observation that recent years have seen the creation of greater democratic spaces in countries throughout the world, the author argues that the democratization trend holds the threat that new types of conflict will appear and that "armed conflicts and criminality may dominate the democratic space available." For instance, democratization accommodates and can actually increase ideological, ethnic, authority, and identity conflicts.

Human Psychology and Decision Making

Bloomfield, Lincoln P. "Nuclear Crisis and Human Frailty," *Bulletin of Atomic Scientists* (October 1985). Bloomfield's article considers the limits of human decision making in military crises, nuclear especially but conventional crises as well, and recommends changes in weapons design, and command and control to take account of such limits. The article is premised on the claim that policymakers have addressed the physical threats to the technical management of future crisis but that "the human component is the least analyzed or even acknowledged." Bloomfield points out that intense crisis situations tend to create levels of stress that far exceed the levels at which humans perform well mentally. For instance, he claims that such stress can lead to increased rigidity that can cause intolerance of ambiguity and fixation on one alternative; to defensive and avoidance mechanisms such as denial or procrastination; to a declining sense of long-term responsibility; to stereotyping of opponents; to poor use of information; and to other problems. Crisis situations can also lead to physical and mental exhaustion, with even more devastating effects on decision making. Bloomfield recommends appointing a person responsible for monitoring the stress, fatigue, and rationality of the decision-making group, and giving preference to weapons and strategies that afford time to deliberate (e.g., less offensive weapons and doctrines).

George, Alexander L. *Forceful Persuasion: Coercive Diplomacy as an Alternative to War* (Washington, D.C.: United States Institute of Peace Press, 1991). "Coercive diplomacy" refers to a defensive strategy that attempts to persuade an opponent to stop or undo an aggressive action through the threat or limited use of force. George describes the general theory and logic behind coercive diplomacy, and then provides seven case studies to illustrate the uses and limitations of this strategy. He concludes that coercive diplomacy, though flexible, is difficult to implement successfully in specific situations.

Janis, Irving. *Groupthink,* 2nd edition (Boston: Houghton Mifflin, 1982). Among the cluster of ideas about the psychology of group behavior relevant to conflict and its resolution, this book develops the idea of groupthink—a condition of conformity among members of a group in response to threatening, stressful, crisis situations. When a dominant view has been expressed, such as by a person in a position of political or moral authority, individuals will hesitate to express doubts. The classic examples of groupthink in action, according to Janis, include Kennedy's advisers in deciding on the Bay of Pigs invasion and President Lyndon B. Johnson's intervention in the Dominican Republic. Strategies for avoiding or checking groupthink include the appointment of a "devil's advocate" to a group in crisis decision making, as a way to institutionalize the expression of critical views.

Jervis, Robert. *Perception and Misperception in International Politics* (Princeton, N.J.: Princeton University Press, 1976). Jervis focuses on how decision makers' perceptions of the world and of other actors diverge from reality in patterns that are detectable and for reasons that are comprehensible. Focusing mainly on concepts developed in psychology and drawing on a wide range of historical cases, Jervis develops a framework for explaining specific decisions and patterns of interaction between states. Among the most important patterns are security dilemmas and conflict spirals, wherein misperception of the intentions of adversaries produces actions by states to improve their security, inspiring similar actions and retaliation on the part of other states and thereby leading to a cycle, or spiral, of escalation.

Lebow, Richard Ned. *Between Peace and War: The Nature of International Crisis* (Baltimore: Johns Hopkins University Press, 1981). In attempting to bridge the gap between history and political science, Lebow integrates both disciplines in his analysis of the role of crisis in international conflict. He first develops a typology of crisis, then analyzes crisis outcomes, and finally examines the relationship between crisis and international relations. Case studies used throughout the book support Lebow's conclusion that crises not only play an important role in international conflict, but also act as turning points for such conflicts.

Lorenz, Konrad. *On Aggression* (New York: Bantam Books, 1966). Lorenz believes that humans have a killer instinct that underlies conflicts, often self-destructive, at all levels of social life, including wars between countries. His argument relies on a variety of human psychology research and on his own comparisons of canine and human biology and psychology. It represents a statement of how pursuit of power at the core of realist theorizing can have origins at the level of animal instinct.

Snyder, Glenn, and Paul Diesing. *Conflict Among Nations: Bargaining, Decision Making, and System Structure in International Crises* (Princeton, N.J.: Princeton University Press, 1977). This book, a culmination of more than a decade of research on negotiation and bargaining in conflict settings, presents a theory of international crisis behavior. Such behavior is conceived mainly as bargaining behavior, but it also includes the effects of international system structures (e.g., multipolarity versus bipolarity) and the decision-making activities of the actors in the bargaining process. The theory was developed "by testing and linking a number of primarily deductive theories and models via sixteen case studies of international crises that occurred from the late nineteenth century to the present."

Overviews and Alternatives

Azar, Edward, and Chung-in Moon, eds. *National Security in the Third World: The Management of Internal and External Threats*, 1988. This collection of essays assesses the concept of statehood and national security in Third World countries. It is premised on the idea that Western conceptions of national security tend to underlie misperceptions of how to promote political development, stability, economic well-being, and, above all, peace within and among Third World nations. According to the editors, conceiving national security as the physical protection of states from external military threats is too narrow and misleading, considering that most Third World security challenges are "endogenous" to the countries, and in the light of human rights, environmental, political, and economic dimensions of security. As the essays based on the security experiences of Argentina, Chile, North Korea, and Iran make clear, "domestic factors such as legitimacy, integration, ideology, and policy capacity" play as important a role as military posture, or perhaps even more so.

Boulding, Elise, ed. *New Agendas for Peace Research: Conflict and Security Reexamined* (Boulder, Colo.: Lynne Rienner Publishers, 1992). This collection of essays provides a peace research consideration of post–Cold War conflict. It is premised on the view that North-South conflicts have superseded those between East and West, and that "boundaries between internal and interstate conflicts have all but disappeared." The book is divided into three parts. Part I, "New Faces, Old Conflicts," develops a variety of European peace research, feminist, and Third World perspectives on post–Cold War challenges. Part II, "Reconceptualizing Security," contains essays that expand the concept of security beyond standard military conceptions. Environmental issues get the largest airing in this section. In Part III, "New Security Technologies," contributors offer insights into creative new approaches to conflict and its resolution, including organized and informal mediation, the use of United Nations' "Good Offices," and a strategy for using education to replace "cultures of militarism with peace cultures."

Boulding, Kenneth Ewart. *Conflict and Defense: A General Theory* (Lanham, Md.: University Press of America, 1962). In its second reprint (in 1988) of the original, this theoretical work is Boulding's classic study of conflict as a social process. Boulding analyzes many models of conflict (including static models, game theory, ecological and epidemiological models, and others) to develop a general theory of conflict. The author demonstrates how he believes conflicts act as a social process in a number of specific cases; he concludes with a personal look at the practical implications of conflicts and the means by which they may be resolved.

Brown, Seyom. *The Causes and Prevention of War* (New York: St. Martin's Press, 1987). Brown ambitiously takes on the question, "How can we reduce the role of large-scale violence in world society?" The conflicts he seeks to understand and to help reduce include intranational strife as well as interstate wars. His approach is interdisciplinary, drawing insights from political science, biology, psychology, and anthropology. The book is divided into three parts: "Violence in Human Affairs," in which he considers essentialist and other arguments about violence being ubiquitous in private and public life; "The Determinants of War," in which he considers domestic and international structural, as well as more contingent technological and cognitive, causes of conflict; and "The Prevention and Control of War," in which he considers conflict-resolution strategies ranging from radical plans "to purge war from the world" to more modest efforts to reduce its role in the international system through international law, statesmanship, collective security, and arms control.

Butterworth, Robert L. *Managing Interstate Conflict, 1945–1974: Data with Synopses* (Pittsburgh, Pa.: University of Pittsburgh Center for International Studies, 1976). Butterworth compiles brief summaries and analyses of 310 cases of interstate and internal conflict. The analysis focuses on causes that promote the abatement of conflict. Each case is also coded for computer analysis.

Klare, Michael T., and Daniel Thomas, eds. *World Security: Challenges for a New Century,* 2d edition (New York: St. Martin's Press, 1994). This reader contains 19 original essays on world security issues in the post–Cold War era, including nonproliferation, democratization, UN peacekeeping, ethnic conflict, hunger, violence against women, arms trade, and environmental degradation.

Levy, Jack. "The Causes of War: A Review of Theories and Evidence," in P. Tetlock et al., eds. *Behavior, Society and Nuclear War,* Vol. 1, 1989. These are probably the clearest and most comprehensive single-essay overviews of the literature on the cause of war. Levy divides the literature into system-level, societal-level, and decision-making theories, broadly consistent with the common levels of analysis distinction. He summarizes and analyzes the strengths and weaknesses of each approach. Throughout the discussion, he gives special attention to the contributions of a particular approach to understanding the prospects of nuclear war. His focus on the causes of interstate war means leaving out intrastate conflicts and giving only peripheral attention to conflict resolution.

Rapaport, Anatol. *The Origins of Violence: Approaches to the Study of Conflict* (New York: Paragon House, 1989). This book is a major primer on the causes of conflict and its resolution. It is premised on the idea that humanity's violent past and present stem "from a lag in the enlightenment process initiated by the natural sciences; that is, the study of peace should be considered a science just like biology." Reflecting his lifetime as a scholar of game theory applied to peace research, most of the book considers different approaches to explaining violence: psychological approaches, such as Freud's theory of the "death wish" and Lorenz's theory of animal aggression; ideological approaches that emphasize how ideals held by groups can fuel disagreements and violence; strategic approaches that emphasize the possibility of conflict and elusiveness of cooperation in the interaction of rational egoists; and the systemic approaches, which focus on characteristics of the international system, such as anarchy. The remaining chapter, "In Quest of Peace," considers a variety of approaches to conflict resolution, including mediation and education, pacifism and reason in art and science, and increasing reliance on world organizations.

Van Evera, S. "The Cult of the Offensive and the Origins of the First World War." *International Security,* Vol. 9, 1984, pp. 58–107. This article describes the origins, nature, and implications of widespread belief in the advantages of offensive military doctrine. Van Evera argues that Europeans in Germany, France, England, and elsewhere embraced a constellation of political and military myths that obscured the advantages of more defensive strategy, and motivated territorial expansionism by Germany and hair-trigger brinksmanship by all European military and political leaders. Thus, in Van Evera's view, the cult of the offensive was a primary cause of World War I.

Van Evera, S. "Primed for Peace: Europe After the Cold War," *International Security,* 1990. Van Evera's article takes issue with the views of John Mearsheimer, Jack Snyder, and other realist pessimists who believe that the end of bipolarity and the dissolution of the Soviet empire spells certain conflict for Europe. His more optimistic view is that the principal causes of Europe's major wars have vanished or are vanishing, and this situation will be slow to reverse. At the international level, he focuses on how nuclear deterrence and a variety of changes in the technology and strategy of war have reversed the dominance of offense over the defense in military strategy; how the United States retains a lasting commitment to the security of Europe; and how knowledge-based economies are less likely to make conquest pay. At the domestic level, Van Evera focuses on the decline of social stratification and the rise of democracy, thereby removing elites with incentives to peddle nationalist myths and lowering incentives for military organizations to propagandize war. He also takes on a series of specific arguments advanced by Mearsheimer and Snyder, two of the most prominent "pessimists" in the academic security studies community (see Mearsheimer above).

Vasquez, J. A. "The Steps to War: Toward a Scientific Explanation of Correlates of War Findings," *World Politics,* Vol. 40, pp. 108–145. This article provides one of the clearest and most succinct statements of findings from the Correlates of War Project. After defending against major criticisms of the project—that it is too inductive, contradictory, and atheoretical—Vasquez summarizes some important conclusions about the causes of war, alliances, and power-balancing. He argues, for instance, that international disputes are most likely to escalate if there is an arms race; if the dispute is triggered by physical threats to vital issues and is the second or third crisis with the same rival; if a hostile interaction cycle (such as security dilemma spirals discussed in Jervis, 1976) emerges during the crisis; and if hardliners dominate in at least one leadership.

Wallensteen, Peter, Johan Galtung, and Carlos Portales, eds. *Global Militarization* (Boulder, Colo.: Westview Press, 1985). This collection of essays seeks to analyze the increasing militarization of the world and to suggest ways of controlling and limiting that militarization. The contributors see militarization as both "a social formation and structure" of relations in which military behavior is seen as appropriate, and a behavior entailing the preference for violent action rather than nonviolent paths of influence. The book is divided into three sections. The first includes broad theoretical treatments of militarization, including Johan Galtung's comprehensive "structural theory" of militarization that sees military formations as embedded in social formations, and Charles Tilly's discussion of European state-making. The second section contains more historical and contemporary essays on militarization in Chile, Thailand, and Ghana, respectively. The final section includes essays on alternatives to militarization, including Paul Wehr's discussion of peaceful protest in Poland, and nonoffensive defense in Switzerland.

Wright, Quincy. *A Study of War,* revised edition (Chicago: University of Chicago Press, 1965). First published in 1942, Wright's book is one of the classic realist definitions and explanations of interstate conflict. The 1965 abridged edition defines war and the different stages of conflict in legal terms, and then examines the causes of war. Wright discusses both structural factors, such as the relative capabilities of states, and the underlying social, political, and cultural attitudes that lead to war. On the avoidance and resolution of war, Wright contends that lasting international peace requires stronger and more inclusive international institutions. He concludes that the attitudes of policymakers and citizens must focus not only on the interests and stability of their nations, but also on those of the world community.

CONFLICT RESOLUTION

International Law and Diplomacy

Clark, Grenville, and Louis Sohn. *Introduction to World Peace Through Law* (Chicago: World Without War Publications, 1983). First published in 1958 and now in its third edition, this book fulfills its title as an introduction to "World Peace Through World Law" by being a sustained proposal for world government. It begins with an introductory essay by the editors, summarizing their full detailed plan to eliminate war as a legitimate means of resolving international conflicts. They argue that eliminating war would be possible by changing existing international organizations into effective instruments of world governance. The book also includes an essay by Robert Woito on "Five Approaches to World Law." The rest of the volume offers a bibliographic introduction to international organizations, a listing of various UN agencies, and a listing of other selected government and nongovernmental world affairs organizations.

Falk, Richard, Friedrich Kratochwil, and Saul H. Mendlovitz, eds. *International Law: A Contemporary Perspective* (Boulder, Colo.: Westview Press, 1985). This large collection of essays (38 articles) provides an ideologically balanced and comprehensive survey of international law's "contributions and limitations . . . in creating a dependable environment in which nations can interact." It is premised on the hope that contemporary international relations may present an opportunity for a "Grotian moment," the rejuvenation of the international legal system to better establish this environment. Included in the collection are essays on the traditional concerns of international lawmaking, the sources of law, problems of compliance, the interaction between power and normative preferences, and "the classical issues relating to the regulation of force." Also addressed are the relationship between international law and demands for ecological protection, resource sharing, demands for distributive justice, and human rights.

Forsythe, David P. *The Internationalization of Human Rights* (Lexington, Mass.: Lexington Books, 1991). Forsythe investigates the development of international principles of human rights, their inclusion in U.S. foreign policy over time, and activities of the United Nations and other regional bodies, such as the Organization of American States. He also considers the role of private organizations in the protection of human rights. The major conclusion of the volume is that human rights is no longer an internal national issue, but is instead increasingly the subject of international focus and action.

Halperin, Morton H., David J. Scheffer, with Patricia L. Small. *Self-determination in the New World Order* (Washington, D.C.: Carnegie Endowment for International Peace, 1992). The authors maintain that the most complex but important issues emerging in the post–Cold War period are the resurgence of movements for self-determination and the breakup of nations. They suggest that industrialized and intact countries like the United States ought to depart from past policies by promoting an expanded role for international law to solve the disputes that emerge from these developments. They propose that the United States and other countries get involved early in managing self-determination conflicts by linking diplomatic recognition to the human rights behavior of existing and new states, and by providing direct protection of minority rights. The book includes a list of more than one hundred self-determination movements around the world.

Henkin, Louis. *How Nations Behave: Law and Foreign Policy,* 2nd ed. (New York: Council on Foreign Relations and Columbia University Press, 1979). Henkin provides a general overview and analysis of international law and its real implications for international relations and foreign policy. Any inquiry into the role of law, he maintains, must take into account the state of the system—the character of international society and of the law at a given time. The first section of the book analyzes the role of law and its limitations, the politics of making international law, and the politics of implementing those laws. The second section considers contemporary political forces and international law, including ideological conflict and politics in the Third World, and the United Nations' institutional role in implementing that law. The third section considers the politics of creating new international laws, including the remaking of the Law of the Sea and the Law of Human Rights. The final empirical section considers the law in operation, focusing on the successes (the Suez problem and crisis) and failures (Vietnam and the case of Adolf Eichmann) of international law.

Janis, Mark W. *An Introduction to International Law* (Boston: Little, Brown, 1988). Janis's book is written for both first-year law students and lay readers. It provides an overview of international law, the international legal process, and the actual role of international law in international relations. Janis discusses the difficulties of regulating the interactions between historically sovereign states and reviews the different kinds of international law that have sought to do so, including treaties, multinational legal institutions, and customary practices. The author is also interested in conflicts of jurisdiction and enforcement between the domestic laws of distinct sovereign nations.

Rapaport, Anatol. *Peace: An Idea Whose Time Has Come* (Ann Arbor: University of Michigan Press, 1992). Rapaport hypothesizes that there is a constant struggle between the institutions of peace and of war. For the past 28 centuries, war has dominated this relationship, but the rationales supporting the institutions of war can now be exposed as superstitions. Therefore, the author concludes that the institutions of peace will gain power because more people are concerned with promoting cooperation than with power struggles among nations.

Walzer, Michael. *Just and Unjust Wars: A Moral Argument with Historical Illustrations* (New York: Basic Books, 1992). Walzer considers a series of moral arguments for and against war, including the "just war" doctrine in the Western liberal tradition. Using historical illustrations, he analyzes the moral claims made by those advocating war, finding most incoherent the hypocrisy of those who have used the moral claims to justify their resort to war.

The United Nations, Collective Security, and Peacekeeping

Betts, Richard K. "Systems for Peace or Causes of War?: Collective Security, Arms Control, and the New Europe," *International Security,* Vol. 17, No. 1, 1992. Betts sounds a cautionary note about the wisdom of pursuing collective security arrangements as a mechanism for preserving peace and resolving conflicts at the core and periphery of the state system. His main argument is that "reborn enthusiasm for collective security is fueled by confusion about which is the cause and which is the effect in the relation between collective security and peace, and by conflation of *present* security *conditions* (absence of threat) with *future* security *functions* (coping with threat)." Betts claims that collective security arrangements that seek to mitigate military instability could actually worsen it: implementing collective commitments could turn minor wars into major ones; and equalizing the military power of individual states through arms control "without reference to their prospective alignment in war might yield unequal forces when alignments congeal."

Claude, Inis L. *Swords into Plowshares: The Problems and Progress of International Organization* (New York: Random House, 1984). Claude's book provides a history of international organizations, focusing mainly on the United Nations but also on other international organizations. It considers several approaches to peace: collective security, preventive diplomacy, disarmament, "grand debate," trusteeship, and peaceful settlement of disputes. The fourth edition includes founding documents for the League of Nations, United Nations, and NATO.

Flynn, Gregory, and David Scheffer. "Limited Collective Security," in *Foreign Policy* (Fall, 1990). Flynn and Scheffer argue that a limited collective security arrangement is the best route to promote stability, democracy, and peace in the post–Cold War era, setting the stage for a draft treaty they offer in the appendix. They claim that the demise of the Soviet Union's rogue-state sphere of influence creates a variety of opportunities and threats to Europe and the world, mostly having to do with the major and sweeping transitions that are being attempted in Russia and the rest of Eastern Europe.

Flynn and Scheffer advocate moving beyond the traditional debate between those supporting traditional alliances as the means to security and those supporting collective security. After explaining why and how some of the historical barriers to successful collective security no longer apply, they contend that the best arrangement for safe-guarding Eastern Europe's transitions and overseeing an enduring peace involves a hybrid of traditional alliances and collective security. Although NATO is a necessary coun-tervailing power to deter and contain the former Soviet Union, they believe that some new collective security arrangement needs to be developed alongside NATO to reas-sure the East that the new Europe is not being built against it and to deal with new sources of instability. They contend that such an arrangement would be an all-European security regime developed within the 35-nation Conference on Security and Coopera-tion in Europe (CSCE).

Kupchan, Charles, and Clifford Kupchan. "Concerts, Collective Security and the Future of Europe," *International Security* (Summer 1991). Collective security is said to work by promoting more effective balancing behavior and by institutionalizing coop-eration. A concert arrangement similar to the Concert of Europe after 1815 is considered the most effective form of collective security for contemporary great powers.

Luard, Evan. *Conflict and Peace in the Modern International System: A Study of the Principles of International Order* (Albany, N.Y.: State University of New York Press, 1988). In its second edition, Luard's book studies various forms of conflict, analyzes the diffi-culties of reaching international agreements, and assesses the record of international orga-nizations and the role of international law in maintaining peace. The management of crisis situations requires more effective and stronger interaction between the interna-tional community and individual states. Luard also argues for a more carefully defined set of rules and conventions in the international community to guide those states that may suffer from regional conflicts within its borders and with other states.

Roberts, Adam. "The United Nations and International Security," *Survival* (Summer 1993). Roberts assesses the UN Secretary General Boutros Boutros-Ghali's *Agenda for Peace,* an attempt to devise a coherent rationale for UN activity. Roberts maintains that this *Agenda* underestimates the wide range of problems the United Nations is asked to address. He argues, for instance, that the organization is overloaded with security issues, that it tends to apply a model developed to address interstate wars to intrastate civil and ethnic wars, that it ignores disagreement among major powers in basic international norms, and that the structure of the Security Council is losing legitimacy. After devel-oping these and other criticisms, Roberts suggests ways of reforming the UN agenda that include devolving some of these responsibilities to other international institutions and to national policy making.

United Nations. *The Blue Helmets: A Review of United Nations Peace-keeping* (New York: United Nations, Department of Public Information, 1990). This volume contains summaries of the first 18 peacekeeping operations sponsored by the United Nations since 1948. The summaries contain background information on the dispute, the process of putting together the peacekeeping force, the implementation of the intervention, and the financial costs of the operation.

Weiss, Thomas, ed. *Collective Security in a Changing World* (Boulder, Colo.: Lynne Rienner Publishers, 1993). This collection of essays considers the prospects for improv-ing collective action to maintain international peace and security in light of the end of the Cold War. Most of the essays maintain that the end of the Cold War has brought dramatic changes in the balance of power and shrinkage "in the boundaries of state sov-ereignty," posing new challenges and possibilities for collective security arrangements. These arrangements include established and new regional security groupings as well as the United Nations. Part One of the volume includes four essays that describe and defend the idea of collective security. This sets the stage for Part Two, which includes essays that deal with more empirical details of UN and regional collective security experiences in the late 1980s and 1990s. Part Three offers "Conclusions and Recommendations" in two essays, one by Lincoln P. Bloomfield on prospective U.S. approaches to collective security in light of recent history, and one by Leon Gordenker and Thomas G. Weiss that reviews "the most salient suggestions emanating from the preceding chapters."

Going It Alone: Intervention, Power-Balancing, and Negotiation

Axelrod, R. *The Evolution of Cooperation* (New York: Basic Books, 1984). Axelrod explores how cooperation can emerge in a world of self-seeking units (individuals, firms, organizations, and states) and under conditions where no central authority exists to encourage and enforce such cooperation. Axelrod focuses on prisoners' dilemma situations, such as often characterized arms race/control situations; in these situations the players tried to maximize their payoffs through repeated interactions (that is, an iterated game). The simplest strategy usually yields the highest outcome: A tit-for-tat strategy in which the player starts by cooperation and thereafter does what the other player did on the previous move. Such a strategy tends to yield the highest payoffs for all players because it is a nice strategy, it is a forgiving strategy on the first interaction, and it involves swift and immediate retaliation. The key condition for such tit-for-tat cooperation to emerge is that the "players" expect to interact in the future. Axelrod illustrates and finds empirical support for the argument in a critical case in which the incentives for conflict were intense: trench warfare among infantrymen during World War I.

Dunn, Lewis A. "Rethinking the Nuclear Equation: The United States and the New Nuclear Powers," *Washington Quarterly* (Spring 1994). Dunn develops a set of principles to guide a nuclear deterrence policy for dealing with countries recently acquiring nuclear weapons. He holds that traditional concpts of deterrence that guided the U.S. nuclear relationship with the USSR are ill-suited to deal with countries with smaller numbers of weapons, different delivery systems, and different and more unstable military and leadership structures. He claims that the United States ought to go back to hitherto discredited ideas such as strategies for using conventional military operations on a nuclear battlefield and damage limitation at home and on the battlefield. He also believes that crisis management, not deterrence, "is likely to become the central theme of US relations with some new nuclear powers."

Fisher, Roger, and William Ury. *Getting to Yes: Negotiating Agreement Without Giving In* (Boston: Houghton Mifflin, 1981). Written for a general audience, this book explores a new strategy for negotiating conflicts, based on the method of principled negotiation developed by the Harvard Negotiation Project. This method has four basic guidelines: to work together, to focus on interests, to generate options for mutual gain, and to insist on objective criteria. The work is intended to provide a usable framework for individual relationships, for business exchanges, and for diplomatic relations between countries—anywhere conflict and the need for cooperation may emerge.

Klare, Michael T. *American Arms Supermarket* (Austin: University of Texas Press, 1984). Klare's book is about U.S. arms sales to Third World countries. By analyzing U.S. policies, practices, and experiences in military sales to the Third World from the 1950s through the mid-1980s, Klare concludes that growing arms sales do not achieve the ends and benefits attributed to them by U.S. policymakers. Instead, they undermine stated U.S. interests and global security. With case studies of sales to Latin America, Iran, and the Middle East, he focuses on the political economy of military sales and develops a theory of the institutional framework for arms export decision making. Klare also considers how arms sales and embargos affect human rights and political development in "pariah regimes," and compares the U.S. experience with that of other major arms exporters, including France, Britain, Germany, and Italy. The book concludes with Klare's own proposals for an alternative arms export policy.

Klare, Michael T., and Peter Kornbluh, eds. *Low-Intensity Warfare: Counterinsurgency, Pro-Insurgency, and Antiterrorism in the Eighties* (New York: Pantheon Books, 1988). This volume collects essays on low-intensity wars within and between countries, focusing on their origins and character, and on existing practices within the countries undergoing the conflicts and on major-power intervention to quell or promote insurgency. The focus on U.S. interventionism is particularly interesting. All the essays are broadly critical of great-power military intervention that is designed either to quell or promote insurgency. Although the book was published before the end of the Cold War, the discussions of insurgency, counterinsurgency, and interventionism provide insights into contemporary conflicts.

Oye, Kenneth, ed. *Deterrence Debates: Problems of Definition, Specification, and Estimation* (Ann Arbor: University of Michigan Press, 1994). This volume contains a collection of articles on the "rational deterrence debate"—a debate concerning the subject of extended deterrence, the attempt by a country to protect another from attack by a third country through the threat of force. For more than two decades, but especially in the late 1980s, scholars have disagreed over whether and under what conditions such deterrence will succeed. This disagreement has sparked a number of other methodological disagreements over how to define deterrence, how to select cases of deterrence, how to measure success and failure, and how to theorize and empirically understand important historical subjects. Contributors include the main partisans to the recent debate, including Paul Huth, Bruce Russett, Richard Ned Lebow, and Janice Stein.

Pastor, Robert. "Preempting Revolutions: The Boundaries of US Influence," *International Security,* Vol. 15 (Spring 1991). Pastor considers whether the United States can prevent revolutions that replace friendly Third World dictatorships with hostile democratic or revolutionary regimes. The cases he reviews include Cuba, Nicaragua, Iran, and the Philippines. Noting that the United States invariably sought to promote political liberalization, he concludes that U.S. power to influence peaceful and friendly democratization of dictatorships is limited, with outcomes depending primarily on local circumstances. He recommends that the United States obtain better information on local actors and develop more contacts with military groups, insurgents, and regional governments. These improvements should be part of a more long-term approach, including a clear multilateral human rights policy, which would facilitate a dictator's departure, assist international supervision of elections, and help consolidate democracy following elections.

Reed, Laura, and Carl Kaysen, eds. *Emerging Norms of Justified Intervention* (Cambridge, Mass.: American Academy of Arts and Sciences, 1993). This collection of essays considers whether, when, and how the international community can justifiably intervene to ameliorate ethnic conflict, civil wars, widespread human rights abuses, and human suffering generally. The essays address the efficacy, legality, and legitimacy of such humanitarian intervention; contributors include political scientists, historians, international legal scholars, and philosophers.

Schelling, T. C. *The Strategy of Conflict* (Cambridge, Mass.: Harvard University Press, 1960). Schelling lays the groundwork for a theory of the strategy of interdependent decision making in international conflict. One of the first analysts to show how such conflicts often take the form of bargaining or mixed-motive games, he goes beyond the traditional game theory of the time to overview elements of games to be considered when constructing theories of international conflict, including interdependent decision, tacit bargaining, manipulation of information to convey commitments, "focal points," and other concepts that have become widely used in contemporary studies of conflict and cooperation.

Schelling, T. C. *Arms and Influence* (New Haven, Conn.: Yale University Press, 1966). In a more accessible and focused book than *The Strategy of Conflict,* Schelling develops a series of principles that underlie the diplomacy of violence and the use of military potential to influence other countries and their people by the harm it could do to them. Throughout history nations have used this potential for evil, for self-protection, and for peacemaking as an integral part of establishing and using bargaining power, "the uglier, less civilized part of diplomacy." The principles he develops concern how nations try to use military capacity for bargaining power, the difficulties and dangers of that use, and the sources of success and failure. The principles are clustered under subjects such as the manipulation of risk, the "art of commitment," and the implicit dialogue of arms races. Although the book is theoretical, it draws on dozens of historical illustrations from past and contemporary cases of deterrence, compellence, and other examples of force-infused diplomacy.

Van Evera, Stephen. "The United States and the Third World: When to Intervene?" in Kenneth Oye et al., eds., *Eagle in a New World: American Grand Strategy in a Post–Cold War Era* (New York: HarperCollins, 1992). Van Evera considers the appropriateness and efficacy of U.S. military intervention into the Third World in the service of national security, democratization, and peacemaking. On the whole, Van Evera states that military intervention in the Third World is rarely justified and is becoming less so. The discussion of national security focuses principally on power-balancing and considers several assumptions underlying interventionism for national security: the USSR sought an empire in the Third World; it could gain such an empire either by direct intervention or by proxy wars; and such an empire would substantially increase Soviet military strength so as to shift the world balance of power. Other national security arguments Van Evera considers as justification for intervention are the pursuit of raw materials; the loss of key strategic locations; credibility in other arenas; and domino effects. In all cases, the article explains why the Third World is likely to be less important for these justifications. Moreover, Van Evera argues that the United States lacks the means to create democracy in countries without necessary preconditions, and that the United States lacks the will to promote democracy when the outcome is a leftist government.

Waltz, Kenneth. "What Will the Spread of Nuclear Weapons Do to the World?," in J. King, ed., *International Political Effects of the Spread of Nuclear Weapons* (Washington, D.C.: National Foreign Assessments Center, CIA, 1979). In this controversial article, Waltz states that contrary to widespread wisdom, the spread of nuclear weapons might mitigate violence and enhance security both for the countries possessing the weapons and for "third" countries. He observes that the acquisition of nuclear weapons exponentially increases the ability to wreak damage on an adversary, and that when both parties to a struggle have such an ability, the stability and certainty of deterrence will be much stronger than if they rely on conventional weaponry. Acknowledging that crisis situations could unravel such stability, he emphasizes that mini balances of power in the U.S.-USSR Cold War model could emerge to moderate confrontation.

Conflict-Resolution Overviews and Alternatives

Bloomfield, L. P., and A. C. Leiss. *Controlling Small Wars* (New York: Alfred A. Knopf, 1969). Bloomfield and Leiss identify conditions for minimizing violence in small wars, both internal and interstate. They distinguish such a task from understanding the conditions for winning a conflict. They discuss cases including civil wars such as the Greek Insurgency, colonial wars such as the Indonesian War of Independence, and several kinds of interstate wars such as the Arab–Israeli conflict and the Soviet–Iranian conflict of 1945–46. All the cases are analyzed in terms of different stages in the character and intensity of violence, and they are discussed theoretically in a chapter entitled "Anatomy of Conflict." They focus on the causes leading to higher or lower levels of violence, and the conclusion presents several of the most common and important factors that minimize violence at different stages, such as preventing violent escalation or promoting peaceful deescalation.

These factors underlie policy prescriptions for the countries and groups involved in hostilities, as well as third countries and international institutions that seek to control those hostilities. Suggestions include lowering unneeded national armaments that threaten combatants, addressing political and economic sources rather than military manifestations of conflict, and formally or informally agreeing with one's adversaries to abstain from fueling a conflict.

Burton, John. *Conflict: Resolution and Provention* (London: Macmillan Press, 1990). This book develops and tests a theory of conflict, its resolution, and "provention," the removal of basic sources of conflict. Burton considers conflict to be a universal phenomenon "affecting all cultures, at all stages of political, social and economic development, and at all societal levels from the interpersonal to the international." Conflict has its origins in "deep-rooted human needs" that cannot be altered by socialization processes or deterred by coercion, although these methods are still relevant. Drawing on a variety of traditions in political psychology and anthropology, Burton approaches conflict resolution and prevention according to what he calls "problem-solving . . . political philosophy," implying a focus on the underlying sources of conflict rather than on its overt, violent manifestations. This approach also emphasizes the importance of third-party mediation to the resolution of intractable conflicts stemming from needs basic to human experience.

Oye, Kenneth, ed. *Cooperation Under Anarchy* (Princeton, N.J.: Princeton University Press, 1986). This volume develops, illustrates, and tests theories of international cooperation in security and economic affairs. As its point of departure, it acknowledges that the anarchic character of the international system militates against interstate cooperation, but that such cooperation is possible and likely under theoretically understandable and empirically observable conditions. These conditions include the existence of repeated interaction between states, interdependence of interests, the internal interests and beliefs of statesmen, and the existence of international institutions and norms that soften anarchy. Illustrations include studies of the Concert of Europe as an example of international security cooperation, of why cooperation failed in 1914, and of arms races and their control through cooperation.

Sharp, Gene. *The Politics of Nonviolent Action* (Boston: P. Sargent Publisher, 1973), 3 vols. This three-volume study concentrates on the politics of nonviolent action as an alternative to war and violent civil conflict. The first volume focuses on political power and its dependence on the cooperation of the populace. Government's dependence on this cooperation is what makes nonviolent action possible. The second volume presents a detailed inventory of 198 methods of nonviolent action and nonviolent weapons, including discussion of how they may be used as part of a larger nonviolent strategy. The third volume analyzes the historical dynamics of nonviolent action.

Weston, Bruce, ed. *Alternative Security: Living Without Nuclear Deterrence* (Boulder, Colo.: Westview Press, 1990). This volume discusses alternatives to nuclear deterrence as a method for preserving and establishing peace between and among industrialized and developing countries. These alternatives include stable conventional military strategy and international law, as well as more wide-ranging strategies of conflict resolution that address domestic political and economic origins of violence. Among these are Bruce Russett's essay, "Toward a More Democratic, Therefore More Peaceful, World," which argues for a foreign policy by Western democracies that uses carrots and sticks to promote democracy in less democratic countries, based on the premise that democracies rarely fight each other (see Doyle above). Another essay is Lloyd Dumas's "Economics and Alternative Security: Toward a Peacekeeping International Economy," which connects international economic development policies to the pursuit of political stability and peace.

Index

Sam·s·kāra. 1. Forming well or thoroughly, making perfect, perfecting; finishing, refining, refinement, accomplishment. 2. Forming in the mind, conception, idea, notion; the power of memory, faculty of recollection, the realizing of past perceptions... 3. Preparation, making ready, preparation of food, etc., cooking, dressing... 4 ... 5. Making sacred, hallowing, consecration, dedication; consecration of a king, etc. 6. Making pure, purification, purity. 7. A sanctifying or purificatory rite or essential ceremony (enjoined on all the first three classes or castes). 8. Any rite or ceremony. 9. Funeral obsequies.

From p. 1479, *A Kannada-English Dictionary*
by the Reverend F. Kittel, Mangalore, 1894

PART ONE

I

HE BATHED Bhagirathi's body, a dried-up wasted pea-pod, and wrapped a fresh sari around it; then he offered food and flowers to the gods as he did every day, put the flowers in her hair, and gave her holy water. She touched his feet, he blessed her. Then he brought her a bowlful of cracked-wheat porridge from the kitchen.

Bhagirathi said in a low voice, "You finish your meal first."

"No, no. Finish your porridge. That first."

The words were part of a twenty-year-old routine between them. A routine that began with the bath at dawn, twilight prayers, cooking, medicines for his wife. And crossing the stream again to the Maruti temple for worship. That was the unfailing daily routine. After their meals, the brahmins of the agrahara would come to the front of his house, one by one, and gather there to listen to his recitation of sacred legends, always new and always dear to them and to him. In the evening he would take another bath, say more twilight prayers, make porridge for his wife, cook, eat dinner. Then there would be more recitations for the brahmins who gathered again on the verandah.

Now and then Bhagirathi would say: "Being married to me is no joy. A house needs a child. Why don't you just get married again?" Praneshacharya would laugh aloud. "A wedding for an old man . . . ."

"Come now, what kind of an old man are you? You haven't touched forty yet. Any father would love to give you his girl and bless her with wedding water. You studied Sanskrit in Kashi . . . . A house needs a child to make it home. You've had no joy in this marriage."

Praneshacharya would not answer. He would smile and pat his

9

wife who was trying to get up, and ask her to try and go to sleep. Didn't Lord Krishna say: Do what's to be done with no thought of fruit? The Lord definitely means to test him on his way to salvation; that's why He has given him a brahmin birth this time and set him up in this kind of family. The Acharya is filled with pleasure and a sense of worth as sweet as the five-fold nectar of holy days; he is filled with compassion for his ailing wife. He proudly swells a little at his lot, thinking, "By marrying an invalid, I get ripe and ready."

Before he sat down to his meal, he picked up the fodder for Gowri, the cow, on a banana leaf and placed it in front of Gowri who was grazing in the backyard. Worshipfully he caressed the cow's body, till the hair on her hide rose in pleasure. In a gesture of respect, he touched his own eyes with the hand that had touched the holy animal. As he came in, he heard a woman's voice calling out, "Acharya, Acharya."

It sounded like Chandri's voice. Chandri was Naranappa's concubine. If the Acharya talked to her, he would be polluted; he would have to bathe again before his meal. But how can a morsel go down the gullet with a woman waiting in the yard?

He came out. Chandri quickly pulled the end of her sari over her head, blanched, and stood there, afraid.

"What's the matter?"

"He...He..."

Chandri shivered; words stuck in her mouth. She held on to the pillar.

"What? Naranappa? What happened?"

"Gone..."

She covered her face with her hands.

"Narayana, Narayana—when was that?"

"Just now."

Between sobs Chandri answered:

"He came back from Shivamogge and took to bed in a fever. Four days of fever, that's all. He had a painful lump on his side, the kind they get with fever."

"Narayana."

Praneshacharya ran out, still wrapped in the ritual raw silk, ran to Garudacharya's house and went straight to the kitchen calling out, "Garuda, Garuda!"

The dead Naranappa had been related to Garuda for five generations. Naranappa's great-grandfather's grandmother and Garuda's great-grandfather's grandmother were sisters.

Garudacharya was in the act of raising a handful of rice mixed with *saru* to his mouth, when Praneshacharya entered, wiping the sweat of midday from his face, and said, "Narayana. Don't. Garuda, don't eat. I hear Naranappa is dead." Dumbstruck, Garuda threw down the mixed rice in his hand on the leaf before him, took a gulp of consecrated water and rose from his seat. He couldn't eat, even though he had quarrelled with Naranappa, severed all relations with him, and shed his kinship long ago. His wife, Sitadevi, stood there motionless, ladle in hand. He said to her, "It's all right for the children. They can eat. Only we adults shouldn't, till the funeral rites are done." He came out with Praneshacharya. They feared that the kinsmen next door might eat before they got the news, so they ran from house to house—Praneshacharya to Udupi Lakshmanacharya, Garudacharya to Lakshmidevamma the half-wit and to Durgabhatta down the street. The news of death spread like a fire to the other ten houses of the agrahara. Doors and windows were shut, with children inside. By god's grace, no brahmin had yet eaten. Not a human soul there felt a pang at Naranappa's death, not even women and children. Still in everyone's heart an obscure fear, an unclean anxiety. Alive, Naranappa was an enemy; dead, a preventer of meals; as a corpse, a problem, a nuisance. Soon the men moved towards the Acharya's house-front. The wives blew words of warning into their husbands' ears:

"Don't be in a hurry. Wait till Praneshacharya gives you a decision. Don't agree too quickly to perform the rites. You may do the wrong thing. The guru will excommunicate you."

The brahmins gathered again, just as they did for the daily reading of the holy legends, crowded one against the other. But today an obscure anxiety brooded among them. Fingering the basil-bead rosary round his neck, Praneshacharya said to them, almost as if to himself:

"Naranappa's death-rites have to be done: that's problem one. He has no children. Someone should do it: that's problem two."

Chandri, standing against the pillar in the yard, waited anxiously for the brahmins' verdict. The brahmin wives had come in through the backdoor into the middle hall, unable to contain their curiosity, afraid their husbands might do something rash.

Fondling his fat black naked arms, Garudacharya said as usual:

"Yes. Ye ... es. Ye ... es."

"No one can eat anything until the body's cremated," said Dasacharya, one of the poorer brahmins, thin, bony as a sick cow.

"True ... true ... quite true," said Lakshmanacharya, rubbing his belly—jerking his face forwards and backwards, batting his eyelids rapidly. The only well-fed part of his body was his belly, swollen with malarial bubo. Sunken cheeks, yellow eyes deep in sockets, ribs protruding, a leg twisted—altogether an unbalanced body. The rival brahmins of Parijatapura mocked at him for walking with his buttocks out.

No one had a direct suggestion. Praneshacharya said:

"So the problem before us is—who should perform the rites? The Books say, any relative can. Failing that, any brahmin can offer to do them."

When relatives were mentioned, everyone looked at Garuda and Lakshmana. Lakshmana closed his eyes, as if to say it's not for him. But Garuda was familiar with law courts, having walked up and down many; he felt it was his turn to speak up. So he raised a pinch of snuff to his nose and cleared his throat:

"It's but right we should go by the ancient Law Books. Acharya, you are our greatest scholar, your word is vedic gospel to us. Give us the word, we'll do it. Between Naranappa and me, it's true, there's a bond of kinship going back several generations. But, as you know, his father and I fought over that orchard and went to court. After his father's death, I appealed to the guru at the Dharmasthala monastery. He decreed in my favour. Yet Naranappa defied it, even god's word—what do you say?—So we swore we'd have nothing between us for generations to come, nothing, no exchange of words, no wedding, no rite, no meal, no hospitality. That's what we swore—what do you say…"

Garudacharya's nasal sentences punctuated by his what-do-you-says suddenly halted, but were spurred on again by two more pinches of snuff. He gathered courage, looked around, saw Chandri's face and said boldly:

"The guru will also agree to what you say. What do you say? Let's set aside the question of whether I should do the rites. The real question is: is he a brahmin at all? What do you say?—He slept regularly with a lowcaste woman…"

There was only one man from the Smarta sect, Durgabhatta, in this colony of Madhva brahmins. He was always checking and measuring the rival sect's orthodoxy with a questioning eye. He looked sideways at Chandri and cackled:

"Chi Chi Chi, don't be too rash, Acharya. O no, a brahmin isn't lost because he takes a lowborn prostitute. Our ancestors after all came from the North—you can ask Praneshacharya if you wish—history says they cohabited with Dravidian women. Don't think I am being facetious. Think of all the people who go to the brothels of Basrur in South Kanara…"

Garudacharya got angry. This fellow was mischievous.

"Not so fast, not so fast, Durgabhatta! The question here is not simply one of carnal desire. We don't have to advise our great Praneshacharya. He knows all about alliances and misalliances, has studied it all in Kashi, he knows all the scriptures, earned the title Crest-Jewel of Vedic Learning. What do you say?…Our Acharya has won all sorts of arguments with all the super-pundits, yours and ours, won honours at every seat of learning in the South, fifteen lace shawls and silver platters…our Acharya…what do you say?…"

Embarrassed by the way this conversation had turned away from the question at hand towards his own praise, Praneshacharya said:

"Lakshmana, what do *you* say? Naranappa was married to your wife's sister, after all."

Lakshmana closed his eyes.

"It's your word, your command. What do we know of the subtleties of dharma? As Garuda says, Naranappa had contacts with a low-caste . . ." He stopped in the middle of his sentence, opened his eyes wide, and dug into his nose with his upper cloth. "As you know, he even ate what she cooked . . ."

Padmanabhacharya who lived right opposite Naranappa's house added:

"And he drank too."

"Besides drinking, he ate animal flesh." Turning to Durgabhatta, Garudacharya said, "Maybe even that doesn't matter too much *to you* people. Shankara, your great founder, in his hunger for full experience, exchanged his body for a dead king's and enjoyed himself with the queen, didn't he?"

Praneshacharya thought that the talk was getting out of hand. He said, "Garuda. Stop talking for a while, please."

"Naranappa abandoned his lawful wife after tying the wedding-string round her neck. You may condone even that . . ." Lakshmana had closed his eyes again and started talking. "He went and got mixed up with some woman. My wife's sister became hysterical and died: he didn't even come to the funeral rites. You may condone even that; but he didn't care to observe the death-anniversaries of his own father and mother. I'm not the sort who would hide anything about him just because he was my close relative. He was my wife's uncle's son. We tolerated things and sheltered him in our lap as long as we could. In return, what does he do? He comes to the river in full view of all the brahmins and takes the holy stone that we've worshipped for generations and throws it in the water and spits after it! Condone everything if you wish—but didn't he, wilfully, before our very eyes, bring Muslims over and eat and drink forbidden things in the wide-open front yard? If any of us questioned him in good faith, he would turn on us, cover us with abuse from head to foot. As long as he lived, we just had to walk in fear of him."

Lakshmana's wife, Anasuya, listening to him from inside the house, felt proud that her husband said all the right things. Her eyes fell on Chandri sitting against the pillar, and she cursed her to her heart's content: may tigers trample her at midnight, may snakes bite her, this whore, this seducing witch! If she had not given him potions, why should he, Anasuya's own maternal uncle's son, why should he push aside his own kinswoman, call her an invalid, squander all his property, and throw all the ancestral gold and jewels on the neck of this evil witch! She looked at the four-strand gold chain round Chandri's neck and the thick gold bracelet on her wrist, and could not bear to think of it. She wept loudly. If only her sister had been alive, that gold chain would have been round *her* neck—would a blood-relative's corpse lie around like this without even the benefit of a rite? All because of this filthy whore—won't someone brand her face! Anasuya simmered and simmered till she boiled over and cried.

Dasacharya lived entirely on the meals that brahmins get at death-rites and anniversaries. He would walk ten miles for such a meal any day. He complained: "As you all know, we let him stay in our agrahara, so for two whole years we didn't get calls for any meal or banquet. If we do the rites for him now or anything rash like that, no one will ever invite us for a brahmin meal. But then we can't keep his dead body uncremated here in the agrahara either, and fast forever. This is a terrible dilemma. Praneshacharya should tell us precisely what's right and what's wrong. Who in our sect can dispute his word?"

For Durgabhatta, this was an internal issue. He sat unconcerned in his place, ogling Chandri. For the first time his connoisseur eyes had the chance to appraise this precious object which did not normally stir out of the house, this choice object that Naranappa had brought from Kundapura. A real "sharp" type, exactly as described in Vatsyayana's manual of love—look at her, toes longer than the big toe, just as the Love Manual says. Look at those breasts. In sex she's the type who sucks the male dry. Her eyes, which should be fickle, are now misty with grief and fear, but she looks good that way. Like Matsyagandhi, the Fisherwoman in the Ravi Varma print hung up in Durgabhatta's bedroom, shyly trying to hide her breasts bursting through her poor rag of a sari. The same eyes and nose: no wonder Naranappa threw away the worship-stone for her, ate taboo meat and drank taboo liquor. One wonders at his daring. One remembers Jagannatha the brahmin poet who married the Muslim girl, and his verses about the alien's breasts. If Praneshacharya were not present, if Naranappa weren't lying dead right there, he would have happily quoted the stanza and expanded on it even to these barren brahmins. "To the lustful"—that is, to Naranappa and his like—"there's no fear, no shame," as the saying goes.

Noticing that the audience was silent, Durgabhatta spoke up:

"We've anyway said whatever needs to be said. What's the use of raking up dead men's faults? Let Praneshacharya speak. He is a guru, for me as for you, regardless of what Garudacharya may say in his passion."

Praneshacharya was weighing every word, knowing full well that the protection of the entire brahmin agrahara was now on his shoulders. He spoke haltingly.

"Garuda said: an oath stands between him and Naranappa. Yet the Books of Law have ways of absolving such oaths—you can perform a rite of absolution, give away a cow, make a pilgrimage. But this is an expensive matter, and I've no right to ask anyone to spend his money. And as for the question raised by Lakshmana and Dasa and others that Naranappa didn't behave as a well-born brahmin, that he's a smear on the good name of the agrahara, it's a deep question—I have no clear answer. For one thing, he may have rejected brahminhood, but brahminhood never left him. No one ever excommunicated him officially. He didn't die an outcaste; so he remains a brahmin in his death. Only another brahmin has any right to touch his body. If we let someone else do it, we'd be sullying our brahminhood. Yet I hesitate, I can't tell you dogmatically: go ahead with the rite. I hesitate because you've all seen the way he lived. What shall we do? What do the Law Books really say, is there any real absolution for such violations?..."

Suddenly Chandri did something that stunned the brahmins. She moved forward to stand in the front courtyard. They couldn't believe their own eyes: Chandri loosened her four-strand gold chain, her thick bracelet, her bangles, and placed them all in a heap before

Praneshacharya. She mumbled something about all this jewellery being there for the expenses of the rite, and went back to stand in her place.

The women calculated swiftly: that heap of gold was worth at least two thousand rupees. One after another, the wives scanned their husbands' faces. The brahmins bowed their heads: they were afraid, fearful that the lust for gold might destroy brahmin purity. But in the heart of every one of them flashed the question: if some other brahmin should perform the final rite for Naranappa, he might keep his brahminhood and yet put all that gold on his wife's neck. The new reason inflamed further the jealous hatred between Lakshmana and Garuda: "Suppose this wretch should rake in all that gold giving a poor starving cow as a token gift, insuring both the goods of this world and the other?" Durgabhatta said to himself: "If these Madhvas get tempted and cremate Naranappa, I'll roam the towns, spread the news, expose these so-called brahmins." The eyes of the poorer brahmins like Dasa grew moist, their mouths watered. Would Garuda and Lakshmana let anyone else do the rites?

Praneshacharya grew anxious. Why did Chandri spoil everything with her good intentions?

Every brahmin present was afraid that someone else might be tempted to agree, and vied with the others in lurid accounts of Naranappa's misdeeds—things done not to them but always to others.

"Who induced Garuda's son to run away from home and join the army? Naranappa, who else? Praneshacharya had taught the boy the Vedic scriptures, but what mattered finally was only Naranappa's word. That fellow was hell-bent on corrupting our young people..."

"Look at poor Lakshmana's son-in-law now. Lakshmana picks an orphan, nurses him, brings him up and gives his daughter in marriage to him—then Naranappa comes along and turns the young fellow's head. You hardly see him here once in a month."

"And then those fish in the temple-pond. For generations they were dedicated to Lord Ganesha. People believe that anyone who catches the sacred fish will vomit blood and die. But this outcaste scoundrel didn't care two hoots, he got together his Muslim gang, dynamited the tank and killed off god's own fish. Now even low-caste folk go there and fish. The rascal undermined all good brahmin influence on the others, he saw to it. And then, he wasn't content with ruining our agrahara, he had to go and spoil the boys of Parijatapura too, make them run after dramas and shows."

"The casteless scoundrel should have been excommunicated, what do you say?"

"How could that be Garuda? He threatened to become a Muslim. On the eleventh day of the moon, when every brahmin was fasting, he brought in Muslims to the agrahara and feasted them. He said, 'Try and excommunicate me now. I'll become a Muslim, I'll get you all tied to pillars and cram cow's flesh into your mouths and see to it personally that your sacred brahminism is ground into the mud.' He said that. If he had really become a Muslim no law could have thrown him out of the brahmin agrahara. We would have had to leave. Even Praneshacharya kept quiet then, his hands were tied too."

Dasacharya put in his last word. He was upset he'd had to get up from his meal before he'd a chance to taste one morsel of his mango-rice. He was hungry.

"After his father's death, no brahmin here got a taste of that jack-fruit in his backyard—and it used to taste like honey."

The women kept staring at the heap of gold and they were disappointed by their husbands' words. Garuda's wife, Sita, was outraged by the way Lakshmana had shot his mouth off about her son joining the army. What right did *he* have to talk about her son? Lakshmana's wife, Anasuya, was outraged by Garuda talking about *her* son-in-law being corrupted—what right did he have?

Thinking what an ordeal this whole affair was getting to be, Praneshacharya said almost in soliloquy:

"What's the way out now? Can we just fold our arms and stare at a dead body laid out in the agrahara? According to ancient custom, until the body is properly removed there can be no worship, no bathing, no prayers, no food, nothing. And, because he was not excommunicated, no one but a brahmin can touch his body."

"Not excommunicating him at the right time—that's the cause

of all this mess," said Garuda, who for years had screamed for an excommunication. He got his chance now to say, "I-told-you-so, you-didn't-listen-to-me."

The brahmins countered him as one man: "Yes, yes, if he had actually become a Muslim, we'd have had to leave the polluted agrahara; there'd have been no two ways about it."

Dasa, who had meanwhile been imagining the hardship of a whole day without food, suddenly came out with an idea. He stood up alertly and said:

"I have heard that Naranappa was very friendly with the brahmins of Parijatapura. They ate and hobnobbed together. Why don't we ask them? Their orthodoxy is not as strict as ours, anyway."

Parijatapura's brahmins were Smartas, not quite out of the upper set, their lines being a little mixed. Once upon a time some lecher got one of their widows pregnant and their agrahara tried to hush it up. The rumour was that the guru at Shringeri heard of it and excommunicated the whole colony. On the whole the brahmins of Parijatapura were pleasure-lovers, not so crazy about orthodoxy and strict rules; they were experts at running betelnut farms, and rich too. So, Durgabhatta had a soft spot for the whole clan; furthermore, he was a Smarta himself. He had secretly eaten their flat-rice and *uppittu* and drunk their coffee. He was not brazen enough to eat a whole meal with them, that's all.

Furthermore, he was fascinated by their widows who didn't shave their heads and grew their hair long, who even chewed betel leaf and reddened their mouths. He got into quite a rage at Dasacharya— "Look at this Madhva's gall, though he can't afford a morning meal." He stood up and said:

"Look, that's a foul thing to say. You may think them low hybrid brahmins, but they don't think so themselves. If your sect will be polluted by laying hands on your own dead man, wouldn't it pollute them worse? Go ahead, be cheeky and ask them—you'll get an earful. Do you know that Manjayya of Parijatapura has enough money to buy up every man's son here?"

Praneshacharya tried to pacify Durgabhatta's anger.

"You're quite right. It's not truly brahminical to get someone else to do what you don't do yourself. But friendship is as strong a bond as blood, isn't it? If they and Naranappa were friends, don't you think they should be told of their good friend's death?"

Durgabhatta said, "Agreed, Acharya. The brahminism of your entire sect is in your hands. Your burden is great. Who can go against what you decide?" He had spoken all he felt. He didn't speak again.

The question of the gold ornaments came up again. If the Parijatapura people chose to perform the rites, shouldn't the gold go to them? Lakshmana's wife, Anasuya, could not bear the thought of her sister's rightful jewels falling into the hands of some hybrid brahmin in the next village. Unable to contain herself any more, she blurted out: "Who does she think she is? If things were straight, they should be around my sister's neck." Then she broke into sobs. Lakshmana felt the tightness of his wife's words, but he didn't want his status as a husband to be lowered in public. So he snarled, "You shut up now. Why are you prating in an assembly of menfolk?"

Garuda, angry now, thundered: "What kind of talk is this? According to the decree of the Dharmasthala guru, this gold belongs to me."

Wearily Praneshacharya consoled them.

"Be patient. What's before us is a dead body waiting to be cremated. About the gold—leave the decision to me. First send someone to Parijatapura with the news. If they decide by themselves to perform the rites, let them."

Then he stood up and said, "You may go now. I'll look into Manu and other texts. I'll see if there's a way out of this dilemma." Chandri pulled her sari-end over her head respectfully, and looked imploringly at the Acharya.

II

There were cockroaches in the buttermilk shelves, fat rats in the store-room. In the middle room, ritually washed saris and clothes hung out on a rope stretched for a clothes-line. Fresh *pappadams*, fries, and marinated red peppers spread out to dry on the verandah mat. Sacred balsam plants in the backyard. These were common to all the houses in the agrahara. The differences were only in the flowering trees in the backyards: Bhimacharya had *parijata*, Padmanabhacharya had a jasmine bush, Lakshmana had the *ember-champak*, Garuda had red *ranja*, Dasa had white *mandara*. Durgabhatta had the conch-flower and the *bilva* leaf for Shiva-worship. The brahmins went to each other's yards each morning to get flowers for worship and to ask after each other's welfare. But the flowers that bloomed in Naranappa's yard were reserved solely for Chandri's hair and for a vase in the bedroom. As if that wasn't provocative enough, right in his front yard grew a bush, a favourite of snakes, with flowers unfit for any god's crown—the night-queen bush. In the darkness of night, the bush was thickly clustered with flowers, invading the night like some raging lust, pouring forth its nocturnal fragrance. The agrahara writhed in its hold as in the grip of a magic serpent-binding spell. People with delicate nostrils complained of headaches, walked about with their dhotis held to their noses. Some clever fellows even said Naranappa had grown the bush to guard with snakes the gold he had gathered. While the auspicious brahmin wives, with their dwarfish braids and withered faces, wore *mandara* and jasmine, Chandri wore her black-snake hair coiled in a knot and wore the flowers of the *ember-champak* and the heady fragrant screw-pine. All day the smells were gentle and tranquil, the sandalpaste on the brahmins' bodies and the soft fragrance of *parijata* and other such flowers. But when it grew dark, the night-queen reigned over the agrahara.

The jackfruit and mango in the backyard of each house tasted different from all the others. The fruit and flower were distributed, according to the saying: "Share fruit and eat it, share flowers and wear them." Only Lakshmana was sneaky, he moved out half the yield of his trees and sold it to the Konkani shopkeepers. His was a niggard's spirit. Whenever his wife's people came visiting, he watched his wife's hands with the eyes of a hawk—never sure when or what she was passing on to her mother's house. In the hot months every house put out *kosumbari-salads* and sweet fruit-drinks; in the eighth month they invited each other for lamp-offerings. Naranappa was the only exception to all these exchanges. A total of ten houses stood on either side of the agrahara street. Naranappa's house, bigger than the others, stood at one end. The Tunga river flowed close to the backyards of the houses on one side of the street, with steps to get down to the water, steps built by some pious soul long ago. In the rainy month the river would rise, roar for three or four days, making as if she was going to rush into the agrahara; offer a carnival of swirls and water-noises for the eyes and ears of children, and then subside. By mid-summer she would dry to a mere rustle, a trickle of three strands of water. Then the brahmins raised green and yellow cucumber or watermelon in the sand-bank as vegetables for rainy days. All twelve months of the year colourful cucumbers hung from the ceiling, wrapped in banana-fibre. In the rainy season, they used cucumber for everything, curry, mash, or soup made with the seeds; and like pregnant women, the brahmins longed for the soups of sour mango-mash. All twelve months of the year, they had vows to keep; they had calls for ritual meals occasioned by deaths, weddings, young boys' initiations. On big festival days, like the day of the annual temple celebrations or the death-anniversary of the Great Commentator, there would be a feast in the monastery thirty miles away. The brahmins' lives ran smoothly in this annual cycle of appointments.

The name of the agrahara was Durvasapura. There was a place-legend about it. Right in the middle of the flowing Tunga river stood an island-like hillock, overgrown with a knot of trees. They believed Sage Durvasa still performed his penance on it. In the Second Aeon of the cycle of time, for a short while, the five Pandava brothers had lived ten miles from here, in a place called Kaimara. Once their wife Draupadi had wanted to go for a swim in the water. Bhima, a husband who fulfilled every whim of his wife, had dammed up the Tunga river for her. When Sage Durvasa woke up in the morning and looked for water for his bath and prayers, there wasn't any in his part of the Tunga. He got angry. But Dharmaraja, the eldest, with his divine vision, could see what was happening, and advised his rash brother Bhima to do something about it. Bhima, Son of the Wind-god, forever obedient to this elder brother's words, broke the dam in three places and let the water flow. That's why even today from the Kaimara dam on, the river flows in three strands. The brahmins of Durvasapura often say to their neighbouring agraharas: on the twelfth day of the moon, early in the morning, any truly pious man could hear the conch of Sage Durvasa from his clump of trees. But the brahmins of the agrahara never made any crude claims that they themselves had ever heard the sound of that conch.

So, the agrahara had become famous in all ten directions—because of its legends, and also because of Praneshacharya, the great ascetic, "Crest-Jewel of Vedic Learning," who had settled down there, and certainly because of that scoundrel Naranappa. On special occasions like the birth-anniversary of Lord Rama, people mobbed the place from the neighbouring agraharas to hear Praneshacharya's ancient holy tales. Though Naranappa was a problem, the Acharya nursed his invalid wife to uphold the great mercy of god, bore up with Naranappa's misdeeds, dispersed little by little the darkness in the brahmins' heads filled with chants they did not understand. His duties in this world grew lighter and more fragrant like sandalwood rubbed daily on stone.

The agrahara street was hot, so hot you could pop corn on it. The brahmins walked through it, weak with hunger, their heads covered with their upper cloth; they crossed the three-pronged river and entered the cool forest to reach Parijatapura after an hour's trudging. The green of the betelnut grove lifted the earth's coolness to the heat of the sky. In the airless atmosphere the trees were still. Hot dust burned the brahmins' feet. Invoking Lord Narayana's name, they entered Manjayya's house in which they had never set foot before. Manjayya, a rich man shrewd in worldly affairs, was writing accounts. He spoke loudly and offered right and proper courtesies.

"Oh oh oh, the entire brahmin clan seems to have found its way here. Please come in, please be good enough to sit down. Wouldn't you like to relax a bit, maybe wash your feet?...Look here, bring some plantains for the guests, will you?"

His wife brought ripe plantains on a platter, and said, "Please come in." They thanked her politely, and went in, Garuda made a hissing sound as he sat down and mentioned Naranappa's death.

"O God! What happened to him? He was here eight or nine days ago on some business. Said he was going to Shivamogge. Asked me if I wanted anything done. I asked him to find out if the markets had sold any arecanuts. Shiva, Shiva....He had said he'd be back by Thursday. What, was he sick? With what?"

Dasacharya said, "Just four days of fever—he also had a swelling."

"Shiva, Shiva," exclaimed Manjayya, as he closed his eyes and fanned himself. Knowing Shivamogge town as he did, he suddenly remembered the one-syllable name of the dread epidemic; and not daring to utter it even to himself, merely said, "Shiva, Shiva."

In the blink of an eye, all the lower-caste brahmins of Parijata-pura gathered on the bund.

"You know—" began Garuda, shrewd man of the world, "we agrahara people had a bad fight with Naranappa, we didn't exchange even water and rice. But you here were all his friends, what do you say, now he's dead, his rites have to be done, what do you say?..."

The Parijatapura folks were unhappy over their friend's death, but quite happy they were getting a chance to cremate a highcaste brahmin. They were partly pleased because Naranappa ate in their houses with no show of caste pride.

Shankarayya, priest of Parijatapura, intervened. "According to brahmin thinking, 'a snake is also a twice-born'; if you happen to see a dead snake, you've to perform the proper rites for it; you shouldn't eat till you've done so. As that's the case, it's absolutely wrong to sit back with folded arms when a brahmin has passed on to the bosom of God. Don't you think so?"

He said this really to display his knowledge of the texts, to tell those Madhvas "we here are no less than you," and to bring down their pride.

Durgabhatta was very agitated by this man's words.

"Look at this stupid brahmin, rashly opening his stupid mouth. He'll bring a bad name to the whole Smarta clan," he thought, and spoke in his own crooked way.

"Yes yes yes, we understand all that. That's exactly what Praneshacharya also says. But our dilemma is something else: is Naranappa, who drank liquor and ate meat, who threw the holy stone into the river, is he a brahmin or is he not? Tell me, which of us is willing to lose his brahminhood here? Yet it's not at all right, I agree, to keep a dead brahmin's body waiting, uncremated."

Shankarayya's heart panicked and missed a beat. His clan had already been classed low, and he didn't like them to fall lower by doing something unbrahminical. So he said:

"If that's so, wait, we can't do anything rash. You, of course, have in Praneshacharya a man known all over the South. Let him look into it and tell us what's right in this crisis. He can untangle the delicate strands of right and wrong."

But Manjayya didn't hesitate to say, "Don't worry about the expenses. Wasn't he my friend? I'll personally see to it that all the necessary charities etcetera are done," meaning really to jibe at the niggardly Madhva crowd.

III

When the brahmins left for Parijatapura, Praneshacharya asked Chandri to sit down, came into the dining-room where his wife lay, and proceeded to tell her how pure Chandri's heart was, how she'd laid down all her gold and what new complications arose from that generous act. Then he sat down among his palm-leaf texts, riffling them for the right and lawful answer. As far back as he could remember Naranappa had always been a problem. The real challenge was to test which would finally win the agrahara: his own penance and faith in ancient ways, or Naranappa's demoniac ways. He wondered by what evil influence Naranappa had got this way, and prayed

that god's grace should bring him redemption. The Acharya fasted
two nights in the week for him. His painful concern and compassion for Naranappa had stemmed also from a promise he had made
to the dead man's mother. He had consoled the dying woman: "I'll
take care of your son's welfare, and bring him to the right path.
Don't worry about him." But Naranappa hadn't walked the path, he
had turned a deaf ear to all counsel. By sheer power of example, he'd
even stolen Praneshacharya's own wards and Sanskrit pupils—Garuda's son Shyama, Lakshmana's son-in-law Shripati. Naranappa
had incited Shyama to run away from home and join the army. The
Acharya, wearied by complaints, had gone to see Naranappa one
day. He was lolling on a soft mattress, and showed some courtesy by
getting up. He didn't take counsel well, and talked his head off;
sneered at the Acharya and brahmin ways.

"Your texts and rites don't work any more. The Congress Party is
coming to power, you'll have to open up the temples to all outcastes,"
and so on irreverently.

The Acharya had even said, "Stop it, it isn't good for you. Don't
separate Shripati from his wife."

A guffaw was the answer. "O Acharya, who in the world can live
with a girl who gives no pleasure—except of course some barren
brahmins!" "You fellows—you brahmins—you want to tie me down
to a hysterical female, just because she is some relative, right? Just
keep your dharma to yourself—we've but one life—I belong to the
'Hedonist School' which says—borrow, if you must, but drink your
ghee."

The Acharya pleaded, "Do whatever you want to do yourself.
Please, please don't corrupt these boys."

He just laughed. "Your Garuda, he robs shaven widows, he plots
evil with black magic men, and he is one of your brahmins, isn't
he?... All right, let's see who wins, Acharya. You or me? Let's see
how long all this brahmin business will last. All your brahmin respectability. I'll roll it up and throw it all ways for a little bit of pleasure with one female. You better leave now—I don't really want to
talk and hurt you either," he said finally.

Why had he, the Acharya, objected to excommunicating such a creature? Was it fear, or compassion? Or the obstinate thought he could win some day? Anyway, here is Naranappa testing out his brahminhood in death, as he did in life.

The last time he saw Naranappa was three months ago, one evening on the fourteenth day of the moon. Garuda had brought in a complaint. Naranappa had taken Muslims with him that morning to the Ganapati temple stream, and before everyone's eyes he'd caught and carried away the sacred fish. Those free-swimming man-length fish, they came to the banks and ate rice from the hand—if any man caught them he would cough up blood and die. At least that's what everyone believed. Naranappa had broken the taboo. The Acharya was afraid of the bad example. With this kind of rebellious example, how will fair play and righteousness prevail? Won't the lower castes get out of hand? In this decadent age, common men follow the right paths out of fear—if that were destroyed, where could we find the strength to uphold the world? He had to speak out. So he had walked quickly to Naranappa's place and confronted him on the verandah.

Naranappa was probably drunk; his eyes were bloodshot, his hair was dishevelled. And yet, didn't he, as soon as he saw the Acharya, put a cloth to his mouth?

The Acharya felt a dawning of hope when he saw this gesture of respect and fear. He sometimes felt that Naranappa's nature was a tricky maze he had no way of entering. But here in this gesture, he saw a crack, a chink in the man's demoniac pride, and felt his forces of virtue rush towards him.

He knew that words were useless. He knew, unless his goodness flowed like the Ganges silently into Naranappa, he would not become open. Yet, a desire welled up in the Acharya, a lust, to swoop on Naranappa like a sacred eagle, to shake him up, tear open the inward springs of ambrosia till they really flowed.

He looked at Naranappa cruelly. Any ordinary sinner would have been terror-struck and fallen to the ground under that gaze. Just two repentant drops from this sinner's eyes, and that would be enough: he'd hug him as a brother—and he looked at Naranappa with desire.

Naranappa bowed his head. He looked as if the sacred bird of prey had swooped and held him in its talons, as if he'd been turned to a worm that minute, bewildered as when a closed door suddenly opens.

Yet, no; he put aside the cloth that covered his mouth, threw it on the chair, and laughed out aloud: "Chandri! Where's the bottle? Let's give the Acharya a little of this holy water!" "Shut up!" Praneshacharya was shaking from head to foot.

He was angered at the way the man slipped from under his influence, and felt he had missed a step on the stairs he was descending.

"Aha! The Acharya too can get angry! Lust and anger, I thought, were only for the likes of us. But then anger plays on the nose-tips of people who try to hold down lust. That's what they say. Durvasa, Parashara, Bhrigu, Brihaspati, Kashyapa, all the sages were given to anger. Chandri, where's the bottle? Look, Acharya—those are the great sages who set the tradition, right? Quite a lusty lot, those sages. What was the name of the fellow who ravished the fisherwoman smelling of fish, right in the boat and gave her body a permanent perfume? And now, look at these poor brahmins, descended from such sages!"

"Naranappa, shut your mouth."

Naranappa, now angry that Chandri didn't bring the liquor to him, ran upstairs making a big noise, brought the bottle down and filled his cup. Chandri tried to stop him, but he pushed her aside. Praneshacharya closed his eyes and tried to leave.

"Acharya, stop, stay a while," said Naranappa. Praneshacharya stayed, mechanically; if he left now he would seem to be afraid. The stench of liquor disgusted him. "Listen," said Naranappa in a voice of authority. Taking a draught from his cup, he laughed wickedly.

"Let's see who wins in the end—you or me. I'll destroy brahminism, I certainly will. My only sorrow is that there's no brahminism really left to destroy in this place—except you. Garuda, Lakshmana, Durgabhatta—ahaha—what brahmins! If I were still a brahmin, that fellow Garudacharya would have washed me down with his *aposhana* water. Or that Lakshmana—he loves money so much he'll lick a copper coin off a heap of shit. He will tie another wilted sister-in-law round my neck, just to get at my property. And I'd have had to cut my hair to a tuft, smear charcoal on my face, sit on your verandah and listen to your holy-holy yarns."

Naranappa took another draught and belched. Chandri stood inside watching everything fearfully, folded her hands and gestured to the Acharya to go away. Praneshacharya turned to go—what's the point of talking with a drunkard?

"Acharya, listen to this. Why this vanity, why should the agra-hara listen to your words all the time? Why don't you listen to a thing or two I say? I'll tell you a holy yarn myself.

"Once, in an agrahara, there lived a very holy Achari—that is, once upon a time. His wife was always ill and he didn't know what it was to have pleasure with a woman—but his lustre, his fame had travelled far and wide to many towns. The other brahmins in the agrahara were awful sinners—they knew every kind of sin, sins of gluttony, sins of avarice, love of gold. But then, this Achari's terrific virtue covered up all their sins; so they sinned some more. As the Achari's virtue grew, so did the sins of everyone else in the agrahara. One day a funny thing happened. What, Acharya-re are you listen-ing? There's a moral at the end—every action results not in what is expected but in its exact opposite. Listen to the lesson and you can go tell the other brahmins too.

"Here comes the funny part. There was a young fellow in the agrahara. He never once slept with his one lawfully wedded wife be-cause she wouldn't sleep with him—out of sheer obedience to her mother's orders. But this young man didn't miss an evening of this Achari's recitations of holy legends—every evening he was there. He'd good reason. It's true, that Achari had no direct experience of life, but he was quite a sport with erotic poetry and things like that. One day he got into a description of Kalidasa's heroine, Shakuntala, in some detail. This young man listened. He was already disgusted with his wife, because the stupid girl complained to her mother that he came to her bed only to pinch her at night. But now the young man felt the Achari's description in his own body, felt a whole female grow inside him, a fire burn in his loins—you know what it means, don't you, Acharya-re?—He couldn't stand it, he leapt from the Achari's verandah and ran. He couldn't bear to hear any more, he ran straight to plunge his heat in the cold water of the river. Luckily, an outcaste woman was bathing there, in the moonlight. Luckily, too, she wasn't wearing too much, all the limbs and parts he craved to see were right before his eyes. She certainly was the fish-scented fisherwoman type, the type your great sage fell for. He fantasied she was the Shakuntala of the Achari's description and this pure brahmin youth made love to her right there—with the moon for witness.

"Now, you explicate it, Acharya-re—didn't the Achari himself corrupt the brahminism of the place? Did he or didn't he? That's why our elders always said: read the Vedas, read the Puranas, but don't try to interpret them. Acharya-re, you are the one who's studied in Kashi—you tell me, who ruined brahminism?"

As Praneshacharya stood silently listening to Naranappa's words, he began to worry: is this a drunkard's rigmarole? Could it be he himself was responsible for such awful things?

With a sigh, he said: "Only sin has a tongue, virtue has none. God have mercy on you—that's all."

"You read those lush sexy Puranas, but you preach a life of barrenness. But my words, they say what they mean: if I say *sleep with a woman*, it means *sleep with a woman*; if I say *eat fish*, it means *eat fish*. Can I give you brahmins a piece of advice, Acharya-re? Push those sickly wives of yours into the river. Be like the sages of your holy legends—get hold of a fish-scented fisherwoman who can cook you fish-soup, and go to sleep in her arms. And if you don't experience god when you wake up, my name isn't Naranappa." Then he winked at the Acharya, quaffed the liquor in his cup and let out a loud long belch.

The Acharya, angered by Naranappa's sneering at his invalid wife, scolded him, called him a low-born scoundrel, and came home. That night, when he sat down for his prayers, he couldn't "still the waves of his mind." He said, "O God," in distress. He gave up telling the luscious Puranic stories in the evenings and started on moral tales of penance. The result—his own enthusiasm for reciting the Puranas faded and died. The young listeners who used to look at him with lively eyes and bring joy to his heart, stopped coming. Only women bent on earning merit, uttering the names of god over yawns in the middle of the stories, and old men, were his audience now.

As he sat reading and contemplating his palm-leaves, he heard his wife's moan and remembered he hadn't given her the afternoon's medicine. He brought it in a small cup, and leaning her head against his chest, poured it into her mouth, and said, "You'd better sleep now." He came back into the hall, muttering to himself obstinately, "What do I mean by saying there's no answer to this dilemma in the Books?" And started reading through them again.

IV

The brahmins came back from Parijatapura, muttering "Hari Hari Hari" as they walked hungry in the sun, thinking of a little rest in the afternoon. But the wives, especially Garuda's wife and Lakshmana's, wouldn't let them rest, and treated them to the Lord's Counsel.

In the agrahara they gave all sorts of reasons why Garuda's single son and heir, Shyama, had run away from home and joined the army. Garuda's enemies said, that the son couldn't take his father's punishments any more. Naranappa's enemies said he had incited Shyama to join the army. Lakshmana's opinion was different—the black magic Garuda used against Naranappa's father must have boomeranged back on himself, why else should Shyama go wrong and run away in spite of Praneshacharya's teaching? Anyone who uses black magic, like the Ash-Demon who wanted to burn his own creator, ends up burning himself. Lakshmana's wife, Anasuya, smarting over Naranappa who had sullied her mother's family name, used to blame him also on Garuda: if Garuda didn't resort to black magic why would a well-born man like Naranappa have gone astray and become an out-caste?

Garuda's wife, Sitadevi, had given up food and drink, and pined away, for her son was "ruined by that scoundrel Naranappa." She'd waited night and day, and groaned for three months. At last a letter came from Shyama—he was in Poona, had joined the army. He was bonded to them by a signature on legal paper, so he couldn't leave unless he put down six hundred rupees as penalty. After that Sita-devi had accosted Naranappa on the street, her arms akimbo, and scolded and wept. Then she'd got a letter written to her son saying, "Don't ever eat meat, don't give up your baths and twilight prayers." She'd fasted Friday nights so that her son's heart might turn good and clean. Garudacharya had raged like Durvasa, and jumped about as if overrun by red ants, shouting, "He's as good as dead to me, if he so much as shows his face here I'll break his head." Sitadevi had of-fered vows to the goddess: "Give my husband peace, may his love be constant for his son." And had given up her food even on Saturday nights. Durgabhatta, that hater of Madhvas, had fuelled the already burning fire, shaming Garuda into lying low forever, by saying, "He's in the army, he'll have no baths, no prayers; and they'll force him to eat meat now."

Today Sitadevi came home happy thinking they might even be able to buy off her son from the military bond, if only Chandri's jewellery came into their hands. The Law Books must have it some-where that her husband could perform Naranappa's rites. But she was worried. Would Lakshmana forestall her own husband and of-fer to do the rites?—Or those people of Parijatapura? They seemed to have no sense of pollution at all, clean and unclean seemed all one to them. She vowed offerings of fruit and coconut to Maruti—"O God, please let my husband be the one to do the rites, please." Now, Naranappa's meat-eating didn't look too heinous. One of these days her son would return from the army—will the cruel tongues of the agrahara keep quiet about it? What'll happen if he gets excommuni-cated? She'd once maligned Praneshacharya for hesitating to excom-municate Naranappa. Now she thought of him worshipfully: he's truly a man of loving kindness, surely he'll take on her son's sins also and protect him. No doubt about it.

Garudacharya had hardly come home and tried to rest on the floor when Sitadevi began to nag him tearfully. But he said severely, "To me he's as good as dead. Don't let me hear a word about that scoundrel." Yet his wife's suggestion entered him like a tick and troubled him. Let everything go to hell, let his son go to hell, he wasn't ready to kill his brahminhood. Yet if only Praneshacharya would say "Yes," the path would be clear. Then he could even rescue his only son and heir from the army. Only a son could offer his fatherly soul any consolations after death.

Though he had growled at his wife "Shut up, impossible," Garuda stepped like a thief into Praneshacharya's house. Without looking at the face of Chandri who was sitting on the raised verandah, he walked into the middle hall.

"Sit down, Garuda. I hear that the Parijatapura folks said they'd do as the Books say. That's right, of course," said Praneshacharya and returned to his palm-leaves. Garuda cleared his throat and asked:

"What do Manu's *Laws* say, Acharya-re?"

Praneshacharya silently shook his head. Garuda went on.

"Sir, what's there in the Books that *you* don't know? I am not asking you about that. Haven't I heard you in controversy with great pundits—what do you say—in the monastery that day—what do you say—on the death-anniversary of the Great Commentator—argue with those pundits from the Vyasaraya monastery? Those fellows were beaten by your challenge—to interpret the sentence, 'Thou art the Original, and me the reflection'—according to our Madhva school. The feast that day went on for four hours. So you mustn't misunderstand me; I haven't come to offer *you* any suggestions. In your presence, I'm a lout, a clumsy bear."

The Acharya felt disgust rising in him at Garuda's attempts to flatter and cajole him. This man wasn't really interested in what was in the Books. All the fellow wanted to hear was: "Yes you can do it." So this Garuda is now raising him, the Acharya, to the skies, for a "Yes" that would silence all fault-finding tongues. The motive: gold.

Generosity creates its exact opposite; just what Naranappa said once. You shouldn't melt in pity now; you should stand firm, see what the Books say, and do accordingly.

"What do you say, the ancient sages knew past, present and future. Is it possible they didn't think about this problem, or what?"

The Acharya didn't answer and continued to read. "Acharya-re, you once said—our Philosophy is called Vedanta, because it's the end, the *anta*, of all thinking. Is it ever possible that such Vedanta has no solution for us? Especially when—what do you say—a brahmin corpse lies untouched in the agrahara, thwarting every daily duty for a whole colony of brahmins—what do you say—they can't eat till they take care of the body—I don't mean just that—"

Praneshacharya didn't answer. Garuda was returning all the Vedanta, Purana, and logic he'd heard from him—for what? Gold. Alas for men's lives.

"Furthermore, what you said was very right. He abandoned brahminhood, but brahminhood didn't abandon him, did it? We didn't get him excommunicated, did we? What do you say—if we had really excommunicated him, he'd have become a Muslim and we'd have had to leave the unclean agrahara, what?"

The Acharya lifted his eyes and said, "Garuda, I've decided to do just what the Books say—" and continued to read, hoping to end the conversation.

"Suppose one didn't get an answer in the Books. Not that I mean we can't get it there. Suppose we didn't. Haven't you yourself said, there's such a thing as a dharma, a rule for emergencies? Didn't you—what—once suggest that—if a man's life depended on it we could feed him even cow's flesh—such a thing wouldn't be a sin— didn't you say? What do you say—a story you told us once—Sage Vishvamitra, when the earth was famine-stricken, found hunger unbearable, and ate dog-meat, because the supreme dharma is the saving of a life?—What do you say? ..."

"I understand, Garuda. Why don't you just come out and say what you have in mind?" said Praneshacharya, wearily closing his palm-leaf books.

"Nothing, nothing at all really," said Garuda and looked at the ground. Then he abruptly prostrated himself full length before the Acharya, stood up, and said:

"Who'll get my son Shyama out of the army, Acharya-re? And tell me, who but my son can do my rites when I die? So, if you'd kindly give me permission, what ...?"

As he said these words, Lakshmana entered and stood next to him.

Lakshmana's wife Anasuya had come home in tears that day; her sister's ornaments were now someone else's; because of that whore, Chandri, her sister had died. Her tears flowed for Naranappa too. Wasn't he, after all, her maternal uncle's son? If only Uncle were alive, if only her sister were alive, if only Garuda hadn't used black magic against our Naranappa and driven him out of his mind, would he have thrown away so much gold, would he have died like a vagabond, a homeless wretch? Would he be lying there now, rotting without last rites? These thoughts made her cry out aloud. She leaned against the wall and shed tears, saying, "O God, O God, whatever he might have done, how can we cut the family bond that binds us?" The very next minute her eye fell on her daughter Lila-vati—short, plump and round, a nose-ring in one nostril and a long vermilion mark on the brow, wearing a dwarfish braid of hair very tight—and her heart hardened again.

She asked for the tenth time, "Did Shripati say when he was coming back?"

Lilavati said, "I don't know." She had married her daughter to orphan Shripati, but then her own blood-kin Naranappa had misled him and perverted him. That serpent eats its own eggs. Who knows what awful things he poured into her son-in-law's head? Shripati hardly stays home, hardly two days in a month. Roams from town to town, on the heels of Yakshagana players' troupes; keeps the company of Parijatapura boys. News had reached her through Durga-bhatta's wife that he even had a prostitute or two. She knew long ago

he would come to ruin; ever since she'd seen him one day sneak fur-
tively in and out of Naranappa's house; she knew he'd gone astray.
Who knows what godawful things he ate and drank in that house?
No one could escape falling for that woman Chandri. So Anasuya
had taught her daughter a trick, just to teach her roving son-in-law a
lesson: "Don't you give in to your husband when he wants it. Knot
up your thighs, like this, and sleep aloof. Teach him a lesson." Lila-
vati had done exactly as she was told. When her husband came at
night to embrace her, she would come crying to her mother, com-
plaining that he pinched and bit her—and she started sleeping next
to her mother.

Shripati didn't learn his lesson. Anasuya's methods didn't work
with him, though these had once worked on her husband and forced
him to give in to her. Shripati cut off his brahmin tuft, wore his hair
in a crop, Western style, like Naranappa. He saved money and
bought a flashlight. He had taken to roaming round the agrahara
every evening, whistling obscenely.

Lakshmanacharya came home and fell on his bed, looking leaner
than ever, wearied by heat and hunger—his frame already thinned
by fevers, eyes sunk in their sockets. He seemed to be counting his
days. Anasuya nagged him. "Wasn't Naranappa my own maternal
uncle's son? Sinner he may be. But if any lowcaste man is allowed to
pick up his dead body, I'll die of shame. Praneshacharya is much too
soft-hearted. That Garuda is clever, quite ready to gobble up the
whole town. He's no milksop like you. If he should get permission to
do the death-rite, all that jewellery will go to his wife Sita; she already struts about so proudly. God has pretty well taken care of their
mean hearts, though—why else would their son Shyama run away
and join the army? These same people say such things about Naranappa, my cousin, my uncle's son—these very people—where's the
guarantee their son is keeping the faith in those army barracks?
Don't you let that man Garuda go to Praneshacharya and win over
his heart. You'd better go too. You lie here like a log and that fellow
is out there—don't I know it?"

Then she came out and carefully examined the back and front of Garuda's house, and pushed her husband out.

Garuda felt tremendous rage when he saw the thin Kuchela-like form of Lakshmana right next to him, appearing suddenly like a bear let loose in the middle of a service for Shiva. Lakshmana sat down, gasping, holding in his protruding heavy belly with one hand, and leaning on the ground with the other. Garuda looked at him as if he would devour him whole. He wanted to call him all sorts of names like niggard of niggards, emperor of penny-pinchers, mother-deceiver, but held them in because Praneshacharya was sitting right there. This fellow doesn't buy a spoon of oil for his bath, his fist is rigid as stone, this is the meanest of brahmins. Who in the agrahara doesn't know it? When his wife nags him about an oil-bath he gets up in the morning and walks four miles to the Konkani man's shop. "Hey, Kamat, have you any fresh sesame oil? Is it any good? What does it sell for? It isn't musty, is it? Let me see." With such patter, he cups his hands and gets a couple of spoons as sample, pretends to smell it and says: "It's all right, still a bit impure. Tell me when you get real fresh stuff, we need a can of oil for our house." And smears the oil all over his head. Then he puts his hands into the sack of red peppers, and while asking the price, picks up a fistful and transfers it to his bag, all the while chatting casually. From there he walks a mile to Shenoy's shop; there he slanders Kamat's shop, and picks up another couple of spoons of oil for his bath and for a fresh-cooked meal. Then he forages again in someone or other's grove, brings home some cuts of banana-leaf to dry them in the sun and make leaf-cups which he will sell for a few pice. Or sells sacred thread to make a few more pice. Waits like a vulture to get invited to meals. Now his eyes are on the gold. Come what may—one must see to it that he doesn't get the loot.

Lakshmana gasped. "Narayana, Narayana." He wiped the sweat off his body, closed his eyes, and said, "Acharya-re, if the Books have no objection, I've none either. Naranappa is my wife's sister's husband, isn't he, after all? If you don't mind, no one but me has the right to perform the death-rites." And opened his eyes.

Garuda was nonplussed. How can he counter this? It was his turn.

"If it's the problem of who's qualified to perform the rite—what do you say. You can do it yourself. After all we are born as brahmins only to take on others' sins. But that gold must be submitted to the court. Or else, according to the decree at Dharmasthala, it must come to me."

Praneshacharya felt disturbed. Even if the problem of the dead man's rites should be solved, the problem of the gold ornaments would not be easy to solve. Minute by minute his own responsibilities seemed to grow. Naranappa's challenge was growing, growing enormous like God Trivikrama who started out as a dwarf and ended up measuring the cosmos with his giant feet.

Just then the poor brahmins came over in a group, led by poor Dasacharya.

Dasacharya fondled his belly as a mother fondles a crying child. He said: "You know I'm not well. I'll die if I miss meals. You must find a way. This is an emergency and there must be a special rule for it. Tell us if we can eat while there's a dead body in the agrahara. In a day the body will begin to stink. My house is quite close to his. This isn't good for anyone. For the sake of the whole agrahara, Lakshmanacharya or Garudacharya should come to some clear decision. . . ."

He stopped and looked round at everybody. What lust was to Naranappa, hunger was to Dasacharya. At this moment, hunger saved him, gave him a large heart.

"All it takes is a word from you, Acharya-re. Your word is gospel; it's like the Vedas. We don't want the gold, or anything. You tell us. Four of us will pick up the body this minute and finish the cremation rites. You can take the gold, make a crown, offer it to Lord Maruti on our behalf."

Goodness suddenly stirred within Praneshacharya. Only Garuda and Lakshmana were crestfallen. Garuda thought hard and searched for the right thing to say. It would be sinful to contradict Dasacharya's suggestion that the gold should go to God Maruti.

"Let our Acharya do as the dharma dictates. Some people won't like it. When the Acharya searches for the answer—what do you say—it shouldn't seem wrong to the guru—what—then what'll be our fate? Nothing should hurt the good name of our Acharya also. What do you say? We shouldn't fall out of favour like the Parijatapura people, with the highcaste brahmins..."—said Garuda, smiling, pretending to agree with Dasacharya. Even Lakshmana, who didn't know how to sweet-talk his way out, was pleased.

"Please. Go home now, all of you. I'll find the answer even if I've to turn the whole science of dharma upside down. I'll sit up all night," said Praneshacharya, very tired.

It was evening. He hadn't yet offered his prayers or had his dinner. Agitated, Praneshacharya walked up and down, indoors, outdoors, and back. He asked Chandri, who was in the verandah, to come in and sit inside. He lifted his ailing wife with both hands like a baby, took her to the backyard, let her pass water, brought her back to her bed and made her drink her evening dose of medicine. Then he came back to the middle hall and sat there turning over and over the ancient books in the light of the kerosene lantern.

V

Shripati had gone to Shirnali the night before, to see *Jambavati's Wedding* performed by the troupe from Kelur. He didn't really know anything about Naranappa's return from Shivamogge or about his being sick in bed, or his dying. If he'd known it, he would have been grief-stricken. For Naranappa had been his one secret friend in the whole agrahara. He'd left home over a week ago. He made friends with the balladeer of the Kelur troupe, stayed with him wherever the troupe stopped, ate with them, went to their night shows, slept all day. In his spare time he'd gone to the neighbouring villages and persuaded them to invite the troupe for performances. He'd forgotten the whole world for a week, happy in greetings and casual conversations. And tonight he was returning, flashlight in hand, singing loudly, in the scary forest dark. His hair was brushed back, uncut; he'd grown it long; down his neckline, because the balladeer had promised him a girl's role in next year's play. After all, his tongue had been trained by Praneshacharya, hadn't it? The balladeer had admired his pure enunciation, his clear voice. Shripati had heard enough Sanskrit and logic and ancient epics from the Acharya to give him enough culture for the ad-lib dialogues and profundities of these players of epic plays. If only he could get a part in the troupe, he could escape the brahmin dump, escape the endless funeral cakes and funeral porridge, escape all that living and dying for jackfruit curry. The thought filled Shripati with joy; so he wasn't scared any more of the dark forest. He'd also had a drink of toddy in shaman Shina's hut, and being a little high on it, didn't shiver any more at the fearful silence of the forest. Two bottles of toddy; a flashlight pouring forth brilliant light at the touch of a button to the great amazement of peasants—what ghost or demon can touch a man armed with these weapons? As he neared Durvasapura, his body warmed to the thought of the pleasures awaiting him. Who cares if his wife tightens and twines up her thighs? There was Belli. An outcaste, so what? As Naranappa would say—who cares if she's a goddess or a shaven widow? But Belli was neither. Which brahmin girl,—cheek sunken, breast withered, mouth stinking of lentil soup,—which brahmin girl was equal to Belli? Her thighs are full. When she's with him she twists like a snake coupling with another, writhing in the sands. She'd have bathed by now in water heated in mudpots outside her hut; she'd have drunk her father's sour toddy, she'd be warm and ready—like a tuned-up drum. Not utterly black-skinned, nor pale white, her body is the colour of the earth, fertile, ready for seed, warmed by an early sun. Shripati's footfall stopped dead. With pleasure, he squeezed the flashlight button, turning it on and off. He turned it around in the forest, happy like the actors in demon roles. *Ththai ththai thaka ththai ththai:* he danced to their rhythms. He tried a quick sit-down like them, rotating his knees like them, but hurt a knee and stood up. The forest was empty. Birds flapped their wings, wakened and frightened by the flashlight. He got a little more drunk with it. As he called on them, the Nine Essences of feeling presented themselves to him as to any artist—rage, disgust, terror, tender devotion, love, whichever. His fancy glided from one to the other. Now Goddess Lakshmi wakes at dawn her lord, Vishnu, asleep on the serpent-coil, with her morning song:

> Wake, wake, O Narayana
> Wake, O Lord of Lakshmi
> Wa … aa … ke, it's morni … ii … ng. …

Shripati's eyes filled and glowed with tears. Garuda, Lord Vishnu's carrier-bird, comes to wake Him up. "Wake up, O Narayana." Narada, messenger and sage, comes strumming on his strings to wake Him. "Get up, O Lord of Lakshmi." Birds and beasts, monkeys, and singing orders of supernaturals, come and beg of Him to wake up. "O wake, it's mo … oo … rni … ing!" Shripati, in a dancing measure, held his dhoti as if it were a woman's sari, and shook it, moved his neck to one side, and danced. Shina's toddy had really made him high. He should go to Naranappa's and drink some more. He remembered all the heroines. In the legends there isn't a sage who doesn't fall for some woman. That temptress Menaka, who destroyed the penance of Sage Vishvamitra. What a wench she must have been. Must have been lovelier than Chandri. It's amazing that no one's eye had fallen on Belli; she walked around everywhere in rags, picking up manure. But then it wasn't surprising either. How can brahmin eyes see anything, dimmed by looking for meals everywhere? Praneshacharya describes women again and again, talking as if to infants: "The sage must have been thrilled, as he looked at the goddess of dawn. The Lord put these words into his mouth: 'Like the thighs of a blossoming woman, pure after her monthly baths.'

What a bold conception, what a lovely simile!" But then, to these barren brahmins it's one more chant, one more formula for making a living. That Nagappa of Kundapura who plays king's roles, how haughtily, how seductively he speaks! "O what bees, what blossoming *parijata* and *champak* and jasmine and scented screw-pine in this garden! O who are you, lovely woman, alone, downcast? You seem so burdened with sorrow, O who are you?" Shripati walked on, smiling. In the entire agrahara, only two people had an eye for beautiful things: Naranappa and Chandri. Chandri was utterly beautiful, beyond compare. In a hundred-mile radius, show me such a doll, and I'll say you're a man. That fellow Durgabhatta does have some good taste. But he doesn't have the guts to do more than paw at a cooliewoman's breast. Actually, the best connoisseur of them all is Praneshacharya, really one in a million. Every evening, as he reads the Puranas and expounds the stanzas, the beauty of his style is enough to make any balladeer turn green with envy. What delicate phrasing, what gentle smiles and what striking handsomeness. His tuft of hair, the caste-mark—circlet and stripe—on his forehead. Really, only he can don a gold-embroidered shawl, and it looks becoming. He's supposed to have fifteen such shawls—all won in argument and controversy in eight monasteries, against great southern pundits. But he doesn't brag about it. Poor man, his wife's a chronic invalid— no children, nothing. This man who speaks so beautifully about Kalidasa's women, does he feel any desire himself? Actually, Shripati had taken Belli at the river when she had come to get water, only after he had heard the Acharya speak of Shakuntala's beauty. He couldn't stand it any more. Belli was carrying a pitcher of water on her head, the rag on her body had slipped, and as she stood in the moonlight bouncing her breasts, the colour of earth—she'd looked like Shakuntala herself. He had then personally, carnally, enjoyed the Acharya's description.

Tonight Shripati took an inside trail and walked straight to the outcaste hutments on the hillside. In the black new-moon night he saw a hut on fire, burning away. In the light of that fire, various inky forms. He looked from a distance, listened. No one seemed too anxious to put out the fire. Baffled, he waited behind a stump. The hut, built out of bamboo frames, thatched with mats, covered with coconut fronds, burned to cinders in the dry summer heat. It was razed to the ground before his eyes. The inky silhouettes returned to their nests. Shripati stepped softly and clapped his hands a little outside Belli's hut.

Belli, her hair washed in warm water, wearing only a piece below her waist, naked above, waves of hair pouring over her back and face—came quietly out of her hut, and moved into the bushes in the distance. Shripati waited behind a tree till she disappeared, looked this way and that to make sure no one else was about, then went to the bush where Belli crouched. He turned his flashlight on and off and embraced her, panting hard.

"*Ayya*, please, not today."

Belli had never talked like that. Shripati was amazed, but disregarded her words and undid her waist-cloth.

"I don't know what's the matter—Pilla and his woman died today—struck by a demon or something, *ayya*."

Shripati had no use for words right now. She was naked. He pulled her down to the ground.

"Because both of them died, we left the bodies right there and fired the hut. Some kind of fever. They never opened their eyes."

Shripati was impatient. She was saying something, was somewhere else. He had come to her with such urgent desire, here she was prating about someone croaking. She had never talked like that at such times. She had always been like ripe ears of corn bending before the falling rain.

Belli, wrapping the cloth round herself, said:

"*Ayya*, I want to tell you something. I've never seen such a thing before. Why should rats and mice come to our poor huts? Nothing there to eat. Our huts aren't like brahmin houses. Now the rats come like relatives looking for a place to stay. They fall pattering from the roof, run round and round, and die. Like folks running for life from a hut on fire, they run into the forest. I've never seen the likes of it. We must get the shaman possessed with the demon and ask him about it. Why do rats come to pariah huts and pop off? Snap! Like that! Like breaking a twig. We must ask the demon."

Shripati wrapped on his dhoti again, put on his shirt, took out a pocket comb, combed his cropped hair and ran in a hurry, flashing his light. Belli was all right for sleeping with, she was no good for talk. If she opens her mouth, she talks only ghosts and demons.

Anxious to see Naranappa, he tucked his dhoti up to knee-length and ran downhill. He could drink a glass of water there, sleep there that night and go to Nagaraja's place in Parijatapura in the morning. He stood quietly before Naranappa's door and pushed it. It wasn't latched. "He's still up," he thought, and went in happily. He turned his flashlight on and called out, "Naranappa, Naranappa." No answer. There was a stench of something rotting, enough to make one sick in the stomach. He wanted to go upstairs, knock at the door of his room; he walked in the dark towards the stairs he knew so well. When he turned the corner, his bare foot swished on something soft and cold. Startled, he flashed his light on it. A dead rat, dead on its back, its legs up in the air. The flies on it buzzed in the beam of the flashlight. He ran up the steps to the room upstairs; the steps rattled under his feet. Why is Naranappa sleeping on the floor with the blanket over his head? He must have drunk till the liquor came out of his nose. Shripati smiled and pulled down the blanket and shook Naranappa, calling, "Naranappa, Naranappa." Like the rat, the body was cold. He pulled back his hand in a hurry and turned on his flashlight. Open-lidded, sightless eyes, turned upwards forever. In the circle of his flashlight, flies, small insects. And a stench.

VI

Lakshmidevamma, turned sixty over ten years ago, the eldest human in the agrahara, pushed the main door with a big groan and let out a long resounding belch: *Heeey!* She got down into the agrahara street, stood leaning on her staff, and belched again long and loud: *Heeey!* When she couldn't sleep, or when her mind was disturbed, she would come out at night into the street and walk up-down down-up three times, stand in front of Garudacharya's house, invoke sons and grandsons and ancestors, summon gods and goddesses for witness, throw fistfuls of curses at him, go back to her house, draw in her wooden main door with a big scratching noise and go to sleep. Especially as it got close to new moon or full moon, her cursing bouts would reach a pitch. Her door and her belch were famous in the agrahara. Both could be heard from one end to the other. Her fame had spread to the brahmin colonies in all four directions. Because she was a child-widow, they called her Lakshmidevamma the Ill-Omen. She cursed and drove away with her stick all the naughty boys, and also the brahmins who, any time they met her head-on, walked back four paces to undo the ill-luck. But no one really cared. They all called her Sour Belch. But her best known name was Half-Wit Lakshmidevamma. Her life was a Purana by itself. Married at eight, widowed at ten. Her mother-in-law and father-in-law had died when she was fifteen. The agrahara had sneered at her as the ill-starred girl. Before she was twenty her father and mother had died. And then, Garuda's father had taken custody of the little property and jewellery she had. He'd brought the woman over to his own house. That was his way always. He had managed similarly Naranappa's father's property too, saying the man wasn't bright enough to manage it himself. Lakshmidevamma had spent twenty-five years under that roof. Garuda took over when his father died. His wife pinched pennies, never fed anybody a full meal. Lakshmidevamma and she regularly had got into fights and even come to blows. Then the couple had thrown her out, pushed her into her husband's old ruined house. From then on she had lived there alone. She'd taken her complaints to Praneshacharya. He'd called Garuda and counselled him. Garuda decided to give her a monthly allowance of a single rupee. So she'd become all venom towards Garuda. Praneshacharya now and then got her some rice from the brahmins. As Lakshmidevamma had got on in years, her misanthropy had risen like poison in the system.

Lakshmidevamma now stood before Garuda's house, belching long and loud, and started her abuse as usual.

"May your house be haunted; may your eyes go white; you ruiner of towns, you widow-taker, you got black magic done to Naranappa's father. Get up and come out if you've any manhood left. You ate up a poor old shaven widow's money, didn't you? Do you think you can digest it? Do you? I'll die and come back as a ghost to torment your children—I'm that sort, don't you know?"

She wheezed and belched again.

"You villain! A golden man like Naranappa became an outcaste, got himself a harlot. You fellows call yourselves brahmins, you sit there and don't want to take out a dead man's body. Where has your brahminism gone, you rascals! Don't you know you'll fall into the lowest hell reserved for outcastes and perish there? In this agrahara, in all my born days, have I seen a body kept uncremated all night? Not once. Rama, Rama, the times are rotten, rotten. Brahminism is in ruins. Why don't you shave your heads and become Muslims, why do you need to be brahmins, you!"

Ayyayyoo...shrieked Shripati, rushing out of Naranappa's verandah, forgetting even to close the door, leaping into the street and breaking into a run.

"Look, look, look! It's Naranappa's ghost! Ghost!" cried Half-Wit Lakshmidevamma, running from door to door, beating on it, hobbling on her stick. His heart in his mouth, Shripati crossed the stream in a hurry and ran to Parijatapura, to Nagaraja's house.

Chandri was lying on Praneshacharya's raised verandah, and she was the only one who recognized the running man as Shripati. She hadn't slept, she was hungry. She wasn't the fasting kind, not in any of her births; nor the kind that lies down alone outside a house. Ever since she left Kundapura and joined Naranappa, she had always enjoyed soft mattresses in a room perfumed by joss-sticks. Now she couldn't stand her hunger any more, so she got up and walked through the backyard to the plantain grove. She plucked a bunch of bananas left on the tree for ripening, ate them till she was full, went to the stream and drank a lot of water. She was afraid of going home—she had never seen a dead man's face. If only Naranappa's body had been properly cremated, all her love for him would have welled up in her and she would have dissolved in tears. But now her heart had nothing but fear in it. Only fear, and anxiety. If Naranappa's body didn't get the proper rituals, he could become a tormenting ghost. She had enjoyed life with him for ten years. How could she rest till he got a proper funeral? Her heart revolted. It's true, Naranappa had given up brahminhood. Ate with Muslims. She too did. But no sin will ever rub off on her. Born to a family of prostitutes, she was an exception to all rules. She was ever-auspicious, daily-wedded, the one without widowhood. How can sin defile a running river? It's good for a drink when a man's thirsty, it's good for a wash when a man's filthy, and it's good for bathing the god's images with; it says Yes to everything, never a No. Like her. Doesn't dry up, doesn't tire. Tunga, river that doesn't dry, doesn't tire.

But these brahmin women, before they bear two brats, their eyes sink, cheeks become hollow, breasts sag and fall—not hers. Perennial Tunga, river that doesn't dry up, doesn't tire. Naranappa had guzzled at her body like a ten-year old, tearing and devouring like a gluttonous bear at a honeycomb. Sometimes he leaped like a raging striped tiger. All we need now is a proper funeral for him. Then she could go away to Kundapura and weep for him there. This can be done only by brahmin hands. It's true Naranappa had thrown out brahmin ways, but they had still clung to him. Angry, mad, strong-willed man—he had capered and somersaulted, said he would turn Muslim if they excommunicated him. But who knows what was going on inside him? She certainly didn't. Whatever his capers, he never used obscenities against Praneshacharya. Though he did talk out of turn, say rash things, he was quite afraid inside. He forgot his quarrels quickly. Someone like herself, who knew jealousy, couldn't fathom such hatred. When she joined him first, she had begged of him: "Don't eat my cooking, don't eat meat and stuff. I'll give it up myself; if I crave for it, I'll go to the Shetti's and I'll eat my fish there, not in the agrahara." But he hadn't listened, he wasn't the kind who would. Sheer pig-headedness. And his hysterical wife didn't have the guts to stand up to his strong will; she'd gone back to her mother's place, cursed him and died there. Who wants complications? Once the rites get done, she could offer her salutes and go home.

But something gnawed at her now. It was weird. Naranappa, who wouldn't fold his hand before a god any time, had started talking strangely as his fever rose to his brain. As coma set in, he mumbled, "O mother! O God Ramachandra, Narayana!" Cried out, "Rama Rama." Holy names. Not words that come out of a sinner's or an out-caste's mouth. She hadn't quite understood what was going on deep inside him. If they don't give him a death-rite according to the Books, he'll surely become an evil spirit. She'd eaten his salt, she, Chandri ...

Everything now depended on Praneshacharya. How gentle he was, how kind. Like Lord Sri Krishna in the play, who came smiling to His devotee Draupadi, when she cried out for Him. How he glows. Poor man, he probably knew nothing of the body's pleasures, his wife lay there like a dry log, the good woman. Yet how patient he was, what a halo around him. Not even once had he raised his eyes and looked at her. Her mother used to say: prostitutes should get pregnant by such holy men. Such a man was the Acharya, he had such looks, vir-tues; he glowed. But one had to be lucky to be blessed by such people.

She had eaten her fill of plantains and her eyes drooped. Sleep hovered close, now far, now near. She could hear some sounds now and then in her drowsiness. Praneshacharya's wakeful pacing in the hall, reading aloud his mantras. How could she sleep when he was awake? She tried to push her sleep away. Worrying about things, she lay on the verandah, head pillowed in her forearm, shyly pulling up her knees to her belly, curled up—and slept, her sari over her face.

Every palm-leaf text had been turned over, looked into, end to end. No solutions there, nothing acceptable to his conscience. Pranesha-charya was afraid of admitting that the Book of Dharma had no solution to the present dilemma. Another fear too hovered over him: wouldn't the other pundits scornfully ask, is that all you know? What would he say if they mock him—you've had the ultimate lessons, is this all your knowledge? He sat there thinking, "Whatever one loses, one shouldn't lose one's good name, it can never be retrieved." But he felt ashamed at the drift of his thinking. Even in this situation, thinking only of his reputation! He wished he could burn out his egotism. He opened the palm-leaves again, devotedly. Meditating for a second, he shut his eyes, picked up a single leaf and read. No, it didn't work. Closed his eyes again, picked up another leaf and read it. Nothing there, either. His wife groaned as she lay in the kitchen. He got up, leaned her to himself, and fed her two mouthfuls of lemon juice. His wife moaned, "Why didn't I die instead of Naranappa? Why doesn't death come to me? I would like to die as an auspicious wife...." He made her unsay it; he made her say, "May it only be good," to undo her self-cursing; consoled her, came back to the hall and sat in the lantern light, distraught. If there's no answer in the ancient code-books, it's truly victory for Naranappa, and defeat for him, the Acharya. The original question was really why he hadn't helped excommunicate Naranappa all these years. It was because of Naranappa's threat to turn Muslim. By that threat, the ancient codes had already been defiled. There was a time when the brahmin's power of penance ruled the world. Then one didn't buckle under any such threat. It's because the times are getting worse such dilemmas torment us...

If one looks at it, was it only his threat to become a Muslim and pollute the agrahara that had kept the Acharya from excommunicating him? No, there was also compassion. The infinite compassion in his heart. As the thought flashed, Praneshacharya reproached himself, saying, "Che! Che! that's self-deception." That wasn't pure pity, it covered a terrible wilfulness. His wilfulness couldn't give in to Naranappa's. "I must bring him back to the right paths; I will, by the power of my virtue, my austerities, my two fasts a week. I'll draw him to right thinking." Such was his uncontrollable wilfulness.

The wilfulness had taken a shape all its own—the shape of a

resolution to use love, compassion, austerity, to make Naranappa walk the narrow path. In such a resolve, how much was wilfulness, and how much the kindness in his bowels? His nature's main impulse seemed to be kindness. When this body wilts in age, lust will leave it but not compassion. For a human, compassion is deeper-rooted than desire. If such compassion hadn't worked in him, how could he have tended an ailing wife through the years, uncomplaining, and never once falling for other women? No, no, only compassion had saved his humane brahmin nature.

Compassion, the right way of dharma, being humane—brahminhood. They all twist together into knots and torment him. The original question was, why had Naranappa gone sour, become venomous? The Books say, one gets to be a brahmin only by merit earned in many past lives. If so, why had Naranappa thrown his brahminhood into the gutter with his own two hands? It's amazing how, to the end, one works out one's nature. Praneshacharya remembered a tale from the Rigveda.

Once there was a brahmin who was addicted to gambling. Whatever he did, he couldn't overcome his nature. The well-bred brahmins debarred him from places of sacrifice. They shooed him away, like a dog. He called upon gods and angels and wept, "O Lord, why did you make me a gambler? Why did you give me such a vicious need? O guardians of the eight directions, give me an answer. Indra! Yama! Varuna! you gods! come and give me an answer."

In the places of sacrifice, the other brahmins held out their offerings and called upon the gods, Indra, Yama, Varuna and the rest, to come and receive them.

But the gods went to answer the gambler's call. The brahmins had to swallow their brahminical pride and go where he, the scoundrel, was. It's hard to know the inner workings of dharma. An arch-sinner, an outcaste, reaches salvation and paradise by merely uttering the name Narayana with his dying breath. The Lord once asked his gatekeepers, Jaya and Vijaya, to choose between reaching Him in seven lives as devotees and reaching Him in just three lives as enemies, and they chose the latter. The quicker way of salvation was through conflict. For such as us, wearing away our karma like a log of sandalwood by daily worship and ritual, it takes life after life to work our salvation. The inner meanings of dharma are inscrutable. Who knows in what storms Naranappa's inmost life was involved? He leaped and played, but died in a twinkle.

If only the Lord would give him the power to know! Suddenly, like a sign from the Unknown, a thought struck him, and he thrilled to it. Early next morning after his baths etc., he should go to the Maruti temple and ask Him, "O Son of the Wind-god, what's right in this dilemma?" His heart lightened, he paced up and down in the inner room. He remembered suddenly. "Che! That young woman is sleeping in the verandah without even a mat." He brought out a mat, a blanket, a pillow and called out, "Chandri!" Chandri, who had been thinking of what her mother had said, got up with a start, and pulled her sari-end over her head. Praneshacharya felt it wasn't proper to stand in the dark like that before a woman, and so he said, "Take this mat and pillow," and went back. Chandri seemed to have lost the use of her tongue. Praneshacharya stopped as he crossed the threshold. In the lantern light, he saw the woman sitting embarrassed and her body was drawn-in like a bud. As he came in, another thought flashed. He came out with the jewels she had taken off her body earlier in the day, and said, "Chandri." She sat up quickly, anxiously.

"Look here, Chandri. Your generosity complicates the question. The brahmin has to follow whatever is right for an emergency. Keep this gold with you. Naranappa's dead. But you've your life to live." He stood near her, lantern in hand, bent down in the light, looked kindly into her large dark eyes lifted meekly towards him and he put the gold in her hands. Then he went in.

VII

Dasacharya couldn't bear his hunger. In his distress he invoked the name of god. Narayana Narayana! Sighing loudly, he kneaded his belly, he tossed in bed. His son, unable to sleep, woke his mother up.

"Amma, it stinks, it stinks," he said.

Dasacharya, in the distress of unbearable hunger, smelled no smells. But his wife said, "Yes, it's true it stinks." And tapped her husband and said, "Look, that stench. It's summer time, the dead body has rotted. It's stinking up the whole agrahara."

Then she heard Half-Wit Lakshmidevamma cry out, "Naranappa's ghost! Naranappa's ghost!" She screamed. She shivered. The dead man's ghost must be roaming about, spreading the stench.

In the hut, Belli couldn't sleep. She sat up. It was a dark night, she could see nothing. She came out. The hut had been fired to cremate the dead outcaste and his woman; it had burned all the way down to cinders. Sparks glimmered within the ash at each movement of the wind. In the distant bush, she saw a great many fireflies twinkling. She tiptoed softly towards them, unwrapped her piece of cloth, stood naked, pleasured by the soft wind; then carefully spread out the cloth and captured the lightning-bugs, their twinkling lights; and ran back to her hut and shook them out on the floor. Twinkling and darkening, they lit the hut dimly and flew about. Belli groped for them on the floor with her hand. Her groaning father and mother, when Belli's groping hand touched them, grumbled, "What's this bandicoot doing here?"

"Dead rats, it stinks, *isshi!*" cried Belli, as her searching hand touched a chilling-cold dead rat; she saw it in the light of the fireflies, and cried out, "*Ayya...Ayya...yapaa!*" She picked it up by its tail and threw it out. She cursed them. "What's come upon these damned bastard rats to run about and die like this all over!" Then she wrapped the cloth around herself, lay on the floor and fell asleep.

Hunger beat drums in their bellies and banished sleep, giving red eyes to the brahmins. They got up in the morning, washed their faces, and came to the village-court, cursing Naranappa for the awful things now happening to the agrahara. Because of the stench indoors, children jumped about in the verandahs and backyards. The women were scared that Naranappa's ghost now roaming the streets would touch their children. So, the unwilling urchins had to be spanked, pushed in and the doors had to be shut. Never before had they shut a door in broad daylight like this. There were no sacred designs to bless and decorate the threshold, nor any sprinkling of cowdung water for the yard without them. The agrahara didn't feel that morning had dawned yet. Things looked empty, desolate. Bikoooo! they seemed to cry. It felt as if there was a dead body in every house, in some dark room. The brahmins sat in the village hall, their heads in their hands, not knowing what to do next.

Only Venkataramanacharya's naughty children defied their mother's orders, and stood in the backyard counting the rats leaping and tumbling from the store-room into the yard. They clapped hands and jumped about. They counted, in the style of their fathers counting measures of paddy:

gain-O gain
two-O two
three-O three
four-O four
five-O five
six-O six
one-more-O one-more

When mother came down, broom in hand, to spank them, they shrieked, clapping and leaping, "Look Ma, look, eight-O eight, nine-O nine, ten-O ten. Ten rats! Look Ma, look!"

Mother responded angrily.

"The rice you've wolfed down has gone to your head, hasn't it? What's all this business of counting filthy rats? Get in, or else I'll beat you till you have welts all over. The store-room is full of them, the filthy things. The rice and the lentils are covered with rat droppings."

Grumbling, she drove her kids inside and shut them up. In there, a rat appeared from nowhere, and turned like a kid turning round and round himself, and fell dead on his back. The children were delighted.

Slowly the brahmins got down from their verandahs, walked towards Praneshacharya's house, holding their noses. Durgabhatta stopped everyone and said, "What the half-wit granny said could be true, couldn't it, Acharya?"

The brahmins, quite scared in their hearts, said, "Let's wait and see," and walked softly to Naranappa's house. They stopped outside, gripped by fear when they saw that the big door was open. The corpse was certainly walking about as a ghost. If the correct rites are not done, he would certainly become a brahmin-demon and terrorize the whole place. Dasacharya, eyes full of tears, blamed the other brahmins.

"We're ruined by your lust for gold. Didn't I say so? That's a brahmin corpse. Unless the funeral rites are properly done, he'll become a demon. Who cares here for a poor man's words? Will it not rot in this summer heat and stink up the place? How long can one fast and not perish—with a dead body out there. . . ."

Durgabhatta, raging in hunger, said, "What sort of Madhvas are you? What sort of orthodoxy is this? You can't think of a way out on such an occasion!"

Garuda had mellowed. "I've no objection, if Praneshacharya says Yes. What do you say—let's set aside the problem of the gold and jewellery. What. Let's first get the dead body to the cremation ground. What do you say. It's enough if Praneshacharya saves our brahminhood."

Everyone went straight to Praneshacharya and stood humbly in the hall. The Acharya carried his wife to the backyard, waited for her to pass water, helped her wash up, gave her medicine, came out and saw the gathered brahmins. He explained to them his decision of the previous night. Garuda submitted the opinion of the entire group in a humble voice.

"Our brahminhood is really in your hands. You must save us from accusations and bad names. We may get blamed whether we take out the dead man or don't, either way. What do you say. We'll wait here for you to bring back Maruti's divine decree."

The Acharya, starting out, said, "You all know, don't you, that your children can eat; there's no objection."

Wicker basket in hand, he plucked jasmine and champak flowers from the trees of the agrahara. He filled the basket with leaves of the sacred basil. After a bath in the river, he wrapped a wet cloth round himself, changed his sacred thread in preparation for this special visit to Lord Maruti. He crossed the water, walked in the woods for two miles, and came to the Maruti temple, which stood peacefully in the silence of the forest trees. He drew some water from the temple well, poured two pitcherfuls over his body to purify himself of any pollution that might have besmirched him on the way. He carried another pitcherful to the man-sized Maruti idol; removed all the old dry petals and basil leaves from the god's body, and bathed it thoroughly. Then he sat in front of the image, and uttering sacred chants for a whole hour, he rubbed sandalwood on the wet stone and made sandalpaste. He covered the idol with the fragrant paste, and adorned it with flowers and basil leaves. He meditated with eyes closed, and presented the conflicts in his mind to the Lord.

"If your orders are Yes, give me the flower at your right; if you forbid the death-rite, give me the flower on the left. I'm limited, I come to you." Thus he formed his thoughts behind closed eyes in utter devotion, and sat there gazing at Monkey-god Maruti in the light of the oil lamp.

The heat of the day was fierce, though it was hardly ten in the morning. Even in the dark temple, it was sultry and sweaty. The Acharya poured another pitcher of water over himself and sat there waiting, his body still wet. "Till you give me an answer, I'll not rise," he said.

When Praneshacharya left his house, Chandri, who was afraid of facing the angry brahmin faces, returned to the plantain grove. After a clean scrub in the river, she filled the lap of her sari with ripe sweet plantains, and walked on—her glossy black hair loose on her wet body, her wet sari clinging to her limbs. She now sat against a tree, at a little distance from the Maruti temple. From the distant shrine she could hear the sound of the bells rung by the Acharya. The holy sound of temple bells took her back to an experience that had moved her. Just as she was remembering her mother's words, hadn't the Acharya come close with mat and pillow, holding a lantern in the darkness, and called her "Chandri," ever so softly? Suddenly she regretted that she was past thirty. Ten years she'd lived with Naranappa, she still hadn't had a child. If she had borne a son, he could have become a great musician; if a daughter, she could have taught her to dance, classical style. She had got everything, yet had nothing. She sat there looking at the little birds that whirred and perched on the trees.

VIII

Dasacharya was afraid he would die if he didn't eat right away. The smells of all that food cooking for the children, O to smell them on this fasting day! It was like melted butter poured into a burning fire. He spat out some of the rising spittle in his mouth, and swallowed some of it. Finally, unable to bear it any more, he got up and left. Unseen by anyone, he went into the waters of the Tunga river, bathed in the burning sun, and walked towards Parijatapura. He soon stood in the shade of Manjayya's thatched canopy. How could he ask here openly for food? In all his born days, he hadn't even touched water in the houses of these crosslined brahmins. After all, he was a brahmin who lived on ritual meals. Bad things would happen if others heard about it. Yet his legs brought him, faster than thought, to Manjayya who was eating spicy *uppittu*, made of flattened rice.

"O O O, come in, come in, Acharya. How come you brought yourself so far? Did Praneshacharya come to some decision or what? Really a pity. Unless the body is disposed of, none of you can eat, can you? Please sit down. Rest a while. Look here, bring a seat for the Acharya!" And so on, Manjayya rolled out his courtesies.

Dasacharya stood there in a trance, looking only at the *uppittu*. Manjayya looked at him kindly and said, "Are you feeling dizzy, or something, Acharya-re, shall I get you some fruit-drink?"

Dasacharya said neither yes nor no, but squatted on the low seat. How could he open his mouth and ask him? Mustering enough courage, he started beating about the bush; Manjayya listened, eating his *uppittu*.

"I didn't really like the way our folks talked here yesterday, Manjayya."

"Che Che Che, you shouldn't say such things," said Manjayya for politeness' sake.

"If you really look—how many real brahmins are there in this *kali* age, Manjayya?"

"I agree, I agree, Acharya-re. The times are rotten, it's true."

"How are you less than any other brahmin, Manjayya, in orthodoxy and in keeping to the rules? Here you are, ready to perform the funeral rites without a pice. But Garuda and Lakshmana of our agrahara fight there like crows, over a piece of gold...."

"*Ayyo ayyo*, is that so?" said Manjayya, glossing over things, not interested in getting into anyone's bad books.

"Manjayya, one thing, between ourselves—everyone says Garuda's black magic ruined Naranappa. It back-fired, so his own son ran away and joined the army. Look, he even swallowed up that poor widow Lakshmidevamma's jewellery and money."

Manjayya, though pleased, said nothing.

"I ask you, where are the real brahmins today? I've nothing against Garuda, really. Just because we get stamped and branded five ways by the guru once a year, do all our sins get burned away? I didn't like those fellows wanting you to do what they themselves won't do. Whatever you may say, Manjayya, Praneshacharya is our one true brahmin. What lustre, what ascetic penance!" he clucked.

"True, true; very true, isn't it?" agreed Manjayya, and asked, "You've had your bath, Acharya-re?"

"O yes, I've just had a dip in the river," he said.

"Then, eat something with us, Acharya-re."

"I don't really mind eating in your house. But if those rascals in our agrahara hear about it, no one will invite me to a ceremony again. What can I do, Manjayya?"

Responding to the pathetic words of Dasacharya, Manjayya came close to him, secretly delighted that another of the agrahara brahmins had come to eat with him, and said softly:

"Why should I tell anyone, Acharya-re, that you ate with us? Just get up, wash your hands and feet. Look here, hey, get us some *uppittu* here...."

As soon as the word *uppittu* was uttered, the bowels in Dasacharya's belly turned and made loud gurgling noises. Still, he was afraid to eat cooked stuff in a Smarta house; so he suggested:

"No, no, *uppittu* doesn't really agree with me. Just a little plain flat-rice, and some milk and jaggery will do."

Manjayya understood, was amused. He gave Dasacharya some water to wash his feet with, brought him as if in secret to the kitchen, sat him down. And himself sitting down next to him, he made him take milk, jaggery, flat-rice, plantains and honey. Dasacharya got a little intoxicated as he ate; finally Manjayya persuaded him to eat even a spoonful of *uppittu*, saying, "Where's the harm in one spoonful?" Manjayya's wife gleefully served another four spoonfuls of it; Dasacharya rubbed his belly to the rhythm of the name of the Supreme Spirit, and didn't say No. Just for courtesy's sake, he pretended to cover his leaf with his hands, saying, "Enough. Enough. Must leave some for you."

IX

Chinni, instead of Belli, came that day to pick up the cowdung. She said, "Belli's father and mother are both sick in bed." The brahmin women of the agrahara, too full of their own problems, didn't listen to her. But Chinni, who was picking up the manure, told her story anyway, not caring whether anyone heard it or not. "Chowda died, his woman too died. We set fire to his hut and finished that too.

Who knows if the Demon is angry with us, who knows?" Sitadevi, Garuda's wife, stood with her hand on her waist, and worried ceaselessly about her son: what could they do if something happened to him in the army? Chinni begged, standing at a distance: "Please, *avva*, throw a morsel for my mouth, *avva*!" Sitadevi went in, brought out some betel leaf, betelnut and a quid of tobacco, threw them at her and stood there thinking her own precious thoughts. Chinni, tucking away the tobacco and betel in her lap, said:

"*Avva*, what a lot of rats are coming out now! Like a wedding procession. Who knows what they're up to?" Then lifted her cowdung basket to her head and walked away.

When she went back, she thought she could break some tobacco and share it with Belli. As she walked to Belli's hut, she heard Belli's father and mother crying out aloud.

"Look how the fellow cries in fever. Don't know if the Demon is treading on him too," she thought and came out calling Belli. She saw Belli sitting next to her parents, her head in her hands. Chinni was about to say, "Look, even in the agrahara the rats are taking out a procession." Instead she broke off a piece of tobacco and said, "Take a bite, Sitavva gave me some." Belli rubbed the tobacco on her palms and put it in her mouth.

"If Pilla gets the Demon on him today, we must ask about this. I'm quite scared, Chinni. What's all this, rats coming like an army to our poor pariah huts! Chowda and his wife popping off, snap! Like that! And now papa and mama trodden all over by the Demon. We must ask Him."

"*Ayy*, you idiot—just be quiet," said Chinni, trying to hearten Belli.

By two in the afternoon, the sun rose over the head, and burned like the angry third eye of Lord Shiva, stupefying the brahmins already half-dead with hunger. Mirages, horses of the sun, danced before their eyes as they stared at the shimmering heat of the street; they were waiting for Praneshacharya. Fear and hunger, both acute, worked in their bellies like succubi. Dissolved into formless anxiety, these brahmins' spirits hung around Praneshacharya who had gone to Lord Maruti for counsel—hung around him like bats. A dim hope: maybe they would not really have to wait another night with Naranappa's dead body. Sitadevi found a rat lying dead in the rice vessel in her store-room; she picked it up by the tail, held her nose with her sari-end, and brought it out to fling it, when a vulture swooped towards her, and glided away to perch on their roof. She screamed, "*Ayyayyo*, look, look!" A vulture on the roof was an omen of death. Nothing like it had ever happened before. Garudacharya came running, took one look at the vulture and sank down. Sitadevi started weeping, "*Ayyo*, what could have happened to my son!" Garuda thought at once he was being punished for refusing in his heart Dasacharya's suggestion that the gold should go to Lord Maruti. In fear, he held on to his wife's hand, came in, placed an offering before his household god, prostrated himself, and prayed: "I've done wrong. May your gold be yours, may it be for you. Forgive me." Then came out saying, "Ussh! Ussh!" to the vulture, trying to chase it off his roof. The vulture had by now picked up the rat that Sitadevi had flung out and was pecking at it on the roof. The bird sat there, unafraid, defiant, like a shameless kinsman. Garudacharya lifted his head and looked into the dazzling heat above. He saw vultures, vultures, vultures in the blue blue sky reeling, gliding, spiralling circle below circle, descending. "Look, look there!" he called out to his wife. Sitadevi came running. She shielded her eyes with her palms and looked, and she let out a long sigh: "Usshsh".... As they looked on, the vulture on their roof curved his neck around like a danseuse, looked around and whirred right down to their feet to peck at and pick up another rat which had run out from the store-room to the backyard, and flew back to his perch on the roof. Both husband and wife, their life-breaths shaken up together as never before, sank down to a sitting position. Another vulture, flying far in the sky, came down to sit on Naranappa's house. He lifted his head, flapped his demon wings loudly, came to a standstill and inspected the whole agrahara with his eagle eyes. After that, more flying vultures came down to sit, two by two, two on each house, as if they had agreed upon it earlier. Some would whirr to the ground unpredictably, pick up rats in their beak and perch back on the roof to pick at their prey at leisure. The birds of prey had left their burial grounds to descend on the agrahara, as if at the Last Deluge, and everyone in the agrahara came out and gathered in the street, with their hands on their mouths. Sitadevi saw that every house had its bird of ill-omen and felt consoled; the omens weren't directed in particular at her son. The brahmins, their women and children, had stood there in unspeakable dread only for two seconds, when Durgabhatta shrieked, "Hoo Hoo Hoo!" at the birds, trying to scare them away. In vain. All the brahmins shouted in unison—but even that didn't work.

But Dasacharya, who had just returned beaming, after filling his belly with *uppittu*, had an idea. "Bring out the sacred gongs and beat them," he said. The men, happy at the thought, ran into the household gods' rooms, brought out the bronze gongs and the conches. The dreadful auspicious din, like the din during the great offerings of flaming camphor, shattered the grim silence of the afternoon like grisly wardrums. For anyone who heard it in the villages five or six miles around, it created the illusion that in Durvasapura it was worship time, that they were making an offering of flaming camphor in the temple and beating the huge temple drum. The vultures looked this way and that, as if astonished; then they unfurled their wings and flew, with rats in their beaks; turned into floating glimmering dots in the sky. The brahmins, tired out, uttering the holy name of Narayana, climbed their front yards, covered their noses with their upper cloths and wiped the sweat off their faces. Sitadevi and Anasuya went to their husbands and begged tearfully: "Let the gold go to hell! Why do we need other people's property? Please take out the body and get to the rites. Naranappa's spirit is calling out these vultures." There was not a breath of wind; the stench stood stagnant in each house, and like a bodyless ghost it troubled everyone—wretched already with heat, hunger and dread. The orthodox brahmins were distraught, as if nothing in lives to come would wash the filth of their day.

The burning sun climbed the sky. Chandri, sitting in the shade of a tree, was very tired. When her hand fumbled at the plantains in her lap, she thought of Praneshacharya in the temple, fasting and worshipping the god; she couldn't eat. She was surprised by the sound of gongs and conches in the distance. She looked around. The air was still, not a leaf was stirring. The only moving things were the gently gliding vultures in the clear blue sky. When she saw Praneshacharya pouring over his body another pitcher of water, she thought, "All this trouble is because of me." And it hurt her to think so. Before she knew it, her hand had peeled the plantains and put them in her mouth. "These things don't apply to me," she consoled herself.

Again and again the obstinate vultures came back and sat on the roofs. The brahmins came out again and again and beat their gongs, blew their conches. The battle was on till evening. But it was the brahmins who got exhausted. In spite of all their humble waiting, Praneshacharya didn't appear. The thought of another night was unbearable. The agrahara grew dark, and the vultures vanished.

X

Praneshacharya waited desperately for the god's favour, His solution. "Without a proper rite, the dead body is rotting; Maruti, how long is this ordeal going to last?"—he pleaded. "If it shouldn't be done, give me a sign, at least the flower on the left, please," he begged. He entreated. He sang devotional love-songs to the god. He became a child, a beloved, a mother. He recalled the holy songs that blamed the Lord, listed His hundred and one faults. The man-sized Monkey-god Maruti just stood still, carrying on His palm the mountain with the life-giving herb that He carried to save the wounded hero in the epic war. Praneshacharya prostrated himself, laying the entire length of his body on the ground, and prayed. It was evening. Night fell. In the lamplight, the flower-decked Maruti didn't yield; gave neither the right flower nor the left. "I didn't get the answer in the Books, and didn't get it here, do I not deserve it then?"—the supplicant doubted himself. "How can I face the people who have put their trust in me?"—he said, mortified. "You're testing me, teasing me"—he scolded Maruti. As the darkness thickened, he realized it was the darkness of the new-moon night. He tried to persuade Maruti: "Don't you think it's my test. Keep in mind the rotting corpse, don't forget that." Maruti, unhearing, unyielding, stood there, His profile turned forever towards the mountain on His palm. The Acharya suddenly remembered it was time for his wife's medicine. His legs had gone numb with all that sitting. He walked out weakly with slow steps.

As he walked a little, he heard footsteps behind him in the forest dark, and he stopped. The sound of bangles. He listened. "Who's that?" he asked. And waited.

"Me," said Chandri, in an embarrassed low voice.

Praneshacharya felt strange standing like that all on a sudden with a woman in the dark of the forest. He searched for words. Remembering his own helplessness, overcome with sadness, he stood there murmuring, "Maruti ... Maruti."

Listening to his gentle grief-stricken voice, Chandri suddenly overflowed with compassion. The poor man. Famished, distressed, he had suffered and grown so lean in a single day for me. The poor brahmin. She wanted to hold his feet and offer him her devotion. The next second, she was falling at his feet. It was pitch dark, nothing was visible. As she bent over as if overcome with grief, she didn't quite fall at his feet. Her breast touched his knee. In the vehemence of her stumbling, the buttons on her blouse caught and tore open. She leaned her head on his thigh and embraced his legs. Overwhelmed with tender feeling, filled with pity at this brahmin who had perhaps never known the pleasure of woman, helpless at her thought that there was no one but him for her in the agrahara—overcome, she wept. Praneshacharya, full of compassion, bewildered by the tight hold of a young female not his own, bent forward to bless her with his hands. His bending hand felt her hot breath, her warm tears; his hair rose in a thrill of tenderness and he caressed her loosened hair. The Sanskrit formula of blessing got stuck in his throat. As his hand played on her hair, Chandri's intensity doubled. She held his hands tightly and stood up and she pressed them to her breasts now beating away like a pair of doves.

Touching full breasts he had never touched, Praneshacharya felt faint. As in a dream, he pressed them. As the strength in his legs was ebbing, Chandri sat the Acharya down, holding him close. The Acharya's hunger, so far unconscious, suddenly raged, and he cried out like a child in distress, "Amma!" Chandri leaned him against her breasts, took the plantains out of her lap, peeled them and fed them to him. Then she took off her sari, spread it on the ground, and lay on it hugging Praneshacharya close to her, weeping, flowing in helpless tears.

PART TWO

I

IT WAS midnight when the Acharya woke up. His head was in Chandri's lap. His cheek was pressed into her low naked belly. Chandri's fingers caressed his back, his ears, his head.

As if he had become a stranger to himself, the Acharya opened his eyes and asked himself: Where am I? How did I get here? What's this dark? Which forest is this? Who is this woman?

It felt as though he'd turned over and fallen into his childhood, lying in his mother's lap and finding rest there after great fatigue. He looked about wonderingly. A night of undying stars, spread out like a peacock's tail. The constellation of the Seven Sages. Next to the sage Agastya was Arundhati, paragon of faithful wives, twinkling shyly. Below were green grass smells, wet earth, the wild *vishnukranti* with its sky-blue flowers and the country sarsaparilla, and the smell of a woman's body-sweat. Darkness, sky, the tranquillity of standing trees. He rubbed his eyes, maybe it's all a dream. I clean forgot where I came from and where I should go from here, he thought anxiously. He said, "Chandri," and his wakefulness was complete. In the forest, in the silence, the dark was full of secret whispers. Chirping sounds, from a bush that suddenly appeared outlined like a chariot, a formation of twinkling lightning-bugs. He gazed, he listened, till his eyes were filled with the sights, his ears with the sounds all around him, a formation of fireflies. "Chandri," he said, touched her belly and sat up.

Chandri was afraid that Praneshacharya might scold her, despise her. There was also a hope in her that his touch might bear fruit in her body. And a gratefulness that she too might have earned merit. But she didn't say anything.

Praneshacharya didn't say anything for a long time. Finally he got up and said:

"Chandri, get up. Let's go. Tomorrow morning when the brahmins gather, we'll say this happened. You tell them yourself. As for my authority to decide for the agrahara, I have...."

Not knowing what to say, Praneshacharya stood there in confusion.

"I've lost it. If I don't have the courage to speak tomorrow you must speak out. I'm ready to do the funeral rites myself. I've no authority to tell any other brahmin to do them, that's all." Having said the words, Praneshacharya felt all his fatigue drop from him.

They crossed the stream together. Out of embarrassment she let Praneshacharya go ahead, and when she reached the agrahara a little later, she had anxious thoughts: Why is it everything I do turns out this way? I gave the gold out of my good will, and it made nothing but trouble. And now the Acharya is in trouble, trying so hard to get the funeral rites performed right. But Chandri was a natural in pleasure, unaccustomed to self-reproach. As she walked the agrahara street in the dark she remembered—the dark forest—the standing, the bending—the giving, the taking—and it brought her only a sense of worthwhileness, like the fragrance of flowers hidden. The poor Acharya, it may not strike him the same way. Now one should not go back to his verandah and trouble him further. A great good fortune had suddenly rushed into her life. She couldn't speak of it in broad daylight before those dry brahmin folk as the Acharya asked her to, and expose him to their mercy—she couldn't do it. But then,—what was she going to do now? It wasn't right to go to the Acharya again, and she dreaded going to her dead master's house. What could she do?

After all, he'd lived with her so long—she said to herself, and plucked up courage. "Let's go there and see, if I feel strong enough I can sleep on the outer verandah. If not I can go again to the Acharya's verandah. What else can be done in an emergency?" So arguing with herself she went straight home. She stood under the thatch and listened. Dogs barked tonight like any other night. She started climbing the steps. Her groping hand felt the open door. "*Ayyo* O God, hope no fox or dog has entered the house and done things to the body...." She felt distressed, forgot her fears, went in swiftly, found by habit the box of matches in the wall-niche and lit the lantern. A horrid stench. Dead rotting rats. She was grief-stricken that she'd left the body orphaned, unprotected, the body of the man who'd antagonized the whole agrahara for her sake. She went upstairs, thinking, "We should have burned some incense and filled the place with sweet smoke." The dead body was reeking. The belly was swollen, the face of the dead man was grisly, disfigured. She let out a scream and ran out. Her spirit cried out: what's up there, that thing, that's not the man who loved her, no no no there's no connection. Like one possessed, she gripped the lantern and ran a mile all the way to the farmers' section. She recognized cartman Sheshappa's house by the white oxen tied up in the yard—he used to deliver eggs to their house. She went in. The oxen reacted to the unfamiliar shape, stood up, breathed out in hisses and tugged at their halters, the dogs barked. Sheshappa got up and came down. Chandri hastily described the situation and said to him, "You must come with your ox-cart and take the dead body to the cremation ground. There's firewood in the house, we can cremate him."

Sheshappa had woken up from a happy sleep after a swig of toddy. He panicked.

"Chandramma, that can't be done. Do you want me to go to hell, meddling with a brahmin corpse? Even if you give me all eight kinds of riches, I can't. Please. If you're scared, come sleep in this poor man's house, and go home in the morning," he said, all courtesy.

Chandri came out without a word. What was she going to do? Only one thought burned clear: it's rotting there, that thing, it's stinking there, its belly swollen. That's not her lover, Naranappa. It's neither brahmin nor shudra. A carcass. A stinking rotting carcass.

She walked straight to the Muslim section. She offered them money. She went to Ahmad Bari, the fish merchant. His late master,

Naranappa, had once loaned him money to buy oxen when he was bankrupt. He remembered that, and came at once with his bullock-cart, secretly loaded both the body and the firewood into it, drove to the cremation ground before anyone knew, kindled a flapping flaming fire in the dark night and burned it to ashes—and left, twisting his bullocks' tails, goading them with various noises to run faster. Chandri wept, came back home, collected a few of her silk saris in a bag, bundled up the cash in the box and the gold ornaments the Acharya had returned, and came out. Suppressing her desire to wake up the Acharya and touch his feet, she decided to catch the morning bus to Kundapura and walked towards the motor route in the forest path with her bundle in her hands.

II

Meanwhile, in Parijatapura, in Rich Man Manjayya's spacious terrace, several young men from four or five agraharas—Shripati, Ganesha, Ganganna, Manjunatha and others—had gathered to rehearse a play. Right in the middle was a harmonium, donated by Naranappa to their drama troupe.

When he was alive, he had to be present for every play. Without his encouragement, the Parijata Drama Group would never have been born. He was the prime mover; he added some money of his own to what the young fellows got together and bought them "sceneries"—backdrops—from Shivamogge. He also gave them ideas about acting style. In the whole neighbourhood, he alone owned a gramophone. And had with him all the records from Hirannayya's plays. He would wind up the gramophone and play them all to his young friends. When he heard about the Congress Party here and there, he came to the village and taught the boys the new fashion of Congress uniform, of handspun knee-length shirts, loose pajamas and white caps. Now all the young fellows were in grief over his death. But they were quiet, afraid of the elders. They'd shuttered all the doors, lit *Passing Show* cigarettes. A rehearsal was on, somewhat half-heartedly. Shripati, who had a passion for dance-drama, was present, though he had no acting part. He loved anything in make-up. While the rehearsal was going on, they also consumed a small wicker tray full of spicy crisp-rice and a vessel full of hot coffee. Thinking of Naranappa now and then, eating the spiced rice and drinking the coffee, they rehearsed their play till midnight. When it ended, Nagaraja winked at Ganesha. Ganesha pinched Manjunatha who did female roles. Manjunatha passed it on to Ganganna of the Malera caste. Ganganna gave Shripati's dhoti a tug. After these secret "in" signals, the rest of the boys were told that the rehearsal was over for the day, and packed off. When everyone was gone Nagaraja bolted the door, opened the lid of the trunk very importantly and held up two bottles of liquor. He hummed a drinking song from an old play in memory of mentor Naranappa. After that, they put the bottles in a sack; tied up the spiced rice in a banana leaf; carefully, without making a sound, glasses were packed. "Ready?" asked Nagaraja. "Ready," said the others. One by one, as they went down the stairs, Manjunatha said, "Hold on," like a bus conductor and put a sliced lemon in his pocket. The young men silently closed the door behind them, and crossed the agrahara. Delighted by their own nefarious activity, they walked in the dark towards the river by the light of Shripati's torch. "Our guru could down a whole bottle and still play the drum without missing a beat!" said Nagaraja on the way, remembering Naranappa. They came to a large sand-heap, sat on it in a circle, placing the bottle, the glasses, the rice in the centre. They felt the world contained only the five of them; the stars for witness, they wanted to shed the dwarfish Vamana natures of the agrahara and prepare to grow, with the help of liquor, into giant Trivikrama forms. The river gurgled in the silences between their words and assured them of their privacy.

As the liquor went warmly to his head, Shripati said, his voice breaking, "Our companion, he's dead."

"Yes, yes," said Nagaraja, his hand reaching for the crisp-rice. "A pillar of our company broken. In this whole area, who kept time like him on the drums?"

In spite of several squeezes of lemon, Manjunatha's head was light. Trying to say something, all he could say was, "Chandri, Chandri."

Shripati waxed quite enthusiastic: "Whatever anybody may say, whatever brahmins bray—I swear—what do you say?—in a hundred-mile radius is there any woman as lovely, as bright, as good, as Chandri? Take a count. If you find one, I'll give up my caste. What does it matter if she's a whore? You tell me, didn't she behave better than any wife with Naranappa? If he drank too much and vomited, she wiped up the mess. She even wiped ours up, didn't she? Anytime, even at midnight, when he woke her up she cooked and served him, all smiles. Which brahmin woman would do so much? Stupid shaven widows!" He spat out the last words.

Manjunatha uttered one of the three English words he knew: "Yus, yus."

"If you give Manjunatha a drink, he'll speak English," Nagaraja laughed.

The talk turned again to girls. They measured and judged all the lowcaste women. Only Naranappa had known anything about his affair with Belli, so Shripati listened to their conversation quite calmly. It was good these fellows didn't set their eyes on Belli. Even if they did, they would be afraid to touch an untouchable. All for the best.

Shripati, uncorking the second bottle, said, "Our best friend is lying there dead, rotting! No one to take care of his rites. And what are we doing here, having a good time?" Then he started crying. His crying fit spread contagiously to the other young men. They embraced each other.

Shripati said, "Who are the real he-men here?"

"Me, me, me, me," shouted all four.

Nagaraja looked at the girl-faced Manjunatha who did all the girls' roles, and said, "Che, Che, you're our heroine, you're Sadarame, Shakuntale," and gave him a kiss.

"If you're real men, I'll tell you something. If you agree, I'll say you're great. Okay? Naranappa was our dear friend. What have we

given him in return? Let's take his body secretly and cremate it ourselves. What do you say? Get up," said Shripati, egging them on, filling their glasses. They drank noisily; then, without a thought, they
staggered and weaved across the river, guided by Shripati's flashlight. In the dark night, there was not a soul anywhere. The liquor
had gone straight to their heads; they went into the agrahara, to Naranappa's door, gave it a push, and went in fearlessly. The liquor had
made them insensitive to the stench. They went upstairs. Shripati
beamed his flashlight all around. Where? Where? Naranappa's
corpse was nowhere. All five of them suddenly feared for their lives.
Nagaraja said, "Ha, Naranappa has become a spirit, and has walked
away!" As soon as he said that, they dropped the bag of liquor bottles
and all five ran for their lives.

When Half-Wit Lakshmidevamma, sleepless, opened her thun-
derous door and came out into the agrahara street to curse everybody, she saw them. She shrieked, "Look, look at the demons!" And
let out a long belch: *Hee...eey!*

III

The brahmins, miserable that Praneshacharya did not return even
late at night, shut their doors and windows tight, held their noses
against the horrid stench that turned and brought their bowels up
into their mouths, and tried to sleep. They tossed about on the cold
floors in hunger and fear. As if from another world, there were footsteps in the night, the sound of cartwheels, the pitiful wail of Lakshmidevamma's dog-like howl and her belches. Their very life-breaths
quaked, as if the agrahara had suddenly emptied itself into a desolate
forest, as if the protecting gods had left them to their own devices. In
house after house, children, mother and father seemed to become
one shapeless mass, hugging each other and shivering in the dark.
When night was over, the sun's rays descended through the holes in
the rafters and brought courage in little circles of light in the dark
houses. They all got up slowly, unbolted the doors and looked out.

Vultures, birds of carrion. Again, the vultures, driving away the crows, sitting obstinately on the rooftops. The men tried to shoo them away, clap at them. But they didn't budge. Downhearted, the brahmins blew their sacred conches and beat their gongs. Hearing in the dawn the auspicious sounds heard only on the twelfth day of the moon, Praneshacharya came out baffled. In a perplexity he couldn't undo, he walked in and out, out and in, snapping his fingers, saying, "What shall I do? What shall I do?' When he gave his wife her usual medicine as she lay groaning in the dining room, his hands trembled and spilled the medicine. As he held it to her lips, as he looked into his broken wife's pitted eyes, those helpless visionless symbols of his self-sacrifice and duty as a householder—he felt his legs twitch and double-up, as if in troubled sleep, as if in a dream he fell dizzily into bottomless nether-worlds. At the end of the beaten path of a quarter-century of doctor-patient relations, of affection and compassion,—he seemed to see an abyss. He shivered in an attack of nausea. He imagined all the stinks assailing his nostrils, all issuing from that source. Like a baby monkey losing hold of his grip on the mother's body as she leaps from branch to branch, he felt he had lost hold and fallen from the rites and actions he had clutched till now.

Did he clutch this duty, this dharma, to protect this wife lying here lifeless, a pathetic beggar-woman—or did the dharma, clinging to him through the action and culture of his past, guide him hand in hand through these ways? He did not know. When he married her he was sixteen, she twelve. He had thought he should renounce the world, become a *sanyasi*, live a life of self-sacrifice. That was the ideal, the challenge, of his boyhood days. So he had married a born invalid deliberately. He'd left her in the grateful house of her father, gone to Benares, studied to become "the Crest-Jewel of Vedanta Philosophy," and had come back. Here was the Lord's ordeal for him, waiting, to test him whether he had the strength to live and act by non-attachment—that was why He had given an ailing invalid wife into his hands. He would serve her, delighting in that knowledge. He had cooked for her, fed her the wheat-gruel he had himself made, done meticulously every act of daily worship for the gods, read and explicated the holy texts for the brahmins—Ramayana, Bharata, Bhagavata, etc.—hoarded his penances like a miser his money. A hundred thousand mantras chanted and counted this month, another hundred thousand the next, a couple of hundred thousand for the eleventh day of the moon. Million by million, he counted his earnings, penances reckoned on the beads of his basil-bead rosary.

Once a Smarta pundit had gone and argued: Your idea that only men of "Goodness" can reach salvation, isn't that only a form of hopelessness? Doesn't it mean the disappointment of a human hope, desiring a thing and not getting it? In men of "Darkness" (he had replied) there's no desire for salvation in the first place. How can such clods feel disappointed by not getting what they don't want? No one can say, "I'll become a 'Man of Goodness'; one can only say truly "I am a 'Man of Goodness.'" Only such natures crave and hunger for the Lord's grace.

"I am born with one such 'Good' nature. This invalid wife is the sacrificial altar for my sacrifice." With such thoughts had he begun to cultivate his salvation. Naranappa too was a test of his "Good" nature. Now every one of his beliefs seemed to have turned topsy-turvy, returning him to where he had started in his sixteenth year. Which is the way? Where is the path that will not lead to the brink of an abyss?

Bewildered, he lifted her as he did every day in his arms to take her for her bath, though he was bothered by the conches and gongs out in the street. When he poured the bath water over her, he noticed her sunken breasts, her bulbous nose, her short narrow braid, and they disgusted him. He felt like screaming, "Stop it! Stop it!" to the brahmins out there blowing conches and beating gongs against the vultures. For the first time his eyes were beginning to see the beautiful and the ugly. He had not so far desired any of the beauty he'd read about in the classics. All earthly fragrance was like the flowers that go only to adorn the god's hair. All female beauty was the beauty of Goddess Lakshmi, queen and servant of Lord Vishnu. All sexual enjoyment was Krishna's when he stole the bathing cowgirls' garments, and left them naked in the water. Now he wanted for himself a share of all that. He wiped the water off his wife's body, laid her on the bed he'd made, and came out again. The din of conch and gong abruptly stopped; his ears seemed to drown in a sudden depth of silent water. "Why did I come here? Did I come looking for Chandri? But Chandri isn't here." This bedridden woman, and that other woman who suddenly pressed his hand to her breast—what if both should leave him? For the first time, a desolation, a feeling of being orphaned, entered his inmost sense.

The brahmins, who had finally chased off the birds of prey, lifted their cadaver faces, came in a herd to climb his verandah and looked at him questioningly. When they saw the Acharya unresponsive and hesitant, they were afraid. The Acharya looked into the brahmins' eyes looking up to him for guidance, like homeless orphans; they had transferred on to his head the whole burden of their brahminhood. Looking into those eyes, the Acharya felt not only remorse, but a lightness in the thought he was now a free man, relieved of his responsibility to lead the way, relieved of all authority. "What manner of man am I? I am just like you—a soul driven by lust and hate. Is this my first lesson in humility? Come, Chandri, tell them, relieve me of the guru's burden," he thought, and looked around. No, she wasn't there. She wasn't anywhere there. Urvashi, she had walked away. He was afraid to say openly, to say explicitly that he too had shared in Naranappa's pleasure. His hand sweated and grew cold. The desire, natural to mere mortals, to tell lies, to hide things, to think of one's own welfare, arose in him for the first time. He couldn't find the courage to shatter the respect and faith these people had placed in him. Is this pity, self-preservation, habit, inertia, sheer hypocrisy? The Sanskrit chant, learned by heart and recited daily, turned over and over in his mind: "I am sin, my work is sin, my soul is sin, my birth is in sin." No, no, even that is a lie. Must forget all words learned by heart, the heart must flow free like a child's. When he caressed Chandri's breast, it didn't occur to him to say, "I am sin." Now he was quite happy Chandri wasn't here to shame him. Thoughts after waking are different from the thoughts when one is unaware. He became aware, this life is duplicity. Now he's really involved in the wheel of karma. To relieve this misery, he must lose awareness again and embrace her, must wake up in that misery, for absolution one must return to her. The wheel, the wheel of karma. This is the life of "Passion." Even if he had left desire, desire had not left him.

Troubled, unable to bring out a word, he left the seated brahmins where they were and went into the worship room. He recited God's many names—according to routine. If he didn't tell the truth—if it burns like embers poured into one's lap—he could never face Maruti again, could not tend the invalid woman with a clear heart. "O Lord, tide me over this confusion—has Chandri come? Will she blurt it out?" Anxious, in dread, he came out. The brahmins were still waiting. The vultures had returned to sit on the rooftops. The Acharya closed his eyes, drew a long breath, and gathered courage. But the words that came out of his mouth were: "I'm lost. I couldn't get Maruti to say anything. I know nothing. You do whatever your hearts say."

The brahmins were startled. Garudacharya exclaimed, "Che, Che! That cannot be." Dasacharya, who had some life in him today because he had eaten a bellyful the previous day, said:

"What shall we do then? Let's go to the Kaimara agrahara. Let's ask Pundit Subbannacharya there. Not that he would know what our own Acharya couldn't find. If he doesn't know, we can go straight to the monastery and see the Swami. How long can we creep about in this agrahara, without food, keeping a dead body in this stench? It also gives us a chance to visit our guru. Also, the thirteenth day is a public worship day at the monastery. What do you say? We'll walk to Kaimara and change our polluted sacred threads. Won't the brahmins there offer us a meal? You shouldn't eat in the agrahara where a dead body lies uncremated, but is there any objection to eating in Kaimara? What do you say?"

All the brahmins said, "Yes, Yes." Lakshmanacharya remembered that Venkannacharya in Kaimara had said he would buy from him a hundred leaf-cups and a thousand dry eating-leaves. He could take those when he went there. And Garudacharya had some business with the guru. Praneshacharya felt relieved by this suggestion; a burden lifted, his fatigue vanished.

Dasacharya, very happy at his words being accepted, said: "We'll have to leave the agrahara for at least three days. What will happen to our women and children? Let's send our families to our in-laws!"

Everyone agreed.

IV

Durgabhatta got back home, full of curses; he felt he was being dirtied by the company of these Madhva bastards, lovers of shaven widows; he got his bullock-carts ready and went away to his mother-in-law's place with his wife and children. Lakshmanacharya packed his banana leaves and leaf-cups. Dasacharya packed some puffed rice for the road, roused wife and children for their journey, packed off Lakshmidevamma also to Lakshmana's in-laws! By the time all the brahmins came to Praneshacharya's front yard, his wife had started her period. The Acharya said, "I can't come with you now, I can't leave my bedridden wife." The brahmins understood, and started out on the road to Kaimara hurriedly, not worrying any more about the vultures on the roofs.

When they reached Kaimara, the heat of day had cooled into evening. They bathed, changed their sacred threads, wore their sandal-paste caste-marks and gathered on Subbannacharya's verandah. The pundit said, "You must eat first." The brahmins, waiting just for that suggestion, poured down hot steaming rice and *saru* into their bellies till it touched the Supreme Spirit inside. Then they crowded around Subbannacharya in a state of happy languor. Subbannacharya was an astrologer: he had to know whether the time of Naranappa's dying was malignant or benign, then he could think about the proper rites. So he put on his spectacles, spread out the almanac, counted and consulted some sea-shells, and said, "Malignant." He shook his head, saying, "How can I advise when Praneshacharya himself couldn't?" Dasacharya was pleased by this, and they started out again for the monastery, happy that they could get a share of the offerings of the great worship there.

"It's already dark. Stay here tonight and go early in the morning," the Kaimara people said, and the brahmins didn't refuse their hospitality. But when they woke up early in the morning, Dasacharya lay weak in bed, running a fever. They tried to rouse him. He was in a coma.

Garudacharya explained that it might be mere indigestion, maybe he ate too much. The poorer brahmins felt sorry that the poor man would miss the great worship-service and the feast. They got up in a hurry, had a wash, ate flattened rice in yoghurt, and walked twenty miles to reach another agrahara by nightfall. They stayed and dined there that night, but when they woke up early next morning, Padmanabhacharya was down with high fever. It must be the fatigue of all that walking, they thought; and left him there. They had to walk another ten miles to reach the monastery. Whey they reached there, the big drum was sounding for noon-time worship.

V

Not a creature was visible in the agrahara except his bedridden menstruating wife, some crows and vultures. Praneshacharya was alone. No sounds of worship or ritual. A terrible leery silence had settled on the place. Assaulting the nostrils with the fact that seven houses away a human corpse was rotting, lodging itself in the very sources of breath was the horrible stench; with the vultures sitting on house after house, it pestered the mind, not permitting any oblivion. When he went to the gods' room, he saw to his disgust a rat reel inauspiciously counter-clockwise, fall on its back and die. He picked it up by its tail and threw it to a vulture outside. As he came in, he was startled by the raucous cries of crows and vultures; so he came out again. He couldn't bear to lift his eyes to the deathly silent noonday heat of the sun. He shooed at the birds ineffectively and came in. Distressed by hunger, unable to bear it any longer, he gathered some plantains into the lap of his dhoti, bathed, crossed the stream, and ate them in the shade of a tree. His hunger was stilled. He remembered the darkness in which Chandri had fed him the plantains from her lap.

Did he take her then out of compassion? That is doubtful. His body's tigerish lust, taking on the form of pity and compassion, tamed by a righteousness which had brought him this far—it could be nothing else. At the touch of Chandri's breast, the animal leaped to its natural self and bared its teeth. Naranappa's words came to his mind: "Let's see who'll win, you or me . . . go to sleep in the arms of Matsyagandhi, the fragrant fisherwoman." He'd also told him a parable about how every act of ours reverses itself in its results. Not through Naranappa, but through him and his wilfulness, his action, the life of this agrahara must have turned topsy-turvy. He'd heard that a young lad went to the riverbank and slept with an outcaste girl there, after hearing his description of Shakuntala. The Acharya's fantasy dragged in all the untouchable girls he'd never thought of; stripped them and looked at them. Who is it? Who could it be? Belli, of course; yes, Belli. Imagining her earth-coloured breasts he had never before reckoned with, his body grew warm. He felt wretched at his fantasy. Naranappa had said mockingly: to keep your brahminhood, you must read the Vedas and holy legends without understanding, without responding to their passion. Embedded in his compassion, in his learning, was an explosive spark, which was not there in the others' stupidity. Now the tamed tiger is leaping out, baring its teeth. . . .

His hands itched to go caress Belli's breasts, thirsting for new experience. So far he didn't even live; doing only what was done, chanting the same old mantra, he had remained inexperienced. Experience is risk, assault. A thing not done before, a joining in the dark of the jungle. He'd thought experience was fulfilment of what one wanted, but now it seemed it was the unseen, the unpredicted, thrust into our life like breasts, entering it. Just as *he* had received the touch of woman, did Naranappa receive the touch of God in the dark, unbidden? Responding gently to rainfall, stirring in the soft pressure of the earth, the hard seed breaks into sprout. If one is wilful, it dries into a hard shell. Naranappa was such a wilful shell; now dead, he rots. Till I touched Chandri, I too was a shell, counterwill to his will. Just as naturally as the body's desires reach out to me, not leaving me even when I think I have left them, why shouldn't God come and touch me, unwilled by me?"

Where is Chandri now? Did she go sit with the dead body so that he may not be troubled? How will she stand that stench? He worried. He dived into the stream and swam around. Let me, he felt, let me stay here forever, swimming in the water. He remembered his boyhood days when he used to escape his mother's overseeing eyes and run to the river. He was astonished that, after so many years, his boyhood desires had returned to him. To escape mother's suspicion, he used to lie in the sand after the swim, dry himself before he went home. Is there any pleasure equal to rolling in the sun-warmed sands after a swim in the cold water? He didn't want to go back to the agrahara. He got out on the bank and lay on the sands. In the heat of noon, the body dried quickly and the back began to burn.

Something occurred to him and he got up. Like an animal with his snout to the ground, he entered the woods where he had made love to Chandri. Even in broad daylight, it was shady and dusky there. In the bushes, it was quite dark, a humming dark. He stood at the place where his life had turned over. The weight and shape of their bodies still visible on the green grass. He sat down. Like an idiot, he pulled out blades of grass and smelled them. He had come from the death-stench in the agrahara; the smell of grass-roots smeared with wet earth held him in its power like an addiction. Like a hen pecking at and raking the ground, he pulled at everything that came to his hand and smelled it. Just sitting coolly under a tree had become a fulfilment, a value. To be, just to be. To be; keen, in the heat, the cool, to the grass, the green, the flower, the pang, the heat, the shade. Putting aside both desire and value. Not leaping, when the invisible says "Here!" To receive it gratefully. Not climbing, not reaching out, not scrambling. A small sprout of sarsaparilla touched his hand. He pulled at it. The sarsaparilla was a firmly rooted, long creeper, and it did not yield to him. Unlike the grass, it had sunk roots into the hard ground beneath the soft topsoil. He sat up and tugged with both hands. He severed half the length of the mother root, and the sarsaparilla creeper came to his hand. He smelled it. The root had earned a fragrance, existing there, a kin knotted into the heat and the shade, sod of the earth and the space above it. The smell of it reached into him, sinking into his five-fold breath of life. He sat there, smelling it like a greedy man. The smell settled in the nostril, the sweetness entered his blood; soon the experience of fragrance passed, and he was left unsatisfied. He put aside the root and smelled the forest smells, and returned to the sarsaparilla, its smell made new. He came out of the forest and stood looking at the *vishnukranti* flowers, now become as sapphires dotting the shade—looking at them as if mere looking was wealth. Got into the stream once again and swam around. Stood in the deeper part where the water came to his chin. Fishes mobbed him, prickled at his ticklish toe-spaces, armpits and ribs. Like a ticklish boy, Praneshacharya exclaimed, "Ahaha," and fell then swimming into the water, climbed onto the bank and stood in the sun till he was dry. He remembered it was time to give his wife her gruel, and walked quickly back to the agrahara.

All at once he saw again the crows, the vultures—felt a sudden slap on his face. When he came home, his wife's face looked hot and flushed. "Look here, look here!" he cried to her. Had the fever risen? How can I touch a woman polluted by her menstrual blood? "Che!," he said to himself in self-disgust, catching himself at his own hesitation; he touched her brow and drew back startled. Not knowing what to do, he put a wet cloth to her brow, he pulled her blanket aside suspiciously and examined her body. There was a swelling, a bubo on the side of her stomach. Was it the same fever that took Naranappa? He rubbed on a stone all the herbs he knew, separated her lips and poured emulsions into her mouth. None of the medicines went down her throat. "What's this new ordeal now?" he thought, pacing up and down. The din of crows and vultures grew unbearable, the stench seemed to craze his wits. He ran into the backyard. Stood there in a dimness, not seeing the passage of time. Evening came. He was relieved to see the crows and vultures disappear, came in distraught that he had left his sick wife alone all this while. In fear, he lit the lamp and called to her. "Look here, look here!" No answer. The silence seemed to howl. But suddenly his wife let out a shriek that left him speechless. The long raucous pitiful cry touched him in the rawest flesh, and he shivered. When the howling stopped, it was like darkness after a flash of lightning. He could not bear to be alone there. Before he knew what he was doing, he was running to Naranappa's house, calling out to Chandri. "Chandri! Chandri!" But there was no response. He went in. It was dark. He searched in the middle room, the kitchen. No one. Just as he was about to climb the stairs, he remembered there was a corpse in there; a fear returned, as in childhood when he had been afraid to enter a dark room, fearing a goblin there; he came home running. When he touched his wife's forehead, it was cold.

He walked all the way to Kaimara in the dead of night with a lantern, and as he entered Subbannacharya's house, behind him came the four brahmins saying, "Narayana, Narayana"; they had wet dhotis on their heads after the cremation of Dasacharya. He brought them back with him, took his wife's body to the burning ground, and she was ritually cremated before dawn. As if to himself, he murmured to the brahmins, "There's another dead body in the agrahara waiting to be cremated. Anyway its fate will be decided at the guru's monastery. You'd better be on your way." They left him looking on at the burning body of his wife—at the best of times no more than a small fistful, the field of his life's penance—now burning down to ash. He did not try to hold back his tears; he wept till all his weariness flowed away from him.

VI

At the monastery, the brahmins didn't want to say anything inauspicious till the holy feast was over. Silently they took the sacred water, and finished the big meal of special dishes and sweet porridge. The guru gave them all a gift, a fee, of a mere anna each. Lakshmanacharya was disappointed; grumbling at this niggardly ascetic, he tucked away the nickel in his waistcloth. "He has no kids, no family—yet the man hangs on to money for dear life." After the feast was over, in the main yard of the monastery the brahmins sat on the cool cement floor, and the guru sat in their midst on a chair. He was wearing an ochre robe, a rosary of basil beads, a sandal-mark on his brow. Sitting like a round doll, ruddy-cheeked, and massaging his tiny feet, he asked courtesy questions: "Why didn't Praneshacharya come? How is he? Is he well? Why, didn't our announcement reach him?"

Garudacharya cleared his throat and submitted the entire situation.

The guru listened to everything carefully and said decisively:

"Even if he gave up brahminism, brahminism cannot leave Naranappa. Which means, the right and proper duty is to perform the death-rites. But the impurity must also be cleared—therefore all his property, silver and gold must be offered to the monastery, to Lord Krishna."

Garuda plucked up courage and wiped his face with his dhoti.

"Your Holiness, you already know about the fight between him and my father. Three hundred betelnut trees of his grove must come to me."

Lakshmanacharya said, "Ah," and interrupted him.

"Your Holiness, is there no justice in this matter? As you know, Naranappa's wife and my wife are sisters...."

Anger appeared on the face of the round red-faced Swami.

"What kind of scoundrels are you? It's an age-old rule that all orphan property should be given over to the Lord's service. Don't you forget that! You'll have to leave the agrahara yourselves if we don't give you permission for his death-rites," he thundered.

The two brahmins confessed they had done wrong and asked forgiveness; prostrated themselves before the Swami with all the others. When they stood up, they missed Gundacharya who had come with them. They found him lying down with a high fever, in an attic of the monastery; he had eaten nothing. But they were in a hurry to finish the funeral rites. They took to the road, leaving Gundacharya behind.

The Acharya did not return to the agrahara after his wife's cremation. He thought of nothing, neither the fifteen gold-lace shawls in his box, the two hundred rupees, nor the basil-bead rosary done in gold given by the monastery.

Meaning to walk wherever his legs took him, he walked towards the east.

PART THREE

I

THE MORNING sunshine had descended into the forest in dotted patterns. Praneshacharya, dragging his feet wearily as he walked, didn't think of place and direction for a long time. For a fleeting minute he felt remorse that he didn't have the patience to wait and pick out the leftover unburned bones, the remains of his wife's body, and throw them in the stream; he had the shocking thought they might be picked and worried by dogs and foxes. But he consoled himself that he had walked away free, leaving everything behind; he had no more duties, no debts. "I said I would walk where my legs took me, now I must walk according to that decision." So he walked, trying to bring some balance into his mind. Whenever in the past his mind had become overactive, he would chant the names of Lord Vishnu to give it a single point and to still its streaming distractions. "Achyuta, Ananta, Govinda." He wanted now to do likewise. He remembered the first maxim of yoga, "Yoga is the stilling of the waves of the mind." "But No!" he said to himself. "Put aside even the consolations of recitations and God's holy names, stand alone," he said to himself. May the mind be like the patterns of light and shade, the forms the branching trees give naturally to sunshine. Light in the sky, shadow under the trees, patterns on the ground. If, luckily, there's a spray of water—rainbows. May one's life be like that sunshine. A mere awareness, a sheer astonishment, still, floating still and self-content, like the sacred Brahmani-kite in the sky. Legs walk, eyes see, ears hear. O to be without any desire. Then one's life becomes receptive. Or else, in desire it dries to a shell, it withers, becomes a set of multiplication tables learned by rote. That Kanaka, illiterate saint—his mind was just one awareness, one wonder. That's why he came to his Master and asked: "You want me to eat the plantain where there's no one. Where can I go, where can I do that? God is everywhere, what shall I do?" God has become to me a set of tables, learned by rote. Not an awareness, a wonder as He was to Kanaka—so no more God for me.

Once you leave God, you must leave all concern for all the debts, to ancestors, to gurus, to the gods; must stand apart from the community of men. That's why it's right, this decision to walk where the legs lead. Walk in this pathless forest like this. What about fatigue, hunger, thirst—Praneshacharya's stream of thought stopped abruptly. He was entering another cave of self-deception. Even though he had decided he would walk where the legs lead him, why had he walked all this way within earshot of those bamboo cowbells, that cowherd boy's fluting sounds? Whatever his decision, his feet still walked him close to the habitations of men. This is the limit of his world, his freedom. Can't seem to live outside the contacts of men. Like the folktale hermit's g-string: lest mice should gnaw at the g-string, he reared a cat; for the cat's milk, he kept a cow; to look after the cow, he found a woman; and married her and ceased to be a hermit.

Praneshacharya sat under a jackfruit tree. "I must look at this matter squarely. I must conduct my future differently, not deceive myself even one little bit. Why did I walk away after cremating my wife? The agrahara was stinking, one couldn't bear to return to it. Certainly a good reason: the intolerable stench in my nostril, the sense of pollution, certainly. Then what? Why didn't I want to meet again the brahmins who were waiting for my guidance? Why?" Praneshacharya stretched his legs, trying to shed his fatigue, waiting for his mind to clear itself. Unseen by him, a calf came and stood beside him; lifted its face and smelled his neck and breathed on it. Praneshacharya shuddered and turned around. The friendly piteous eyes of the maturing calf moved him, feelings welled up from within. He ran his fingers on its dewlap. The calf lifted its neck, came closer and closer, offered its body to the caressing hand, its hair rising in pleasure, and began to lick his ears and cheeks with its warm rough-textured tongue. Tickled, Praneshacharya rose to his feet, and felt like playing with the calf; he put his hands under its neck and said, *uppuppuppu....* The calf lifted both its legs, leaped at him, then leaped away into the sunshine and disappeared. Praneshacharya tried to remember what he was thinking. "Yes, the question was why didn't I go back and see the brahmins?" But the mind didn't settle on it. He was hungry, he should go get some food in some nearby village. So he got up and walked, following the cowdung and the footprints of cattle. After an hour of wandering, he came to a Mari temple. Which meant it wasn't a brahmin agrahara. He went on and sat under a tree on the edge of the village.

The sun had begun to climb, it was getting hot even in the shade and he was thirsty. If some farmer saw him, he would bring some fruit and milk. A farmer, herding buffaloes to the tank, did look at him from under his hand shading his eyes; came close and stood near him. His mouth was full of chewed betel leaf and betelnut, his moustache was magnificent, his head was wrapped in a check-patterned turban cloth. Praneshacharya guessed that this was really a village chief. There was comfort in finding someone unknown. Because his mouth was full of betel leaf, the farmer lifted his chin to keep the juice from dribbling, and asked with his hands where the stranger came from. If he had known he was Praneshacharya, that farmer wouldn't have stood there, his mouth full of betel, and asked discourteously the way he did. When you shed your past, your history, the world sees you as just one more brahmin. He was a little disturbed by the thought. As he didn't get a reply, the farmer went aside and spat out the quid of betel in his mouth, came back humbly, wiping the red juice from his moustache with his cloth, looked at him questioningly and asked,

"Which way is the gentleman going?"

Praneshacharya was a bit relieved that the villager had shown respect. He knew it would be inauspicious to ask a brahmin directly, "Where are you going?" But Praneshacharya was not able to answer directly. "O, just this way..." he said, waving his hand vaguely in some direction, and wiping his sweat. He felt peaceful that by god's grace the farmer didn't recognize him.

"Does the gentleman come from down the valley or what?" the villager asked curiously. Praneshacharya's mouth, unaccustomed to lying, simply said "Ha."

"Must be someone going for his collection."

Praneshacharya felt like bowing his head. Look, this villager took him for a mendicant brahmin going on his rounds. All his lustre and influence lost, he really must look like a brahmin going around for his collection. The lesson of humility had begun. Better bow down, bend, he said to himself; and assented with another "Ha." That he could take on the shape he desired in the eyes of a stranger, seemed to extend the limits of his freedom.

The villager stood leaning against his buffalo and said, "There's no brahmin house anywhere near here."

"Oh?" said Praneshacharya rather indifferently.

"About ten-twelve miles from here, there's a brahmin agrahara."

"Oh really?"

"If you go by the cart road, it's even farther. By the inner path, it's much closer." "Good."

"There's a well here. I'll give you a pitcher. You can draw some water and take a bath. I'll give you rice and lentils, you can cook it on three bricks, and eat. You must be tired, poor man. If you really want to get to the agrahara, tell me; the cartman Sheshappa is here to see a relative, his cart will go home empty. He lives near the agrahara.... But from what he said, I don't know if you'd want to go to that agrahara. A body is lying there dead, rotting for three nights, it seems. A brahmin corpse. *Ush*... Sheshappa said. By dead of night that good man's mistress came all the way to Sheshappa's house asking him to help her burn the dead body. It seems there was no rightful heir to that body. How can a dead brahmin rot like that? When Sheshappa came that way in the morning in his cart, he said there were vultures sitting on the roofs of the agrahara houses...."

The villager rubbed his tobacco on his palm and sat there talking. When Praneshacharya heard that Sheshappa was nearby, his heart missed a beat. He didn't want Sheshappa to see him in the state he was in. It would be disastrous to stay there any longer.

"If you can give me some milk and a few plantains, I'll move on," he said looking at the villager.

"That's no trouble, sir. I'll get it for you this minute. I can't eat when a brahmin is hungry in the village; so I offered you rice, that's all...."

And he left. Praneshacharya felt he was sitting on thorns. What will happen if Sheshappa should see him? He looked around, growing small in his fear. "Why this fear in me when I've shed all things?" he asked himself, disturbed, unable to contain the rising dread within. The villager brought a cup of cold milk and a bunch of plantains, put them before the Acharya and said:

"A brahmin seems to have come to the village at a good time. Could you read me a bit of the future? I brought a bride for my son, paying a hundred rupees as bride-price. But ever since she came, she's been sitting dully in a corner, possessed by some she-demon. If only you can give me something with a spell on it...."

Praneshacharya reined his mind and stopped it dead, while it was about to get into action, ready to perform brahmin functions by sheer habit. "Even if I leave everything behind, the community clings to me, asking me to fulfil duties the brahmin is born to. It isn't easy to free oneself of this. What shall I say to this villager who has brought milk and fruit to an utter stranger with such concern? Shall I tell him I've sinned and lost the merits of penance? that I am no brahmin? or just the simple truth?"

"Today I'm not in a position to use my chants. A close relative died, and I'm in a period of pollution yet," he said, happy at the right answer occurring to him. He drank the milk and returned the cup, tied up the fruit in his cloth and stood up.

"If you walk this way about ten miles, you'll come to a place called Melige. A car-festival is on at the temple today, tomorrow and the day after. If you go there, you'll really get a good collection," said the villager and walked on, chewing his betel and driving his buffaloes on.

As he faded out of sight, Praneshacharya entered the forest again, and walked along the footpath. He was worried that his problem had become more critical. "I'd never experienced such dread before. A fear of being discovered, of being caught. A fear that I may not be able to keep a secret from others' eyes. I lost my original fearlessness. How, why? I couldn't return to the agrahara because of fear, the fear of not being able to live in full view, in front of those brahmins. O the anxiety, I couldn't live with a lie knotted in my lap."

As the forest silence deepened, his heart began to clear. He dragged his feet slowly as he peeled the plantains and ate them. Since he saw the villager, the problem had touched deeper. One must hold it by its tuft of hair, look at it face to face. The origin of it all was a thing that had to be burned. That thing was Naranappa, who had lived kicking away at brahminism. Waiting to be burned; among all things that had to be burned some day, it stood out as a problem. Thinking that the problem belonged to the realm of the Law of Dharma, he had run to the ancient Law Books; he had run to God; but at last in the forest, in the dark. . . .

He stopped. To know fully and exactly, he waited balancing his heart.

When one tries to recreate what exactly happened and how, one has the feeling of pursuing a dream.

"I was roused by the unexpected touch of her breasts, I ate the plantains she took out of the end of her sari. Hunger, weariness, and the disappointment that Lord Maruti gave no answer. That was the reason why. Undesired, as if it were God's will, the moment had arrived—that was the reason why. It was a sacred moment. Nothing before it, nothing after it. That moment brought into being what never was and then itself went out of being. Formless before, formless after. In between, the embodiment, the moment. Which means I'm absolutely not responsible for making love to her. Not responsible for that moment. But the moment altered me—why? I'm responsible now for someone who's changed—that's the present distress. Has that experience become a mere memory? And as memory is roused, I begin to desire it again. Once again I press forward to embrace Chandri."

As desire stirred in it, the Acharya's body craved for touch. His eyes grew dim. He thought of going to Kundapura and searching out Chandri. The usually undisturbed logic of his self-examining seemed disturbed. The waves were broken. "If I went now in search of her and enjoyed her, I would be fully responsible for my act, wouldn't I? At least then I might be released from this agony, this awareness that I turned over suddenly, unbidden. This is me, this, this is the new truth I create, the new person I make. So I can look God squarely in the eye. Now my person has lost form, has found no new form, it is like a demoniac premature foetus taken hastily out of the womb. I must examine unafraid even my belief that the moment occurred suddenly by itself, without my stir, in the darkness of the forest. It's true it occurred suddenly; I didn't go after it and get it. The outstretched hands touched the breasts—desire was born— there, there's the secret. That was the moment that decided which way to turn, No, a moment when I could have decided which way to turn. The answer is not that my body accepted it, but in the darkness my hands fumbled urgently, searched for Chandri's thighs and but- tocks as I had never searched any dharma. In that moment, decisive of which way I should turn, the decision was taken to take Chandri. Even if I lost control, the responsibility to decide was still mine. Man's decision is valid only because it's possible to lose control, not because it's easy. We shape ourselves through our choices, bring form and line to this thing we call our person. Naranappa became the person he chose to be. I chose to be something else and lived by it. But suddenly I turned at some turning. I'm not free till I realize that the turning is also my act, I'm to answer for it. What happened at that turning? Dualities, conflict, rushed into my life. I hung sus- pended between two truths, like Trishanku. How did the ancient sages face such experiences? Without dualities, conflict? One won- ders. The great sage who impregnated Matsyagandhi the fisher- woman in the boat and fathered Vyasa—did he agonize over it like me? Did Vishvamitra suffer, when he lost all the merits of penance for a woman? Could they have lived, seeing life itself as renunciation, staying with God, going beyond conflicts and opposites by living through them, taking on every changing shape that earth carves and offers, flowing finally into formlessness in the ocean like a river? As for me, God never became such an immediate urgency. If it had for anyone, it might have for my friend Mahabala. Among all my childhood friends, only for him was God a hunger. We went together to Kashi. He had a superb brain. He was tall, slim, fair-skinned. There wasn't a thing beyond his grasp. He guessed the next step even while the guru was explaining this one. Only for him did I have a terrible jealousy, a terrible love. The deeper friendship was not hindered in any way because I was a Madhva and he a Smarta. While I was busy establishing the Madhva view, only the experience of God was important to him, nothing else was. I argued, 'Don't you need a path to the experience of God? It's through dualism of God and soul you reach him.' He would say, 'What do you mean by a path? Is God's heaven a city or a village so you can find it on a road? One should reach it from where one stands.' He loved music more than logic or philosophy. When he sang poet Jayadeva's song about Krishna, one was transported to Krishna's garden. 'Southern breezes from sandalwood mountains caress delicate vines of clove'—the verse sprang within him. Praneshacharya's voice choked on the memory of his dear friend. "I've never experienced such love of God. What happened to Mahabala? When we were in Kashi he gradually withdrew and became distant. I didn't understand why. I fell into great grief. My studies didn't touch me. The fellow who was once always with me, now evaded me and roamed about. Never quite knew why. I never longed for anyone as I longed then for Mahabala. I was infatuated. Some days, his sad reddish face with a black mole on his left cheek would haunt my eyes and I'd long for his friendship. But if I went near he would elude me on some pretext or other. One day he suddenly vanished, stopped coming for the lessons. I roamed the streets of Kashi looking for him. I was distraught with the thought someone might have killed him for a human sacrifice somewhere. One day he was sitting on the front verandah of a house. I was amazed. He sat there alone, smoking a hubble-bubble. Unable to bear it, I ran to him, I pulled him by the hand. Lifting his heavy eyes, he said, 'Pranesha, go your way.' That's all. I pulled at him. In a fit of anger he stood up and said, 'You want the truth, don't you? I've given up studies. Do you know for what I live now? Come in, I'll show you.' He dragged me inside and pointed to a young woman sleeping on a mattress after her lunch. She lay there, her arms spread out. From her clothes and cosmetics I could see she was a prostitute. I was startled. I shivered in fear. Mahabala said, 'Now you know, Pranesha. Don't worry about me, go now.' I walked away in a daze, not knowing what to say. Then my heart hardened to stone. I came away with a vow: I will not go the way of the fallen Mahabala, I'll be his opposite. And came away. Whenever I see Naranappa I remember Mahabala, even though the two are as different as goat and elephant, worlds apart.

"Now I feel like seeing Mahabala again and asking him: 'Did you change your course on your own? What experience, what need, what craving moved you this way? What would you advise me now? Did woman and pleasure bring you every satisfaction? Could that aristocratic spirit of yours be satisfied by a mere woman?'

"Aha, now I know." Praneshacharya rose to his feet and started walking. "Yes, that's the root of it. My disappointment with Mahabala remained with me. Unawares, I have seen Mahabala in Naranappa. To make up for my defeat there, I tried to win a victory here over Naranappa. But I was defeated, defeated—fell flat on my face. Whatever it was I fought all along, I turned into it myself. Why? Where, how, did I lose? In this search, everything gets tangled up again.

"Look at it, one is twined with the other. From Mahabala to Naranappa, from Naranappa to my wilfulness, the holy legends I recite, their effects, finally the way I lusted for Belli's breasts myself. The form I'm getting now was being forged all along, obliquely, unknown to me. I doubt now if even the moment I united with Chandri came unbidden. It must have been the moment for everything within to come out of hiding—like the rats leaping out of the storeroom. The agrahara comes to mind again and revives the nausea. The agrahara stands there, explicit form for what I'm facing within, an entire chapter on the verse that's me. The only thing clear to me is that I should run. Maybe go to where Chandri is. Become like Mahabala. Like him, find a clear-cut way for oneself. Escape this ambiguous Trishanku state. I must go away now, undetected, unseen by any familiar eye."

He walked on and as he walked he sensed someone coming behind him in the forest. He felt a pair of eyes riveted on his back. He straightened up and strode on. He wanted to turn and see who it was, but he was afraid. He heard a noise, he turned. At a distance, he could see a young man taking quick steps toward him. Praneshacharya too quickened his step. Every time he turned, he found the young man quickening his. He walked faster. But the young man didn't seem to give up. Being younger he gained on him. What'll happen if he is no stranger? The young man got closer and closer. Praneshacharya's legs ached, and he had to slow down. The young man joined him. Panting for breath, he started walking alongside. Praneshacharya looked at him, curious. No one he knew.

"I am Putta, of the Maleras. Going for the car-festival at Melige. How about you?" the stranger asked, beginning the conversation himself.

Praneshacharya didn't wish to talk. Not knowing what to say, he looked into the young man's face—dark and a little withered, with beads of sweat. A very long nose gave the face the look of a strong-willed man. His close-set eyes sharpened his gaze and made one squirm under it. He had cropped his hair, wore a shirt over his dhoti. Obviously a young fellow from the town.

"I saw you from behind and thought you were someone I knew from your gait. Now I look at your face, you do look familiar...."

Though Putta spoke the usual words of any villager opening a conversation, Praneshacharya squirmed.

"I came from down the valley. Going for my collections," he said, trying to close the conversation.

"Oh—oh—I know people from down the valley. Actually my father-in-law lives there. I go there often. Where exactly down the mountain?"

"Kundapura."

"Oh—oh. Kundapura, really? Do you know Shinappayya there?"

"No," said Praneshacharya and walked faster. But Putta, eager for talk, didn't seem to be contented with little.

"You know, Shinappayya is close to us. Good friend of my father-in-law's. He arranged for his second son to marry my wife's younger sister...."

"Hm...Hm..." grunted Praneshacharya as he walked on. But this creature next to him didn't give up easily. Thinking he might move on, minding his own business, Praneshacharya sat down under a tree as if utterly tired. Putta seemed quite pleased, he too sat down with a loud sigh. He took out matches and bidis from his pocket and offered a bidi to him. Praneshacharya said, "No." Putta lit his bidi. Praneshacharya, pretending that he was less tired already, rose to his feet and started walking again. Putta too got up and started walking. "You know if you've someone to talk to, on the road, you forget the road. I, for one, always need someone to talk to," said Putta, all smiles, eyeing Praneshacharya inquisitively.

II

Within a couple of hours after his wife's death-rite, and the Acharya's decision to go where his legs took him, the people of Parijatapura came to know everything—everything except that actually a Muslim cremated Naranappa's body. The young fellows of Parijatapura who had, in a brief moment of heroism, meant to perform their friend Naranappa's final rites, but had fled for their dear lives—they had sealed their lips, unable to speak of what they had seen. The thing that had disturbed Rich Manjayya was really the series of deaths occurring one after another. Naranappa first, then Dasacharya, then Praneshacharya's wife. It meant only one thing, an epidemic. Experienced in affairs as he was, in the exchanges, the markets, the law courts and offices of Shivamogge, he'd just laughed at the other brahmins' explanations. They all believed that these disasters were due to Naranappa's untimely death and the brahmins' dereliction of duty in not performing his final rites. Of course Manjayya had said unhappily, "How awful! Dasacharya is dead! He came and ate *uppittu* here only the day before yesterday." But he was fearful inside that he'd let that brahmin into his house. He'd had his suspicions already when they came to tell him that Naranappa died of fever and a bubo, after a trip to Shivamogge. And now he was afraid even to name the dread disease. Why overreach oneself, he felt. But when he heard that rats had been running out of the agrahara and falling dead, and carrion birds had arrived to eat them, his suspicions became certainties. His guess was correct, as surely as there are sixteen annas to a rupee. The *Tayinadu* newspaper that came yesterday, though a week old, had printed the news in a corner: "Plague in Shivamogge." Naranappa did bring the plague into the agrahara, and plague spreads like wildfire. Being inert all this while, bound to some blind belief and not doing the dead man's last rites— was like drawing a slab of stone over one's own head. Fools. Even he had been an idiot. Standing in the front yard, he suddenly called out, "Fix the carts, at once! Can't waste a minute. The plague will cross the river and come to our agrahara. It's enough if a crow or vulture brings in its beak a single plague rat and drops it—everything will be finished here." He stood outside his house and announced in a shouting voice so that everyone could hear: "Till I return from the city no one should go near Durvasapura." As the leader of the agrahara, he didn't have the heart to scare them with his suspicions of plague. The bullock cart was ready. He sat against the pillow inside the curved wagon, and ordered the cartman to drive to Tirthahalli. In his very practical brain, the decisions were well-formed already: one, to tell the municipality and get the dead body removed; two, to call in doctors and get everybody inoculated; three, to get rat exterminators and pumps, fill the ratholes with poison gas and stop them up; four, if necessary, to evacuate the people from the agrahara. For quite some time he muttered to himself like a chant—"The idiots, the idiots!"—between words of encouragement to the cartman to twist the bullocks' tails and drive the cart faster. The cart soon got on to the Tirthahalli road and moved swiftly on it.

Leaving the monastery in disappointment, Garudacharya, Lakshmanacharya and others came to the agrahara, chanting "Hari Hari." Padmanabhacharya lay in a high fever. When they arrived, he was in a coma. One of them had gone to the sick man's in-laws in another village to inform his wife of his condition. Another ran to the city to get a doctor. Garudacharya was scared. In the monastery, Gundacharya took to bed with a fever; in Kaimara Dasacharya was sick. Here Padmanabhacharya's tongue was hanging out. The agrahara was in some kind of danger. In front of everyone, Lakshmana abused Garuda for preventing Naranappa's funeral rites. But no one cared, this was no time for abuse, it was better to hurry and finish the rites and offer to God the whole property as penalty. Reluctantly they left the sick Padmanabhacharya behind, and started out. Garuda folded his hands to the others and pleaded, "Please take the monastery doctor with you and get some medicine for Gundacharya lying there." On the way, no one had the courage to utter a word. A dullness fell on them like a pall. Garuda prayed inside himself to Maruti, "I'll pay the penalty, please forgive me." They walked with a heavy heart to Kaimara, and what did they find? Dasacharya's cremated ashes, the news of the death of Praneshacharya's wife. They were bewildered. Their familiar world was in a confusion. They felt they'd seen demons in the dark. Like children they leaned on walls, tears flowing from their eyes. The elder, Subbannacharya, tried to console and hearten them. Garuda, after sitting dully for a long time, said in a faint voice: "Are the rats still dying?" Subbannacharya asked, "What do you mean?" "Nothing, vultures were sitting on our roofs," said Garudacharya. The elder answered, "Finish the rites, everything will turn out well." "I won't go back to the agrahara," said Garudacharya. The other brahmins also murmured, "How can we do rites to a body already decomposed? Even four cartloads of firewood may not burn it down." Lakshmanacharya said, "Let's get going."

Garudacharya said, "I'm tired; one of you must do it." Subbanna-charya said, "If grown-up people like you get scared and confused, what about the rest?" "I just can't," said Garudacharya. "Get up, get up," urged Lakshmanacharya. "There's no one in the agrahara. What'll happen to the cows, the calves? No one's there to herd them to the shed or milk them." "Yes, yes, true," agreed the others. Mut-tering God's name, "Hari, Hari," they started out. All along the way they chanted the praise of Raghavendra.

Belli's people sacrificed a cock to the demon and vowed they would sacrifice a sheep at the next new moon; yet both Belli's parents died the same night. Praneshacharya's wife passed away. Hearing Belli's screams the neighbouring outcastes came and joined her. Near-naked black bodies sat around the hut silently and wept in the dark for half an hour. Then the dry palm-leaf-thatched hut was set on fire. In a minute the fire burned high and licked up the bodies of Belli's father and mother. Belli, who was standing there frightened, ran out of the village in the dark, thinking nothing of directions, like the rats themselves.

Putta of the Maleras stuck to Praneshacharya like a sin of the past. That was his way: if you stop, he'll stop too; sit, he'll sit. Walk faster, he'll walk faster; if slower, slower. Won't leave your side. Pranesh-acharya was getting quite upset. He'd like to be alone, sit with his eyes shut, and think for himself—but this fellow Putta is rattling away ceaselessly. The Acharya gives him no quarter, yet he clings. Because he doesn't know this is Praneshacharya, Crest-Jewel of Ve-danta, etc., he is behaving as he would with a common mendicant brahmin on his beggarly rounds. He advised the Acharya it wasn't a good idea to walk barefoot so far. He said, "You can get a hand-sewn pair of sandals in Tirthahalli for three rupees." He asked didactic-ally, "What's more important, money or comfort? Look at my san-dals, over a year old, haven't worn down a bit." He pulled them off his feet and displayed them. "I like talking," he said. "Come, answer me a riddle, if you can," he challenged. Praneshacharya held his tongue, controlling his rising anger. "A river, a boat, a man. With him, the man has a bundle of grass, a tiger, a cow. He's to cross the river with one at a time in the boat. He must see to it that the cow doesn't eat the grass, and the tiger doesn't eat the cow. He must transfer all three from this bank of the river to that. How does he do it? Let's see how sharp you are," he said, setting out the riddle, and merrily lit his bidi. Though angry, Praneshacharya's brain was teased by the riddle. Putta walked beside him, taunting the Acharya: "Did you get it, did you get the answer?" Praneshacharya got the answer, but he was too embarrassed to tell it. If he really solved the riddle, he'd be holding out a hand of friendship to Putta. If he didn't, Putta will think him dull-witted. It was a dilemma. Should he become a dull-witted thing in this fellow's eyes? "Got it?" Putta asked, sucking at his bidi. Praneshacharya shook his head. Putta guffawed "Ho ho ho!" and instantly solved the riddle. He felt immense affection for this good, not-too-clever brahmin. "Here, another riddle," he said. "No, no," said Praneshacharya. "All right then, you better tell me one. You defeat me. Tit for Tat." "I don't know any," said Praneshacharya. "Poor fellow," thought Putta. Casting about for conversation, Putta's tongue itched. He started a new topic, "Acharya-re, do you know? Shyama, the actor in the Kundapura troupe—poor fellow, he died." "Che, poor man, I didn't know," said the Acharya. "Then you probably left town a long time ago," said Putta. Praneshacharya was delighted to see the path branching in front of him. He stopped and asked Putta, "Which way are you going?" "This way," he said, pointing to one path. The Acharya pointed to the other footpath and said, "This is mine." "Both go to Melige. One is a little roundabout, that's all. I'm in no hurry. I'll come with you," said Putta. He took out a chunk of brown sugar and some coconut pieces, saying "Come, have some." He gave some to Praneshacharya, and ate some himself. Praneshacharya was hungry, and quite grateful to Putta. Wherever he went, whatever happened, human company seemed to cling to his back like one's lot earned in a past life.

Putta moved on to more familiar terms, while he chewed coconut and hard sugar. "You must be married, right? Who isn't? I'm asking like a fool. How many children? None at all? I'm sorry. I have two kids. I did tell you, didn't I, my wife is from Kundapura. One thing, you know. I don't know whether to laugh or cry, thinking about it. She just loves her parents. She throws tantrums every month, or every other, insisting on a visit to her mother's place. In these times, who can spend two rupees for the bus so often? You tell me. She just doesn't listen. A mother of two children, she's still childish. But then, she's really very young. My mother-in-law is a fusspot, but my father-in-law, he's large-hearted, I tell you. After all, he knows the world. My mother-in-law says at times, 'What right has my son-in-law to beat my daughter?' But my father-in-law hasn't mentioned it, not once. But then my wife hasn't learned the lesson, despite the beating. She threatens to jump into the well if I don't send her home to her mother. What can I do? She's so neat, so good in everything else—but for this one trouble. Whether she cooks a dish, or washes a pot, she's neat. Just this one trouble. What do you say to this?"

Praneshacharya laughed, not knowing what to say. Putta too laughed. "Understanding the way of a woman is just like tracing the track of a fish darting in the water—that's what the elders say. They know," he said.

"That's true, quite true," added Praneshacharya.

At last Putta's stream of words stopped. The Acharya felt, Putta must be searching for an answer to his woman's ways in some world beyond language. "Now here's my riddle. I didn't look at it squarely earlier. My life's decisive moment—the moment that would describe every relation of mine, with Naranappa, with Mahabala, with my wife, with the other brahmins, with the entire dharma I leaned on—it was born without my stir. I suddenly turned in the dark of the forest. But, my dilemma, my decision, my problem wasn't just mine, it included the entire agrahara. This is the root of the difficulty, the anxiety, the double-bind of dharma. When the question of Naranappa's death-rites came up, I didn't try to solve it for myself. I depended on God, on the old Law Books. Isn't this precisely why we have created the Books? Because there's this deep relation between our decisions and the whole community. In every act we involve our forefathers, our gurus, our gods, our fellow humans. Hence this conflict. Did I feel such conflict when I lay with Chandri? Did I decide it after pouring and measuring and weighing? Now it's become dusky, unclear. That decision, that act gouged me out of my past world, the world of the brahmins, from my wife's existence, my very faith. The consequence, I'm shaking in the wind like a piece of string.

"Is there any release from it?"

Putta said, "Acharya-re!"

"What's it?"

"Would you like some coconut and jaggery?" "Give me some."

Putta gave him some more coconut and jaggery and said, "It's hard to pass the time on the road, right? If you're getting bored, I'll tell you another riddle. Solve it. One plays, one runs, one stands and stares. What is it? Tell me." Then he lit another bidi.

"Therefore the root of all my anxiety is because I slept with Chandri as in a dream. Hence the present ambiguity, this Trishanku-state. I'll be free from it only through a free deliberate wide-awake fully-willed act. Otherwise, a piece of string in the wind, a cloud taking on shapes according to the wind. I've become a mere thing. By an act of will I'll become human again. I'll become responsible for myself. That is . . . that is . . . I'll give up this decision to go where the legs take me, I'll catch a bus to Kundapura and live with Chandri. I'll then end all my troubles. I'll remake myself in full wakefulness. . . ."

"Did you get it?" asked Putta, laughing.

"The fish plays, the water runs, the stone stands and stares," said Praneshacharya.

"Great! You win. Do you know what they call me at home? Riddleman Putta is what they call me. I'll give you a new riddle for every mile," he said, and threw away the bidi stub.

By the time Garuda, Lakshmana and the others reached Durvasapura walking all the way in the sun, the sun was going down. They entered the agrahara hesitantly, but they were relieved to see no vultures sitting on the rooftops. Lakshmanacharya said softly, "I'll go look at what's happened to my cattle, you go on." Garudacharya got angry and scowled, "The death-rite had better be your first concern. After that, your household affairs!" Lakshmanacharya didn't dare to talk back. Everyone came to Praneshacharya's house. Everyone felt, "Poor man, we must offer him sympathies." But when they called, there was only the smell of dead rats. After that, no one had the courage to enter even his own house. When they came to the main street, a stupor came over them. It had a dead, haunted look. They huddled together and thought of what they should do next. "The death-rite," said one. But no one had the courage to enter Naranappa's house and take a look at a rotted body, probably grotesque and fearful. Garudacharya thought of something: "Praneshacharya must have gone to the river, or somewhere. Let's wait for him." Lakshmanacharya said, "No time to lose, let's at least begin preparations for the cremation." "Firewood," one said. "Must cut down a mango tree," said another. "How will a rotting body burn in wet green firewood," said still another. Lakshmanacharya said, "Well, we can burn him in wood from his own house." Garuda taunted: "No one asked you anyway for firewood from your house." But when they went round to Naranappa's backyard, there was not enough firewood there. They called out, "Chandri! Chandri!" There was no answer. "Probably ran away to Kundapura, after ruining the entire village, the Mari!" muttered the brahmins. "What else can we do? Everyone should bring a bundle of firewood from his house to the cremation ground. Everyone," ordered Garudacharya. Everyone agreed and carried on his head a bundle to the cremation ground two miles away. When they returned to the agrahara, there was still no sign of Praneshacharya. "The body," said one. "Let Praneshacharya come," said Garuda. "All right," said Lakshmanacharya. Everyone was afraid to go look inside. Garuda said, "Let's not be rash. It isn't right to do anything without asking Praneshacharya." The other brahmins meanwhile said, "Let's get things ready and wait." They kindled a fire in a clay pitcher outside Naranappa's house, brought bamboos, started making a stretcher for the body, and waited—for Praneshacharya.

It was about three in the afternoon when Praneshacharya reached the Melige tank with Putta. They had walked on the big road meant for carts; their bodies were covered with red dust. When he climbed down into the tank to wash his hands and feet, Putta said, "Look, I talked so much, but never told you anything of my own affairs." As he washed his face, the Acharya felt a twinge of fear that someone in Melige might recognize him. He was disturbed at the renewal of fear. But one consolation: all the Melige brahmins were Smartas, therefore strangers. Who will really attend to him in the bustle of the festivals? Anyway, where's the occasion for fear once he has truly decided? Yet fear is natural. But why, if there's no reason for it? One must look for its roots. Must pull it out from the roots and destroy it. How fearlessly, how royally Naranappa lived with Chandri in the heart of the agrahara! Even if he should join Chandri, he'll probably cover his face, who knows? What sort of existence is this!

"You must be wondering why I'm prattling so much. You must have thought 'What a leech!' I'll tell you why. Though you don't talk much, you too need people, conversation. You're a meek person, quite a suffering type," said Putta, wiping the water off his face. "Am I right or wrong, you tell me. I can tell from the face, who's what type. Why should I hide anything? I hope you didn't get the impression I'm a low-class fellow. I told you I'm a Malera, didn't I? My father was a high-class brahmin. He took care of my mother whom he lived with, better than his lawfully wedded wife. He even performed a sacred-thread ceremony for me. Look, if you wish," he said, pulling out his sacred thread from under his shirt. "Therefore, all my buddies are brahmin boys. Let's go now," he said. As he climbed the bund of the tank into the street, he laughed and said, "I'm exactly what people call me. One of my names is Riddleman Putta, another is Prattling Putta. On the whole, I like people."

The bustle of the festival had made Melige very colourful. The temple chariot stood in the middle of town, its pinnacle adorned with zodiac pictures of virgo, scorpio, gemini and others. All along the road, two heavy ropes hung from the chariot. The devotees had pulled the chariot halfway from its shed and left it there for offerings of coconut and fruit. A young brahmin took the devotee's coconut and fruit offerings up and down a ladder to the priest who had already gone up and taken his seat inside the chariot. All around was a big crowd, waiting with the offerings. Praneshacharya scanned the crowd anxiously lest there should be some acquaintance who would recognize him. The crowd was so thick that, if you scattered a handful of sesame, not a seed would fall to the ground. Through such a milling crowd, Putta led Praneshacharya by the hand to a shop, and bought coconuts and bananas to offer to the god. "Let the crowd thin a bit, we'll offer our worship later. Let's walk around. Come, Acharya-re," he suggested. When they came out of the crowd there was a noise of reed-pipes everywhere. Every village boy's mouth held a pipe with a different noise. Pipes bought with small change wrested from the parents after much nagging. Also the smells of burning camphor and joss-sticks. The smell of new clothes. The song of the balloon-seller. In one corner was the Bombay Box. If you give the man a coin, he dances, and drums on a box with jingling anklets tied to it, and shows you pictures through a hole. "Look at Delhi City, look at the Eighteen Courts, look at the Bangalore bazaar, look at the Mysore rajah! Ahaa, take a look at the rajah holding court, look at the god of Tirupati! Aha, look at the Bombay concubine, aha, look at the Bombay concubine, look, look!" The sound of dancing anklets stops. He shouts: "The Bombay Box, the Box! Just one little coin, just one!" Putta couldn't bear to walk on without looking in. "Acharya-re, I must look," he said. "Yes, do," said Praneshacharya. "Don't go away and leave me behind. Just stay here," said Putta, as he pulled the black curtain of the box over his head and sat there looking into the peepshow. The Acharya toyed with the idea of leaving him there and walking off. He thought, "Poor fellow, can't do that to him. Yet he gives me no peace, I must be alone now." So he walked away. After a few paces, he heard a voice call, "Acharya-re!" He turned, it was Putta. "I was really afraid you'd left me behind and walked off. But that Bombay Box man showed me the way you went. Let's go." Praneshacharya felt like scratching himself blue all over in sheer exasperation. Should he scold him? But how can one hurt a human being holding out his hand in friendship without one's bidding or asking? Just bear it, he said to himself. "Aha, look there," said Putta. An acrobat show was in progress. A shapely serpentine woman, all curves, had spread-eagled her hands and legs, swaying, balancing herself on her bare belly at the end of a bamboo pole. The acrobat gypsy beat a drum. The next minute the girl on the bamboo had slid down to the ground to dance. The crowd threw copper coins. Putta too threw a coin. As they neared the temple, writhing on the ground on either side were beggars begging, beggars with stumps for hands or legs, blind men, people with two holes in place of a nose, cripples of every kind. Putta threw a coin to the most attractive of the cripples. Further on, he bought a yard of ribbon for his wife's hair from a mobile shop with multi-coloured ribbons hung in a maypole. "She loves these," he said. He bought two coloured pipes for his kids, blew on them, and said, "Let's go." Praneshacharya felt like a hovering demon, a rootless object in the hustle and noise. As soon as Putta saw a sodawater shop he said, "Come, let's have an orange drink." Praneshacharya declined, "No, I don't drink those things." Putta stood in the thatched sodawater shop of a Konkani man, carefully examined a bottle of red liquid and said, "A bottle of this for me." The shop was full of village women, shyly drinking soda-pop from the sweet-smelling bottles. Farmers, children. Their heads, oiled and combed sleek. Knots of flowers in their hair. New saris on the women. New shirts on the farmers. The squeak and gurgle of the sodawater as they push down the glass marbles in the soda bottles; the belch that comes up the throat after a drink of the sweet-coloured aerated waters—the whole thing was a matter of expectation, experience, contentment. Of the many pleasures of a temple festival, this too was one. Everyone thinks of it early and earmarks enough money for it. Praneshacharya stood outside this world of ordinary pleasures and looked at the gathered crowd. Putta belched with a sudden snort and his face blossomed. "Let's go." he said. "But you didn't drink anything!"

In all this bustle and busyness, amid noises of balloons and pipes, the soda-pop and the sweetmeats, the peal of temple bells, the gorgeous spectacle of women's bangle shops, Praneshacharya walked as one entranced, following Putta. Purposeful eyes everywhere, engaged in things. His eyes, the only disengaged ones, incapable of involvement in anything. Putta was right. "Even my meeting him here must have been destined. To fulfil my resolution I should be capable of his involvement in living. Chandri's too is the same world. But I am neither here, nor there. I am caught in this play of opposites." A smell of coffee and spiced *dose* assailed his nostrils. Putta stopped. The Acharya too stopped.

"Come along. Let's drink a cup of coffee," said Putta.

"Not for me," said Praneshacharya.

"This is a brahmin restaurant. They've brought it along all the way from Tirthahalli just for the festival. It won't pollute you. There's a special place inside for orthodox brahmins like you."

"No, I don't want any coffee."

"That won't do. Come. I have to buy you some coffee," said Putta, and dragged him in by the hand. Praneshacharya squatted on a low seat unwillingly. He looked around timidly, fearing the presence of some familiar person. If someone sees the Crest-Jewel of Vedanta Philosophy drinking a cup of polluted restaurant coffee.... "*Thuth*, I must first rid myself of such fears," he cursed himself. Putta stood a little further off, respecting the Acharya's brahminhood. "Two special coffees," he said to the waiter standing in front of him. He paid two annas, drank the tumbler of coffee, cursing it. "Awful coffee at these festivals." Praneshacharya was quite thirsty; he even liked his coffee. With a new access of spirit, he came out. Putta said, "Why don't you go and eat in the temple? They serve festival meals for brahmins till six o'clock today." Praneshacharya hadn't had a meal for days; he felt a craving to eat a hot meal of rice and *saru*. But at once he remembered, the mourning period for his wife's death was not over yet. One couldn't just enter a holy temple and eat there, one would pollute the temple; and as people say, the festival chariot will not move an inch. But didn't Naranappa manage even to eat the holy fish in the Ganapati tank and get away with it? He would never have the courage to defy brahmin practice as Naranappa did. His mind mocked: "What price your resolve to join Chandri and live with her? If you must, do it fully; if you let go, let go utterly. That's the only way to go beyond the play of opposites, that's the way of liberation from fear. Look, how Mahabala willed and acted."

"Wait a bit, Acharya-re. Look there," said Putta. At a distance on a hill was a group of lowcaste folk standing in some kind of trance. "Come, let's go there. I'm sure it's a cock-fight." Praneshacharya's heart missed a beat. Yet he walked with Putta, troubled by a sense of fate. Standing at a little distance away from the group, he looked on. The smell of cheap toddy made him gag a little. The people sat on their heels watching two roosters snapping at each other with knives tied to their legs, leaping at each other, flapping their wings. People squatted on their toes all around the fighting roosters, mouths gaping. Praneshacharya had never seen such concentration, such sharp cruel looks. All their five vital breaths seemed to converge in the eyes of those squatting people. And then, the two roosters: a swirl of wings, four wings, four knives. Kokk, kokk, kokk, kokk. All around them, forty, fifty eyes. Red-combed roosters, flashing knives. The sun, flash, flash. Flicker. Glint. Spark as from flintstone. Ah, what skill. One of them struck, struck, and struck. Swooped and sat on top of the other. Praneshacharya was in a panic. He had abruptly dropped into a demoniac world. He sat down, in utter fear: if in that nether-world where he decided to live with Chandri, if in that depth of darkness, in that cave, if the cruel engagement glinting in the eyes of these entranced creatures is just a part of that world, a brahmin like him will wilt. The two masters were making throaty sounds to egg their roosters on, and the sounds didn't seem to issue from human throats. It became clear that he didn't have the skills to live in this world of sharp and cruel feelings. One part of lust is tenderness, the other part a demoniac will. Cowardice returned, the cowardice he had felt the day Naranappa had defied him, when his whole person seemed to shrink before that arrogance. The men forcibly pulled the fighting cocks apart, put stitches on the bloody wounds and set them up again for the fight. Meanwhile, Putta, who was looking on with enthusiasm, had wagered with a stranger. "That rooster is mine," he said, "if he wins, two annas." The stranger said, "If mine wins, four annas." Putta said, "Eight annas." The other man said, "Ten annas." Putta said, "Twelve annas." "All right, let's see," said the other. Praneshacharya waited anxiously. What shall we do if this callow youth should lose all his money? To his amazement, it was Putta who won. Then Putta got up to leave. The man who had lost said, "Another bet." Putta said, "No." The other man, who was drunk, got up to beat him. Praneshacharya held out his hand. Seeing a brahmin in front of him, the man gulped down his anger. The others started lowering on them, saying, "What's going on? What it is?" Before anything could happen, Praneshacharya dragged Putta out of the crowd and led him away.

Putta didn't seem to be bothered; he had won twelve annas. He was beaming. Praneshacharya was filled suddenly with a fatherly affection for Putta. If I'd a son I could have brought him up lovingly, he thought.

"Now, Putta, let me go my way," said Praneshacharya, trying to close off his feelings of friendship.

Putta's face fell. He asked, "Which way do you go?" The Acharya searched suspiciously for some reason why this fellow might want to hang on.

"Somewhere. I'm not sure yet," he said.

"Then I'll walk with you some distance. You can at least eat a meal at the temple," insisted Putta.

Praneshacharya thought all this was getting to be a nuisance.

"I've got to see a goldsmith," he said. "Why?" asked Putta, not giving up. "I've to sell a piece of gold."

"Why do you have to do that? If you don't have enough money on you, I'll loan you twelve annas. You can return it to me sometime."

Praneshacharya racked his brains for a way to release himself from this man. This man's sympathies were like creepers that tangle up your feet.

"No, Putta. The money I need isn't a small amount. I've to catch the Kundapura bus. And there are other expenses," said Praneshacharya, unable to release himself from Putta's hold.

"O, is that so? Come then, I know a goldsmith here. What do you want to sell?"

"The ring on my sacred thread," said Praneshacharya, unable to evade him.

"Let me see it," said Putta, stretching out his hand. Praneshacharya untied the ring on his sacred thread and handed it to him. Putta held it in his hand, examined it, and said, "Don't you accept anything less than fifteen rupees." Then they entered a *keri* and went to a goldsmith's house. The goldsmith was sitting before a wooden box, filing away at a ring. He straightened his silver-rimmed glasses and asked, "What do you want?" Then he recognized Putta, and spoke words of courtesy: "What's happening here, our Puttayya's feet have brought him all the way here?" The ring was handed over. The goldsmith weighed it in his balance with little red seeds for weights, rubbed it on a touchstone, and said, "Ten rupees." Putta said, "If it's less than fifteen rupees, let's not even talk about it." The Acharya was disturbed by such business talk. The goldsmith said, "The price of gold has come down." "I don't know about all that. Can you give us fifteen rupees or not?" asked Putta. Then he looked at the Acharya and shot up his eyebrows as if to say, "See how I do business, and admire it." But the Acharya, trying to put an end to the argument, said, "If it's ten rupees, then ten it is. That'll do for expenses." Putta felt let down. The goldsmith's face beamed. He counted out ten rupees and folded his hands in farewell. "That was a help," said Praneshacharya, and came out.

As soon as they came out Putta started nagging—almost like a lawfully wedded wife: "What's the matter with you? Here I try to be useful to you and you make *me* lose face. He'll never value my word any more now. Of course I could say 'Okay, it's you who lost five rupees down the drain!' But look, in this iron age of *kali*, you can't be that dumb and survive. Haven't you heard, goldsmiths will cheat even on their sisters' gold?"

"I needed money desperately. I was rash. Forgive me," said Praneshacharya meekly, not wishing to hurt Putta. Putta softened and said,

"I knew, the minute I looked at you. You've a very simple soul. You shouldn't be sent out alone anywhere. I'll put you on the bus personally and then go back. Now you'd better do as I tell you. I've to go see someone. You come with me. After that you can go eat at the temple, there's plenty of time, they serve food till evening to line after line of guests. You can sleep somewhere here tonight. In the morning we can walk to Tirthahalli, it's only five miles. There's a bus from there to Agumbe. If you go straight down the mountain in a taxi, you can catch the bus to Kundapura."

"All right," said the Acharya, tucking into his waist the money, the fare for Kundapura which he had got by selling the ring. Putta warned, "Careful, that's money."

The Acharya thought, "It shouldn't be hard to give this fellow the slip when they get to the temple feast. Here is Putta, willing to involve himself in another's life for no reason at all. Who knows, what debts from what past life are being cleared this way? There seems to be no escaping this man's company. A creeper winding around one's feet. Who dare say one's life is one's own?"

"Come this way," said Putta, and led him through the crowded temple road to a narrow alley. They walked till they came to a deserted place. There was a small stream; across it was a bamboo bridge-piece. Crossing a fence, they came to a wet crop field. As he walked on the edges of it, Praneshacharya remembered the cockfight. How one rooster trod on another, what excitement of wing and feather! How one mastered the other, tearing it, getting into it, deeper, deeper. The knives glinting sharply in the sunshine. Then those eyes. The smell of country liquor. Even when pulled apart, laid on their backs, their wounds stitched, the roosters were pressing forward, crying kokk, kokk, throbbing. A demon world of pressing need, revenge, greed. I was there like a futile ghost. Panic-stricken. I tried wilfully to change and move into that world. And there was that acrobat gypsy girl. Swinging in her exercises in the sky, at the end of a bamboo pole, wearing body-tight clothes, showing off. She glided down suddenly. She danced. The sodawater bottles, with marbles in their necks squeaking when squeezed; the coloured liquids, the abrupt belches, desire, experience, satisfaction. Those purposive eyes. Eyes engaged in things: in the midst of multi-coloured ribbons, balloons, around the pinnacle of the temple chariot, eyes everywhere, behind my back, in front, on either side. Eyes all around —the wings—the knives—the beaks—the talons. Immersed. The oneness, the monism, of desire and fulfilment. That art Thou.

"I dread it. It's the dread of being transformed from ghost to demon."

Putta lit up a bidi and asked laughingly, in mischief, "Do you know where we are going?" Praneshacharya shook his head.

"My good sir, I like your ways. You really will go anywhere, you ask no questions. I'm also a little like that. I once went with a friend of mine just like this, all the way to Shivamogge. My father-in-law complains, 'Wherever Putta goes, there he stays put. O Putta? Our Putta: if you let him go, you'll lose him; but find him, he'll never leave you,' he says."

"You said you've to see someone, didn't you?"

"Acharya-re, please address me in the singular. It's not good for my longevity to be addressed in the plural by an elder like you."

"All right."

"There's a grove near here. There, that one. A woman we know stays there, running it as a tenant. She's all alone, quite a courageous woman. Really a beautiful woman; you've to wash your hands clean to touch her, so neat. Distant relative of mine. She's very respectful to orthodox brahmins like you. Let's say hello to her for a minute and then we'll leave. If I don't look her up, she'll say, 'I heard you were in town, Putta, you didn't even show your face. Didn't inquire if I were dead or alive, did you? You've become that busy, ha?' You know, I don't really like to hurt anyone. Man's life is here this second, gone the next. Tell me, why should we hurt anyone? That's why I say Yes to everything. Still, you know, Acharya-re: my wife is a nuisance. Every month she wants to visit her mother. I said Yes to her at first. Later I said No. I even beat her. But then I feel pity for her. You must have heard the village song:

> He beats his wife
>> But cries in his heart,
> so falls at her feet
>> and at her feet he pleads
> Who's sweeter, tell me,
>> Me or your Mother's place?

I'm like that.... We're here now."

They had reached the tile-covered house beyond the grove. "Is she in or not? She might've gone to the festival," said Putta, and called out, "Padmavati." Praneshacharya, who sat down on the pyol mat, heard a sweet female voice answer, "Coming!" Warm attractive voice. Fear: who's she? Why did Putta bring me all the way here? The same voice said courteously: "O you, you've come." Praneshacharya started, turned around. She had crossed the threshold and stood there holding the pillar with one raised hand. As his eyes fell on her, she pulled her sari over her breast. Putta said, "Look, who do you think I've brought here? An Acharya." "O you came this far," she said again shyly. "Shall I get some Ganges water?" she asked. "You must take some milk and fruit at least," she insisted, and went in. Praneshacharya was sweating all over. There was no doubt—she was a half-caste Malera woman. Living alone. Why did Putta bring me here? Not a word from Putta. All his chatter had been stilled. The Acharya had suddenly the scary feeling that two eyes were getting at him from behind. For those onlooking eyes I'm a wide-open thing. Afraid to turn around, yet wanting to do so. Who knows what those eyes will say? As soon as eye meets eye, who knows what shape the unformed will take? Elongated dark eyes. A black snake braid coming down her shoulder, over her breast. The girl swaying at the end of the bamboo pole. Knives—wings—beaks—feathers. In the forest dark, the offering of full breasts. Belli's earth-coloured breasts. An unblinking eye that'll see everything as if it is wide-open. Behind him. The bird is paralysed by the stare of the black serpent. Dread. He turned around. It was true. The eyes were looking at him stealthily, her hands were holding a platter; the eyes peeping from the door suddenly retreated into the dark indoors. Bangles jingled. Again she came into the light. It was peaceful now. An expectation turned in his body, cutting a path inside. She bent forward to put down the platter, the top of her sari sliding, breasts thrust forward, eyes heavy with a look of pleading. A stirring of fire in his chest. His eyes looked on, fiery. The sense vanished of having become a wide-open object for staring eyes. Now he was those eyes. That art Thou. She asked, "Where is the gentleman from?" Looking at the Acharya, his glowing person. Putta said, "He's from Kundapura," and added a lie, "He knows Shinappa." "Looks after temple affairs," adding another lie. When he said, "He's come to this province to collect dues," Putta gave him an entirely new personality. In the eyes of strangers, one gets a new form, a new makeup. "Even to the point of doubting who I really am, I have become many persons in one single day. All right, let things happen as they will." He sat waiting. "Bird ravaging, bird ravaged, the knives. Wife Bhagirathi screamed as if the very quick of her life had been touched, before she fell back utterly motionless, dead. Then she burned in the cremation fire, Bhagirathi, the altar of my sacrifice. I lost her and entered limbo, a lost soul. Seen by these eyes. I have moved to the next stage of soul, leaving the ghostly stage behind. Perhaps."

Padmavati, evading any possible direct gaze, went and sat at the foot of the door. Praneshacharya was disturbed again that she was staring at him from that vantage point. Plucking up courage he turned his head. His heart was pounding. Padmavati got up, and brought a platter of betelnut and betel leaf. Putta smeared lime on the betel leaves, folded and tucked several between his fingers, threw a piece of betelnut into his mouth and started speaking. Padmavati went back to sit at the foot of the door. Putta said:

"I met the Acharya on the road. We came chatting all the way. He'd started out for Kundapura. I said: why not stay here tonight and go to Tirthahalli tomorrow and catch a bus? Don't you agree that's a good idea?"

Padmavati too insisted, a little embarrassed:

"Right. Why not sleep here tonight and go tomorrow?"

Praneshacharya felt faint. His ears seemed to roar, his hands were clammy. "No, no, not today. Tomorrow. I didn't reckon on the decisive moment being now, here. Not today, I'm in a period of mourning and pollution, I've just cremated my wife. Haven't yet disposed of Naranappa's body. I must tell them. I must speak the truth. I must get up and leave here. I must vanish." But the body stayed there, solid, an object of Padmavati's expectant gaze. Putta said:

"All right then. He hasn't had his dinner yet. He'll go to the temple feast and come back here." Then he asked Padmavati, familiarly, "The Dharmasthala troupe has come here, hasn't it? Are you going to see their show?"

"O no. I'll just visit the temple in the evening, get God's *darshan* and come back here. I'll wait for you people."

Without any move on his part, without so much as a grunt from him sitting between Putta and Padmavati, Putta said, "Let's get up." The Acharya stood up, looked at Padmavati. Long hair, not yet oiled after a bath; plump fleshy thighs, buttocks, breasts. Tall, long-limbed. A gleam in the eyes, an expectation. A waiting. Must have had a ritual bath in the river after her monthly period. Breasts rise and fall as she breathes in and out. They'll harden at the tips if caressed in the dark. The scent of grass and country sarsaparilla. Floating chariots of lightning-bugs. Fire. The crematory flames licking the firewood, reaching the hands and feet, simmering in the stomach and hissing, exploding, splitting the bony skull, stretching tongues of flame to the chest of the dead. The fire. Naranappa's dead body. Unburned yet. How he sat there once, on his front verandah pulling on his hubble-bubble. The body swung on the bamboo-stretcher, curving it with its weight. The Vedic sage Yajnavalkya said: "Love. Love for whom? Love for one's wife is love for oneself. Love for God is love for oneself." He'll search out the roots. He'll win. He looked on, he admired. Sage Vyasa was born in a pot, born complete with an ascetic's waterpot. The Acharya took a step. "All right, then you go and come back. I'll wait for you," said Padmavati. "Lord Maruti really gave me the slip. Friend Mahabala played a trick on me. Naranappa took his revenge. The brahmins were greedy for the gold. Chandri waiting in the dark—took what she wanted—walked away. Bhagirathi shrieked and died." Putta put his hand on his shoulder, stopped him at the edge of a wet field. Asked, "What do you say?" Then he said, "It turned out as I thought. Don't think that the woman's a common prostitute. No, sir. No lowcaste man has been near her. And she isn't the kind of spirit that'll accept any ordinary brahmin either. Not for money, not for a few coins. Didn't you see for yourself? She has an estate. Even the ancient sages would fall for her, she's like that. I was scared for a minute you might expose my lie. You liked her, didn't you? This Putta will do anything for a friend. Putta, the Altruist, that's my title," he said, laughing, patting the Acharya's back.

Crossing the wet field, the fences, walking over the makeshift bridge, through the lane, again into the bustle of the crowded fair. A crowd milled around the temple chariot. Another crowd around the sodawater shop. Still another, around the man with the performing monkey. Children's toy trumpets, balloons. In the midst of these noises, a demon, an evil spirit. A town-crier. Beating his tom-tom, he announced in his loud town-crier voice: "There's a plague in Shivamogge! The epidemic of Mari! Anyone going to Shivamogge should stop at Tirthahalli and get an inoculation! That's the order of the Municipality!" People listened to him with interest, and drank more sodawater. Laughed in guffaws at the antics of the monkey. A bilingual expert spoke in Urdu and Kannada, selling his medicine to the gathered crowd: "Just one anna, one anna, *ek ana, ek ana*. For stomach-aches, ear-aches, diabetes, arthritis, children's diseases, menstrual troubles, itches and typhoid—take this pill. Pundits from Kerala have prepared this pill with magic chants. Just one anna, *ek ana, ek ana . . .*" The Bombay Box man was dancing: "Look, look at the Tirupati God, Timmappa! Look, look at the courtesan of

Bombay!" An acrobat slid in a flash down the slope of a rope tied between a branch above and a peg on the floor, and came to his feet with a salute. A man suddenly slapped a little boy for wanting a balloon. The boy cried loudly. A gramophone song from the coffee shop. Sweetmeats of many colours in the Muslim shop. The drawling intonation of the peasants and their women. An incessant priestly jumble of Sanskrit scripture on the temple chariot, the raucous talk of the Smarta brahmins. In between he must decide, here, now. Decide to give up a quarter-century of discipline and become a man of the world? No, no. Naranappa's funeral comes before all else. After that come all other decisions. Garuda and Lakshmana would have returned today after consulting the Guru. What should he say if the Guru said No? The same dilemma, all over again.

He stood near the temple. A blind beggar was singing to the tune of a drone-box. A devotional song. "O how shall I please you, how shall I serve you, O Lord?" When Putta threw a coin into his platter, another beggar with only stumps for hands and legs came crawling towards him, flailing his stumps, crying "No hands, no legs for this sinner!" He whined and pleaded, lay flat on the floor, lifted his dwarfed arms and legs, and beat himself, displaying the places where the fingers had been eaten away and become stubs. Seeing this body decomposing in leprosy, Praneshacharya thought again of Naranappa's body rotting, uncremated. Putta threw a coin for the beggar. More deformed bodies rushed towards him, crawling, beating their stomachs, beating their mouths. "Let's go, let's go," said the Acharya.

Putta said, "You go in and eat your temple dinner."

"Why don't you come along?" invited Praneshacharya. All of a sudden, he'd felt panic at the thought of being seen, alone, unaccompanied, by the rows of brahmins sitting down for the feast in the temple hall. "I can't stir without Putta," he thought. He'd never before felt such a dread of being alone.

"What are you talking about? Did you forget I'm no brahmin, but a Malera?" said Putta, to which the Acharya said,

"Never mind, come along."

"What, are you joking? This place is full of people who know me.

If not, I'd have tried it. You know, don't you, of the time a goldsmith boy told lies and got a job in the monastery? But then, we Maleras too have our sacred threads, don't we? I'm just talking for talking's sake. I really don't have the gall, the guts to sit and eat a meal with you. You'd better go, I'll wait here."

Praneshacharya, not able to stand the pathetic cries of the invading beggars all around him, walked into the temple in a daze.

On all the four raised verandahs of the temple, they had set rows of banana leaves. Before each leaf sat a food-seeking brahmin. As he saw their faces, Praneshacharya's heart sank. What would happen if they spot me? Let me run. But he couldn't lift his feet. He stood there rooted, and thought: "What am I doing? What lowborn misdeed am I committing? I'm in the unclean period of mourning and can I in full knowledge sit with the brahmins and eat a meal? And pollute them all with my impurity? These people believe that the temple chariot will not move an inch if there's any pollution around. If I seat myself here and eat with them, it's as heinous a sin as Naranappa catching temple-fish to destroy brahmin ways. If they discover, in the middle of the meal, that this is Praneshacharya ... that he's still in the pollution period after his wife's death ... it'll be a scandal. The entire chariot-festival will get cancelled. Thousands of eyes will devour him."

"Here, here's a free leaf, come here," said somebody. He was startled. He looked. A brahmin sitting at one end of the row was inviting him. What should he do? O Lord, what should he do? He just stood there. "Didn't you hear me?" said the inviting brahmin, laughing, reaching out for Praneshacharya's hand, and pointing to the free place and the leaf. "Look there. I reserved that leaf for you, and left a cup on it for you. If I had not, you'd have had to wait for the next meal-line," he said. The Acharya mechanically walked to it and sat down. He felt dizzy in the head.

Trying to calm down his mind, he thought, "O God, what's the root of this dread? Are these the first pains of a rebirth? Is it the kind of fear that will be quenched if I sleep with Padmavati tonight? Will it be quenched if I go live with Chandri? What's my decision worth?

Am I forever to be a ghost of a man, hovering in indecision? I wish Putta was here. Shall I get up, walk out? What will the brahmin next to me think?"

A brahmin walked through the row of seated diners, touching each leaf-end with holy water. Another poured a spoonful of milk-porridge on the edge of each leaf. From behind him, two robust brahmins came serving rice, crying out, "Clear the way, the way, the way." Then there was a salad of lentils and cucumbers. There were new fears at the appearance of each face, as they came close to serve the food: "Maybe this one knows me and will recognize me, what will I do?"

The brahmin who sat next to him, who gave him the place, was a huge dark figure like Bhimasena. A Smarta, with sandalpaste marks drawn lengthwise on his forehead. The Acharya feared him as soon as he set eyes on him. Furthermore, he had questions that made the Acharya nervous.

"Can I ask from where you come?"

"I'm right from this place."

"From where exactly? From down the mountain?"

"Kundapura."

"What community, if I may ask?"

"Vaishnava."

"What sub-group?"

"Shivalli."

"I'm of the Kota group. What's your descent-line?"

"Bharadvaja."

"I'm of the Angirasa line. O sir, I'm really glad I met you. We've a young girl, getting ready for marriage. In a year or two, she'll reach puberty. We can't let our girls reach puberty, before we find them husbands; we're not yet that spoiled. So we're really looking now for a suitable bridegroom. Sir, do let me know if there's any suitable groom in your group. Relieving a father's burden is a great help. After we finish this meal, let's go to our house. I'll give you a copy of the girl's horoscope. You can stay with us tonight."

Praneshacharya, getting his *saru* served into a leaf-cup, lifted his head and looked up. The man serving it was intently looking at him. He stood still for a second, then moved on.

"All right," said Praneshacharya, trying to cut the conversation short. Is it possible that this man serving *saru* knows his face? He has a charcoal caste-mark on his forehead, obviously a Madhva, like himself—it's quite likely the man would know the Acharya. He can't even get up now, after taking the holy water in his palm, after imbibing it in the name of the Lord, chanting with all the others: "Shrimad Ramaramana Govinda... aa... Govinda." He mixed the *saru* with the hot steaming rice and ate it. It was some days since he'd had a regular meal. "O Lord, tide me over this calamity. See to it that I am not detected today. I cannot decide and say, 'This is my own decision.' I seem to involve everyone else in what I do. After what happened, I should have performed the rites for Naranappa myself. But how could I do it alone? The ritual needs three more, even to carry the body out. I have to ask three others. Which means, I involve three others in my decision. This is the root of my agony, my anxiety. Even when I slept with Chandri, unknown to everyone, I involved the life of the entire agrahara in my act. As a result, my life is open to the world." The man serving *saru* came again, shouting, "*Saru, saru*, who wants *saru*?" He stood before the Acharya's leaf and said, "*Saru*." The Acharya looked up, timidly.

The man said, "I think I've seen you somewhere."

"Quite possible," said the Acharya. But by God's grace the man went to the next row, to attend to their leaves. "But his eyes are thinking of me. They're sending my image to his brain and trying to check out my identity. Even if I went with Chandri, someone will waylay me and ask, 'Who are you? Which sub-caste? Which descent? Which group?' Unless I shed brahminhood altogether I cannot stand aside, liberated from all this. If I shed it, I'll fall into the tigerish world of cock-fights, I'll burn like a worm. How shall I escape this state of neither-here-nor-there, this ghostliness?"

The brahmin next to him grumbled, "They've watered down the *saru* this time.... What, you are filling your belly with mere *saru*. Do wait, sweets and things are yet to come."

The fellow who had brought the *saru,* came back this time with a vessel full of vegetable curry. He stopped in front of the Acharya and said, "I can't remember where. Could it be in the monastery? On worship days I often go there for cooking jobs. Our agrahara is beyond the river. I did go to the monastery the day before yesterday to do some cooking, then I came here."

Then, in a hurry, he walked off to serve the next row, announcing, "Curry, curry, curry."

The Acharya thought he should get up now and walk out, but his legs had gone numb. The brahmin next to him said, "You know, our girl is a very good cook. Very obedient to elders. We want very much to give her to a respectable family where the father- and mother-in-law are still alive to guide family affairs."

"There's only one way out of the present fear. I must take on the responsibility of Naranappa's last rites. I must stand upright in the eyes of the brahmins, in the very agrahara where I grew up to be respected, an elder. Must call in Garuda and Lakshmana and tell them: 'This is how it went. My decision is such and such. I'll shed the respectability I acquired here before your eyes. I've come back to tear it and throw it down, right here before your eyes.' If I don't, my fear will dog me everywhere, I won't be free. What then?

"Just like Naranappa who turned the agrahara upside down by fishing in the temple-tank, I too would have turned the brahmin lives upside down. I'd be giving their faith a shattering blow. What shall I tell them? 'I slept with Chandri. I felt disgust for my wife. I drank coffee in a common shop in a fair. I went to see a cock-fight. I lusted after Padmavati. Even at a time of mourning and pollution, I sat in a temple-line with brahmins and ate a holy feast. I even invited a Malera boy to come into the temple and join me. This is my truth. Not a confession of wrongs done. Not a repentance for sins committed. Just plain truth. My truth. The truth of my inner life. Therefore this is my decision. Through my decision, here! I cut myself off.'"

"If necessary, we won't object to giving her a dowry, sir. You know, the times are wicked; dark-skinned girls have a hard time getting husbands. You come and see the girl yourself. The only defect is her dark complexion, but her eyes and nose are very shapely. According to her horoscope, she has a rare Lion-Elephant combination for a good future. She'll be the very Goddess of Good Luck to any house she sets foot in," said the brahmin next to him, eating his curry and rice.

"But if I don't tell the agrahara brahmins, if Naranappa's body is not properly cremated, I cannot escape fear. If I decide to live with Chandri without telling anyone, the decision is not complete, not fearless. I must come now to a final decision. All things indirect must become direct. Must pierce straight in the eye. But it's agony either way. If I hide things, all through life I'll be agonized by the fear of discovery, by some onlooking eye. If I don't, I'll muddy the lives of others by opening up and exposing the truth to the very eyes my brahminhood has lived and grown by. Have I the authority to include another's life in my decision? The pain of it, the cowardice of it. O God, take from me the burden of decision. Just as it happened in the dark of the jungle, without my will, may this decision too happen. May it happen all at once. May a new life come into being before I blink my eye. Naranappa, did you go through this agony? Mahabala, did you go through it?"

The man who had brought *saru* came this time with a basket of sweets. The brahmin next to the Acharya didn't want the sweets served on his leaf, but received them in his left hand and put them aside. The man was again standing in front of his leaf. The Acharya's heart heaved.

"O yes, my memory be damned. You are Praneshacharya from Durvasapura, aren't you? O how can someone like you come for a humble meal here? There was a big feast in the Sahukar's house. For all the big people like you, they arranged the feast there. Because you didn't have any mark on your forehead, I didn't recognize you right away. Neither did you tell me. If I don't tell the Sahukar, I'll really get it in the neck—that I seated and fed a great Pundit at the end of a meal-line. I'll be back in a minute. Wait. Please." Saying which he ran, leaving the basket of sweets behind. Praneshacharya quickly took a palmful of ritual water, drank it up, ending his meal thereby. He leapt to his feet and walked away. "Swami, Swami, the milk-porridge is yet to come," screamed the brahmin of the next leaf. But he didn't turn back till he came out of the temple. He had come out, his hands yet unwashed—away from people, far away. Before he had gone far, he heard a voice: "Acharya-re . . . Acharya-re!" Putta's voice. He came running and stood close to Praneshacharya, who quickened his pace.

"What's this, Swami? Not a word, and you're running like someone in a hurry to go to the bathroom for a big job," laughed Putta. When he was far from the crowd, the Acharya stopped. He looked at his unwashed hands and was disgusted.

"What, the call was so urgent you couldn't even wait to wash your hands! It's happened to me too. Come let's go to the tank, you can do it there."

They walked to the tank. Putta said, on the way:

"I decided one thing, Acharya-re. I'll come with you to Kundapura. I didn't tell you earlier, my wife and children went to their mother's place over a month ago. Haven't had a letter from them. I've to talk to her and bring her back. You're an elder. You must do me a favour. Come and give my wife some good advice. She'll listen to you. You became my life's companion in a single day. One more thing, Acharya-re. I don't carry tales. I won't breathe a word about your sleeping in Padmavati's house—I'll take an oath on my mother's body, I won't tattle. There I was standing, watching the monkey's dance. Then I saw you running, it made me laugh. These things do happen. Calls of nature become most urgent right in the middle of dinner. I thought that's what happened to you, so I felt like laughing."

Praneshacharya climbed down into the tank, and washed his hands. Above him, Putta stood, his back against the tank bricks. When Praneshacharya came back and stood next to him, he said,

"What? Back so soon?"

"One thing, Putta."

Praneshacharya looked up. The long evening of a summer day. Streaks of red on the west. Line after line of white birds returning to their nests. Down below, at the edge of the tank, a stork is gurgling. It's almost time for lighting the lamps. How many days ago was it that the lamps were lit in the agrahara, that the returning evening cows and calves were tied up and milked, and the milk offered to the Lord? The clear faraway forms of the western hills grow dim, like a world melting in a dream. The colours of this moment fading the next, the sky grows bare. As the new-moon day is left behind, in a little while a sliver of the moon will appear over the hills, like the edge of a silver chalice bent over an idol for an inaugural libation. Silence will fill the valleys between the hills. The torches lit for the night service will die down as the service gets over, and the noises of the fair will fade. Again, the drama troupe's drums will raise and spread their din. "If I begin walking now, I'll reach the agrahara by midnight, far away from this world. In full view of the frightened brahmins, I'll stand exposed like the naked quick of life; and I, elder in their midst, will turn into a new man at midnight. Maybe when the fire leaps and dances around Naranappa's dead body, there'll be a certain consolation. When I tell them about myself, there should be no taint of repentance in me, no trace of any sorrow that I am a sinner. If not, I cannot go beyond conflict and dualities. I must see Mahabala. Must tell him: only the form we forge for ourselves in our inmost will is ours without question. If that's true, don't you really have any craving for good any more?—I must ask him." That melodious Sanskrit line came into his mind again: "Southern breezes from sandalwood mountains caress delicate vines of clove." Praneshacharya was quite moved. Affection moved him. He put a hand over Putta's shoulders, and drew him closer. And patting his back for the first time, he said, "What was I about to say?"

"O sir, when I met you on the road, your talk was so stiff that I thought this gentleman will never be friends with me," said Putta, delighted that the Acharya put a friendly hand on his shoulder.

"Look here, Putta. Do you know why I left that dinner in a hurry? I've to get back to Durvasapura at once."

"Oho, how can you do that, Acharya-re? Your Padmavati will be waiting there for you, with a soft bed all ready; joss-sticks all lit up, and flowers in her hair. If you aren't there with me, how can I face her? Whatever your urgent business, you must stay here tonight and go only by morning. A curse on my head if you leave now," said Putta, and tugged at Praneshacharya. Praneshacharya got a little frightened. He doubted the firmness of his own will. He might slide back. He must now escape Putta.

"No, Putta. Impossible. Shall I tell you the truth? I didn't want to involve your feelings, so I didn't tell you so far." He thought for a moment, and decided it was best to tell a lie. "My brother is deathly sick in Durvasapura. I heard the news while I was sitting there in the temple. It may be any minute now, how can I . . . ?"

Putta sighed. Disappointed, he agreed, "All right then."

Praneshacharya, preparing to go, said, "When do I see you again? Tell Padmavati I'll see her on my way back to Kundapura. Shall I move on then?"

Putta stood there, thinking. "How can I send you alone through the dark forest? I'll come with you," he said.

Praneshacharya was nonplussed. It seemed impossible to chase away this man by any tactic. "I don't really want you to be bothered on my account," he said. Putta didn't budge.

"No bother, no trouble. I too have some business in Durvasapura. I've cousins in Parijatapura. You probably know my friend Naranappa there. When I went to Parijatapura once, I got to know him just as I got to know you now. O yes! I'm glad I remembered. The whole town knows Naranappa squandered his property. He can't pass up anything wrapped in a sari, he's that type. This is strictly between ourselves, Acharya-re. If you happen to know him, please don't mention anything about Padmavati, and the way she invited you. Okay, why hide it from you? As soon as I got acquainted with Naranappa, he stuck to me like a leech, insisting I introduce him to Padmavati. But I don't do such things, I'm not that cheap. Still, you know, what can you do when a brahmin falls all over you? Padmavati didn't like his ways. He was such a horrible drunkard, she told me later. 'Don't you bring him here any more,' she said. You'd better keep all this to yourself. I started on something and ended somewhere else. I told you, didn't I, my village is a little beyond Tirthahalli. Naranappa owns an orchard there. It's now razed to the ground, ruined out of sheer neglect. It's years since he received from it a single arecanut due to him. Knowing him as I do, will he say No to me if I ask? So I'd like to try and ask him: 'Rent out the orchard to me. I'll work on it, improve it, it'll also bring you some profit.' That's why I said, I'll come with you, Acharya-re. You too will have company on the dark road. And I'll get some work done."

Praneshacharya listened to Putta restlessly. "Shall I tell him Naranappa is dead? Shall I tell him my true dilemma?" But he didn't want to raise a big storm in that simple heart. In case he really decides to come along, it would be impossible not to tell him. Then it suddenly seemed a good thing to have Putta for company. "How can I face all those brahmins alone? First, let me try it all on Putta, bosom-friend of the present. Let's see how I look in his eyes—that may be a good way of doing it." Now the sky had become cloudless, bare. From the temple issued noises of gongs beaten, conches blown for worship. Must go now. "Let's go then," he said.

Just then a covered wagon came trundling along. Putta said, "Wait a minute." He held out his hand and stopped the cart. From within the cart, a Smarta man in a gold-lace shawl put out his head and asked, "What do you want?"

"Does your cart, by any chance, go via Agumbe?" said Putta.

"Ha," nodded the lace-shawled gentleman from within the cart.

"Do you have place for two? We want to get to Durvasapura," said Putta.

"But we've place only for one."

Putta took hold of his hand and said, "You'd better go, Acharya-re."

"No, no. Let's go together, on foot," said the Acharya.

"Che, Che, you shouldn't walk all the way and tire yourself out. I'll come and see you tomorrow," said Putta. The man in the shawl wanted them to hurry. "Then, are you coming? We'll turn off a mile or two before we reach Durvasapura. One of you can come with us. Get into the cart. Quick."

Putta insisted on Praneshacharya getting in, and pushed him in. Praneshacharya, not seeing any way out, climbed into the cart and sat down. The cart started moving. "I'll see you tomorrow," said Putta. "All right," said Praneshacharya. Four or five more hours of travel. Then, what?

The sky was full of stars. The moon, a sliver. A perfectly clear constellation of the Seven Sages. A sudden noise of drum beats. Here and there, the flames of a torch. The hard breathing of the bullocks climbing the hillock. The sound of the cowbells round their necks. He will travel, for another four or five hours. Then, after that, what?

Praneshacharya waited, anxious, expectant.

NOTES

THESE rather minimal notes are part of the translator's effort to "translate" and a confession of failures. They include:

(a) glosses on myth, ritual, flora, food, names, quotations (exx. Madhva, Matsyagandhi, *saru*);

(b) the original Kannada or Sanskrit words (exx. *tamas, ekadashi*), which I have replaced in the text by English glosses (exx. "Darkness," "eleventh day of the moon").

(a) is meant for the unspecialized non-Indian or non-Kannada reader,

(b) for fellow-Indians and Indianists.

No transliterations, only approximate Roman spellings, have been used.

9   *Maruti:* name of Hanuman, Monkey-god, and devotee of Rama (an incarnation of Vishnu). Hanuman is worshipped by devotees of Vishnu; his temple is usually outside the village, as here.

agrahara: "villages or land assigned to Brahmins for their maintenance" (Kittel); an exclusive settlement of brahmins.

Praneshacharya: the title acharya, "spiritual guide, learned man," is added to certain brahmin names, especially among the Madhva sect (see notes to p. 13) to which most of the brahmins in this book belong.

Kashi or Benares: a holy city of North India, especially known for Sanskrit scholarship.

10   *five-fold nectar: Panchamrita,* the five nectarious substances: milk, curd, ghee, honey, and sugar, and a compound made of them, offered to gods and distributed to devotees on special days.

Narayana: one of the many names of the god Vishnu, uttered frequently as exclamation, blessing, etc. Such names have the power to redeem and protect.

11   *saru:* a well-seasoned sauce regularly eaten with rice.

consecrated water: aposhana, a ritual sipping of water from the palm of the hand at the beginning and end of a meal.

holy legends: Purana, a tale of the past, about gods, saints, etc.

13   *lowcaste: shudra*, the fourth caste.

Madhva and *Smarta:* brahmin sects, traditional rivals. Madhvas are the followers of the philosopher Madhva (13th century) who taught *dvaita* or dualism (soul and godhead are two entities, not one). Smartas follow Shankara (7th century) who taught *advaita* or monism (soul and godhead are one and the same). Madhvas are strict worshippers of Vishnu, and bear only Vaishnava names. For instance, Durgabhatta (a Smarta) is named after Durga the goddess, a manifestation of Shiva's consort; nor does his name carry the suffix *acharya*. Note also how the name of heretic Naranappa (set against the entire brahmin community) is a form of Narayana (or Vishnu), localized to Naranappa, with none of the Sanskritic "markers" of orthodoxy like *acharya, bhatta*.

14   *dharma:* a central word in Hinduism, therefore multi-vocal, untranslatable; usually glossed "law, righteousness, duty, code, etc."

Shankara: philosopher of monism: according to legend, the celibate philosopher was challenged in argument by a woman-philosopher and disqualified because he had experienced no sex. He qualified himself, without losing his celibate status, by magically entering the body of a king just dead and having intercourse with the queen—and returned to finish the argument.

wedding-string: tali, ceremonially tied by the bridegroom around the bride's neck, as part of the wedding-ritual.

holy stone: saligrama, a black river-stone, worshipped as sacred to Vishnu.

15   *"sharp": cittini*, "intelligent woman," one of the eight types of women in Vatsyayana's Kamasutra (manual of love).

18   *eleventh day of the moon: ekadasi*, a day of fasting for orthodox brahmins.

19   *uppittu:* salted (and spiced) dish made out of cream of wheat, rice, flattened rice, etc.

  widows: some brahmin orthodox sects like the Smarta (Durgabhatta's sect) insist on certain austerities for their widows; one of them is a shaven head.

20   *Manu:* "a generic name for fourteen successive mythical progenitors and sovereigns of the earth"; the first of these is supposed to be the author of the Code of Manu, the most influential codification of Hindu laws and rules of conduct.

21   *parijata:* the coral tree, one of the five trees in heaven. Note that all these flowers are sacred to Vishnu, as Durgabhatta's are sacred to Shiva.

  Konkani: a person from Konkan on the west coast.

  hot months: Chaitra (March–April), the first month of the Hindu year, a month of spring, and *Vaishakha* (April–May), the second month.

22   *eighth month: Kartika* (October–November).

  rainy month: Shravana (July–August), the fifth lunar month.

  Great Commentator: Tikacharya, a revered commentator on Madhva's (see notes to p. 13) works.

  Durvasa: a sage notorious for his chronic bad temper. The five Pandava brothers are the exiled heroes of the epic *Mahabharata*. Draupadi is their wife. Dharmaraja is the eldest, known for his patience and fairness; Bhima, the second brother, is known for his rashness and strength.

23   *twelfth day of the moon: dvadasi*: on this day orthodox brahmins break their fast begun on the previous day (*ekadasi*, the eleventh day).

24   *bund:* embanked causeway.

  twice-born: dvija: the epithet applies not only to brahmins and the other two upper-castes (kshatriya, "warrior," vaisya, "tradesman") but also to birds, snakes, various grains, and to teeth, etc.—anything that may be said to have two births (e.g. birds and snakes are born as eggs and reborn from them). Snakes are considered sacred and therefore should be cremated ceremoniously.

26 *Hedonist School:* the Charvaka School, materialists and hedonist philosophers, who believed in the slogan quoted—equivalent to "Enjoy yourself, even if it's on borrowed money."

ghee: clarified butter.

27 *decadent age: kali,* the present age, the last and the most decadent of the four ages.

28 *permanent perfume:* a classic precedent for a sage lusting after a lowcaste woman. Sage Parashara took Matsyagandhi ("the fish-scented woman") on the river as she rowed him across—and blessed her body with a perennial fragrance.

29 *aposhana:* see notes to p. 11.

Achari: a vulgar disrespectful form of Acharya. In Acharya-re "-re" is a respectful vocative suffix. Naranappa plays with both forms here.

Kalidasa's heroine, Shakuntala: Kalidasa, the great Sanskrit poet and dramatist (5th century?). His most celebrated heroine is Shakuntala.

31 *Hari:* another name of Narayana or Vishnu.

Ash-Demon: Bhasmasura obtained from Shiva a boon—that he could burn to cinders anyone on whose head he placed his hands. As soon as he received the boon, he wished to test it on Shiva himself who ran to Vishnu for rescue. Vishnu assumed the form of a seductive woman, and enticed Bhasmasura to learn Indian dancing. One of the dance postures required him to place his palm on his own head, which sent the gullible demon up in flames.

33 *raised verandah: jagali,* pyol.

34 *Vedanta:* "the end of the Vedas," or the essential creed, expounded by three great Hindu philosophers, Shankara, Ramanuja, and Madhva.

rule for emergencies: apaddharma, a relaxation of ethical or other rules (dharma) during an emergency.

35 *Yakshagana:* a popular dance-drama of South Kannada country on classical themes.

37 *Kuchela:* a poor thin brahmin, who was a devotee and a friend of Lord Krishna.

38   *Trivikrama:* one of the ten incarnations of Vishnu: Vishnu appears as a dwarf (*Vamana*) to demon-king Bali and asks only for a small gift of land, measured by three paces of his small feet, which Bali unwittingly grants him, whereupon the dwarf grows to cosmic proportions (*Trivikrama*) and measures all of earth with one step, all the heavens with another, and with his third step pushes the awe-struck but enlightened demon Bali into the nether-world.

41   *Nine Essences: rasa*, "flavour, essence," a central concept in Indian aesthetics. The business of art is to compose, make, evoke, present, etc. one or more *rasas* in the listener, reader, etc. The feelings of real life are *bhavas*, the raw material; the work of art composes, refines, structures, generalizes, etc. these into *rasas*. There are, traditionally, nine *rasas*.

    Menaka, Vishvamitra: see notes to p. 95.

47   *ever-auspicious, daily-wedded: nitya-sumangali*, etc., traditional (and often ironic) description of prostitutes.

48   *Draupadi:* in the epic *Mahabharata*, Draupadi, wife of the five Pandava brothers, is wagered and lost to their rivals and cousins, the Kauravas, in a dice game. One of the Kaurava brothers drags her into court by her sari. She cries out to Lord Krishna for help, who miraculously makes the sari endless—so the molester finds it impossible to disrobe her. On other occasions, too, Draupadi prays to Krishna for help, never in vain—a common theme in mythological plays.

50   *Indra, Yama, Varuna:* Vedic gods. Indra: God of Heaven, the Rain-God; Yama: God of Death; Varuna: God of the Seas.

53   *sacred designs: rangavalli, rangoli*, auspicious and ornamental designs drawn with various coloured powders on the floor, in front of a house or an idol.

    gain-O gain: in measuring numbers one and seven are taboo. One is called "gain" (*jabha*), and seven "one more."

56   FOOD TABOOS (for brahmins): Dasacharya, a Madhva, would be breaking a taboo and would lose ritual status by eating cooked food in a Smarta house. For Madhva and Smarta, see notes to p. 13.

59   *Sitavva: avva* or "mother" is a respectful suffix added to women's names by servants, etc. So Sitadevi is called Sitavva here.

61 *flaming camphor: mangalarati*, the lamp-service in a temple, when gongs and drums are beaten, conches blown; flowers, fruits and flaming camphor are offered to the deity's image.

63 *epic war:* in the epic *Ramayana*, Maruti, or Hanumana, the monkey-devotee of Rama, carried a whole mountain on which grew life-giving herbal plants which alone could save Lakshmana (Rama's brother) who had received a death-wound. In Maruti's temples, the Monkey-god is often represented with a mountain on the palm of his hand.

64 *amma:* an intimate form of address for one's mother, like mom, mummy, etc., in English.

67 *constellation of the Seven Sages:* the constellation Ursa Major, the Big Dipper. The seven stars are supposed to be Seven Sages.

69 *farmers' section: keri*, usually any exclusive street or section where the lower castes (farmers, etc.) live; the non-brahmin counterpart of the brahmin agrahara.

70 *Hirannayya:* once a famous actor on the Kannada stage.

71 *Vamana, Trivikrama:* see notes to p. 38.

72 *Sadarame, Shakuntale:* Kannada names of heroines in popular plays; see notes to p. 29.

73 *life-breaths: prana*, the soul (as opposed to the body), vital power. Tradition lists five such vital "breaths."

74 *baby monkey:* probably a reference to the way of the Monkey, or *markatanyaya*. The soul has two possible kinds of relations with the Lord: (a) like a baby monkey (*markata*) he may hold on to the mother-monkey as she goes about her business, indifferent to the little dependent, (b) like a kitten (*marjara*) he may do nothing, letting the mother-cat pick him up and move him where she will; (a) is the analogue of the way of Works, and (b) of the way of Faith (and surrender to God's grace).

75 *mantras:* the *gayatri* mantra, a Vedic prayer/hymn, repeated by every brahmin at his morning and evening devotions; also chanted thousands of times to accumulate merit.

75   *Goodness: sattvika, rajasika, tamasika,* "Men of Goodness, Energy, or Darkness" (Zaehner's tr.). There are three constituents or "strands" (*guna*) in all natural beings: *sattva* (goodness), *rajas* (passion, energy), *tamas* (darkness). Human beings differ according to the predominance of one or the other. For a clear text, cf. *The Bhagavadgita* 8.40: "There is no existent thing in heaven or earth nor yet among the gods which is or ever could be free from these three constituents from Nature sprang." References to *gunas* are translated here by "Good" nature, "Energy" etc. with capitals.

76   *Urvashi:* a celestial nymph (*apsara*). The sight of her beauty is said to have caused the generation of certain sages. She was also cursed by the gods to live upon the earth, and became the love of Pururavas. Kalidasa (see notes to p. 29) wrote a play about their love. Like the myth of Parashara earlier, here is another myth connecting human and divine, beauty and sanctity, erotic and ascetic,—sharpening one of the central themes of this novel.

79   *counter-clockwise:* ritually speaking, clockwise (moving to the right) circumambulations (of an idol, a brahmin, a holy place, etc.) are auspicious, counter-clockwise movements are not.

80   *Matsyagandhi:* the fish-scented woman, see note to p. 28.

82   *five-fold breath of life:* see note to p. 73.

83   *wet dhotis:* after a cremation, the brahmins have to bathe and wash their clothes. *Dhotis* are unstitched pieces of cloth worn by men wrapped round the waist.

89   *remains of his wife's body:* the remains after a cremation, the ashes, bones, etc. are immersed in a running stream.

91   *Mari:* the dark goddess of death, plague, etc.; often a term of abuse.

95   *dualities: dvandvas,* like pain/pleasure, love/hate, are to be transcended, cf. *The Bhagavadgita* 2.45.

    Trishanku: a king who engaged Sage Vishvamitra (see note to p. 95, below) to send him to heaven against the will of the King of Heaven, Indra. Vishvamitra rocketed him heavenwards with his spiritual power, but Indra didn't accept him. So Trishanku hung between two worlds and became the symbol for all those who hang similarly.

95 *Vyasa:* the sage and compiler of the epic *Mahabharata* was the off-spring of an illicit union between the fisherwoman Matsyagandhi and Sage Parashara.

Vishvamitra: a king turned sage, often given to passions of lust, pride and rage; was frequently tempted and lost his spiritual earnings. A celestial nymph, Menaka, was once sent to tempt him away from his penances which imperilled Indra, the Rain-God.

96 *Jayadeva's song about Krishna: Gitagovinda,* Jayadeva's celebrated (12th century) religious/erotic poem about Krishna and his loves. The Sanskrit line quoted runs as follows: *Lalitalavangalataparishilanako-malamalayasamire.*

98 *Malera:* a community (as suggested later) rather low in others' esteem, allegedly the offspring of brahmins and their mistresses, out of wedlock.

99 *bidi:* small Indian cigarette, tobacco rolled in dried leaves.

100 *Tayinadu:* a Kannada newspaper, well known a few decades ago. *Tayinadu* means "Motherland." The novelist identifies the time of the novel by such references.

102 *Raghavendra:* another name of Rama, "king of the dynasty of Raghus," specially worshipped by Madhvas of this region.

110 *dose:* "a holed, i.e. spongy cake of rice-flour, pulses, etc. baked on a potsherd or ironplate" (Kittel).

low seat: mane, a low wooden seat.

113 *keri:* see note to p. 69.

114 *kali:* see note to p. 27.

115 *monism, advaita:* see notes to p. 13.

That art Thou: tattvamasi, the famous monistic formula.

118 *darshan:* the sight of a holy object, image, deity or person—such a glimpse is participatory, rewarding.

119 *ek ana:* "one anna" (anna being a small coin, a nickel, now obsolete) in Urdu or Hindustani. Such references mark the story as non-

NOTES · 139

contemporary, strengthening the effect of an allegory in a densely realistic setting.

122 *Bhimasena:* the second of the Pandava brothers, known for his strength, size and appetite, see notes to p. 22.

125 *Sahukar:* "the rich man," here obviously a rich local donor.

127 *Southern breezes . . . clove:* line from *Gitagovinda,* see note to p. 96.

143 *"Just as a work . . . prescribed rites":* Parashara, quoted by P. V. Kane, *History of Dharmashastra,* Volume II, Part I (Poona, 1941), pp. 189–90.

"perpetually deferred reply": Roland Barthes, on Balzac's *Sarrasine,* in *S/Z,* tr. Richard Miller (New York, 1974), p. 84.

144 *rite de passage:* see Arnold van Gennep, *Rites of Passage* (London, 1960; first published 1908). For further explorations of the "liminal," see Victor Turner, *The Ritual Process* (Chicago, 1969).

145 *the god-heretic:* cf. Wendy O'Flaherty's *Asceticism and Eroticism in the Mythology of Siva* (London, 1973).

148 *decadent Hinduism:* M. G. Krishnamurti, *Adhunika Bharatiya Sahitya* (1970). Here, and elsewhere in these pages, I am indebted to G. H. Nayak's and S. Nagarajan's articles in *Sakshi 11* (1971), and to M. G. Krishnamurti's essay.

AFTERWORD

THE TITLE, *Samskara*, refers to a concept central to Hinduism. Our epigraph lists some of the denotations.

"A rite of passage or life-cycle ceremony," "forming well, making perfect," "the realizing of past perceptions," "preparation, making ready," are some of the meanings of the multi-vocal Sanskrit word. Even "Sanskrit" (*samskṛta*, the "remade, refined, perfected" language) is part of the *samskara*-paradigm. The sub-title for this translation, "A Rite for a Dead Man," is the most concrete of these many concentric senses that spread through the work.

The opening event is a death, an anti-brahminical brahmin's death—and it brings in its wake a plague, many deaths, questions without answers, old answers that do not fit the new questions, and the rebirth of one good brahmin, Praneshacharya. In trying to resolve the dilemma of who, if any, should perform the heretic's death-rite (a *samskara*), the Acharya begins a *samskara* (a transformation) for himself. A rite for a dead man becomes a rite of passage for the living.

In life as in death, Naranappa questioned the brahmins of the village, exposed their *samskara* (refinement of spirit, maturation through many lives) or lack of it. He lived the life of a libertine in the heart of an exclusive orthodox colony (*agrahara*), broke every known taboo; drank liquor, ate flesh, caught fish with his Muslim friends in the holy temple-tank, and lived with a lowcaste woman. He had cast off his lawfully wedded brahmin wife, and antagonized his kin.

Protected fully by modern secular laws, and even more fully by the brahmins' own bad conscience, he lived defiantly in their midst. If they could exorcize him, they would have found in him a fitting scapegoat to carry their own inmost unspoken libidinous desires. He was their mocking anti-self and he knew it. Now that he is dead, they could punish him at least in death, by disowning him.

Was he brahmin enough in life to be treated as one in death? Did he have the necessary "preparation" (*samskara*) to deserve a proper "ceremony" (*samskara*)? Once a brahmin, always a brahmin? Age-old questions, human questions in Hindu form, they are treacherous and double-edged: once raised, they turn on the questioner.

Naranappa's targets are the strait-laced village brahmins who attend to the "rituals" (*samskaras*), but have not earned by any means their "refinement of spirit" (*samskara*). They are greedy, gluttonous, mean-spirited; they love gold, betray orphans and widows; they are jealous of Naranappa's every forbidden pleasure. They turn for answers to Praneshacharya, Naranappa's opposite number. But, ironically, in the very act of seeking the answer in the Books, and later in seeking a sign from Maruti the chaste Monkey-god, the Acharya abandons everything and becomes one with his opposite: contrary to all his "preparation" he sleeps with Chandri, Naranappa's lowcaste mistress. By what authority now can he judge Naranappa or advise his brahmin followers? So far his *samskara* consisted of Sanskrit learning and ascetic practice. He had turned even marriage into a penance, immolated himself by marrying an invalid. His sudden sexual experience with the forbidden Chandri becomes an unorthodox "rite of initiation." So the question, "Who is a brahmin, how is he made?" finally turns even against this irreproachable brahmin of brahmins, brahmin by birth as by *samskara* (in its many senses). Through crisis, through a breach in the old "formations," he begins to transform himself. With the rightness of paradox, he is initiated through an illicit deed, a misdeed, totally counter to his past. He participates in the condition of his opposite, Naranappa, through Naranappa's own hand-picked whore.

All the battles of tradition and defiance, asceticism and sensuality, the meaning and meaninglessness of ritual, dharma as nature and law, desire (*kama*) and salvation (*moksha*), have now become internal to Praneshacharya. The arena shifts from a Hindu village community to the body and spirit of the protagonist.

Though the word *samskara* does not occur obtrusively or too frequently in the narrative, its meanings implicitly inform the action. Furthermore, the action depends on the several meanings being at loggerheads with each other. It is significant that, in the brahminical texts, there is no division between "outer" and "inner," "social" and "individual," "ritual" and "spiritual" aspects: they imply and follow each other in one seamless unity. "Just as a work of painting gradually unfolds itself on account of the several colours (with which it is drawn), so *brahmanya* (brahminhood) is similarly brought out by *samskaras* performed according to prescribed rites."

As in many traditional tales a question is raised; kept alive, despite possible solutions; maintained, till profounder questions are raised. Answers are delayed until the question is no longer relevant. The delay is filled with "promised answers, suspended, jammed or partial answers, snares and ambiguities." The "perpetually deferred reply" plots the story. Question, Delay and Answer (or its absence) form the overt strategy for another exploration, for covering (and uncovering) psychological ground. Meanwhile, the physical problem of the body's disposal has, ironically, ceased to be relevant; the body is simply, unceremoniously carried in a cart and burned in a field by Chandri and her Muslim friends, though the Acharya does not know it.

In Praneshacharya, brahminism questions itself in a modern existentialist mode (a mode rather alien to it, in fact); and the questioning leads him into new and ordinary worlds. These include not only Naranappa's world but also Putta's. Naranappa has an ideology; Putta has none. In the guided tour through temple festival and fair, whorehouse and pawnshop, the Acharya sees a demoniac world of passion and sensation, where the human watchers of cock-fights are one with the fighting roosters. Putta is a denizen of this world; he is riddle-master, expert bargainer, pimp without any *samskara*; he is so completely and thoughtlessly at one with this world that he is a marvel. He is Praneshacharya's initiator into the mysteries of the ordinary and the familiar, the purity of the unregenerate, the wholeness of the crude. The vision of this world is part of the Acharya's new *samskara*, his "passage."

Indeed, the story moves very much like a *rite de passage*. It is well known that many types of ritual, especially rites of initiation, have three stages: "separation," "transition" ("margin or limen") and "reincorporation." In and through such rituals, individuals and groups change their state or status. Such a change of state is often symbolized (as in this book) by a change of place—a going-away, a seclusion and a coming back.

Particularly rich in symbols of "tradition" is the Acharya's flight from his accustomed village: he wanders through forests and lonely roads, meets with the riddling Putta, journeys through a non-verbal world of fairs, festivals, and performances where he is the marginal man, liminal like the unhoused dead, "betwixt and between." Again, he experiences in himself the condition of Naranappa, once his opposite.

So a *samskara* is not only the subject of the work but the form as well. The Acharya moves through the three stages—though we see him not entirely into the third stage, but only on its threshold.

Will he, can he, ever integrate it with his old ways, his past *samskara*? We do not know. We only see him mutating, changing from a fully evolved socialized brahmin at one with his tradition towards a new kind of person; choosing himself, individuating himself, and "alienating" himself. We are left "anxious, expectant," like the Acharya himself at the end of the novel. Thus, a traditional pattern, like Question, Delay and Answer, or a three-part ritual, appears here without the usual climax or closure. Such inconclusive, anti-climactic use of tradition is very much a part of this modern tale.

I think I have said enough, perhaps too much, about the resonances of the title. *Samskara* is a religious novel, a contemporary reworking of ancient themes. So, naturally (according to some, too easily), the work tends to allegory, and finds continuous use for mythology. The characters are somewhat simplified, and represent polar opposites. The characters come in sets: e.g. Praneshacharya v. Mahabala-Naranappa-Shripati; their lowcaste mistresses v. the brahmin women. Neatly, schematically, the opposites are mediated. Praneshacharya merges with his opposite number through Chandri, the latter's lover; the Acharya's erotic description of a classical heroine rouses Shripati, and he makes love to an outcaste woman on the riverbank.

The complex relations between asceticism and eroticism are well-worked in Hindu thought and mythology. The mythology of Shiva details the paradoxes of the erotic ascetic, the god-heretic. The erotic plagues and tempts the ascetic; the two are also seen as alternative modes of quest, represented here by Naranappa and the Acharya. They speak the same language.

Naranappa's mischief revels in mythological reminders and precedents. Didn't Parashara the great ascetic put a cloud on the holy Ganges as the fisherwoman ferried him across, take her in the boat, bless her body with perpetual fragrance? Out of this union of sage and fishwife came Vyasa the seer, compiler of the Vedas and epic poet of the *Mahabharata*. Didn't Vishvamitra the warrior-sage succumb to the celestial Menaka and lose all his accumulated powers? He once ate even dog-meat to survive a famine and became the proverbial example of "emergency ethics" (*apaddharma*). And didn't Shankara, the celibate philosopher, use his yogic powers to enter a dead king's body, to experience sex, to qualify for a debate on the subject with a woman?

Praneshacharya often wonders whether there is not a serious side to Naranappa's mockery and sensuality; whether sacrilege is not a "left-handed" way of attaining the sacred. By an ancient inversion, salvation is as possible through intoxication as by self-discipline, through violation as through observance of the Law. The Lord may even be reached sooner through hate than by devotion. Naranappa's way gathers strength by enlisting, not defying, instinctual urges. Praneshacharya himself remembers out of his past in Benares, another Naranappa-like figure, fellow-pupil Mahabala. Mahabala gave up the "strait and narrow" path of Sanskrit learning and found "reality" in a whore in the holy city itself.

The other polarity is quite blatant: while all the brahmin wives are sexless, unappetizing, smelly, invalids at best, the women of other castes are seen as glowing sex-objects and temptations to the brahmin. Lowcaste and outcaste women like Chandri and Belli are hallowed and romanticized by references to classical heroines like Shakuntala, and Menaka, the temptress of sages. Besides being classical, women like Chandri are also earthly and amoral, ideals of untroubled sexuality.

As in an early Bergman film, the characters are frankly allegorical, but the setting is realistic. An abstract human theme is reincarnated in just enough particulars of a space, a time, a society. Though the name of the village is allegoric, named after Durvasa the angry sage—all the nearby villages and cities are real places on the map, Shivamogge, Basrur, etc. Several details suggest that the time of action could be the early '30s or '40s: references to older coins (*anna*), and to the then-popular daily *Tayinadu*, the rise of the Congress Party, etc. Yet the time is a stereotype of what might be called Indian Village Time—indefinite, continuous, anywhere between a few decades ago and the medieval centuries. The cycles of natural season and the calendar of human ceremony are interlocked in Village Time. The rigid greedy brahmins mindlessly live off it, while Praneshacharya mindfully lives in it until it is interrupted and cancelled; then he drifts out of the accustomed village spaces and cycles into the outer world and comes back. The dead man, the heretic, defied it all and lived in his own time and territory, his body.

"Realism" and "allegory" (I hope the terms are clear in context) are generic patterns of expectations; the attempted realism of place, time and custom raises certain expectations in the reader. Occasionally, this felt mixture of modes makes uneasy reading. "Realistically" speaking, there are many things wrong with the story. I have heard it said that the central dilemma regarding the death-rite need be no dilemma to a learned brahmin like the Acharya, "Crest-Jewel of Vedic Learning"; there is an answer to this very question in a text, the *Dharmasindhu*. Certain simple ritual modifications and offerings would have solved the problem, as the guru of Dharmasthala clearly suggests. And every villager is supposed to know that no crow or vulture would touch a plague-ridden rat. Several dramatic pages on the plague flout such native knowledge.

But the book's allegoric and narrative power marshals enough poetic images, ideas, stereotypes, and caricatures around the central *human* figure of the Acharya and his mutation, so that most readers are "bounced" into the novel and ask no questions. Indeed, in the Acharya, we see "allegory" wrestling with "realism"; in him an archetype wrestles with himself, and becomes atypical.

Not every reader is so taken. Certain brahmin communities in South India were offended by the picture of decadent brahminism. They felt that brahmin men and women were unfairly caricatured; they were offended by the novelist's rather intrusive partiality for Naranappa and the sudra women.

A more serious objection is that the central figure projects a narrow part of the Hindu ideal—not the integrity of the four stages of life, in which desire (*kama*) and the goods of this world (*artha*) are affirmed and celebrated in their time and place and it is part of the design of dharma to do so. To this way of thinking, the Acharya's brand of self-denial is aberrant. As his invalid wife Bhagirathi reminds him in the opening pages, he is in the second stage of life, a married householder. Yet he lives as one arrested in the first stage (celibate student), or as having progressed to the third (forest-dweller), or even the fourth (ascetic renouncer). As an Acharya he ought to have known better than to marry an invalid, a barren woman who would only cripple him in all the pursuits necessary for an able-bodied, able-spirited brahmin. Neither the author, nor his one rather idealized brahmin, seems to be aware of such discrepancies.

Yet it is such a discrepancy that makes the entire action possible. Despite all his virtue, the Acharya does not have the virtue of living out fully his present *stage.* Having exiled *kama* from his house and family, he had to find it outside his customary space, in the forest; his sense of dharma had to be undone and remade by it.

One could reasonably take the view that this novel, written in the '60s, is really presenting a decadent Hinduism through the career of a limited hero, capable only of arcs, not full circles. As said earlier, the last phase of the Acharya's initiation is an anxious return, a waiting on the threshold; his questions seem to find no restful answers. What is suggested is a movement, not a closure. The novel ends, but does not conclude.

A. K. RAMANUJAN

"*SAMSKARA* DOES NOT EXIST IN FREE SPACE...IT EXISTS IN MY CONTEXT"

In Conversation with U. R. Ananthamurthy

SUSHEELA PUNITHA

WHOSE English? What kind of English? So much depends on what a translator considers English.

An open-ended conversation with the author in the thirty-fifth year of the English translation of *Samskara* brought new insights to the ever-shifting world of English renderings of regional language texts in India.

To me, reading *Samskara* in Kannada was like stirring a hornet's nest. My head swarmed with questions. I saw the relevance of the novel as an indictment of people of any religion (though brahmins are used as a prototype here) who think they are superior to the set of spiritual beliefs to which they belong and therefore manipulate it to boost their ego. While Naranappa makes a great show of defying the dictates of his dharma with his wanton ways, Praneshacharya flouts them subversively. By marrying the invalid Bhagirathi, he desecrates his *grihasthashrama*[1] to bolster his ego: "He oozes smug self-righteousness as he gloats, 'Good she's an invalid; I'm ripening well.'"[2] Wouldn't he have matured better if he had chosen to be celibate? While Naranappa putrefies openly, Praneshacharya does so secretly with his self-imposed impotency. He impresses the other

---

1. A reference to the four stages of the Hindu way of life; *grihasthashrama* is the second stage, that of a householder.
2. All translations from *Samskara* seen here are mine.

brahmins of the agrahara[3] with an outward show of regard for the *niyamas*[4] yet he lacks the inner humility that goes beyond egoism to practice what he preaches. No wonder then that he could not find the right advice from the Scriptures on Naranappa's *samskara*.[5] No wonder he could not shepherd his flock across an arid patch. The brahmins of Durvasapura are like mindless sheep, lost and wandering from shepherd to shepherd to be led towards green pastures when all they wanted was the permission to eat to assuage their hunger. Hunger and satiation provide the "infra-structure" on which the novel rests, but space does not allow me to probe this theme. I have focused mainly on the man and the writer in U. R. Ananthamurthy (URA) coming together or standing apart, looking at each other. So, set against these two non-heroic protagonists is Chandri, wholesome and honest, the only person who lives her dharma to the fullest. Born to a prostitute, she is exempt from the dharma of the two-in-one main character but she is faithful to her own; she fulfils her responsibilities as mistress by living with Naranappa for ten years. After his death, she fortifies her progeny by sleeping with Praneshacharya.

And then, when I read *Samskara* in English, I found it wanting. I felt the English version lacked the natural voluptuousness of Kannada that this novel needs, without the negative connotation associated with the word "voluptuous"; here it is fulsomeness, vitality. I read out my translation of some lines to URA as I felt A. K. Ramanujan's (AKR) translation misrepresented the spirit of his text. For instance, in the passage where Chandri thinks of how she feels about Praneshacharya, the English version reads: "Her mother used to say: prostitutes should get pregnant by such holy men." A more faithful rendition of the original would be, "Chandri tells herself, 'Remember what Amma used to say about the kind of men from whom a prostitute should receive the fruit of the womb? Such a man

3. Colony where the brahmins of a village or small town live.
4. Vow; observance.
5. Funeral rites.

is Acharya, in looks, in character and in charisma.'" My version brings out the essence of URA's text: that Chandri was seeing Praneshacharya as a stud. It is an image of the primeval desire to procreate, so natural and therefore so pure. AKR changes the impact by making it moral, by making a prostitute feel the need to be redeemed by a "holy" man. URA's text does not imply that at all. And so I asked him how he felt about AKR's translation and he said, "Well, not everyone would agree but that was the problem with Ramanujan. He tried to write English like an Englishman." URA's answer affirmed my feeling about translation that each text has to be translated into the style appropriate to it. Much of the success of a translation into English depends on what the translator considers "English" proper to the text. His reply also explains many of his statements made in the interview because they refer to the text in Kannada. People who can read the novel only in English may not be able to appreciate the intensity in the novel because AKR's style plays it down.

I wanted URA's free-flowing responses to take precedence over the interview structure. I provided the questions all together at the beginning of the interview, asking him to answer only those he chose. The open-ended process brought forth a deeper perspective on the novel. These were my questions:

1. As a writer, are you aware of the hidden texts your novel posits? Are you aware of patterns surfacing from your unconscious self, patterns you had not thought of, perhaps?

2. Have you deliberately made your women characters like Chandri in *Samskara* and Chikki in *Bharathipura* minor yet more wholesome than the male protagonists to draw attention to them by not spotlighting them? Is that a part of your technique?

3. Why is your image of orthodoxy so withered and withering an influence? What is the contradiction we are asked to see and understand?

4. How do you feel about *Samskara* now in terms of its relevance? Have mores changed much for a lot of people since the time-period in the novel?

5. What does Vedanta say about inner purity? Is it criticizing Praneshacharya's type of egoism?

6. Is *Samskara* a critique of a vision of life which says we are all manifestations of the great reality and yet privileges a section of rule-makers over the others or is it a condemnation of people who subvert the vision of life to justify the social hierarchy and its exploitative tendencies?

I could see he was eager to answer my questions, to reset my eyes to see the novel as an allegory. Here is what he said:

"I was intensely conscious of a single great episode in the *Mahabharata*.[6] The great sage Parashara, while in a boat, falls in love with the fish-smelling Matsyagandhi. Vedavyasa is the *sadyojatha*, the immediately-born, born with a *kamandala*.[7] He makes her a *yojanagandhi*, the sweet-smelling one. Strangely, even after begetting a child, she remains a virgin. And grows up to be a beautiful woman and Shantanu falls in love with her. Then she poses a condition that the child born to her must become the king. Bhishma comes in the way but he becomes a great character by sacrificing his position for his father's love. So the only thing in my head as a subtext was Parashara meeting Matsyagandhi.

"In the 1960s, I felt our great epics saw 'right' as a whole and didn't take positions as shaped by reality. For instance, people in those days could have a love affair and not make it a guilt-ridden experience. Neither the woman nor the man ever thought of it as desecration. Here too, in the novel, Praneshacharya meets Chandri most unpreparedly, and here too, when Praneshacharya touches Chandri, something is aroused in him and he touches her breasts and unites with her. I am reminded of Parashara meeting

6. Epic written by sage Vedavyasa.
7. A hand-held container used by sages to carry water.

Matsyagandhi. Praneshacharya has a whole set of absurd questions before he meets her and a whole set of absurd questions after he meets her. The only thing that is pure in the novel is the meeting. His sexual self is aroused and there is no question of right or wrong, only pure joy. I was made aware of this by my friend Rajiv Taranath. He said, 'You create a whole set of absurd events like whether the body of Naranappa should be burnt or not and afterwards you make Praneshacharya wonder if what he did was right. And in between the two sets of episodes there is an experience that is neither right nor wrong. It is beyond right and wrong.'

"I think my novel goes beyond questions of caste and gains an epic dimension; it becomes an allegorical tale. I am not writing a novel, but an allegorical tale. Meenakshi Mukherjee was the only person who recognized this. Here is a novel that cannot be realistically abandoned. It cannot be realistically interpreted either. It has realism but it is an allegory. In allegory, realism gets changed. But in realism there is no place for allegory. So she said this is a new Indian form. I came to know this from a critic. I was not aware of this when I wrote the novel. But since I am also a professor of English, I began to see this as an insider.

"Many caste brahmins who attacked my novel did not know something that I knew. They have become unaware of the rules from the *Manu Dharma Shastra* because they live in the Victorian era. Now, for a brahmin, to do *samskara* to a body is not merely to burn it. First, there is a mantra which says that the body which came from the *panchabhoothas*[8] goes back to the *panchabhoothas*. It is a *kriya*[9] which does not call for love or emotion. It is the giving up of the body to the five elements from which it has come. But since we are human beings, we cannot give up the body objectively, so there is *vyamoha*.[10] And so there is a whole set of beliefs to cater to it: the

8. The five elements, viz., earth, fire, water, air, and ether.
9. Ritual.
10. Affection; attachment.

dead person has become a *pretha*[11] and the *pretha* has to become a *pithru*.[12] To make him a *pithru*, you invoke different parts of his body—thighs, sexual organs, chest…and then you say, '*gachcha gachcha pretha*' which means 'go away, go away, *pretha*.' And then you have two rice balls, one for the *pithru* and the other for the *pretha*. At that point you mix the two rice balls. You keep some thread and a bowl of milk for the *pretha* who we believe is hovering around us. The first *kriya* of dissolving the body in the *panchabhoothas* is very *nishtoora*[13] but the second one of making it a *pithru* is very human. Nehru, who knew this, did not want the *shraddha*[14] but he wanted the first *kriya* to be preformed, that of dissolving the body in the *panchabhoothas*.

"So, coming back to the novel, when the brahmins are asked to perform the cremation, they refuse to do it, not because they do not want to dispose of the body; they don't want him as a *pithru*. Now comes my awareness of caste and other things like a social context. Manu said, if a man has flouted the norms of caste, he should be excommunicated. Then he is as good as dead. But here, they don't want to cremate him because they can't imagine him becoming a *pithru*. So when I say Praneshacharya did not find an answer in the religious texts, people said, 'There is no answer, that's why he did not find one.' But that is not true. There is an answer, but only a conditional one. If you could throw him out, why didn't Praneshacharya throw him out? Because Naranappa threatened to become a Muslim. If he converted to Islam and continued to live in the agrahara, could they have thrown him out? They couldn't. The British were ruling the country and no man could be thrown out of his house. And so the brahmins would have become polluted if Naranappa had converted to Islam and continued to live in the agrahara.

"Here is a problem that has been created metaphysically but has

11. Spirit of a dead person.
12. Spirit of an ancestor.
13. Harsh; fiercely frank.
14. Death ceremony performed invoking the spirit of the dead.

political implications. Hence, no shastra came to their rescue. No one understood this crucial dimension of the novel. My text does not exist in free space that some Westerner can read and understand; it exists in my context. I am a critical insider. If I were a Christian, I would have questioned Christianity from the inside like Martin Luther did.

"Actually, in the novel, Chandri fails to get Naranappa cremated even by a sudra because they too conform to brahminical beliefs: '"I can't do it, Chandramma. Should I go to hell for touching a brahmin dead body? Not for all the wealth you may give me," says Seshappa in a drunken stupor.' So she gets a Muslim to do it. This is the truly shastric basis of the novel. Even the best of readers did not get it. This happens even in *Ghatashraddha* (The Ritual, 1963). The widow, Yamunakka, is excommunicated when she becomes pregnant. As a widow, her head had been shaved with the assumption that she was now pure; she would not be desired by men nor could she labour under the illusion that she was desirable to men. But once she is cast out of her caste, she may have grown back her hair. Gandhi did this to Miss Slade, an extraordinarily beautiful woman who came to live in the ashram. She was a great musician, a close friend of Vinobha Bhave. She went back after Gandhi died. Shaving the head is a denial of femininity. But, after being excommunicated, the woman could grow back her hair. We suffer when we flout the rules, but then, why do we flout them? Because *prakrithi*[15] is greater than *purusha*.[16] I believe that we have to go on learning from nature. As a writer, I am aware of all the social laws with all their implications, but with the belief that *prakrithi* is superior to them.

"Sometimes *prakrithi* manifests itself as desire. Parashara may have been a great sage but he had to submit to the desire of a woman, Matsyagandhi. Praneshacharya is not a hypocrite in renouncing marital pleasure but he is guilty of bad faith. Many people have asked me about this. He may have flouted the four stages but not as

15. Nature (imagined as female).
16. An individual; a male.

a hypocrite, only out of wilfulness. In the Shakuntala episode, he can speak of Shakuntala in a very evocative manner without his own sexual appetite being triggered. So, he has 'will.'

"But Naranappa has a different kind of will. When he is dying, he calls out the name of god, 'Narayana! Narayana!' In the *Bhagavadgita*, Krishna says, 'Those who remember me at the moment of death will attain me.' T. S. Eliot quotes this line in *Four Quartets* and in brackets, he says, 'The moment of death is every moment.' So, both Praneshacharya and Naranappa are two sides of the same coin. Both of them live a life of will. If there is one character in the novel who has no will, he is Putta. He is the counterpoint. Hence my novel is about *wilfulness* and *willessness*.

"I had sent my novel to Adiga and others and they said it seemed incomplete. I sat down to rework it and I heard footsteps. It was a magical moment and Putta came in. My novel was transformed completely after his entry. Any person who lives in wilfulness is a person who lives in bad faith or in hypocrisy; I would call it plain bad faith. When there is tiredness in what you do, even being good, it is not genuine. In Chandri, there was no tiredness. She was faithful to Naranappa but desired Praneshacharya. In her there was no guilt. People want to read the novel as sudra and brahmin coming together but I feel it diminishes the novel by restricting it to our context. In the Indian civilization, there must have been a time when brahmin and sudra were one. Otherwise, our colour would not have been these beautiful shades of brown. There must have been so much of mixing in the past that someone must have thought of the caste system.

"I was reading *Mahabharata* and in that Vedavyasa says there was no rule that a woman had to be faithful to one man. Her sexuality was so abundant that even after being taken by many men, there was more of it. It is like many rivers joining the ocean and the ocean still not being full. On the other hand, the sexuality of man is like firewood. He says this in *Adhiparva*[17] and he also says that all the rules

17. First canto of the *Mahabharata*.

for the woman were made much later by man because he could not handle her sexuality. Chandri represents that kind of abundant sexuality.

"The structure of this novel came to me magically. I was caught by it unawares. I have written nothing else with such abandon and discovery. While Naranappa and Praneshacharya form one end of the spectrum, Putta and Chandri form the other. Praneshacharya's sexuality which had, perhaps, been accumulating, found release in Chandri. And this is release in more than one sense.

"When I situate my novel in a realistic situation, there is a strong inner text. It allows for all kinds of emotions in authenticity. So to study the novel as a caste and religious text is to diminish it, to underrate its metaphysical dimension. To say Chandri is a sudra woman is to say nothing. My friend Paul Green, a historian, said the person who takes Praneshacharya around and introduces him to things he has never done in his life is Putta. Now Putta is a Malera by caste. Maleras are a brahmin-sudra caste. In fact, even in *Ghatashraddha*, after Yamunakka is cast out of the community, she will perhaps grow her hair, marry someone, and become a Malera. This happens everywhere. There must have been some brahmins who flouted the rules and became lower in the hierarchy.

"Putta takes Praneshacharya to *koli-anka*,[18] gets him to drink coffee, and arranges for him to visit Padmavathi. So, in a way, Praneshacharya is living Naranappa's life and, in doing so, he is performing Naranappa's *shraddha*. It is completed in Praneshacharya sleeping with Chandri. The Muslim burnt his body and Praneshacharya performs his *shraddha*.

"I wonder how at that age, with all my foolish ideas, I could write this novel which has meant so much to so many over the years. I was reading a lot of Hegel at that time. And here, the Hegelian metaphysics of opposites becomes true. The *shanka*[19] and *jagte*[20] which

18. A cock-fight.
19. Conch.
20. A gong sounded at time of worship.

are ritually used to produce sound during worship become tools to frighten away the crows and vultures that hover over the dying in the agrahara!"

TITLES IN SERIES

For a complete list of titles, visit www.nyrb.com or write to:
Catalog Requests, NYRB, 435 Hudson Street, New York, NY 10014

J.R. ACKERLEY Hindoo Holiday*
J.R. ACKERLEY My Dog Tulip*
J.R. ACKERLEY My Father and Myself*
J.R. ACKERLEY We Think the World of You*
HENRY ADAMS The Jeffersonian Transformation
RENATA ADLER Pitch Dark*
RENATA ADLER Speedboat*
AESCHYLUS Prometheus Bound; translated by Joel Agee*
LEOPOLDO ALAS His Only Son *with* Doña Berta*
CÉLESTE ALBARET Monsieur Proust
DANTE ALIGHIERI The Inferno
KINGSLEY AMIS The Alteration*
KINGSLEY AMIS Dear Illusion: Collected Stories*
KINGSLEY AMIS Ending Up*
KINGSLEY AMIS Girl, 20*
KINGSLEY AMIS The Green Man*
KINGSLEY AMIS Lucky Jim*
KINGSLEY AMIS The Old Devils*
KINGSLEY AMIS One Fat Englishman*
KINGSLEY AMIS Take a Girl Like You*
ROBERTO ARLT The Seven Madmen*
U.R. ANANTHAMURTHY Samskara: A Rite for a Dead Man*
WILLIAM ATTAWAY Blood on the Forge
W.H. AUDEN (EDITOR) The Living Thoughts of Kierkegaard
W.H. AUDEN W.H. Auden's Book of Light Verse
ERICH AUERBACH Dante: Poet of the Secular World
EVE BABITZ Eve's Hollywood*
EVE BABITZ Slow Days, Fast Company: The World, the Flesh, and L.A.*
DOROTHY BAKER Cassandra at the Wedding*
DOROTHY BAKER Young Man with a Horn*
J.A. BAKER The Peregrine
S. JOSEPHINE BAKER Fighting for Life*
HONORÉ DE BALZAC The Human Comedy: Selected Stories*
HONORÉ DE BALZAC The Unknown Masterpiece *and* Gambara*
VICKI BAUM Grand Hotel*
SYBILLE BEDFORD A Legacy*
SYBILLE BEDFORD A Visit to Don Otavio: A Mexican Journey*
MAX BEERBOHM The Prince of Minor Writers: The Selected Essays of Max Beerbohm*
MAX BEERBOHM Seven Men
STEPHEN BENATAR Wish Her Safe at Home*
FRANS G. BENGTSSON The Long Ships*
ALEXANDER BERKMAN Prison Memoirs of an Anarchist
GEORGES BERNANOS Mouchette
MIRON BIAŁOSZEWSKI A Memoir of the Warsaw Uprising*
ADOLFO BIOY CASARES Asleep in the Sun
ADOLFO BIOY CASARES The Invention of Morel
PAUL BLACKBURN (TRANSLATOR) Proensa*

* Also available as an electronic book.

FR. ROLFE Hadrian the Seventh
GILLIAN ROSE Love's Work
LINDA ROSENKRANTZ Talk*
WILLIAM ROUGHEAD Classic Crimes
CONSTANCE ROURKE American Humor: A Study of the National Character
SAKI The Unrest-Cure and Other Stories; illustrated by Edward Gorey
TAYEB SALIH Season of Migration to the North
TAYEB SALIH The Wedding of Zein*
JEAN-PAUL SARTRE We Have Only This Life to Live: Selected Essays. 1939–1975
GERSHOM SCHOLEM Walter Benjamin: The Story of a Friendship*
DANIEL PAUL SCHREBER Memoirs of My Nervous Illness
JAMES SCHUYLER Alfred and Guinevere
JAMES SCHUYLER What's for Dinner?*
SIMONE SCHWARZ-BART The Bridge of Beyond*
LEONARDO SCIASCIA The Day of the Owl
LEONARDO SCIASCIA Equal Danger
LEONARDO SCIASCIA The Moro Affair
LEONARDO SCIASCIA To Each His Own
LEONARDO SCIASCIA The Wine-Dark Sea
VICTOR SEGALEN René Leys*
ANNA SEGHERS Transit*
PHILIPE-PAUL DE SÉGUR Defeat: Napoleon's Russian Campaign
GILBERT SELDES The Stammering Century*
VICTOR SERGE The Case of Comrade Tulayev*
VICTOR SERGE Conquered City*
VICTOR SERGE Memoirs of a Revolutionary
VICTOR SERGE Midnight in the Century*
VICTOR SERGE Unforgiving Years
SHCHEDRIN The Golovlyov Family
ROBERT SHECKLEY The Store of the Worlds: The Stories of Robert Sheckley*
GEORGES SIMENON Act of Passion*
GEORGES SIMENON Dirty Snow*
GEORGES SIMENON Monsieur Monde Vanishes*
GEORGES SIMENON Pedigree*
GEORGES SIMENON Three Bedrooms in Manhattan*
GEORGES SIMENON Tropic Moon*
GEORGES SIMENON The Widow*
CHARLES SIMIC Dime-Store Alchemy: The Art of Joseph Cornell
MAY SINCLAIR Mary Olivier: A Life*
WILLIAM SLOANE The Rim of Morning: Two Tales of Cosmic Horror*
SASHA SOKOLOV A School for Fools*
VLADIMIR SOROKIN Ice Trilogy*
VLADIMIR SOROKIN The Queue
NATSUME SŌSEKI The Gate*
DAVID STACTON The Judges of the Secret Court*
JEAN STAFFORD The Mountain Lion
CHRISTINA STEAD Letty Fox: Her Luck
GEORGE R. STEWART Names on the Land
STENDHAL The Life of Henry Brulard
ADALBERT STIFTER Rock Crystal*
THEODOR STORM The Rider on the White Horse
JEAN STROUSE Alice James: A Biography*
HOWARD STURGIS Belchamber